Quantum Information Concepts in Open Quantum Systems

Quantum Information Concepts in Open Quantum Systems

Editors

Bassano Vacchini
Andrea Smirne
Nina Megier

MDPI • Basel • Beijing • Wuhan • Barcelona • Belgrade • Manchester • Tokyo • Cluj • Tianjin

Editors

Bassano Vacchini
Università degli Studi di Milano
Italy

Andrea Smirne
Università degli Studi di Milano
Italy

Nina Megier
Università degli Studi di Milano
Italy

Editorial Office
MDPI
St. Alban-Anlage 66
4052 Basel, Switzerland

This is a reprint of articles from the Special Issue published online in the open access journal *Entropy* (ISSN 1099-4300) (available at: https://www.mdpi.com/journal/entropy/special_issues/quantum_OQS).

For citation purposes, cite each article independently as indicated on the article page online and as indicated below:

LastName, A.A.; LastName, B.B.; LastName, C.C. Article Title. *Journal Name* **Year**, *Volume Number*, Page Range.

ISBN 978-3-0365-6497-5 (Hbk)
ISBN 978-3-0365-6498-2 (PDF)

© 2023 by the authors. Articles in this book are Open Access and distributed under the Creative Commons Attribution (CC BY) license, which allows users to download, copy and build upon published articles, as long as the author and publisher are properly credited, which ensures maximum dissemination and a wider impact of our publications.

The book as a whole is distributed by MDPI under the terms and conditions of the Creative Commons license CC BY-NC-ND.

Contents

About the Editors vii

Preface to "Quantum Information Concepts in Open Quantum Systems" ix

Jose Teittinen and Sabrina Maniscalco
Quantum Speed Limit and Divisibility of the Dynamical Map
Reprinted from: *Entropy* 2021, 23, 331, doi:10.3390/e23030331 1

Stefano Cusumano and Łukasz Rudnicki
Thermodynamics of Reduced State of the Field
Reprinted from: *Entropy* 2021, 23, 1198, doi:10.3390/e23091198 9

Katarzyna Siudzińska, Arpan Das and Anindita Bera
Engineering Classical Capacity of Generalized Pauli Channels with Admissible Memory Kernels
Reprinted from: *Entropy* 2021, 23, 1382, doi:10.3390/e23111382 21

Nina Megier, Andrea Smirne, Steve Campbell and Bassano Vacchini
Correlations, Information Backflow, and Objectivity in a Class of Pure Dephasing Models
Reprinted from: *Entropy* 2022, 24, 304, doi:10.3390/e24020304 35

Valentin Link, Walter T. Strunz and Kimmo Luoma
Non-Markovian Quantum Dynamics in a Squeezed Reservoir
Reprinted from: *Entropy* 2022, 24, 352, doi:10.3390/e24030352 51

Kobra Mahdavipour, Mahshid Khazaei Shadfar, Hossein Rangani Jahromi, Roberto Morandotti and Rosario Lo Franco
Memory Effects in High-Dimensional Systems Faithfully Identified by Hilbert–Schmidt Speed-Based Witness
Reprinted from: *Entropy* 2022, 24, 395, doi:10.3390/e24030395 65

Kazunari Hashimoto and Chikako Uchiyama
Effect of Quantum Coherence on Landauer's Principle
Reprinted from: *Entropy* 2022, 24, 548, doi:10.3390/e24040548 89

Adrián A. Budini
Quantum Non-Markovian Environment-to-System Backflows of Information:Nonoperational vs. Operational Approaches
Reprinted from: *Entropy* 2022, 24, 649, doi:10.3390/e24050649 103

Mingli Chen, Haonan Chen, Tao Han and Xiangji Cai
Disentanglement Dynamics in Nonequilibrium Environments
Reprinted from: *Entropy* 2022, 24, 1330, doi:10.3390/e24101330 121

Arapat Ablimit, Run-Hong He, Yang-Yang Xie, Lian-Ao Wu and Zhao-Ming Wang
Quantum Energy Current Induced Coherence in a Spin Chain under Non-Markovian Environments
Reprinted from: *Entropy* 2022, 24, 1406, doi:10.3390/e24101406 145

About the Editors

Bassano Vacchini

Bassano Vacchini obtained his PhD in Physics at the University of Milan in 1998 and later moved to the University of Marburg as an Alexander von Humboldt Fellow. Since 2015, he has served as Associate Professor at the Physics Department of the University of Milan. His research activity has been focused on the theoretical study of open quantum systems. Within this field, he has devoted his activity to the microscopic derivation and mathematical characterization of master equations for describing the reduced dynamics of open systems. More recently, he has devoted his activity to exploring the memory properties, namely the so-called Markovianity, of such dynamical evolutions.

Andrea Smirne

Andrea Smirne is Associate Professor at the Physics Department of the University of Milan. He obtained his PhD in Physics at the University of Milan in 2012 and then served as a Postdoc at the University of Trieste, from 2013 to 2014, and at the Institute for Theoretical Physics of the University of Ulm, from 2015 to 2019, before returning to the University of Milan as a Researcher. His research interests are focused on the theoretical investigation of open quantum systems, ranging from foundational questions such as the identification of inherently nonclassical features in multi-time statistics and the characterization of non-Markovianity in the quantum realm to the development of optimal quantum estimation strategies when there is a realistic description of the noise effects.

Nina Megier

Nina Megier did her PhD in theoretical physics at TU Dresden. In her PhD and during the two subsequent research stays at the University of Milan and the ICTQT in Gdańsk, she worked on the theory of open quantum systems, focusing on quantum non-Markovianity. Currently, she develops ion traps at Infineon Austria.

Preface to "Quantum Information Concepts in Open Quantum Systems"

It has long been recognized that a key feature in determining the behavior of a quantum system is the interaction with the other surrounding quantum degrees of freedom. This aspect is crucial in foundational studies of quantum mechanics aimed at describing the quantum measurement process. At the same time, it plays a decisive role in the exploitation of quantum effects, especially in view of the implementation of quantum information schemes, quantum thermodynamic devices, and quantum technology applications. The theory of open quantum systems addresses all these challenges. Recent developments in the field have, however, shifted the activity toward considering and understanding the relevance of correlations, both of classical and quantum nature, in the description of the dynamics and measurement of open quantum systems. Indeed, duly keeping correlations into account both at the initial time and during evolution is a crucial requirement to pave the way for experimental advancements in the field of open quantum systems.

Bassano Vacchini, Andrea Smirne, and Nina Megier
Editors

Article

Quantum Speed Limit and Divisibility of the Dynamical Map

Jose Teittinen [1,*] and Sabrina Maniscalco [1,2,3]

[1] Turku Centre for Quantum Physics, Department of Physics and Astronomy, University of Turku, FI-20014 Turku, Finland; smanis@utu.fi
[2] QTF Centre of Excellence, Department of Applied Physics, School of Science, Aalto University, FI-00076 Aalto, Finland
[3] QTF Centre of Excellence, Department of Physics, Faculty of Science, University of Helsinki, FI-00014 Helsinki, Finland
* Correspondence: jostei@utu.fi

Abstract: The quantum speed limit (QSL) is the theoretical lower limit of the time for a quantum system to evolve from a given state to another one. Interestingly, it has been shown that non-Markovianity can be used to speed-up the dynamics and to lower the QSL time, although this behaviour is not universal. In this paper, we further carry on the investigation on the connection between QSL and non-Markovianity by looking at the effects of P- and CP-divisibility of the dynamical map to the quantum speed limit. We show that the speed-up can also be observed under P- and CP-divisible dynamics, and that the speed-up is not necessarily tied to the transition from P-divisible to non-P-divisible dynamics.

Keywords: quantum speed limit; open quantum system; dynamical map

1. Introduction

The quantum speed limit (QSL) is the theoretical lower bound to the time that is needed for a state to be transformed into another. The concept of QSL was first introduced in [1] as a lower time limit of the evolution between two orthogonal pure states for the harmonic oscillator and it ss shown to be bounded by the variance of energy $\tau_{MT} \geq h/4\Delta E$. This initial perspective was then further developed and connected to the maximal rates of computations for a quantum computer in [2]. In that paper, it was concluded that the minimum interaction time is bounded by the average energy as $\tau_{ML} \geq h/4E$. It can be shown that the two bounds are not ordered and the actual QSL should be the maximum of the two bounds. Since then, the study of QSL has been extended to include mixed states [3] and more general dynamics [4–8].

More recently, the study of the quantum speed limit has gained renewed interest after discovering that it can be lowered by means of memory effects, thus theoretically speeding up the process. Specifically, in [4], it was shown that the quantum speed limit is lowered under certain non-Markovian dynamics in an open qubit system. This result was then experimentally confirmed in [9]. A more thorough analysis on the role of non-Markovianity was performed in [10], where it was shown that its connection with QSL is not as straightforward and the speed-up can be present, even when the dynamics is Markovian.

In this paper, we deepen our investigation by considering other aspects of non-Markovianity, specifically the lack of P-divisibility and CP-divisibility of dynamics. We show that the speed-up, which was previously widely credited to information backflow, as defined in [11], can also be observed with P-divisible and even with CP-divisible dynamics. As a paradigmatic example of dynamics, we consider the phase-covariant master equation, since it includes well-known maps, such as amplitude damping and pure dephasing. The conditions for P-divisibility of the phase-covariant master equation were recently studied in [12]. We consider a specific phase-covariant model that can describe the crossover between P-divisible and non-P-divisible dynamics by tuning a certain parameter.

The paper is structured, as follows. In Section 2, we recall the basic definitions and concepts that were used in this paper, and present the dynamics of the example systems that we used. In Sections 3 and 4, we present the results for the QSL of CP- and P-divisible dynamics. Finally, Section 5 summarises the results and presents conclusions.

2. Open Quantum Systems, Dynamical Maps, Divisibility, and QSL

In textbooks, many elementary examples of a quantum system are of idealised closed system. However, in reality, every quantum system is interacting with its environment, whick makes it an open quantum system. When we study an open quantum system, we are usually interested in the reduced dynamics of the smaller system, for example, a qubit, rather than the environment.

A quantum dynamical map Φ_t is a map describing the time evolution of a quantum system, which is $\rho(t) = \Phi_t(\rho(0))$, where $\rho(t)$ is a time dependent density matrix. In an open quantum system with the system of interest (S) and the environment (E), the reduced dynamics of the system is given by $\rho_S(t) = \Phi_t(\rho_S(0)) = \text{tr}_E[U_{SE}^\dagger \rho_S(t) \otimes \rho_E(0) U_{SE}]$, where U_{SE} is a unitary operator describing the time evolution of the total system, with $\rho_S(0)$ and $\rho_E(0)$ being the system and environment states at $t=0$, respectively.

A dynamical map Φ_t is said to be k-positive if the the map $\Phi_t \otimes \mathbb{I}_k$, where $\mathbb{I}_k$ is the identity operator for a k-dimensional ancillary Hilbert space, is positive. If a map is positive for all k, it is called completely positive (CP) and, if a map is 1-positive, it is called positive (P). A dynamical map is called P- or CP- divisible, if the map can be written using a positive or completely positive intermediate map $V_{s,t}$, s.t. $\Phi_t = V_{s,t}\Phi_s$, for $0 \geq s \geq t$.

The explicit dynamics that are considered in this paper arise from a class of master equations in the time-local GKSL form:

$$\frac{d\rho_S(t)}{dt} = L_t(\rho_S(t)) = \frac{i}{\hbar}[\rho_S(t), H(t)] + \sum_i \gamma_i(t)\left(A_i \rho_S(t) A_i^\dagger - \frac{1}{2}\{A_i^\dagger A_i, \rho_S(t)\}\right), \quad (1)$$

where H is the system Hamiltonian, $\gamma_i(t)$ the time-dependent decay rates, and A_i the Lindblad operators. The GKSL-theorem implies that, for master equations in the form of Equation (1), with $\gamma_i(t) \geq 0$, the resulting dynamics is always completely positive and trace preserving (CPTP) and, thus, always physical [13–15]. One should keep in mind that, in the framework of a microscopic description of system plus environment, the GKSL master equation is the result of a number of approximations. When these approximations do not hold, this master equation fails to grasp some—possibly relevant—features of the studied dynamics. Our examples come from the family of so-called phase-covariant master equations [16–19]:

$$\begin{aligned} L_t(\rho(t)) =& \; i\omega(t)[\rho(t), \sigma_3] + \frac{\gamma_1(t)}{2}\left(\sigma_+ \rho(t)\sigma_- - \frac{1}{2}\{\sigma_-\sigma_+, \rho(t)\}\right) \\ &+ \frac{\gamma_2(t)}{2}\left(\sigma_- \rho(t)\sigma_+ - \frac{1}{2}\{\sigma_+\sigma_-, \rho(t)\}\right) + \frac{\gamma_3(t)}{2}(\sigma_3 \rho(t)\sigma_3 - \rho_t), \end{aligned} \quad (2)$$

where σ_1, σ_2 and σ_3 are the Pauli x, y, and z matrices, respectively, with $\sigma_\pm = \frac{1}{2}(\sigma_1 \pm i\sigma_2)$, and $\gamma_1(t)$, $\gamma_2(t)$, and $\gamma_3(t)$ being the heating, dissipation, and dephasing rates, respectively. This class of master equations contains some widely used models, such as amplitude damping and pure dephasing [16,18,19].

In this paper, we use the definitions of the QSL for open quantum systems, as defined in [4]:

$$\tau_{QSL} = \frac{1}{\Lambda_\tau^{op}} \sin^2(\mathcal{L}(\rho(0), \rho(\tau))), \quad (3)$$

where $\mathcal{L}(\rho(0), \rho(\tau))$ is the Bures angle between the initial pure state $\rho(0) = |\Phi_0\rangle\langle\Phi_0|$ and the time evolved state $\rho(t)$, defined as

$$\mathcal{L}(\rho(0), \rho(\tau)) = \arccos(\sqrt{\langle\Phi_0|\rho(t)|\Phi_0\rangle}), \tag{4}$$

and

$$\Lambda_\tau^{op} = \frac{1}{\tau}\int_0^\tau ||L_t(\rho(t))||_{op}\, dt, \tag{5}$$

where

$$||L_t(\rho(t))||_{op} = \max_i\{s_i\}, \tag{6}$$

is the operator norm, with s_i being the singular values of $L_t(\rho(t))$.

In [4], it was shown that, for an amplitude damping system, as given by master Equation (2) with $\gamma_1(t) = \gamma_3(t) = 0$ and $\gamma_2(t) = \gamma(t)$, the QSL is directly dependent on the information backflow as

$$\tau_{QSL}/\tau = \frac{1 - |b(\tau)|^2}{1 - |b(\tau)| + \mathcal{N}}, \tag{7}$$

where $\Phi_t(|1\rangle\langle 1|) = |b(t)|^2|1\rangle\langle 1|$ and $\mathcal{N}$ is the Breuer–Laine–Piilo (BLP) non-Markovianity measure, as given by

$$\mathcal{N}(\Phi) = \int_{\partial_t|b(t)|^2 > 0} \partial_t|b(t)|^2 dt. \tag{8}$$

This connection was later studied in more detail, and it was found that the speed-up is not always dependent on the information backflow and can sometimes be present without any non-Markovian effects [10]. In this case, the presence of information backflow coincides with the loss of P-divisibility.

3. QSL for the Non-Monotonic Populations

In [12], the authors introduce an always-CP-divisible model with oscillations in the populations. This model can be written in the form of a master Equation (2), with

$$\gamma_1(t) = \nu + \frac{\nu}{\sqrt{4\nu^2 + \omega^2}}(2\nu\sin(\omega t) + \omega\cos(\omega t)), \tag{9}$$

$$\gamma_2(t) = \nu - \frac{\nu}{\sqrt{4\nu^2 + \omega^2}}(2\nu\sin(\omega t) + \omega\cos(\omega t)), \tag{10}$$

$$\gamma_3(t) = 0, \tag{11}$$

where $\nu, \omega \geq 0$. For simplicity, we use a general pure qubit state and parametrize our initial state as

$$\rho(0) = \begin{pmatrix} a & \sqrt{a}\sqrt{1-a} \\ \sqrt{a}\sqrt{1-a} & 1-a \end{pmatrix}, \tag{12}$$

where $a \in [0,1]$. We omit the phase parameter, since it does not affect the results in the phase-covariant case. The time-evolved density matrix is

$$\rho(t) = \begin{pmatrix} 1 - e^{\nu t}(1 - a + \frac{\nu}{16}f(\nu,\omega,t)) & \sqrt{a(a-1)}e^{-\nu t/2} \\ \sqrt{a(a-1)}e^{-\nu t/2} & e^{\nu t}(1 - a + \frac{\nu}{16}f(\nu,\omega,t)) \end{pmatrix}, \tag{13}$$

where

$$f(\nu,\omega,t) = -1 + e^{8t} + \frac{-16(\nu-4)\omega + 8e^{8t}(2(\nu-4)\omega\cos(\omega t) - (16\nu + \omega^2)\sin(\omega t))}{(64 + \omega^2)\sqrt{4\nu^2 + \omega^2}}. \tag{14}$$

As an example, in Figure 1 we show the QSL as a function of the interaction time τ and of a, for some exemplary values of the parameters ν and ω. We see that the QSL oscillates wildly and it is almost always below $\tau_{QSL}/\tau = 1$. Figure 2 shows the state dynamics of this model, as well as the fidelity between $\rho(0)$ and $\rho(t)$ and the QSL for $a = 1$.

Note that the oscillations and the speed-up in QSL are connected to the oscillations of the fidelity (defined as $F(\rho(0), \rho(t)) = \text{Tr}\left[\sqrt{\sqrt{\rho(t)}\rho(0)\sqrt{\rho(t)}}\right]^2$), even in the absence of non-Markovian effects. Indeed, this example shows that, when fidelity increases, the QSL also decreases.

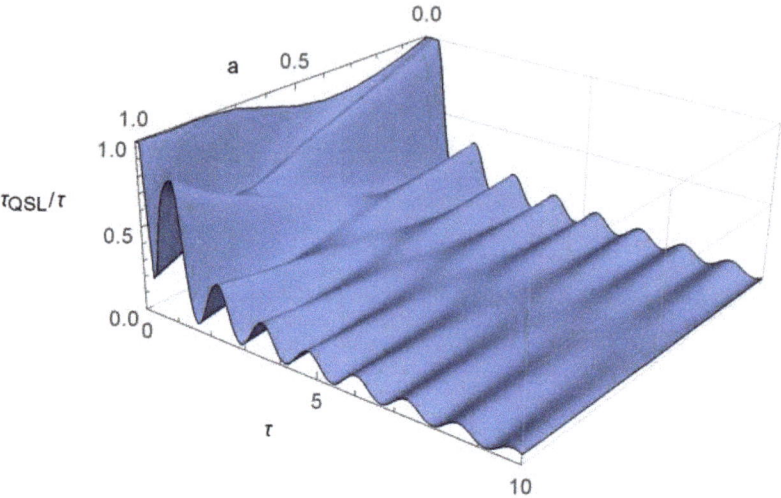

Figure 1. The quantum speed limit (QSL) for the phase-covariant system defined in Equations (9)–(11) for $\nu = 8$ and $\omega = 5$. This system is completely positive (CP)-divisible at all times, but clearly there is significant change in τ_{QSL}/τ for all pure initial states of the form of Equation (12).

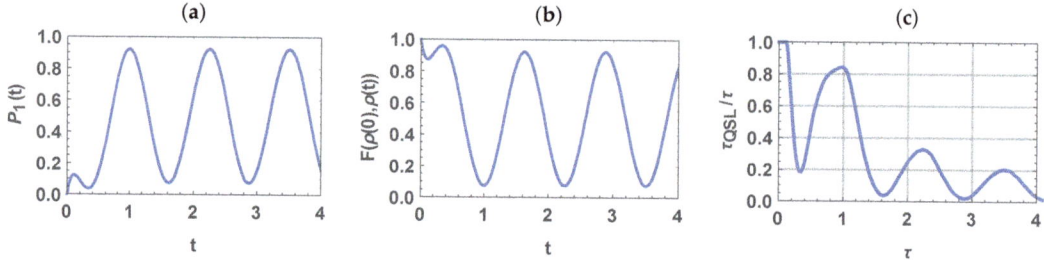

Figure 2. (a) The probability for the qubit to be in the excited state of the model used in Figure 1 for initial ground state ($a = 1$), (b) the fidelity between $\rho(0)$ and $\rho(t)$, and (c) the QSL. The populations undergo oscillations, which results in oscillations in fidelity as well as in QSL. The coherences always remain equal to their initial zero value.

4. P-Divisibility of the Phase-Covariant System

The P-divisibility of this system was studied in [12]. The requirement for P-divisibility is

$$\gamma_{1,2}(t) \geq 0, \tag{15}$$

$$\sqrt{\gamma_1(t)\gamma_2(t)} + 2\gamma_3(t) > 0, \tag{16}$$

where $\gamma_{1,2,3}(t)$ are the decay rates from the master Equation (2). For unital phase-covariant dynamics, which is when $\gamma_1(t) = \gamma_2(t)$, these are equivalent to the BLP non-Markovianity [16]. In the borderline case $\sqrt{\gamma_1(t)\gamma_2(t)} + 2\gamma_3(t) = 0$, a stricter rule

$$\frac{d\gamma_3(t)}{dt} > \gamma_3(t)(\gamma_1(t) + \gamma_2(t)), \quad (17)$$

can be used to determine P-divisibility [12].

As an example, we can use the master Equation (2), with:

$$\gamma_1(t) = e^{-t/2}, \quad (18)$$

$$\gamma_2(t) = e^{-t/4}, \quad (19)$$

$$\gamma_3(t) = \frac{\kappa}{2} e^{-3t/8} \cos(2t) \quad (k \geq 0), \quad (20)$$

which is P-divisible according to Equations (15) and (16) when $\kappa < 1$ and non-P-divisible when $\kappa \geq 1$, whcih is $\exists t \geq 0$ such that $\sqrt{\gamma_1(t)\gamma_2(t)} + 2\gamma_3(t) > 0$. Figure 3 shows the ratio τ_{QSL}/τ as a function of the initial state parameter a and the total interaction time τ for the P-divisible model of Equations (18)–(20) for $\kappa = 0.5$. When the ratio drops below $\tau_{QSL}/\tau = 1$, we know that the theoretical lower limit is lower than the chosen τ and it is possible to speed-up the evolution.

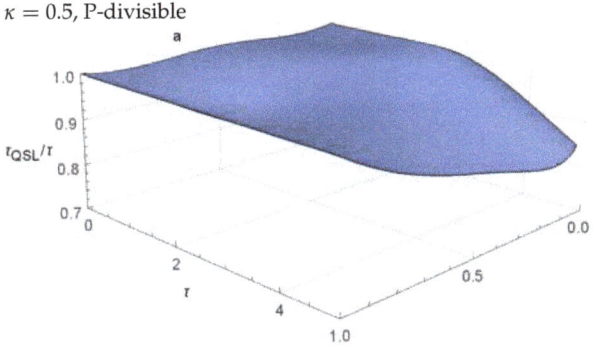

Figure 3. The QSL values for the initial states of (12) with $a \in [0,1]$ and dynamics described by Equations (18)–(20), with $\kappa = 0.5$. Despite being P-divisible according to Equations (15) and (16), we see that the evolution is sped up from the so-called optimal $\tau_{QSL}/\tau = 1$ case for most values of a, similar to the results presented in [4] for non-Markovian dynamics. For $a = 1$, we have $\tau_{QSL}/\tau = 1$ for all values of τ.

Figure 4 shows the same plot with $\kappa = 1$, i.e., when the map is not P-divisible. We see a similar speedup as in Figure 3, with some amplified oscillations. However, the regions where $\tau_{QSL}/\tau = 1$ remains the same in both cases.

We can also break the P-divisibility by choosing $\gamma_1(t)$ and $\gamma_2(t)$, such that Equation (15) is violated, for example:

$$\gamma_1(t) = \gamma_2(t) = e^{-t/2}(\kappa + \cos(2t)) \quad (21)$$

$$\gamma_3(t) = e^{-3/8t}. \quad (22)$$

In this case, when $\kappa < 1$, $\exists t > 0$, such that $\gamma_{1,2}(t) < 0$, which implies non-P-divisible dynamics because of the violation of (15). However, in this case, the dynamics is non-Markovian and the previous results regarding non-Markovianity and quantum speed-up hold [4,16].

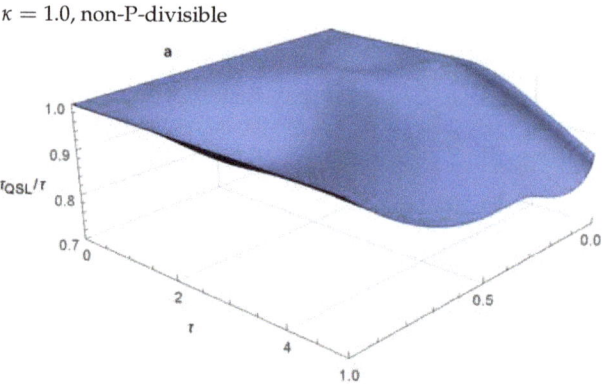

Figure 4. A similar plot as in Figure 3, but with $\kappa = 1$, making the model non-P-divisible. For $a = 1$ the ratio $\tau_{QSL}/\tau = 1$ for all τ, but for other values we can see similar speed-up effects as in Figure 3. All of the areas where $\tau_{QSL}/\tau = 1$ coincide with Figure 3, and changes can only be found when $\tau_{QSL}/\tau < 1$.

In general, for the model that is described by Equations (18)–(20), there is no significant connection between the P-divisbility or non-P-divisible dynamics and the optimality, or non-optimality of the evolution (see Figures 3 and 4 for reference). In both cases, there exists regions where $\tau_{QSL}/\tau = 1$ coincide, as well as the regions where $\tau_{QSL}/\tau < 1$. However, we can numerically find a slight difference between $\kappa = 1/2$ and $\kappa = 1$ for $a = 0.3$, where, for the P-divisible case $\tau_{QSL}/\tau = 1$, and for the non-P-divisible $\tau_{QSL}/\tau < 1$.

In the case of Equations (21) and (22), we see the speedup when κ is greater than the critical value. In Figure 5, we see the QSL as a function of a and τ for $\kappa = 0.5$ and $\kappa = 1.0$. For $a = 1$, we can clearly see that $\tau_{QSL}/\tau = 1$ in the $\kappa = 1$ case, while, for $\kappa < 1$, we have $\tau_{QSL}/\tau = 1$. In this case, the results are consistent with the previous result in [16], since, in this case, $\gamma(t) < 0$ implies BLP non-Markovian dynamics that has been studied and proved to speed up the evolution.

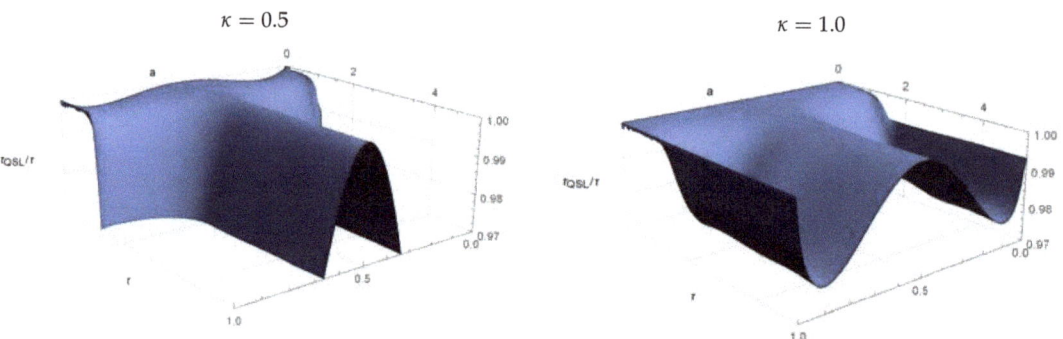

Figure 5. QSL for the dynamics given by Equations (21)–(22). We can see a clear difference for both $a = 0$ and $a = 1$. However, in this case we can explain this using the previous results, since the dynamics is clearly BLP non-Markovian in the left plot, which is when $\kappa = 0.5$, according to [16].

5. Discussion

In this paper, we have studied the quantum speed limit under different phase-covariant dynamics, with both P-divisible and non-P-divisible examples. We have observed that the speed-up effect, which is indicated by $\tau_{QSL}/\tau < 1$, can be seen with non-P-divisible, P-divisible, and even CP-divisible dynamics, further concluding that the speed-up is not simply linked to non-Markovian dynamics. Based on our results, the speed-up is not necessarily connected to non-P- or non-CP-divisible dynamics, and it is possibly linked to oscillations in the populations of a two-level system, which are often present in non-Markovian dynamics.

For the examples that are considered here, there seems to be no difference between P-divisible or non-P-divisible dynamics when considering optimal evolution, which is when $\tau_{QSL}/\tau = 1$. The value of the ratio τ_{QSL}/τ for the regions where $\tau_{QSL}/\tau < 1$ varies, depending on the choice of κ in our examples, but the regions with $\tau_{QSL}/\tau = 1$ are the same. Concluding, we have presented evidence that the speed-up is not generally the result of non-P-divisible dynamics. Moreover, for the model studied, the transition from P-divisible to non-P-divisible dynamics causes speed-up when the transition coincides with the transition between BLP Markovian and non-Markovian.

Author Contributions: J.T. performed most of the research. S.M. directed the study. Plots and numerical data by J.T. Both authors have read and agreed to the published version of the manuscript.

Funding: This research was funded by the Academy of Finland Center of Excellence program (Project no. 312058) and the Vilho, Yrjö and Kalle Väisälä Foundation.

Institutional Review Board Statement: Not applicable.

Informed Consent Statement: Not applicable.

Data Availability Statement: Not applicable.

Acknowledgments: The authors thank Henri Lyyra for helpful discussions during the research.

Conflicts of Interest: The authors declare no conflict of interest.

References

1. Mandelstam, L.; Tamm, I. The uncertainty relation between energy and time in nonrelativistic quantum mechanics. *J. Phys. (USSR)* **1945**, *9*, 249–254. [CrossRef]
2. Margolus, N.; Levitin, L. The maximum speed of dynamical evolution. *Phys. D* **1998**, *120*, 188–195. [CrossRef]
3. Giovannetti, V.; Lloyd, S.; Maccone, L. Quantum limits to dynamical evolution. *Phys. Rev. A* **2003**, *67*, 052109. [CrossRef]
4. Deffner, S.; Lutz, E. Quantum Speed Limit for Non-Markovian Dynamics. *Phys. Rev. Lett.* **2013**, *111*, 010402. [CrossRef] [PubMed]
5. Del Campo, A.; Egusquiza, I.L.; Plenio, M.B.; Huelga, S.F. Quantum Speed Limits in Open System Dynamics. *Phys. Rev. Lett.* **2013**, *110*, 050403. [CrossRef] [PubMed]
6. Taddei, M.M.; Escher, B.M.; Davidovich, L.; de Matos Filho, R.L. Quantum Speed Limit for Physical Processes. *Phys. Rev. Lett.* **2013**, *110*, 050402. [CrossRef] [PubMed]
7. Pires, D.P.; Cianciaruso, M.; Céleri, L.C.; Adesso, G.; Soares-Pinto, D.O. Generalized Geometric Quantum Speed Limits. *Phys. Rev. X* **2016**, *6*, 021031. [CrossRef]
8. Deffner, S. Geometric quantum speed limits: A case for Wigner phase space. *New J. Phys.* **2017**, *19*, 103018. [CrossRef]
9. Cimmarusti, A.D.; Yan, Z.; Patterson, B.D.; Corcos, L.P.; Orozco, L.A.; Deffner, S. Environment-Assisted Speed-up of the Field Evolution in Cavity Quantum Electrodynamics. *Phys. Rev. Lett.* **2015**, *114*, 233602. [CrossRef] [PubMed]
10. Teittinen, J.; Lyyra, H.; Maniscalco, S. There is no general connection between the quantum speed limit and non-Markovianity. *New J. Phys.* **2019**, *21*, 123041. [CrossRef]
11. Breuer, H.P.; Laine, E.M.; Piilo, J. Measure for the Degree of Non-Markovian Behavior of Quantum Processes in Open Systems. *Phys. Rev. Lett.* **2009**, *103*, 210401. [CrossRef] [PubMed]
12. Filippov, S.; Glinov, A.; Leppäjärvi, L. Phase covariant qubit dynamics and divisibility. *Lobachevskii J. Math* **2020**, *41*, 617–630. [CrossRef]
13. Gorini, V.; Kossakowski, A.; Sudarshan, G. Completely positive dynamical semigroups of N-level systems. *J. Math. Phys.* **1976**, *17*, 821. [CrossRef]
14. Lindblad, G. On the generators of quantum dynamical semigroups. *Commun. Math. Phys.* **1976**, *48*, 119–130. [CrossRef]
15. Rivas, A.; Huelga, S.F. *Open Quantum Systems: An Introduction*; Springer: Berlin/Heidelberg, Germany, 2012. [CrossRef]
16. Teittinen, J.; Lyyra, H.; Sokolov, B.; Maniscalco, S. Revealing memory effects in phase-covariant quantum master equations. *New J. Phys.* **2018**, *20*, 073012. [CrossRef]
17. Lankinen, J.; Lyyra, H.; Sokolov, B.; Teittinen, J.; Ziaei, B.; Maniscalco, S. Complete positivity, finite-temperature effects, and additivity of noise for time-local qubit dynamics. *Phys. Rev. A* **2016**, *93*, 052103. [CrossRef]

18. Smirne, A.; Kołodyński, J.; Huelga, S.F.; Demkowicz Dobrzański, R. Ultimate Precision Limits for Noisy Frequency Estimation. *Phys. Rev. Lett.* **2016**, *116*, 120801. [CrossRef] [PubMed]
19. Haase, J.; Smirne, A.; Kołodyński, J.; Demkowicz Dobrzański, R.; Huelga, S.F. Fundamental limits to frequency estimation: A comprehensive microscopic perspective. *New J. Phys.* **2018**, *20*, 053009. [CrossRef]

Article

Thermodynamics of Reduced State of the Field

Stefano Cusumano [1] and Łukasz Rudnicki [1,2,*]

[1] International Center for Theory of Quantum Technologies, University of Gdansk, 80-308 Gdańsk, Poland; stefano.cusumano@ug.edu.pl
[2] Center for Theoretical Physics, Polish Academy of Sciences, 02-668 Warszawa, Poland
* Correspondence: lukasz.rudnicki@ug.edu.pl

Abstract: Recent years have seen the flourishing of research devoted to quantum effects on mesoscopic and macroscopic scales. In this context, in *Entropy* **2019**, *21*, 705, a formalism aiming at describing macroscopic quantum fields, dubbed Reduced State of the Field (RSF), was envisaged. While, in the original work, a proper notion of entropy for macroscopic fields, together with their dynamical equations, was derived, here, we expand thermodynamic analysis of the RSF, discussing the notion of heat, solving dynamical equations in various regimes of interest, and showing the thermodynamic implications of these solutions.

Keywords: reduced state of the field; quantum thermodynamics; macroscopic fields; quantum optics

1. Introduction

In recent years, a considerable attention has been given to the study of quantum phenomena on mesoscopic scale, as many physical systems that are nowadays fundamental for physical applications fall into this regime [1,2]. The main characteristic of mesoscopic systems is that, while they are still large enough not to be considered purely quantum, they are neither small enough to ignore quantum effects.

Furthermore, while the behavior of macroscopic fields is well described by classical wave equations with coherent sources, incorporation of thermal and random sources into the field equations still represents an open problem [3]. As a matter of fact, the most common description of such a situation relies on the introduction of phenomenological terms, for example, terms describing the damping. This solution is not fully satisfactory from a theoretical point of view, as these extra terms do not give a correct thermodynamic description of such systems. On this basis, and on drawing from the fact that the ultimate description of any physical system should be given by quantum mechanics, the Reduced State of the Field (RSF) formalism was conceived [4].

Since a completely quantum picture is generally too complex and, consequently, not convenient to treat macroscopic fields, the RSF aims at describing macroscopic waves using a coarse-grained version of the quantum formalism. Such a description allows one to retain the most important quantum features that would even emanate at macroscopic scale [4], while, at the same time, mitigating the complexity that would have no effect beyond the microscopic realm. Interestingly, in the same spirit, one can answer the question being a sort of opposite to the former one, namely which features of the quantum evolution can be classified as classical [5].

On the other hand, recent years have seen the flourishing of quantum thermodynamics [6], namely the study of thermodynamic phenomena on the quantum scale. This interest has been fostered by progressive miniaturization of electronic and optical devices, at the level where quantum phenomena cannot be ignored [7]. We, therefore, observe a huge development of the field of quantum thermodynamics, where a wide range of topics is being covered, e.g., thermalization and heat transfer [8–11], quantum heat engines and refrigerators [12–18], and quantum batteries [19–21].

The biggest advantage of the RSF formalism is that it provides both a suitable definition of entropy for radiation fields and dynamical equations describing the field which are in a closed form (do not depend on other degrees of freedom). It is, thus, of interest to see how thermodynamics intersects with the description of mesoscopic and macroscopic fields since, especially on the mesoscopic scale, one typically does not have full control over the system, yet quantum effects need to be taken into account in order to describe the system appropriately [22].

In this paper, we want to explore how thermodynamic phenomena, such as heat exchange, fit the RSF formalism. Moreover, we want to analyze the behavior of the entropy of RSF [4], as its definition differs from the one usually found in the classical or quantum realms. The paper is organized as follows. In Section 2, we briefly review the RSF formalism, pointing out its main features. In Section 3, starting from the evolution equations of RSF, we consistently define the main thermodynamic quantities, such as internal energy, heat, and work. Then, in Section 4, we solve the equations of motion in some simple but relevant situations, highlighting the thermodynamic meaning of the different terms present therein. Finally, in Section 5, we give our conclusions and some outlooks for future works.

2. The RSF Formalism

This section mostly follows Reference [4], since we summarize here the most important background and ingredients of the RSF formalism. In particular, all formulas appearing in this section are taken from Reference [4].

We start with classical electromagnetic field which, in a finite volume, is described by a set of modes $f_k(x;t) = e^{-i\omega_k t} f_k(x)$, where x is the position, k is a discrete index, and ω_k is the frequency at which the mode oscillates. In the first quantization picture, these modes represent eigenstates of the single-particle Hamiltonian of quasi-particles associated with the field. Under a proper normalization, these modes form an orthonormal basis of the single-particle Hilbert space, where the energy of each mode is equal to $\hbar\omega_k$.

In the second quantization picture, a pair of operators $\hat{a}_k, \hat{a}_k^\dagger$ is associated to each mode f_k. Standard bosonic commutation relations hold:

$$\left[\hat{a}_k, \hat{a}_{k'}^\dagger\right] = \delta_{kk'} \quad \left[\hat{a}_k, \hat{a}_{k'}\right] = \left[\hat{a}_k^\dagger, \hat{a}_{k'}^\dagger\right] = 0, \tag{1}$$

so that the action of the annihilation and creation operators, on the vectors in the corresponding Fock space spanned by the orthonormal set $\{|n\rangle_k\}$, is

$$\hat{a}_k |n_k\rangle = \sqrt{n_k} |n_k - 1\rangle \quad \hat{a}_k^\dagger |n_k\rangle = \sqrt{n_k + 1} |n_k + 1\rangle. \tag{2}$$

The RSF formalism relies on a correspondence between operators acting on the single-particle Hilbert space and additive operators acting on the Fock space. The former can be written as:

$$\hat{b} = \sum_{k,k'} b_{kk'} |k\rangle\langle k'|, \tag{3}$$

where $|k\rangle \equiv |f_k\rangle$, while the corresponding additive observable in the Fock space is (We follow the convention introduced in Reference [4], according to which operators in the Fock space are denoted by capital letters (with the density operator $\hat{\rho}$ being an exception), while operators acting on a single-particle Hilbert space are denoted by small letters.):

$$\hat{B} = \sum_{k,k'} b_{kk'} \hat{a}_k^\dagger \hat{a}_{k'}. \tag{4}$$

Consequently, unitary operators $\hat{u}$ acting on the single-particle Hilbert space are in correspondence with multiplicative operators on the Fock space via:

$$\hat{u} = e^{i\hat{b}} \rightarrow \hat{U} = e^{i\hat{B}}. \tag{5}$$

From now on, we also use "Tr" for trace operations in the Fock space and "tr" for traces applied to the level of the RSF, i.e., on a single-particle Hilbert space.

The RSF description of the state of a macroscopic field is based on the couple $(\hat{r}, |\alpha\rangle)$, defined from the full quantum state of the field $\hat{\rho}$ in the Fock space as:

$$\hat{r} = \sum_{k,k'} \text{Tr}\left[\hat{\rho}\, \hat{a}_{k'}^\dagger \hat{a}_k\right] |k\rangle\langle k'| := \sum_{k,k'} r_{kk'} |k\rangle\langle k'|, \qquad (6a)$$

$$|\alpha\rangle = \sum_k \text{Tr}[\hat{\rho}\, \hat{a}_k] |k\rangle := \sum_k \alpha_k |k\rangle. \qquad (6b)$$

The matrix $\hat{r}$ is a single-particle density operator, while the vector $|\alpha\rangle$ contains the information about the phase of the macroscopic field.

It is important to observe that the single-particle density operator is not normalized to unity but, rather, to the total number of particles in the state, i.e.,

$$\text{tr}\{\hat{r}\} = N = \text{Tr}\{\hat{\rho}\hat{N}\}, \quad \hat{N} = \sum_k \hat{a}_k^\dagger \hat{a}_k. \qquad (7)$$

In fact, the same expectation-value identification holds for any additive observable

$$\text{tr}\{\hat{r}\hat{b}\} = \text{Tr}\{\hat{\rho}\hat{B}\}. \qquad (8)$$

Furthermore, it turned out beneficial to define an another object, the *correlation matrix*

$$\hat{r}^\alpha = \hat{r} - |\alpha\rangle\langle\alpha|, \quad \text{where} \quad |\alpha\rangle\langle\alpha| = \sum_{k,k'} \alpha_k \alpha_{k'}^* |k\rangle\langle k'|, \qquad (9)$$

which is a positive semi-definite operator being zero if and only if the state is coherent. Using this operator, it is then possible to give a suitable definition of entropy for macroscopic fields, which is

$$S[\hat{r}^\alpha] = k_B \,\text{tr}[(\hat{r}^\alpha + 1)\ln(\hat{r}^\alpha + 1) - \hat{r}^\alpha \ln \hat{r}^\alpha]. \qquad (10)$$

This definition of entropy has an appealing feature of being always greater than or equal to zero, and being zero only when the RSF is coherent. This also highlights the fact that the coherent states are the only pure states in this formalism.

To shortly summarize the above, the RSF formalism is particularly suited to deal with situation where one does not have full quantum control of the system (we just control first and second moments, so to speak), as is in the case of macroscopic fields, but quantum effects are still visible. Having revised the RSF formalism and its main features, we are now ready to start thermodynamic considerations.

3. Thermodynamics of the RSF

In a usual scenario described by thermodynamics, one deals with a system S, often called the working fluid, interacting with one or more thermal baths, i.e., much larger systems with infinite heat capacity that are typically assumed to have a well-defined temperature. By changing the Hamiltonian, i.e., the energy, of the working fluid S and letting it interact appropriately with the thermal baths, it is possible to extract work from the system (i.e., we have a heat engine) or to use work to transfer heat from a cold to a hot bath (i.e., we implement a refrigerator).

As in what follows, we will not be interested in a description of the thermal baths but, rather, in their action on the working fluid S. Therefore, we want to define heat and work only in terms of the state S, in the current context sufficiently well described by the couple $(\hat{r}, |\alpha\rangle)$. In order to study the thermodynamics of a macroscopic field described under the RSF formalism, we first need to recall the dynamical equations describing the behavior of the field when it interacts with an external bath. This was already done in Reference [4], where the system of equation for the RSF was derived from the standard expression for a map belonging to a so-called quasi-free dynamical semigroup [23,24], thus extending this concept to RSF formalism. The set of equations [4] describing the dynamics of the couple $(\hat{r}, |\alpha\rangle)$ can be derived from the equations describing the temporal evolution of the full state in Fock space $\hat{\rho}$ through:

$$\frac{d}{dt}r_{kk'} = \text{Tr}\left\{\hat{a}_{k'}^\dagger \hat{a}_k \frac{d\hat{\rho}}{dt}\right\}, \quad \frac{d}{dt}\alpha_k = \text{Tr}\left\{\hat{a}_k \frac{d\hat{\rho}}{dt}\right\}. \tag{11}$$

Considering a generic model of dynamics for $\hat{\rho}$, given by the evolution equation [4]

$$\frac{d}{dt}\hat{\rho} = -\frac{i}{\hbar}[\hat{H}, \hat{\rho}] + \sum_{k=1}^{N}\left[\zeta_k \hat{a}_k^\dagger - \zeta_k^* \hat{a}_k, \hat{\rho}\right] + \sum_{k,k'=1}^{N} \Gamma_\downarrow^{k'k}\left(\hat{a}_k \hat{\rho} \hat{a}_{k'}^\dagger - \frac{1}{2}\{\hat{a}_{k'}^\dagger \hat{a}_k, \hat{\rho}\}\right)$$
$$+ \sum_{k,k'=1}^{N} \Gamma_\uparrow^{k'k}\left(\hat{a}_{k'}^\dagger \hat{\rho} \hat{a}_k - \frac{1}{2}\{\hat{a}_k \hat{a}_{k'}^\dagger, \hat{\rho}\}\right) + \int \mu(du)\left(\hat{U}\hat{\rho}\hat{U}^\dagger - \hat{\rho}\right), \tag{12}$$

which includes the presence of a coherent source, a thermal bath, and random scattering, one can write the following equations for the couple $(\hat{r}, |\alpha\rangle)$ (Note that the anticommutator terms, in comparison with Reference [4], have been divided by 2. See Reference [5] for details.):

$$\frac{d}{dt}\hat{r} = -\frac{i}{\hbar}[\hat{h}, \hat{r}] + (|\zeta\rangle\langle\alpha| + |\alpha\rangle\langle\zeta|) + \frac{1}{2}\{(\hat{\gamma}_\uparrow - \hat{\gamma}_\downarrow), \hat{r}\} + \hat{\gamma}_\uparrow$$
$$+ \int \mu(du)(\hat{u}\hat{r}\hat{u}^\dagger - \hat{r}), \tag{13a}$$

$$\frac{d}{dt}|\alpha\rangle = -\frac{i}{\hbar}\hat{h}|\alpha\rangle + |\zeta\rangle + \frac{1}{2}(\hat{\gamma}_\uparrow - \hat{\gamma}_\downarrow)|\alpha\rangle + \int \mu(du)(\hat{u} - 1)|\alpha\rangle. \tag{13b}$$

Let us start by explaining the meaning of each term in (12) viz. Equations (13a) and (13b). In the dynamical equation for $\hat{r}$, we first find the commutator of $\hat{r}$ with the single-particle Hamiltonian $\hat{h} = \hbar\sum_k \omega_k |k\rangle\langle k|$ stemming from $\hat{H} = \hbar\sum_k \omega_k \hat{a}_k^\dagger \hat{a}_k$, and this term describes nothing but the standard unitary dynamics induced by the free Hamiltonian. Next, we find the term $|\zeta\rangle\langle\alpha|$, which describes the effect of a coherent source, and, thus, also depends on the phase of the system $|\alpha\rangle$. Then, we can see the anticommutator term with the operators

$$\hat{\gamma}_\updownarrow = \sum_{k,k'} \Gamma_\updownarrow^{kk'} |k\rangle\langle k'|, \tag{14}$$

describing stimulated absorption and emission processes, while the isolated term $\hat{\gamma}_\uparrow$ describes spontaneous emission processes. The coefficients $\Gamma_\updownarrow^{kk'}$ encode the information about the state of the thermal bath and its interaction with the system. Finally, the integral term describes the effect of random scattering phenomena, where the operators $\hat{u}$ are unitary. Similar considerations apply to the dynamical equation for $|\alpha\rangle$. Note also that, although the usual single particle approach is one where recursive systems of equations are truncated through appropriate approximations or boundary conditions, in the RSF approach, one deals with a closed system of equation, a feature that greatly simplifies the study of the dynamics of a macroscopic field.

As the entropy is defined in terms of the correlation matrix $\hat{r}^{(\alpha)}$, it is also useful to derive the dynamical equation for this quantity. Since $\hat{r}^{(\alpha)} = \hat{r} - |\alpha\rangle\langle\alpha|$, we only need to compute the time derivative of $|\alpha\rangle\langle\alpha|$ using Equation (13b):

$$\frac{d}{dt}|\alpha\rangle\langle\alpha| = \left(\frac{d}{dt}|\alpha\rangle\right)\langle\alpha| + |\alpha\rangle\left(\frac{d}{dt}\langle\alpha|\right)$$
$$= -\frac{i}{\hbar}\left[\hat{h}, |\alpha\rangle\langle\alpha|\right] + (|\alpha\rangle\langle\zeta| + |\zeta\rangle\langle\alpha|) + \frac{1}{2}\{(\hat{\gamma}_\uparrow - \hat{\gamma}_\downarrow), |\alpha\rangle\langle\alpha|\}$$
$$+ \int \mu(du)(\hat{u}|\alpha\rangle\langle\alpha| + |\alpha\rangle\langle\alpha|\hat{u}^\dagger) - 2|\alpha\rangle\langle\alpha|), \tag{15}$$

from which we can write the dynamical evolution for the correlation matrix $\hat{r}^{(\alpha)}$ as

$$\frac{d}{dt}\hat{r}^{(\alpha)} = -\frac{i}{\hbar}[\hat{h}, \hat{r}^{(\alpha)}] + \frac{1}{2}\left\{(\hat{\gamma}_\uparrow - \hat{\gamma}_\downarrow), \hat{r}^{(\alpha)}\right\} + \hat{\gamma}_\uparrow$$
$$+ \int \mu(du)\left(\hat{u}\hat{r}^{(\alpha)}\hat{u}^\dagger - \hat{r}^{(\alpha)}\right) + \int \mu(du)(\hat{u}-1)|\alpha\rangle\langle\alpha|(\hat{u}^\dagger - 1). \tag{16}$$

From this equation, we can see that the dynamics of the correlation matrix are not influenced by the presence of coherent sources. Consequently, the entropy $S[\hat{r}^{(\alpha)}]$ is also invariant with respect to coherent evolution. This feature of the theory is associated with the fact that we are dealing with a mesoscopic or macroscopic system, where, in fact, we do not have access to all degrees of freedom [4]. In particular, the single-particle Hamiltonian $\hat{h}$ does not carry the whole content of the Hamiltonian in the Fock space which also contains contributions due to the displacement. In view of this, we define the internal energy as

$$U = \mathrm{tr}\left[\hat{h}\hat{r}^{(\alpha)}\right] \equiv \mathrm{tr}\left[\hat{h}\hat{r}\right] - \langle\alpha|\hat{h}|\alpha\rangle. \tag{17}$$

This definition is motivated by the form of the entropy in Equation (10) and from the related discussion in Reference [4]: as the definition of entropy relies on the effective degree of control that one has over the physical system under examination, the same should apply to other quantities of interest. Since, in the RSF formalism, the entropy is invariant under the application of the Weyl displacement operator, one could expect the internal energy to follow the same behavior. In particular, if, for instance, we were to define the internal energy in the "intuitive" way as $\mathrm{tr}\left[\hat{h}\hat{r}\right]$, then displacement would be a process implying heat absorption from the system, with no change of entropy. In Section 4, we are going to show that this issue is resolved by Equation (17), and that, thanks to this definition, we are able to define properly the free energy of the system. Last but not least, let us emphasize that the internal energy of the system is a notion which depends on an arbitrary choice in which degrees of freedom describe the system and which belong to its environment.

Using the notion of internal energy in Equation (17), one has a natural decomposition

$$dU = \mathrm{tr}\left[\frac{d\hat{h}}{dt}\hat{r}^{(\alpha)}\right]dt + \mathrm{tr}\left[\hat{h}\frac{d\hat{r}^{(\alpha)}}{dt}\right]dt = dW + \delta Q. \tag{18}$$

Two observations are in place here. First of all, the single particle Hamiltonian is time independent by construction. This is because the frequencies, as well as the eigenmode basis, of the Hamiltonian, are not under control and do not vary over time due to the dynamics of the sole field. Therefore, for generic macroscopic fields, there is no work, just the heat. Work would require an engineered variant of time evolution, i.e., one can perform (extract) work on (from) the system only by changing the frequencies ω_k.

Second of all, only the scattering term couples $\hat{r}^{(\alpha)}$ with $|\alpha\rangle$ in Equation (16). This feature in a salient way distinguishes the scattering processes from the other processes subsumed in the dynamical equations. Within a thermodynamic description, which is solely based here on the correlation matrix, the scattering belongs to a different (more complex) class of (likely non-equilibrium) processes. The latter property, however, would strongly depend on the measure $\mu(du)$ chosen. Perhaps, for the invariant Haar measure, the situation would simplify, still, the aforementioned coupling will be there.

Therefore, we believe that the scattering processes deserve a separate and detailed treatment. Consequently, here, we shall neglect random scattering terms, with the goal of delineating the heat exchange and entropy production due to other processes. Under this simplifying assumption, the heat exchanged is equal to

$$\delta Q = \text{tr}\left[\hat{h}\frac{d\hat{r}^{(\alpha)}}{dt}\right]dt = \frac{1}{2}\text{tr}\left[\hat{r}^{(\alpha)}\left\{\hat{\gamma}_\uparrow - \hat{\gamma}_\downarrow, \hat{h}\right\}\right]dt + \text{tr}\left[\hat{h}\hat{\gamma}_\uparrow\right]dt$$

$$= \hbar \sum_{k,k'} \frac{\omega_k + \omega_{k'}}{2} r_{kk'}^{(\alpha)}\left(\Gamma_\uparrow^{k'k} - \Gamma_\downarrow^{k'k}\right)dt + \hbar \omega_k \Gamma_\uparrow^{kk} dt, \qquad (19)$$

that is, it only depends on interactions with the thermal bath. In particular, the second term on the right-hand side of Equation (19) is responsible for the equilibration process towards the equilibrium populations dictated by the bath structure, while the first term describes heat exchanges due to changes in the modes' occupations happening because of the interaction with the bath.

The variation of the entropy in time is also found to be

$$\frac{d}{dt}S[\hat{r}^{(\alpha)}] = k_B \text{tr}\left[\frac{d\hat{r}^{(\alpha)}}{dt}\ln\left(\frac{\hat{r}^{(\alpha)}+1}{\hat{r}^{(\alpha)}}\right)\right]. \qquad (20)$$

We use the notation in which the fraction of non-negative operators needs to be understood in terms of their eigenvalues. This is possible because, whenever some eigenvalue approaches 0, the time derivative also vanishes, killing the potential singularities [25].

Note that the trace of $\hat{r}^{(\alpha)}$ does not need to be constant in time. For a quasi-static process, in which the state $\hat{\rho}$ is always in thermal equilibrium, the correlation matrix is always of the form

$$\hat{r}^{(\alpha)} = \frac{1}{e^{\beta \hat{h}} - 1}. \qquad (21)$$

Since, in this case,

$$\ln\left(\frac{\hat{r}^{(\alpha)}+1}{\hat{r}^{(\alpha)}}\right) = \beta \hat{h}, \qquad (22)$$

we recover the equality from standard thermodynamics

$$dS = k_B \beta \delta Q. \qquad (23)$$

This observation further strengthens our definition of work and heat. Moreover, for a non-quasi-static process, one has that $\hat{r}^{(\alpha)}$ is not of the form in Equation (22); thus, one has also entropy production.

4. Some Examples of RSF Thermodynamics

In the following subsections, we want to solve the dynamical Equations (13a) and (13b) under various circumstances where some of the terms are absent or can be simplified, thus highlighting their thermodynamic meaning.

4.1. Free Dynamics of the RSF

The simplest, and almost trivial, case that one can analyze is the one where no interaction with either a coherent source or a thermal bath is present, so that the dynamics of the RSF is fully described by the Hamiltonian term alone. Assuming the Hamiltonian in the Fock space to be:

$$\hat{H} = \sum_k \hbar \omega_k \hat{a}_k^\dagger \hat{a}_k \to \hat{h} = \sum_k \hbar \omega_k |k\rangle\langle k|, \qquad (24)$$

we can explicitly write down the equations governing the matrix elements $r_{kk'}(t)$ and the vector components $\alpha_k(t)$ as:

$$\frac{d}{dt} r_{kk'}(t) = -i(\omega_k - \omega_{k'}) r_{kk'}(t), \quad \frac{d}{dt} \alpha_k(t) = -i\omega_k \alpha_k(t). \qquad (25)$$

The solutions to these equations are easily found:

$$r_{kk}(t) = r_{kk}(0); \quad r_{kk'} = e^{-i(\omega_k - \omega_{k'})t} r_{kk'}(0); \quad \alpha_k(t) = e^{-i\omega_k t} \alpha_k(0). \qquad (26)$$

These solutions imply that, under purely free dynamics, the populations stay constant, while the coherences among them rotate at a frequency equal to the detuning between the modes. Finally, the components of the phase vector $|\alpha\rangle$ rotate at the corresponding frequency. In accordance with Equation (19), there is no heat exchange, as there is no thermal bath. An important fact to be noted is that, as in Equation (16), the correlation matrix depends on the Hamiltonian $\hat{h}$ only through the commutator term, and the entropy is unchanged under purely Hamiltonian dynamics, since the eigenvalues of $\hat{r}^{(\alpha)}$ are left unchanged.

4.2. RSF Dynamics in Presence of a Coherent Source

We now want to solve Equations (13a) and (13b) subject to a coherent source, but still without a thermal bath, so that we get:

$$\frac{d}{dt}\hat{r} = -\frac{i}{\hbar}[\hat{h}, \hat{r}] + (|\alpha\rangle\langle\zeta| + |\zeta\rangle\langle\alpha|), \qquad (27)$$

$$\frac{d}{dt}|\alpha\rangle = -\frac{i}{\hbar}\hat{h}|\alpha\rangle + |\zeta\rangle, \qquad (28)$$

where $|\zeta\rangle = \sum_k \zeta_k |k\rangle$. We can easily get the dynamical equations for the matrix elements:

$$\frac{d}{dt} r_{kk'} = -i(\omega_k - \omega_{k'}) r_{kk'} + (\alpha_k \zeta_{k'}^* + \alpha_{k'}^* \zeta_k), \qquad (29)$$

$$\frac{d}{dt}\alpha_k = -i\omega_k \alpha_k + \zeta_k. \qquad (30)$$

Solving the second equation first, we get

$$\alpha_k(t) = e^{-i\omega_k t} \alpha_k(0) - i\frac{\zeta_k}{\omega_k}(1 - e^{-i\omega_k t}), \qquad (31)$$

so that the $\hat{r}$ matrix elements are

$$r_{kk'}(t) = e^{-i(\omega_k - \omega_{k'})t}\left[r_{kk'}(0) + \int_0^t ds\, e^{i(\omega_k - \omega_{k'})s}(\alpha_k(s)\zeta_{k'}^* + \alpha_{k'}^*(s)\zeta_k) \right]. \qquad (32)$$

After we perform the integral, we get

$$\begin{aligned} r_{kk'}(t) &= e^{-i(\omega_k - \omega_{k'})t}\left(r_{kk'}(0) + \frac{\zeta_k \zeta_{k'}^*}{\omega_k \omega_{k'}} \right) + \frac{\zeta_k \zeta_{k'}^*}{\omega_k \omega_{k'}}\left(1 - e^{-i\omega_k t} - e^{i\omega_{k'} t}\right) \\ &+ i\left(\frac{\alpha_k(0)\zeta_{k'}^*}{\omega_{k'}} e^{-i\omega_k t} - \frac{\alpha_{k'}^*(0)\zeta_k}{\omega_k} e^{i\omega_{k'} t} \right). \end{aligned} \qquad (33)$$

Let us consider the case where the initial phase vector $|\alpha\rangle$ is null, i.e., $\alpha_k(0) = 0$, for all k. In this case, the solution for the phase and the matrix elements of $\hat{r}$ reads:

$$\alpha_k(t) = -i\frac{\zeta_k}{\omega_k}(1 - e^{-i\omega_k t}), \tag{34}$$

$$r_{kk'}(t) = e^{-i(\omega_k - \omega_{k'})t}\left(r_{kk'}(0) + \frac{\zeta_k \zeta_{k'}^*}{\omega_k \omega_{k'}}\right) + \frac{\zeta_k \zeta_{k'}^*}{\omega_k \omega_{k'}}\left(1 - e^{-i\omega_k t} - e^{i\omega_{k'} t}\right). \tag{35}$$

The latter result, for the diagonal elements $r_{kk}(t)$, reduces to

$$r_{kk}(t) = r_{kk}(0) + 2\frac{|\zeta_k|^2}{\omega_k^2}(1 - \cos\omega_k t). \tag{36}$$

This implies that the populations oscillate around the average values $r_{kk}(0) + |\zeta_k|^2/\omega_k^2$. Of course, the correlation matrix remains constant (also if initial $|\alpha\rangle$ is not null), so does the entropy.

4.3. Dynamics of the RSF in Presence of a Coherent Source and a Thermal Bath

Let us now consider the case where also a dissipation term is present, i.e., we want to analyze the case where the system interacts with both a coherent source and a heat bath. In this case, the dynamical equations for $\hat{r}$ and $|\alpha\rangle$ are:

$$\frac{d\hat{r}}{dt} = -\frac{i}{\hbar}[\hat{h}, \hat{r}] + (|\alpha\rangle\langle\zeta| + |\zeta\rangle\langle\alpha|) + \frac{1}{2}\{(\hat{\gamma}_\uparrow - \hat{\gamma}_\downarrow), \hat{r}\} + \hat{\gamma}_\uparrow, \tag{37}$$

$$\frac{d}{dt}|\alpha\rangle = -\frac{i}{\hbar}\hat{h}|\alpha\rangle + |\zeta\rangle + \frac{1}{2}(\hat{\gamma}_\uparrow - \hat{\gamma}_\downarrow)|\alpha\rangle, \tag{38}$$

where the operators $\hat{\gamma}_\updownarrow$ have already been defined as

$$\hat{\gamma}_\updownarrow = \sum_{k,k'} \Gamma_\updownarrow^{kk'} |k\rangle\langle k'|. \tag{39}$$

Let us remind that the matrix elements $\Gamma_\updownarrow^{kk'}$ are the particle creation and decay rates that can be derived using the Fermi golden rule. Under the typical Born, Markov, and secular approximations, the operators $\hat{\gamma}_\updownarrow$ become diagonal

$$\hat{\gamma}_\updownarrow = \sum_k \Gamma_\updownarrow^k |k\rangle\langle k|, \tag{40}$$

where the rates $\Gamma_\updownarrow^k$, due to the thermal character of the bath, are related via

$$\frac{\Gamma_\uparrow^k}{\Gamma_\downarrow^k} = e^{-\frac{\hbar\omega_k}{k_B T}}, \tag{41}$$

with k_B being the Boltzmann constant, and T being the temperature of the heat bath.

In this case, the dynamical equations for the RSF become:

$$\frac{dr_{kk'}}{dt} = -i(\omega_k - \omega_{k'})r_{kk'} - \frac{1}{2}\left(\frac{\Gamma_\downarrow^k}{Z_k} + \frac{\Gamma_\downarrow^{k'}}{Z_{k'}}\right)r_{kk'} + \delta_{kk'}\Gamma_\uparrow^k + (\alpha_k \zeta_{k'}^* + \alpha_{k'}^* \zeta_k), \tag{42}$$

$$\frac{d\alpha_k}{dt} = -i\omega_k \alpha_k - \frac{\Gamma_\downarrow^k}{2Z_k}\alpha_k + \zeta_k, \tag{43}$$

where we have defined $Z_k = \left(1 - e^{-\beta\hbar\omega_k}\right)^{-1}$. These equations are of the same form as Equations (29) and (30). This can be noted by defining complex frequencies $\tilde{\omega}_k = \omega_k - i\Gamma_\downarrow^k/2Z_k$. In this notation, we get:

$$\frac{dr_{kk'}}{dt} = -i(\tilde{\omega}_k - \tilde{\omega}_{k'}^*)r_{kk'} + \delta_{kk'}\Gamma_\uparrow^k + (\alpha_k\zeta_{k'}^* + \alpha_{k'}^*\zeta_k), \tag{44}$$

$$\frac{d\alpha_k}{dt} = -i\tilde{\omega}_k\alpha_k + \zeta_k, \tag{45}$$

so that one can immediately write down the solution to the second equation as:

$$\alpha_k(t) = e^{-i\tilde{\omega}_k t}\alpha_k(0) - i\frac{\zeta_k}{\tilde{\omega}_k}\left(1 - e^{-i\tilde{\omega}_k t}\right), \tag{46}$$

which implies that the phases α_k are driven towards their steady-state values

$$\alpha_k^{\text{steady}} = -i\frac{\zeta_k}{\tilde{\omega}_k}. \tag{47}$$

As for the matrix elements $r_{kk'}$, one finds:

$$r_{kk'}(t) = e^{-i(\tilde{\omega}_k - \tilde{\omega}_{k'}^*)t}\left[r_{kk'}(0) + \int_0^t ds\, e^{i(\tilde{\omega}_k - \tilde{\omega}_{k'}^*)s}\left(\alpha_k(s)\zeta_{k'}^* + \alpha_{k'}^*(s)\zeta_k + \delta_{kk'}\Gamma_\uparrow^k\right)\right],$$

and, consequently,

$$\begin{aligned}r_{kk'}(t) &= e^{-i(\tilde{\omega}_k - \tilde{\omega}_{k'}^*)t}\left(r_{kk'}(0) + \frac{\zeta_k\zeta_{k'}^*}{\tilde{\omega}_k\tilde{\omega}_{k'}^*}\right) + \frac{\zeta_k\zeta_{k'}^*}{\tilde{\omega}_k\tilde{\omega}_{k'}^*}\left(1 - e^{-i\tilde{\omega}_k t} - e^{i\tilde{\omega}_{k'}^* t}\right) \\ &+ i\left(\frac{\alpha_k(0)\zeta_{k'}^*}{\tilde{\omega}_{k'}^*}e^{-i\tilde{\omega}_k t} - \frac{\alpha_{k'}^*(0)\zeta_k}{\tilde{\omega}_k}e^{i\tilde{\omega}_{k'}^* t}\right) + \delta_{kk'}e^{-\beta\hbar\omega_k}Z_k\left(1 - e^{-\frac{\Gamma_\downarrow^k}{Z_k}t}\right).\end{aligned} \tag{48}$$

It is of particular interest to see the steady values of the matrix elements $r_{kk'}$,

$$r_{kk'}^{\text{steady}} = \frac{\zeta_k\zeta_{k'}^*}{\tilde{\omega}_k\tilde{\omega}_{k'}^*} + \delta_{kk'}e^{-\beta\hbar\omega_k}Z_k. \tag{49}$$

From this steady-state solution, together with Equation (47), we can compute the associated correlation matrix $\hat{r}^{(\alpha)}$, for which one simply obtains:

$$r_{kk'}^{(\alpha)\text{steady}} = r_{kk'}^{\text{steady}} - \left|\alpha^{\text{steady}}\right\rangle\!\!\left\langle\alpha^{\text{steady}}\right|_{kk'} = \delta_{kk'}e^{-\beta\hbar\omega_k}Z_k = \frac{1}{e^{\beta\hbar} - 1}. \tag{50}$$

From this result, one can see clearly what was already noted in Reference [4], namely that, in presence of random scattering (which is absent in this case) or a thermal environment with temperature different from zero, it is impossible to obtain a coherent state, and that only an initial pure state remains pure when the above conditions are met.

Next, we express the entropy of the steady state as a function of β (we set $k_B = 1$):

$$\begin{aligned}S[\hat{r}^{(\alpha)\text{steady}}](\beta) &= \text{tr}\left[(\hat{r}^{(\alpha)\text{steady}} + 1)\ln\left(\hat{r}^{(\alpha)\text{steady}} + 1\right) - \hat{r}^{(\alpha)\text{steady}}\ln\hat{r}^{(\alpha)\text{steady}}\right] \\ &= \text{tr}\left[\beta\hat{h}\hat{r}^{(\alpha)\text{steady}}\right] + \text{tr}\left[\ln\left(\hat{r}^{(\alpha)\text{steady}} + 1\right)\right] \\ &= \beta U + \text{tr}\left[\ln\left(\hat{r}^{(\alpha)\text{steady}} + 1\right)\right],\end{aligned} \tag{51}$$

as it can be found using Equation (50) and going through some algebra. One can immediately see that the entropy depends on the temperature, both through the partition functions and the occupation numbers of the modes. We plot in Figure 1 the entropy as a function of the temperature β for different values of the frequency. From the plot, it can be seen that lower frequency modes have a greater entropy than the modes with higher frequency.

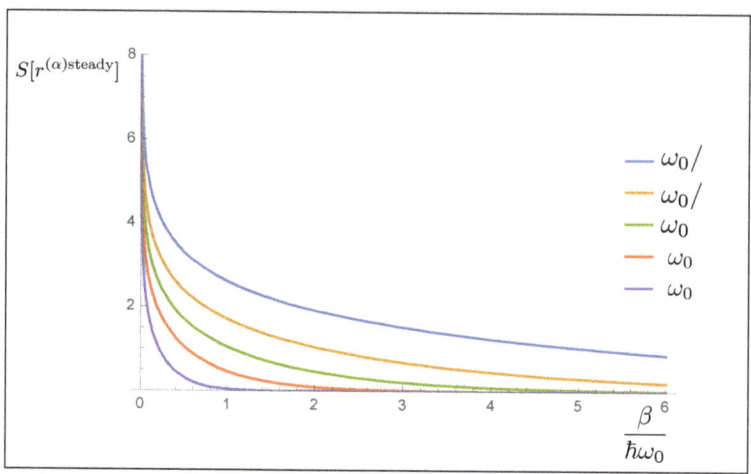

Figure 1. In this plot, the entropy as a function of temperature β is shown. The various lines are plotted using different frequency, so that one can see that the low frequency modes contribute more to the entropy, especially at low temperatures.

The Equation (51) can also be rearranged as:

$$U - \beta^{-1} S = -\frac{1}{\beta} \text{tr}\left[\ln\left(\hat{\rho}^{(\alpha)\text{steady}} + 1\right)\right], \tag{52}$$

so that, in this way, we are driven to define the equilibrium-free energy F_{eq}

$$F_{eq} = -\frac{1}{\beta} \text{tr}\left[\ln\left(\hat{\rho}^{(\alpha)\text{steady}} + 1\right)\right] = -\frac{1}{\beta} \sum_k \ln Z_k. \tag{53}$$

This is exactly the sum of the equilibrium-free energies of each mode. We can then define the free energy as:

$$\begin{aligned} F &= U - \beta^{-1} S = \text{tr}\left[\hat{\rho}^{(\alpha)} \hat{h}\right] - \frac{1}{\beta} \text{tr}\left[(\hat{\rho}^{(\alpha)} + 1) \ln\left(\hat{\rho}^{(\alpha)} + 1\right) - \hat{\rho}^{(\alpha)} \ln \hat{\rho}^{(\alpha)}\right] \\ &= \text{tr}\left[\hat{\rho}^{(\alpha)}\left(\hat{h} - \frac{1}{\beta} \ln\left(\frac{\hat{\rho}^{(\alpha)} + 1}{\hat{\rho}^\alpha}\right)\right)\right] - \frac{1}{\beta} \text{tr}\left[\ln\left(\hat{\rho}^{(\alpha)} + 1\right)\right] \tag{54} \\ &= F_{neq} + F_{eq}, \tag{55} \end{aligned}$$

where we have introduced the non-equilibrium-free energy

$$F_{neq} = \text{tr}\left[\hat{\rho}^{(\alpha)}\left(\hat{h} - \frac{1}{\beta} \ln\left(\frac{\hat{\rho}^{(\alpha)} + 1}{\hat{\rho}^\alpha}\right)\right)\right]. \tag{56}$$

Thus, we see how, in the presence of a thermal bath, and using the definition of internal energy of Equation (17), we are able to define in a reasonable way the free energy, both "in and out" of equilibrium. Clearly, the proposed notion of free energy is somehow attached to the specific case of macroscopic fields. This is to be expected since, in the RSF formalism, one assumes the lack of control over certain (actually, many) degrees of freedom. Therefore, in its spirit, our approach does not differ from descriptions of other physical situations, such as the modeling of magnetic [26,27] and molecular [28,29] systems, where adjustments are necessary in order to account for the specific properties of the system under examination.

5. Conclusions

In this paper, we explored how to define thermodynamic quantities in the RSF formalism, given its definition of entropy. We also showed some examples of dynamical regimes that allowed us to explicitly compute the quantities of our interest, such as energy, heat, work, and other thermodynamic functionals.

Starting from the definition of entropy given in Reference [4], we gave a reasonable definition of internal energy, heat, and work. We were able to show that, in a quasi-static equilibrium process, our definition of heat gave the proper increase of entropy, and then we defined the equilibrium and non-equilibrium-free energy.

It would be interesting in the future to further explore how to describe other thermodynamic phenomena under this formalism, such as work extraction from heat engines and work storage in batteries. This would surely help to further clarify how thermodynamics should be described at mesoscopic scales, as well as to individuate possible issues to be solved in this regime. Last but not least, scattering terms deserve a careful, separate consideration.

Author Contributions: Conceptualization, S.C.; Formal analysis, S.C.; Methodology, Ł.R.; Supervision, Ł.R.; Validation, Ł.R.; Writing—original draft, S.C.; Writing—review & editing, Ł.R. All authors have read and agreed to the published version of the manuscript.

Funding: The authors acknowledge support by the Foundation for Polish Science (IRAP project, ICTQT, Contract No. 2018/MAB/5, co-financed by the EU within the Smart Growth Operational Program).

Data Availability Statement: No new data were created or analyzed in this study. Data sharing is not applicable to this article.

Acknowledgments: We thank Tomasz Linowski for fruitful discussions.

Conflicts of Interest: The authors declare no conflict of interest.

References

1. Datta, S. *Electronic Transport in Mesoscopic Systems*; Cambridge Studies in Semiconductor Physics and Microelectronic Engineering; Cambridge University Press: Cambridge, UK, 1995. [CrossRef]
2. Yamamoto, Y.; Imamoglu, A. *Mesoscopic Quantum Optics*; Wiley-Interscience: New York, NY, USA, 1999. Available online: https://www.wiley.com/en-us/Mesoscopic+Quantum+Optics-p-9780471148746 (accessed on 15 May 2021).
3. Thorne, K.S.; Blandford, R.D. *Modern Classical Physics*; Princeton University Press: Oxford, UK, 2017.
4. Alicki, R. Quantum Features of Macroscopic Fields: Entropy and Dynamics. *Entropy* **2019**, *21*, 705. Available online: https://www.mdpi.com/1099-4300/21/7/705 (accessed on 9 September 2020). [CrossRef]
5. Linowski, T.; Rudnicki, Ł. Classical description of bosonic quantum fields in terms of the reduced-state-of-the-field framework. *arXiv* **2021**, arXiv:2107.03196.
6. Vinjanampathy, S.; Anders, J. Quantum thermodynamics. *Contemp. Phys.* **2016**, *57*, 545. [CrossRef]
7. Pekola, J.P. Towards quantum thermodynamics in electronic circuits. *Nat. Phys.* **2015**, *11*, 118–123. [CrossRef]
8. Reichental, I.; Klempner, A.; Kafri, Y.; Podolsky, D. Thermalization in open quantum systems. *Phys. Rev. B* **2018**, *97*, 134301. [CrossRef]
9. Cusumano, S.; Cavina, V.; Keck, M.; De Pasquale, A.; Giovannetti, V. Entropy production and asymptotic factorization via thermalization: A collisional model approach. *Phys. Rev. A* **2018**, *98*, 032119. [CrossRef]
10. Xu, S.-Z.; Zhao, T.; Chen, Q.; Liang, X.-G.; Guo, Z.-Y. State functions/quantities in thermodynamics and heat transfer. *Fundam. Res.* **2021**, doi:10.1016/j.fmre.2021.07.001. [CrossRef]
11. Ma, Y.-H.; Dong, H.; Quan, H.-T.; Sun, C.-P. The uniqueness of the integration factor associated with the exchanged heat in thermodynamics. *Fundam. Res.* **2021**, *1*, 6–9. [CrossRef]
12. Linden, N.; Popescu, S.; Skrzypczyk, P. How Small Can Thermal Machines Be? The Smallest Possible Refrigerator. *Phys. Rev. Lett.* **2010**, *105*, 130401. [CrossRef] [PubMed]
13. Ono, K.; Shevchenko, S.N.; Mori, T.; Moriyama, S.; Nori, F. Analog of a Quantum Heat Engine Using a Single-Spin Qubit. *Phys. Rev. Lett.* **2020**, *125*, 166802. [CrossRef]

14. Kosloff, R.; Levy, A. Quantum Heat Engines and Refrigerators: Continuous Devices. *Annu. Rev. Phys. Chem.* **2014**, *65*, 365–393. [CrossRef] [PubMed]
15. Peterson, J.P.S. Batalhão, T.B.; Herrera, M.; Souza, A.M.; Sarthour, R.S.; Oliveira, I.S.; Serra, R.M. Experimental Characterization of a Spin Quantum Heat Engine. *Phys. Rev. Lett.* **2019**, *123*, 240601. [CrossRef] [PubMed]
16. Watanabe, G. Heat Engines Using Small Quantum Systems. *AAPPS Bull.* **2019**, *29*, 30. Available online: https://web.b.ebscohost.com/abstract?direct=true&profile=ehost&scope=site&authtype=crawler&jrnl=02182203&AN=142282653&h=ud6Hgx8ol0tq3ntRCMTeewKM4Gh5IV0WRSIgskHgDu4xz%2b2u7ggyrrTRsdefYRSuhsLrQUXwnDOI4yS9EVwEag%3d%3d&crl=c&resultNs=AdminWebAuth&resultLocal=ErrCrlNotAuth&crlhashurl=login.aspx%3fdirect%3dtrue%26profile%3dehost%26scope%3dsite%26authtype%3dcrawler%26jrnl%3d02182203%26AN%3d142282653 (accessed on 3 August 2021).
17. Lu, Y.; Long, G.L. Parity effect and phase transitions in quantum Szilard engines. *Phys. Rev. E* **2012**, *85*, 011125. [CrossRef]
18. Xiao, K.-W.; Xiong, A.; Zhao, N.; Yin, Z.-Q. Quantum ground state cooling of translational and librational modes of an optically trapped nanoparticle coupling cavity. *Quantum Eng.* **2021**, *3*, 62. [CrossRef]
19. Binder, F.C.; Vinjanampathy, S.; Modi, K.; Goold, J. Quantacell: Powerful charging of quantum batteries. *New J. Phys.* **2015**, *17*, 075015. [CrossRef]
20. Campaioli, F.; Pollock, F.A.; Binder, F.C.; Céleri, L.; Goold, J.; Vinjanampathy, S.; Modi, K. Enhancing the Charging Power of Quantum Batteries. *Phys. Rev. Lett.* **2017**, *118*, 150601. [CrossRef]
21. Andolina, G.M.; Keck, M.; Mari, A.; Giovannetti, V.; Polini, M. Quantum versus classical many-body batteries. *Phys. Rev. B* **2019**, *99*, 205437. [CrossRef]
22. Céleri, L.C.; Rudnicki, Ł. Gauge invariant quantum thermodynamics: Consequences for the first law. *arXiv* **2021**, arXiv:2104.10153.
23. Alicki, R.; Lendi, K. *Quantum Dynamical Semigroups and Applications*, 2nd ed.; LNP 717; Springer: Berlin, Germany, 2007.
24. Alicki, R. The Theory of Open Systems in Application to Unstable Particles. *Rep. Math. Phys.* **1978**, *14*, 27–42. [CrossRef]
25. Das, S.; Khatri, S.; Siopsis, G.; Wilde, M.M. Fundamental limits on quantum dynamics based on entropy change. *J. Math. Phys.* **2017**, *59*, 012205. [CrossRef]
26. Zhang, Z.; Scully, M.O.; Agarwal, G.S. Quantum entanglement between two magnon modes via Kerr nonlinearity driven far from equilibrium. *Phys. Rev. Res.* **2019**, *1*, 023021. [CrossRef]
27. Li, J.; Zhu, S.; Agarwal, G.S. Magnon-Photon-Phonon Entanglement in Cavity Magnomechanics. *Phys. Rev. Lett.* **2018**, *121*, 203601. [CrossRef] [PubMed]
28. Zhang, Z.D.; Wang, J. Curl flux, coherence, and population landscape of molecular systems: Nonequilibrium quantum steady state, energy (charge) transport, and thermodynamics. *J. Chem. Phys.* **2014**, *140*, 245101. [CrossRef] [PubMed]
29. Zhang, Z.; Agarwal, G.S.; Scully, M.O. Quantum Fluctuations in the Fröhlich Condensate of Molecular Vibrations Driven Far From Equilibrium. *Phys. Rev. Lett.* **2019**, *122*, 158101. [CrossRef] [PubMed]

Article

Engineering Classical Capacity of Generalized Pauli Channels with Admissible Memory Kernels

Katarzyna Siudzińska *, Arpan Das and Anindita Bera

Institute of Physics, Faculty of Physics, Astronomy and Informatics, Nicolaus Copernicus University in Toruń, ul. Grudziądzka 5, 87-100 Toruń, Poland; arpand@umk.pl (A.D.); anindita.bera@umk.pl (A.B.)
* Correspondence: kasias@umk.pl

Abstract: In this paper, we analyze the classical capacity of the generalized Pauli channels generated via memory kernel master equations. For suitable engineering of the kernel parameters, evolution with non-local noise effects can produce dynamical maps with a higher capacity than a purely Markovian evolution. We provide instructive examples for qubit and qutrit evolution. Interestingly, similar behavior is not observed when analyzing time-local master equations.

Keywords: classical capacity; generalized Pauli channels; non-Markovian evolution; memory kernels

Citation: Siudzińska, K.; Das, A.; Bera, A. Engineering Classical Capacity of Generalized Pauli Channels with Admissible Memory Kernels. *Entropy* **2021**, *23*, 1382. https://doi.org/10.3390/e23111382

Academic Editors: Bassano Vacchini, Andrea Smirne and Nina Megier

Received: 7 October 2021
Accepted: 19 October 2021
Published: 21 October 2021

Publisher's Note: MDPI stays neutral with regard to jurisdictional claims in published maps and institutional affiliations.

Copyright: © 2021 by the authors. Licensee MDPI, Basel, Switzerland. This article is an open access article distributed under the terms and conditions of the Creative Commons Attribution (CC BY) license (https://creativecommons.org/licenses/by/4.0/).

1. Introduction

In quantum information processing, it is crucial to understand how to transmit, manipulate, and preserve quantum information sent through a noisy quantum channel [1,2]. Due to scientific and technological advancements, logic gates and other electronic devices are approaching atomic scales. Therefore, it is becoming increasingly hard to reliably transfer information. This can be remedied if one can minimize the detrimental effects of noise through error correction, error mitigation, or error suppression techniques [3,4].

However, removing errors is only one way to deal with undesirable effects of environmental noise on quantum systems. Another approach to the problem is, instead of reducing the noise, using it to one's advantage. This perception of the role of environmental noise was popularized by the observation that dissipation can be used to enhance quantum information processing [5]. In this way, dissipation has become a quantum resource that is exploited to manipulate quantum systems and engineer specific properties of quantum channels [6–8]. In particular, the memory effects caused by environmental noise have been used for performing quantum information processing tasks, such as improving channel fidelity or preserving quantum entanglement [9]. A decrease in error accumulation was achieved for dissipative Markovian processes and their generalizations [10,11], where adding noises to the Markovian evolution slows down the rate at which the system approaches a steady state.

The goal of this paper is to show how to engineer quantum noise to improve the channel capacity, which is a very important measure in quantum computation and quantum information theory. Through the channel capacity, one can determine the amount of information transmitted coherently through a quantum channel. However, in contrast to the classical channels, which have a unique (Shannon) capacity, the concept of quantum channel capacity is more complex, giving rise to a whole range of informational characteristics. If quantum information is transferred through a noisy channel, then one must consider the quantum capacity, whose lower and upper estimations were determined by Lloyd [12], Shor [13], and Devetak [14]. In quantum cryptography, communication tasks often require the use of private classical capacity [14]. Additionally, quantum correlations are essential to the entanglement-assisted capacity [15], which is the highest rate of classical information transition. The problem of simultaneously transferring classical and quantum information was investigated by Devetak and Shor [16]. More information about channel capacities is available in review works, see e.g., [17,18].

The capacity that directly generalizes the notion of Shannon capacity for classical channels to the quantum scenario is classical capacity [19,20]. In this case, classical information is sent through a quantum channel using separable input states and joint measurements of the outputs. Recently, there has been significant interest in calculating the classical capacity of quantum channels. Rehman et al. used the majorization procedure to provide lower and upper estimations of the Holevo capacity of the Weyl channels [21,22]. Amosov calculated the classical capacity for deformations of classical-quantum Weyl channels [23] and channels generated by irreducible projective unitary representations of finite groups [24].

In this paper, we analyze the time evolution of the classical capacity for the generalized Pauli channels [25,26]. In particular, we compare the capacity for the dynamical maps governed by the memory kernel

$$K(t) = \mathcal{L}\delta(t) + \mathbb{K}(t) \tag{1}$$

with that of the Markovian generator $\mathcal{L}$ alone. In the above formula, $\mathbb{K}(t)$ is the part of the kernel that does not include the local part with the Dirac delta function $\delta(t)$. With the proper choice of parameters, we propose a number of cases where the classical capacity of the map generated by $K(t)$ is better than that of the Markovian semigroup $\Lambda^M(t) = e^{t\mathcal{L}}$. Hence, it is shown that non-local memory effects can be effectively used to decrease the error rate of a quantum channel. We also present a class of quantum evolution where the generator $\mathcal{L}(t)$ is time-local. This implies that improving the channel capacity is possible not only for the Markovian semigroup but for general Markovian dynamics.

2. Generalized Pauli Channels

An important class of quantum channels consists of mixed unitary channels, where a unitary evolution is disrupted by classical errors [27,28]. The channel noise can be corrected with the classical information obtained by measuring the environment [29]. For qubit systems, one considers the Pauli channel [30,31]

$$\Lambda[\rho] = \sum_{\alpha=0}^{3} p_\alpha \sigma_\alpha \rho \sigma_\alpha, \tag{2}$$

where p_α is a probability distribution and $\sigma_0 = \mathbb{I}_2, \sigma_1, \sigma_2, \sigma_3$ are the Pauli matrices. As the Kraus representation of a quantum map is not unique, it is often more convenient to work with its spectrum. One can find the eigenvalues of the Pauli channel through its eigenvalue equations

$$\Lambda[\sigma_\alpha] = \lambda_\alpha \sigma_\alpha, \qquad \lambda_0 = 1. \tag{3}$$

An important property of σ_α, where $\alpha = 1, 2, 3$, is that their eigenvectors $\{\psi_0^{(\alpha)}, \psi_1^{(\alpha)}\}$ form three mutually unbiased bases (MUBs). Recall that two orthonormal bases are mutually unbiased if and only if

$$|\langle \psi_k^{(\alpha)} | \psi_l^{(\beta)} \rangle|^2 = \frac{1}{d} \tag{4}$$

for $\alpha \neq \beta$ and $k, l = 0, \ldots, d-1$, where d is the dimension of the underlying Hilbert space ($d = 2$ for qubits).

The Pauli channels can be generalized in multiple ways [32–35], but only one generalization ensures that the MUB property of its eigenvectors carries over to $d > 2$. Consider the d-dimensional Hilbert space $\mathcal{H}$ that admits the maximal number of $d + 1$ mutually unbiased bases [36]. Using the rank-1 projectors $P_k^{(\alpha)} = |\psi_k^{(\alpha)}\rangle\langle\psi_k^{(\alpha)}|$, one can define $d^2 - 1$ unitary operators

$$U_\alpha^k = \sum_{l=0}^{d-1} \omega^{kl} P_l^{(\alpha)}, \qquad \omega = e^{2\pi i/d}. \tag{5}$$

The generalized Pauli channel is constructed as follows [25,26],

$$\Lambda[\rho] = p_0 \rho + \frac{1}{d-1} \sum_{\alpha=1}^{d+1} p_\alpha \sum_{k=1}^{d-1} U_\alpha^k \rho U_\alpha^{k\dagger}, \qquad (6)$$

where the Pauli channel in Equation (2) is reproduced after setting $d = 2$. The eigenvalues λ_α of Λ are real and $(d-1)$-times degenerated. They satisfy the eigenvalue equations

$$\Lambda[U_\alpha^k] = \lambda_\alpha U_\alpha^k, \qquad k = 1, \ldots, d-1, \qquad (7)$$

and $\Lambda[\mathbb{I}_d] = \mathbb{I}_d$. In terms of the probability distribution p_α,

$$\lambda_\alpha = \frac{1}{d-1}[d(p_0 + p_\alpha) - 1], \qquad (8)$$

whereas the inverse relation reads

$$\begin{aligned} p_0 &= \frac{1}{d^2}\left(1 + (d-1)\sum_{\alpha=1}^{d+1} \lambda_\alpha\right), \\ p_\alpha &= \frac{d-1}{d^2}\left(1 + d\lambda_\alpha - \sum_{\beta=1}^{d+1} \lambda_\beta\right). \end{aligned} \qquad (9)$$

The complete positivity of the generalized Pauli channel is fully controlled by its eigenvalues. Indeed, Λ is completely positive if and only if λ_α satisfies the generalized Fujiwara–Algoet conditions [25,37,38]

$$-\frac{1}{d-1} \leq \sum_{\beta=1}^{d+1} \lambda_\beta \leq 1 + d\min_{\beta>0} \lambda_\beta. \qquad (10)$$

3. Classical Capacity of Generalized Pauli Channels

In the classical theory of information, there exists a unique measure for the amount of information that can be reliably transmitted through a noisy channel. This measure is known as the Shannon capacity, and it is a maximization of the mutual information between the input and output states over all random variable probability distributions [39]. In quantum information theory, however, information can be transmitted in a number of ways. Therefore, there exist many types of channel capacities, such as the quantum capacity [12–14], private classical capacity [14], and entanglement-assisted capacity [15]. A direct analogue of the Shannon capacity in the quantum scenario is the Holevo capacity. It determines the maximal amount of classical information that can be reliably transferred, provided that the input state is separable and the output state is measured via joint measurements [17,40]. The Holevo capacity $\chi(\Lambda)$ is defined as the maximal value of an entropic expression [19,20],

$$\chi(\Lambda) = \max_{\{p_k, \rho_k\}} \left[S\left(\sum_k p_k \Lambda[\rho_k]\right) - \sum_k p_k S(\Lambda[\rho_k]) \right], \qquad (11)$$

where Λ is a quantum channel and $S(\rho) = -\mathrm{Tr}(\rho \ln \rho)$ denotes the von Neumann entropy. Note that the maximum is calculated over the ensembles of separable states ρ_k with the probability of occurrence p_k. The optimal transition rate under infinitely many uses of a channel is given by the classical capacity

$$C(\Lambda) = \lim_{n\to\infty} \frac{1}{n} \chi(\Lambda^{\otimes n}). \qquad (12)$$

In general, $C(\Lambda) \geq \chi(\Lambda)$. However, for a channel Λ with a weakly additive Holevo capacity ($\chi(\Lambda \otimes \Lambda) = 2\chi(\Lambda)$), one has $C(\Lambda) = \chi(\Lambda)$ [20].

In Reference [41], exact values of the classical capacity were found for certain families of the generalized Pauli channels. Namely, if all $\lambda_\alpha \leq 0$ and moreover $\lambda_1 = \ldots = \lambda_d \equiv \lambda_{\max}$, $\lambda_{d+1} = \lambda_{\min}$, then

$$C(\Lambda) = \frac{1 + (d-1)\lambda_{\min}}{d} \ln[1 + (d-1)\lambda_{\min}] + (d-1)\frac{1 - \lambda_{\min}}{d} \ln(1 - \lambda_{\min}). \quad (13)$$

In contrast, if all $\lambda_\alpha \geq 0$ and also $\lambda_1 = \lambda_{\max}$, $\lambda_2 = \ldots = \lambda_{d+1} \equiv \lambda_{\min}$, then

$$C(\Lambda) = \frac{1 + (d-1)\lambda_{\max}}{d} \ln[1 + (d-1)\lambda_{\max}] + (d-1)\frac{1 - \lambda_{\max}}{d} \ln(1 - \lambda_{\max}). \quad (14)$$

In addition, if all of the eigenvalues are equal to one another, meaning that $\lambda_1 = \ldots = \lambda_{d+1} \equiv \lambda$, then one recovers the capacity of the depolarizing channel [42]. For any other combination of eigenvalues, one finds only the lower bound of the classical capacity [41],

$$C_{\text{low}}(\Lambda) = \max_{\alpha > 0} c_\alpha, \quad c_\alpha = \frac{1 + (d-1)\lambda_\alpha}{d} \ln[1 + (d-1)\lambda_\alpha] + \frac{d-1}{d}(1 - \lambda_\alpha)\ln(1 - \lambda_\alpha). \quad (15)$$

In the special case of $d = 2$ (the Pauli channels), the above formula gives the exact value of the capacity [21], meaning that $C(\Lambda) = C_{\text{low}}(\Lambda)$.

Generators vs. Memory Kernels

The evolution $\rho \longmapsto \rho(t) = \Lambda(t)[\rho]$ of an open quantum system is described by a family of time-parameterized quantum channels $\Lambda(t)$, $t \geq 0$, with the initial condition $\Lambda(0) = \mathbb{1}$. Such maps can be obtained as solutions to the master equations. In the simplest scenario, the evolution equation $\dot{\Lambda}(t) = \mathcal{L}\Lambda(t)$, where $\mathcal{L}$ is the Gorini–Kossakowski–Sudarshan–Landblad (GKSL) generator [43,44]. The solution to this equation is the Markovian semigroup $\Lambda(t) = \exp(t\mathcal{L})$. For the generalized Pauli channels, one has [26]

$$\mathcal{L} = \sum_{\alpha=1}^{d+1} \gamma_\alpha \mathcal{L}_\alpha \quad (16)$$

with the decoherence rates $\gamma_\alpha \geq 0$ and

$$\mathcal{L}_\alpha[\rho] = \frac{1}{d}\left[\sum_{k=1}^{d-1} U_\alpha^k \rho U_\alpha^{k\dagger} - (d-1)\rho\right]. \quad (17)$$

Generators that are constant in time are sufficient for open system dynamics with a weak coupling to the environment. When this coupling is relatively strong, however, it becomes essential to consider the master equations that take non-Markovian memory effects into account. One generalization of the semigroup master equation is $\dot{\Lambda}(t) = \mathcal{L}(t)\Lambda(t)$, where the constant generator is replaced with the time-local generator $\mathcal{L}(t)$. In the case of the generalized Pauli channels, one simply has

$$\mathcal{L}(t) = \sum_{\alpha=1}^{d+1} \gamma_\alpha(t) \mathcal{L}_\alpha. \quad (18)$$

The condition on the decoherence rates is relaxed, as they no longer have to be positive for the dynamics to be legitimate. This time, $\gamma_\alpha(t) \geq 0$ is the necessary and sufficient condition for the corresponding (invertible) $\Lambda(t)$ to be Markovian in terms of divisibility [45,46]. A dynamical map is CP-divisible if and only if it is decomposable into $\Lambda(t) = V(t,s)\Lambda(s)$ for any $t \geq s \geq 0$. The propagator $V(t,s)$ is then a completely positive, trace-preserving map, and the corresponding evolution is Markovian.

By solving the evolution equation with the time-local generator, we find that the eigenvalues of the associated dynamical map read [26]

$$\lambda_\alpha(t) = \exp[\Gamma_\alpha(t) - \Gamma_0(t)], \tag{19}$$

where $\Gamma_\alpha(t) = \int_0^t \gamma_\alpha(\tau) \, d\tau$ for $\alpha = 0, \ldots, d+1$ and $\gamma_0(t) = \sum_{\alpha=1}^{d+1} \gamma_\alpha(t)$. Note that the complete positivity conditions from Equation (10) reduce to

$$\sum_{\alpha=1}^{d+1} e^{\Gamma_\alpha(t)} \leq e^{\Gamma(t)} + d \min_\beta e^{\Gamma_\beta(t)}. \tag{20}$$

Another generalization of the Markovian semigroup master equation is realized using memory kernels. In this approach, the GKSL generator is replaced with an integral expression. Now, the evolution of the system is governed by the Nakajima–Zwanzig equation [47,48]

$$\dot{\Lambda}(t) = \int_0^t K(t-\tau) \Lambda(\tau) \, d\tau, \tag{21}$$

where $K(t)$ is the memory kernel. Observe that this is an integro-differential equation; therefore, the evolved state $\rho(t)$ depends on every earlier state $\rho(\tau)$, $\tau < t$. The memory kernel that corresponds to the generalized Pauli channels has a relatively simple form,

$$K(t) = \sum_{\alpha=1}^{d+1} k_\alpha(t) \mathcal{L}_\alpha. \tag{22}$$

Note that $K(t)$ and $\Lambda(t)$ have common eigenvectors,

$$K(t)[U_\alpha^k] = \kappa_\alpha(t) U_\alpha^k, \qquad K(t)[\mathbb{I}] = 0, \tag{23}$$

where

$$\kappa_\alpha(t) = k_\alpha(t) - k_0(t) \tag{24}$$

with $k_0(t) = \sum_{\beta=1}^{d+1} k_\beta(t)$ are the eigenvalues of the kernel. Hence, one can rewrite the Nakajima–Zwanzig equation as

$$\dot{\lambda}_\alpha(t) = \int_0^t \kappa_\alpha(t-\tau) \lambda_\alpha(\tau) \, d\tau. \tag{25}$$

In the Laplace transform domain, the solution reads

$$\tilde{\lambda}_\alpha(s) = \frac{1}{s - \tilde{\kappa}_\alpha(s)}, \tag{26}$$

where $\tilde{f}(s) = \int_0^\infty f(t) e^{-st} dt$ is the Laplace transform of the function $f(t)$.

The necessary and sufficient conditions for legitimate memory kernels are provided in Reference [49]. First, one parameterizes the eigenvalues $\lambda_\alpha(t)$ of the dynamical map by the real function $\ell_\alpha(t)$ in such a way that

$$\lambda_\alpha(t) = 1 - \int_0^t \ell_\alpha(\tau) \, d\tau. \tag{27}$$

Now, the associated kernel is legitimate if and only if its eigenvalues

$$\tilde{\kappa}_\alpha(s) = -\frac{s \tilde{\ell}_\alpha(s)}{1 - \tilde{\ell}_\alpha(s)}, \tag{28}$$

where $\ell_\alpha(t)$ satisfies the additional conditions

$$\int_0^t \ell_\alpha(\tau)\,d\tau \geq 0, \tag{29}$$

$$d\int_0^t \ell_\alpha(\tau)\,d\tau \leq \sum_{\beta=1}^{d+1} \int_0^t \ell_\beta(\tau)\,d\tau \leq \frac{d^2}{d-1}, \tag{30}$$

for $\alpha = 1, 2, \ldots, d+1$.

4. Engineering Capacity through Kernel Manipulations

In this section, we analyze how the classical capacity of the generalized Pauli channels changes in time for the evolution generated by Equation (21) with the memory kernel

$$K(t) = \delta(t)\mathcal{L} + \mathbb{K}(t). \tag{31}$$

Notably, in the formula above, $\mathcal{L}$ is a legitimate Markovian semigroup generator from Equation (18) and $\mathbb{K}(t)$ is a legitimate, purely non-local memory kernel (i.e., it does not involve the Dirac delta function $\delta(t)$). It is shown that, by adding a non-local part $\mathbb{K}(t)$, one can improve the classical capacity of the associated dynamical map $\Lambda(t)$. The addition of purely local and non-local kernels has already been considered in [9,50], where it was proven that the channel fidelity can be temporarily increased by the appropriate engineering of the kernel parameters. In the following, we consider three types of dynamical maps: the Markovian semigroup $\Lambda^M(t) = e^{t\mathcal{L}}$, the non-Markovian noise $\Lambda^N(t)$ that solves $\dot{\Lambda}^N(t) = \int_0^t \mathbb{K}(t-\tau)\Lambda^N(\tau)\,d\tau$, and finally the map $\Lambda(t)$ that satisfies the Nakajima–Zwanzig equation with $K(t) = \delta(t)\mathcal{L} + \mathbb{K}(t)$. The eigenvalues of the corresponding maps are denoted by $\lambda_\alpha^M(t)$, $\lambda_\alpha^N(t)$, and $\lambda_\alpha(t)$, respectively. Interestingly, there is no simple relation between the map eigenvalues, as in the Laplace transform domain

$$\tilde{\lambda}_\alpha(s) = \frac{\tilde{\lambda}_\alpha^M(s)\tilde{\lambda}_\alpha^N(s)}{\tilde{\lambda}_\alpha^M(s) + \tilde{\lambda}_\alpha^N(s) - s\tilde{\lambda}_\alpha^M(s)\tilde{\lambda}_\alpha^N(s)}. \tag{32}$$

In the following examples, the map that describes the noise part is always non-invertible and not kernel non-decreasing–that is,

$$\exists\, 0 \leq \tau \leq t: \quad \ker \Lambda^N(\tau) \not\subseteq \ker \Lambda^N(t). \tag{33}$$

In other words, there exists at least one eigenvalue $\lambda_\alpha^N(t)$ that reaches zero at some finite time t_* but does not remain zero for some $t > t_*$. Such dynamical maps are indivisible, and hence the corresponding evolution is non-Markovian [51].

4.1. Constant Kernel

First, consider the qubit evolutions ($d = 2$) provided by the isotropic Markovian generator

$$\mathcal{L} = \frac{\gamma}{2} \sum_{\alpha=1}^{3} \mathcal{L}_\alpha \tag{34}$$

with a positive decoherence rate γ and the memory kernel $\mathbb{K}(t)$ with constant eigenvalues

$$\kappa_1^N(t) = \kappa_2^N(t) = -\omega^2, \qquad \kappa_3^N(t) = 0, \tag{35}$$

where $\omega > 0$. The corresponding solutions read

$$\lambda_1^M(t) = \lambda_2^M(t) = \lambda_3^M(t) = e^{-\gamma t}, \tag{36}$$

and

$$\lambda_1^N(t) = \lambda_2^N(t) = \cos\omega t, \qquad \lambda_3^N(t) = 1, \tag{37}$$

respectively. Observe that the dynamical maps characterized via $\lambda_\alpha^M(t)$ and $\lambda_\alpha^N(t)$ are always legitimate.

The Pauli dynamical map generated by $K(t) = \delta(t)\mathcal{L} + \mathbb{K}(t)$ is characterized by the following eigenvalues,

$$\lambda_1(t) = \lambda_2(t) = \frac{2\omega}{P} e^{-\gamma t/2} \cos\left(\frac{Pt}{2} + \arctan\frac{\gamma}{P}\right), \qquad \lambda_3(t) = e^{-\gamma t}, \tag{38}$$

where $P = \sqrt{4\omega^2 - \gamma^2}$. The eigenvalues $\lambda_1(t)$ and $\lambda_2(t)$ oscillate if and only if $\gamma < 2\omega$. Additionally, for $\Lambda(t)$ to describe a legitimate evolution, it is sufficient that

$$\frac{2\omega}{P} \leq \cosh\frac{\gamma t_*}{2}, \tag{39}$$

where

$$t_* = \frac{2}{P}\left(\pi - \arctan\frac{\gamma}{P}\right) \tag{40}$$

is the time corresponding to the first local minimum of the cosine function. This is a direct consequence of the Fujiwara–Algoet conditions from Equation (10). Hence, a combination of two legitimate memory kernels does not necessary yield a physical dynamics. Now, using Equation (15), we can calculate the classical capacity of $\Lambda(t)$,

$$C[\Lambda(t)] = \max\left\{c_1(t), c_3(t)\right\}, \tag{41}$$

where $c_1(t) = c_2(t)$ and $c_3(t) = C[\Lambda^M(t)]$. Therefore, whenever $c_1(t) > c_3(t)$, one observes an increase in capacity for the system with additional noise. An exemplary choice of parameters is shown in Figure 1.

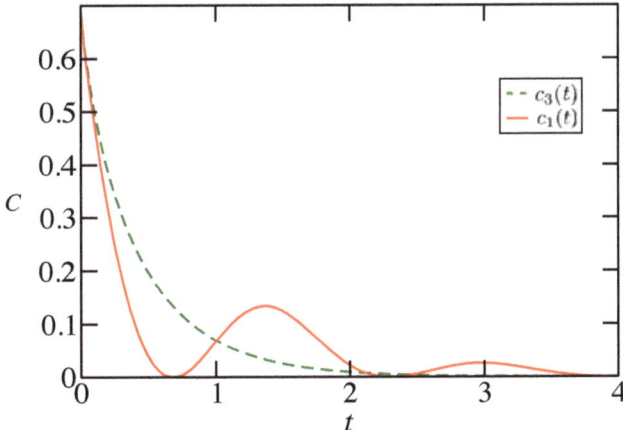

Figure 1. The functions $c_1(t) = c_2(t)$ and $c_3(t)$ are for the qubit evolution with $\gamma = 1/\text{s}$ and $\omega = 2/\text{s}$. The classical capacity of $\Lambda(t)$ is greater than that of $\Lambda^M(t)$ whenever $c_1(t) > c_3(t)$, or when the solid line lies above the dashed line. The maximal increase in capacity that can be observed for this choice of parameters is around 0.1.

4.2. Exponential Decay

Let us take the Markovian semigroup generated by

$$\mathcal{L} = \frac{\gamma}{d}\sum_{\alpha=1}^{d+1} \mathcal{L}_\alpha \tag{42}$$

and the exponentially decaying memory kernel $\mathbb{K}(t)$, similar to the one analyzed in [9,50], with

$$\kappa_\alpha^N(t) = -\omega^2 e^{-Zt}; \qquad \kappa_{\alpha_*}^N(t) = 0, \qquad \alpha \neq \alpha_*. \tag{43}$$

Assume that the constants γ, Z, and ω are positive. By solving the master equations, one can find the associated dynamical maps $\Lambda^M(t)$ and $\Lambda^N(t)$, whose eigenvalues are given by

$$\lambda_\alpha^M(t) = e^{-\gamma t} \tag{44}$$

and $\lambda_{\alpha_*}^N(t) = 1$,

$$\lambda_\alpha^N(t) = \frac{2\omega}{P} e^{-Zt/2} \cos\left(\frac{Pt}{2} - \arctan\frac{Z}{P}\right) \tag{45}$$

for $\alpha \neq \alpha_*$, where $P = \sqrt{4\omega^2 - Z^2}$. Note that for $Z = \gamma$, Equation (45) is very similar to $\lambda_1(t)$ from Equation (38) but differs in the sign before the arcus tangent. The map $\Lambda^M(t)$ is always legitimate, whereas $\Lambda^N(t)$ describes a physical dynamics if

$$e^{Zt_*/2} \geq \frac{2(d-1)\omega}{P}, \tag{46}$$

where

$$t_* = \frac{2}{P}\left(\pi + \arctan\frac{Z}{P}\right) \tag{47}$$

corresponds to the first local minimum of the cosine function.

Now, we analyze the behavior of the dynamical map obtained using $K(t) = \delta(t)\mathcal{L} + \mathbb{K}(t)$. Namely, after adding the non-Markovian noise to the semigroup, the eigenvalue $\lambda_{\alpha_*}(t) = e^{-\gamma t}$ remains unchanged. On the other hand,

$$\lambda_\alpha(t) = \frac{2\omega}{R} e^{-(\gamma+Z)t/2} \cos\left(\frac{Rt}{2} + \arctan\frac{\gamma - Z}{R}\right), \tag{48}$$

for $\alpha \neq \alpha_*$, where $R = \sqrt{4\omega^2 - (\gamma - Z)^2}$. Note that Equation (48) is not a simple shift of Equation (45) by $Z \mapsto \gamma - Z$, as there are two additional sign differences. For $d = 2$, a sufficient condition for $\Lambda(t)$ to produce a legitimate evolution is

$$\frac{2\omega}{R} \leq e^{Zt_*/2} \cosh\frac{\gamma t_*}{2}, \tag{49}$$

where this time

$$t_* = \frac{2}{R}\left(\pi - \arctan\frac{\gamma - Z}{R}\right). \tag{50}$$

Unfortunately, the complete positivity conditions for $d \geq 3$ cannot be simplified in a similar manner. Assuming that $\Lambda(t)$ describes a qudit evolution, Equation (15) gives the following formula for the lower bound of the classical capacity of $\Lambda(t)$,

$$C[\Lambda(t)] = \max\left\{c_\alpha(t), c_{\alpha_*}(t)\right\}. \tag{51}$$

Observe that $c_{\alpha_*}(t) = C[\Lambda^M(t)]$; hence, the channel capacity for $\Lambda(t)$ is greater than for the Markovian evolution if $c_\alpha(t) > c_{\alpha_*}(t)$. Two examples of appropriate parameter engineering are presented in Figure 2.

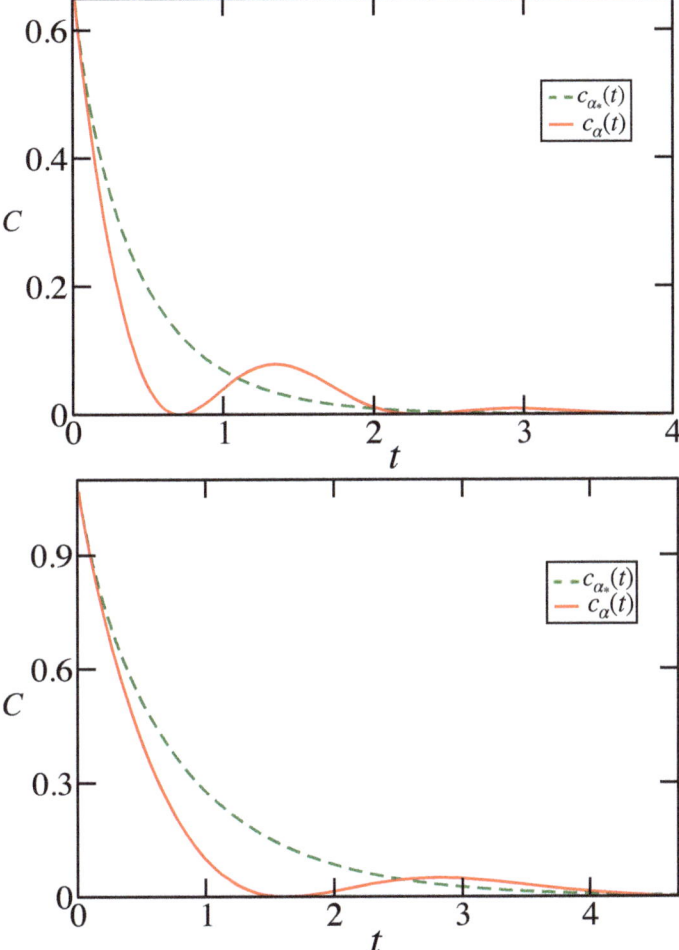

Figure 2. For the functions $c_{\alpha_*}(t)$ and $c_\alpha(t)$, $\alpha \neq \alpha_*$ for the qubit evolution with $\gamma = 1/\text{s}$, $Z = 1/(3\,\text{s})$, and $\omega = 2/\text{s}$ (**top**), as well as for the qutrit evolution with $\gamma = 3/(5\,\text{s})$, $Z = 1/(5\,\text{s})$, and $\omega = 9/(10\,\text{s})$ (**bottom**). The introduction of noise into the Markovian evolution results in an increased classical capacity for the time intervals in which $c_\alpha(t) > c_{\alpha_*}(t)$. This corresponds to the situations when the solid line is above the dashed line. A greater enhancement is observed for the lower-dimensional system.

4.3. Beyond the Semigroup

The classical capacity can also be enhanced in a more general case. Let us consider the Markovian evolution characterized by a dynamical map $\Lambda^M(t)$ that is not a semigroup. Instead, it is generated via the time-local generator $\mathcal{L}^M(t)$ from Equation (18) with $\gamma_\alpha^M(t) \geq 0$. Now, the most natural way to introduce noise is to add the generator $\mathcal{L}^N(t)$ of a non-Markovian evolution, where at least one decoherence rate $\gamma_\alpha^N(t) \not\geq 0$. The resulting dynamical map $\Lambda(t)$ is provided via

$$\mathcal{L}(t) = \mathcal{L}^M(t) + \mathcal{L}^N(t). \tag{52}$$

From a physical point of view, one can add two legitimate generators when the environmental cross-correlations can be ignored [52]. Now, the eigenvalues of the generalized Pauli map $\Lambda(t)$ read

$$\lambda_\alpha(t) = \lambda_\alpha^M(t)\lambda_\alpha^N(t), \tag{53}$$

which means that $\Lambda(t) = \Lambda^M(t)\Lambda^N(t)$ is a composition of two (commutative) generalized Pauli dynamical maps. However, due to the fact that $\lambda_\alpha(t) \geq 0$ for any $\Lambda(t)$ that arises from a legitimate time-local generator, $\lambda_\alpha(t) \leq \lambda_\alpha^M(t)$. Therefore, there can be no increase in the classical capacity. Hence, let us instead consider a more general form of the memory kernel $K(t)$. Namely, we can replace the semigroup generator $\mathcal{L}$ in Equation (31) with the memory kernel $\mathfrak{K}(t)$ that describes the same evolution as the time-local generator $\mathcal{L}(t)$. Then, one has

$$K(t) = \mathfrak{K}(t) + \mathbb{K}(t), \tag{54}$$

where $\mathfrak{K}(t)$ and $\mathbb{K}(t)$ correspond to a Markovian and non-Markovian dynamics, respectively.

As a case study, we analyze the evolution where the Markovian part is given by the generator

$$\mathcal{L}^M(t) = \frac{r}{d+e^{rt}} \sum_{\alpha=1}^{d+1} \mathcal{L}_\alpha \tag{55}$$

with $r > 0$. The solution reads

$$\lambda_\alpha^M(t) = \frac{1+de^{-rt}}{d+1}, \tag{56}$$

and $\Lambda^M(t)$ is always completely positive. One finds that the corresponding kernel has the eigenvalues

$$\kappa_\alpha^M(t) = -\frac{dr}{d+1}\left(\delta(t) - \frac{r}{d+1}e^{-\frac{rt}{d+1}}\right). \tag{57}$$

Therefore, from the kernel point of view, our generalization means that the Markovian part of the kernel not only has terms proportional to the Dirac delta but also has some purely non-local parts. The environmental noise is realized with $\kappa_\alpha^N(t)$ from Equation (43) for a fixed $Z = \frac{r}{d+1}$. The associated solution is $\lambda_{\alpha_*}^N(t) = 1$ and

$$\lambda_\alpha^N(t) = \frac{2\omega}{P}e^{-\frac{rt}{2(d+1)}}\cos\left(\frac{Pt}{2} - \arctan\frac{r}{P(d+1)}\right) \tag{58}$$

for $\alpha \neq \alpha_*$, where $P = \sqrt{4\omega^2 - r^2/(d+1)^2}$. For the complete positivity condition, see Equation (46). Finally, the dynamical map generated by $K(t) = \mathfrak{K}(t) + \mathbb{K}(t)$ is characterized by $\lambda_{\alpha_*}(t) = \lambda_\alpha^M(t)$ and

$$\lambda_\alpha(t) = \frac{2X}{(d+1)Y}e^{-\frac{rt}{2}}\cos\left(\frac{Yt}{2} + \arctan\frac{r(d-1)}{Y(d+1)}\right), \tag{59}$$

where $\alpha \neq \alpha_*$, $Y = \sqrt{4\omega^2 - r^2}$, and $X = \sqrt{(d+1)^2\omega^2 - dr^2}$. For this map to describe a physical evolution in $d = 2$ and $d = 3$, it is sufficient that

$$\frac{X}{Y} \leq \frac{1}{d-1}e^{rt/2} + \frac{1}{2}e^{-rt/2} \tag{60}$$

with the first minimum of the cosine function corresponding to

$$t_* = \frac{2}{Y}\left(\pi - \arctan\frac{(d-1)r}{(d+1)Y}\right). \tag{61}$$

Analogically to the previous example, the lower bound for the classical capacity of $\Lambda(t)$ is given by

$$C[\Lambda(t)] = \max\left\{c_\alpha(t), c_{\alpha_*}(t)\right\}, \tag{62}$$

for $c_\alpha(t)$ defined in Equation (15), where $C[\Lambda^M(t)] = c_{\alpha_*}(t)$ is the capacity of the Markovian evolution. Again, we observe a temporary increase in the channel capacity for a certain set of kernel parameters (see Figure 3 for the qubit evolution).

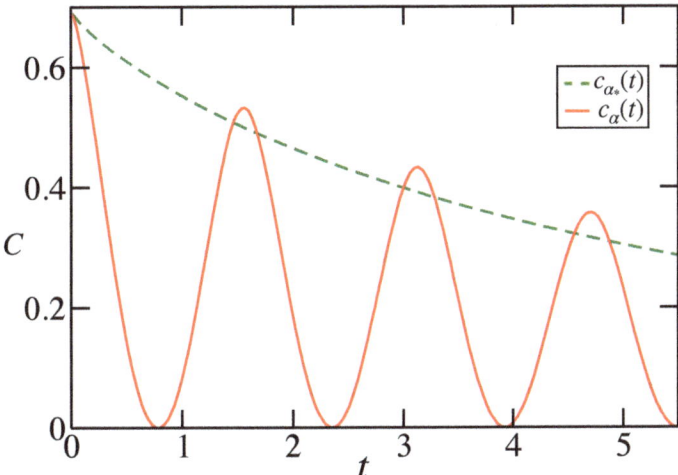

Figure 3. For the functions $c_{\alpha_*}(t)$ and $c_\alpha(t)$, $\alpha \neq \alpha_*$, for the qubit evolution with $r = 1/(10 \text{ s})$, and $\omega = 2/\text{s}$. Observe that $C[\Lambda(t)] > C[\Lambda^M(t)]$ when $c_\alpha(t) > c_{\alpha_*}(t)$, or, in other words, when the dashed line lies below the solid line. Contrary to the semigroup examples, the maximal capacity increase does not occur during the first time range when the classical capacity is enhanced.

5. Conclusions

We analyzed the classical capacity of generalized Pauli channels generated via memory kernel master equations. We compared the evolution of channel capacity for the Markovian semigroup and for the dynamical map generated via a memory kernel that is a sum of the Markovian part and the noise part. Note that the local part is legitimate and identical for both maps. The non-local part, which corresponds to environmental noise, was chosen in such a way that the dynamical map that solves the associated Nakajima–Zwanzig equation describes a valid physical evolution. It was found that the introduction of noise into the master equation could lead to a temporary increase in the classical capacity. In other words, noise effects can be beneficial in quantum information processing, as they result in the enhanced ability of a quantum channel to reliably transmit classical information. Similar results were obtained after a generalization of the Markovian semigroup to a Markovian evolution provided by a time-local generator. However, we showed that analogical observations cannot be made for time-local master equations. A dynamical map generated via the sum of two time-local generators never produces a classical capacity that is higher than that of a map that arises from a single generator.

It would be interesting to further analyze this topic by considering the kernels for noninvertible Markovian dynamical maps mixed with the noise kernels. Another open question concerns the relation between quantum maps that increase classical capacity and maps that increase the channel fidelity. One could expect that capacity enhancement means higher fidelity, but not the other way around. A comparative analysis could also be performed for other important measures, such as output purity, concurrence, logarithmic negativity, and von Neumann entropy.

Author Contributions: Conceptualization, K.S.; methodology, K.S., A.D. and A.B.; validation, K.S., A.D. and A.B.; formal analysis, K.S., A.D. and A.B.; investigation, K.S., A.D. and A.B.; visualization, A.B.; writing—original draft preparation, K.S.; writing—review and editing, K.S., A.D. and A.B.; supervision, K.S. All authors have read and agreed to the published version of the manuscript.

Funding: This research was founded by the Polish National Science Centre project No. 2018/30/A/ST2/00837. Additionally, K.S. was supported by the Foundation for Polish Science (FNP).

Institutional Review Board Statement: Not applicable.

Informed Consent Statement: Not applicable.

Data Availability Statement: Not applicable.

Conflicts of Interest: The authors declare no conflict of interest.

References

1. Nielsen, M.A.; Chuang, I.L. *Quantum Computation and Quantum Information*; Cambridge University Press: Cambridge, UK, 2010.
2. Bruß, D.; Leuchs, G. *Lectures on Quantum Information*; Wiley: Weinheim, Germany, 2006.
3. Lidar, D.A. Review of Decoherence-Free Subspaces, Noiseless Subsystems, and Dynamical Decoupling. *Adv. Chem. Phys.* **2014**, *154*, 295–354.
4. Roffe, J. Quantum error correction: An introductory guide. *Contemp. Phys.* **2019**, *60*, 226–245. [CrossRef]
5. Verstraete, F.; Wolf, M.M.; Cirac, J.I. Quantum computation and quantum-state engineering driven by dissipation. *Nat. Phys.* **2009**, *5*, 633–636. [CrossRef]
6. Zanardi, P.; Venuti, L.C. Coherent Quantum Dynamics in Steady-State Manifolds of Strongly Dissipative Systems. *Phys. Rev. Lett.* **2014**, *113*, 240406. [CrossRef]
7. Marshall, J.; Venuti, L.C.; Zanardi, P. Modular quantum-information processing by dissipation. *Phys. Rev. A* **2016**, *94*, 052339. [CrossRef]
8. Gillard, N.; Belin, E.; Chapeau-Blondeau, F. Enhancing qubit information with quantum thermal noise. *Phys. A Stat. Mech. Appl.* **2018**, *507*, 219–230. [CrossRef]
9. Marshall, J.; Venuti, L.C.; Zanardi, P. Noise suppression via generalized-Markovian processes. *Phys. Rev. A* **2017**, *96*, 052113. [CrossRef]
10. Shabani, A.; Lidar, D.A. Completely positive post-Markovian master equation via a measurement approach. *Phys. Rev. A* **2005**, *71*, 020101. [CrossRef]
11. Chruściński, D.; Kossakowski, A. Generalized semi-Markov quantum evolution. *Phys. Rev. A* **2017**, *95*, 042131. [CrossRef]
12. Lloyd, S. Capacity of the noisy quantum channel. *Phys. Rev. A* **1997**, *55*, 1613–1622. [CrossRef]
13. Shor, P. The quantum channel capacity and coherent information. *MSRI Workshop Quantum Comput. Lect. Notes* **2002**.
14. Devetak, I. The private classical capacity and quantum capacity of a quantum channel. *IEEE Trans. Inf. Theor.* **2005**, *51*, 44–55. [CrossRef]
15. Bennett, C.; Shor, P.W.; Smolin, J.A.; Thapliyal, A.V. Entanglement-assisted capacity of a quantum channel and the reverse Shannon theorem. *IEEE Trans. Inf. Theor.* **2002**, *48*, 2637–2655. [CrossRef]
16. Shor, P.W.; Devetak, I. The Capacity of a Quantum Channel for Simultaneous Transmission of Classical and Quantum Information. *Commun. Math. Phys.* **2005**, *256*, 287.
17. Gyongyosi, L.; Imre, S.; Nguyen, H.V. A Survey on Quantum Channel Capacities. *IEEE Commun. Surv. Tut.* **2018**, *20*, 1149–1205. [CrossRef]
18. Smith, G. Quantum channel capacities. In Proceedings of the IEEE Information Theory Workshop, Dublin, Ireland, 30 August–3 September 2010.
19. Holevo, A.S. The capacity of the quantum channel with general signal states. *IEEE Trans. Inf. Theory* **1998**, *44*, 269–273. [CrossRef]
20. Schumacher, B.; Westmoreland, M.D. Sending classical information via noisy quantum channels. *Phys. Rev. A* **1997**, *56*, 131–138. [CrossRef]
21. ur Rehman, J.; Jeong, Y.; Kim, J.S.; Shin, H. Holevo Capacity of Discrete Weyl Channels. *Sci. Rep.* **2018**, *8*, 17457. [CrossRef] [PubMed]
22. ur Rehman, J.; Jeong, Y.; Shin, H. Directly estimating the Holevo capacity of discrete Weyl channels. *Phys. Rev. A* **2019**, *99*, 042312. [CrossRef]
23. Amosov, G.G. On classical capacity of Weyl channels. *Quantum Inf. Process.* **2020**, *19*, 401. [CrossRef]
24. Amosov, G.G. On capacity of quantum channels generated by irreducible projective unitary representations of finite groups. *arXiv* **2021**, arXiv:2103.08515.
25. Nathanson, M.; Ruskai, M.B. Pauli diagonal channels constant on axes. *J. Phys. A Math. Theor.* **2007**, *40*, 8171. [CrossRef]
26. Chruściński, D.; Siudzińska, K. Generalized Pauli channels and a class of non-Markovian quantum evolution. *Phys. Rev. A* **2016**, *94*, 022118. [CrossRef]
27. Watrous, J. *The Theory of Quantum Information*; Cambridge University Press: Cambridge, UK, 2018.
28. Alicki, R.; Lendi, K. *Quantum Dynamical Semigroups and Applications*; Springer: Berlin, Germany, 1987.
29. Gregoratti, M.; Werner, R.F. Quantum lost and found. *J. Mod. Opt.* **2003**, *50*, 915. [CrossRef]
30. King, C.; Ruskai, M.B. Minimal Entropy of States Emerging from Noisy Quantum Channels. *IEEE Trans. Inf. Theory* **2001**, *47*, 192–209. [CrossRef]

31. Landau, L.J.; Streater, R.F. On Birkhoff's theorem for doubly stochastic completely positive maps of matrix algebras. *Linear Algebra Appl.* **1993**, *193*, 107–127. [CrossRef]
32. Petz, D.; Ohno, H. Generalizations of Pauli channels. *Acta Math. Hungar.* **2009**, *124*, 165.
33. Chruściński, D.; Wudarski, F.A. Non-Markovianity degree for random unitary evolution. *Phys. Rev. A* **2015**, *91*, 012104. [CrossRef]
34. Siudzińska, K. Two Definitions of the Gell-Mann Channels—A Comparative Analysis. *Rep. Math. Phys.* **2018**, *81*, 321–345. [CrossRef]
35. Siudzińska, K. Generalization of Pauli channels through mutually unbiased measurements. *Phys. Rev. A* **2020**, *102*, 032603. [CrossRef]
36. Bandyopadhyay, S.; Boykin, P.; Roychowdhury, V.; Vatan, F. A new proof for the existence of mutually unbiased bases. *Algorithmica* **2002**, *34*, 512.
37. Fujiwara, A.; Algoet, P. One-to-one parametrization of quantum channels. *Phys. Rev. A* **1999**, *59*, 3290. [CrossRef]
38. Bengtsson, I.; Życzkowski, K. *Geometry of Quantum States: An Introduction to Quantum Entanglement*; Cambridge University Press: Cambridge, UK, 2007.
39. Shannon, C.E. A mathematical theory of communication. *Bell Syst. Tech. J.* **1948**, *27*, 379–423. [CrossRef]
40. King, C. Remarks on the Additivity Conjectures for Quantum Channels. *Entropy Quantum Contemp. Math.* **2010**, *529*, 177–188.
41. Siudzińska, K. Classical capacity of generalized Pauli channel. *J. Phys. A Math. Theor.* **2020**, *53*, 445301. [CrossRef]
42. King, C. The capacity of the quantum depolarizing channel. *IEEE Trans. Inf. Theory* **2003**, *49*, 221–229. [CrossRef]
43. Gorini, V.; Kossakowski, A.; Sudarshan, E. Completely positive semigroups of N-level systems. *J. Math. Phys.* **1976**, *17*, 821. [CrossRef]
44. Lindblad, G. On the generators of quantum dynamical semigroups. *Comm. Math. Phys.* **1976**, *48*, 119. [CrossRef]
45. Rivas, A.; Huelga, S.F.; Plenio, M.B. Entanglement and Non-Markovianity of Quantum Evolutions. *Phys. Rev. Lett.* **2010**, *105*, 050403. [CrossRef]
46. Wolf, M.M.; Eisert, J.; Cubitt, T.S.; Cirac, J.I. Assessing Non-Markovian Quantum Dynamics. *Phys. Rev. Lett.* **2008**, *101*, 150402. [CrossRef]
47. Nakajima, S. On Quantum Theory of Transport Phenomena: Steady Diffusion. *Prog. Theor. Phys.* **1958**, *20*, 948. [CrossRef]
48. Zwanzig, R. Ensemble Method in the Theory of Irreversibility. *J. Chem. Phys.* **1960**, *33*, 1338. [CrossRef]
49. Siudzińska, K.; Chruściński, D. Memory kernel approach to generalized Pauli channels: Markovian, semi-Markov, and beyond. *Phys. Rev. A* **2017**, *96*, 022129. [CrossRef]
50. Siudzińska, K.; Chruściński, D. Engineering fidelity of the generalized Pauli channels via legitimate memory kernels. *Phys. Rev. A* **2019**, *100*, 012303. [CrossRef]
51. Chruściński, D.; Rivas, A.; Størmer, E. Divisibility and Information Flow Notions of Quantum Markovianity for Noninvertible Dynamical Maps. *Phys. Rev. Lett.* **2018**, *121*, 080407. [CrossRef]
52. Kołodyński, J.; Brask, J.B.; Perarnau-Llobet, M.; Bylicka, B. Adding dynamical generators in quantum master equations. *Phys. Rev. A* **2018**, *97*, 062124. [CrossRef]

Article

Correlations, Information Backflow, and Objectivity in a Class of Pure Dephasing Models

Nina Megier [1,2,3,*], Andrea Smirne [1,2], Steve Campbell [4,5,*] and Bassano Vacchini [1,2]

1. Dipartimento di Fisica "Aldo Pontremoli", Università degli Studi di Milano, Via Celoria 16, 20133 Milan, Italy; andrea.smirne@unimi.it (A.S.); bassano.vacchini@mi.infn.it (B.V.)
2. Istituto Nazionale di Fisica Nucleare, Sezione di Milano, Via Celoria 16, 20133 Milan, Italy
3. International Centre for Theory of Quantum Technologies (ICTQT), University of Gdansk, 80-308 Gdansk, Poland
4. School of Physics, University College Dublin, Belfield, D04 Dublin, Ireland
5. Centre for Quantum Engineering, Science, and Technology, University College Dublin, Belfield, D04 Dublin, Ireland
* Correspondence: nina.megier@mi.infn.it (N.M.); steve.campbell@ucd.ie (S.C.)

Abstract: We critically examine the role that correlations established between a system and fragments of its environment play in characterising the ensuing dynamics. We employ a dephasing model with different initial conditions, where the state of the initial environment represents a tunable degree of freedom that qualitatively and quantitatively affects the correlation profiles, but nevertheless results in the same reduced dynamics for the system. We apply recently developed tools for the characterisation of non-Markovianity to carefully assess the role that correlations, as quantified by the (quantum) Jensen–Shannon divergence and relative entropy, as well as changes in the environmental state, play in whether the conditions for classical objectivity within the quantum Darwinism paradigm are met. We demonstrate that for precisely the same non-Markovian reduced dynamics of the system arising from different microscopic models, some exhibit quantum Darwinistic features, while others show that no meaningful notion of classical objectivity is present. Furthermore, our results highlight that the non-Markovian nature of an environment does not a priori prevent a system from redundantly proliferating relevant information, but rather it is the system's ability to establish the requisite correlations that is the crucial factor in the manifestation of classical objectivity.

Keywords: non-Markovianity; quantum Darwinism; dephasing; correlations; Jensen–Shannon divergence

1. Introduction

The necessity for effective means to describe how a quantum system interacts with its surrounding environment has precipitated a burgeoning area of research. In many instances, one is solely focused on the dynamics of the system of interest, and therefore, environmental effects can be phenomenologically modelled, rendering the complex system dynamics tractable [1,2]. While highly effective, such an approach neglects to account for the root cause of the ensuing dynamics of the system. Reverting to a full microscopic description, where the system and environment interact and evolve according to an overall unitary dynamics, reveals that the correlations established between the system and the environment during their interaction play an important role in the resulting open dynamics of the system [1,2]. These correlations are the basis for notions of classical objectivity [3–7] and are also known to play a key role in the characterisation of the dynamics, in particular, if the system undergoes a Markovian (memoryless) or non-Markovian evolution [8,9]. Both notions of classical objectivity and non-Markovian evolution have been the object of experimental investigations; see, for example, [10–13] and [14–20], respectively.

However, a given open system dynamics does not arise from a unique microscopic system–environment model, and rather, there are infinitely many system–environment models that result in the same system evolution [21]. Such an insight calls for a more careful analysis of the information exchanges between the system and its environment, allowing to more precisely pin down the relevant contributions which give rise to, for example, Markovian vs. non-Markovian dynamics [22], or establish the conditions for classical objectivity [23–25]. This becomes particularly subtle since under such a microscopic picture, the environment is typically composed of many constituent subsystems, and therefore it is relevant to assess the complementary role that global correlations established between the system and the whole environment play compared to correlations shared between the system and smaller environmental fragments. With regards to the former, it was recently demonstrated that without the creation of strong global correlations in the form of entanglement, reasonable conditions for objectivity are not satisfied [24,25], while for the latter, it appears that only the correlations shared between the system and a small subset of the environmental degrees of freedom are relevant for the characterisation of the system dynamics [22,26].

In this work, we attempt to unravel the contribution that various correlations play in the characterisation of an open system dynamics. To that end, we consider a spin-star dephasing model, where several different initial environmental states, which in turn lead to significantly different correlation profiles, nevertheless produce the same reduced dynamics for the system [21]. We employ recently developed tools for understanding the emergence of non-Markovianity in terms of the correlations established between the system and environment, as well as changes in the environmental state [22,27], to put into evidence the quite different role that these features play when characterising the dynamics, either in terms of its non-Markovian character or its ability to establish the conditions necessary for classical objectivity. We show that two different microscopic descriptions of the evolution that lead to the same reduced dynamics of the system can exhibit significant differences with regards to classical objectivity within the quantum Darwinism framework. Our work therefore demonstrates that the non-Markovian character of an evolution does not necessarily affect a system's ability to redundantly proliferate information to the environment, thus contributing to the ongoing efforts to unravel their relation [28–31] or possible lack thereof [32,33]; note, in particular, the recent analysis in [34] complementary to ours.

The remainder of the paper is organised as follows. In Section 2, we introduce the spin-star model with different initial conditions that is our focus. Section 3 introduces the correlation measures that are our key figures of merit and examines how they spread in the dependence on the initial condition. We analyse various information fluxes in Section 4 and their dual role characterising the non-Markovian nature of the dynamics and the redundant spreading of relevant system information to environmental constituents. Finally, we draw our conclusions in Section 5.

2. Dephasing Models

Let us introduce the models for which we want to study the role of correlations in determining important features of the overall and reduced dynamics. We recall that in being interested in the reduced dynamics of the system in a system–environment setting, the full specification of a model includes the choice of the initial environmental state. We therefore consider a set of N two-level systems with frequency ω_E, interacting with a two-level system with frequency ω_S, via the microscopic Hamiltonian

$$H = \frac{\hbar \omega_S}{2}\sigma_z \otimes \mathbb{1}_{2^N} + \sum_{k=1}^{N} g_k \sigma_z \otimes \sigma_z^k + \sum_{k=1}^{N} \frac{\hbar \omega_E}{2} \mathbb{1}_2 \otimes \sigma_z^k. \tag{1}$$

With σ_z^k, we denote the operator $\mathbb{1}_{2^{(k-1)}} \otimes \sigma_z \otimes \mathbb{1}_{2^{(N-k)}}$, where the Pauli matrix σ_z acts on the k-th environmental qubit, while $\mathbb{1}_d$ indicates the identity operator in a space of dimension d, and the g_k's are the system environment coupling constants. Such an interaction corresponds to a so-called spin-star setting, in which a central spin is coupled to neighbouring environmental degrees of freedom, which can be described by a collection of non-interacting spins. In particular, the considered coupling term is such that it only affects the coherences of the system since $\sigma_z \otimes \mathbb{1}_{2N}$ is a constant of motion, thus describing a dephasing dynamics. We investigate the time evolution of these degrees of freedom in the hypothesis of the existence of a closed reduced dynamics for the central spin system, that is to say, assuming the initial overall state factorised according to $\rho_{SE}(0) = \rho_S(0) \otimes \rho_E(0)$. We consider models in which the initial environmental state is given by a tensor product of identical states, namely

$$\rho_E(0) = \bigotimes_{k=1}^{N} \varrho_E, \tag{2}$$

with

$$\varrho_E = \begin{pmatrix} p & c \\ c & 1-p \end{pmatrix}, \tag{3}$$

where $p \in [0,1]$ and without loss of generality, we can take c real in the range $|c| \leq \sqrt{p(1-p)}$. This initial environmental state allows us to explore not only the total correlations, but also their establishment as a function of the fraction of environmental degrees of freedom we are taking into consideration.

Starting from the fact that the total unitary evolution operator in the interaction picture can be written in the form

$$U(s) = \sum_{\{m_k\}} e^{-i\sigma_z (\sum_{k=1}^{N} g_k m_k)s} \otimes |\{m_k\}\rangle\langle\{m_k\}|, \tag{4}$$

where the vectors $\{|\{m_k\}\rangle = |m_1\rangle \otimes \ldots \otimes |m_N\rangle\}$, such that $\sigma_z^k |m_k\rangle = m_k|m_k\rangle$ with $m_k \in \{-1,1\}$, denote the basis of eigenvectors of the operator $\bigotimes_{k=1}^{N} \sigma_z^k$ in the environmental space, we obtain for the evolved state of system and environment the expression

$$\rho_{SE}(s) = \begin{pmatrix} \rho_{11}(0) \bigotimes_{k=1}^{N} \rho_k(s) & \rho_{10}(0) \bigotimes_{k=1}^{N} \sigma_k(s) \\ \rho_{01}(0) \bigotimes_{k=1}^{N} \sigma_k^*(s) & \rho_{00}(0) \bigotimes_{k=1}^{N} \rho_k^*(s) \end{pmatrix}, \tag{5}$$

where

$$\rho_k(s) = \begin{pmatrix} p & ce^{-i2g_k s} \\ ce^{i2g_k s} & 1-p \end{pmatrix} \tag{6}$$

and

$$\sigma_k(s) = \begin{pmatrix} pe^{-i2g_k s} & c \\ c & (1-p)e^{i2g_k s} \end{pmatrix}. \tag{7}$$

An important feature of the considered class of evolutions appears when considering the associated reduced dynamics. Indeed, taking the partial trace with respect to the environmental degrees of freedom, one immediately obtains

$$\rho_S(s) = \begin{pmatrix} \rho_{11}(0) & \rho_{10}(0)\chi(s) \\ \rho_{01}(0)\chi^*(s) & \rho_{00}(0) \end{pmatrix} \tag{8}$$

with

$$\chi(s) = \prod_{k=1}^{N} [\cos(2g_k s) - i(2p-1)\sin(2g_k s)], \tag{9}$$

where we have used the identity

$$\sum_{\{m_k\}} e^{-i2(\sum_{k=1}^{N} g_k m_k)s} \langle \{m_k\} | \rho_E(0) | \{m_k\} \rangle = \prod_{k=1}^{N} [\cos(2g_k s) - i \langle \sigma_z^k \rangle_{\varrho_E} \sin(2g_k s)], \qquad (10)$$

and $\langle \ldots \rangle_{\varrho_E}$ denotes the expectation value with respect to the state ϱ_E given in Equation (3), so that the reduced dynamics is exactly the same for all initial environmental states with the same diagonal matrix elements. Therefore, we have a whole class of dephasing models, parametrised by the coherence, c, of the environmental state given by Equation (3), leading to exactly the same reduced dynamics. The existence of different environments equally affecting a given system has been studied in different contexts, with the purpose of allowing for more convenient numerical treatments [35–38]. The occurrence of the very same reduced evolution starting from different microscopic dynamics in a controlled setting was recently considered also in [21], in order to investigate the physical mechanism behind memory effects in quantum dynamics.

For the sake of simplicity, and in order to allow for analytical results, we consider the case in which all coupling constants are taken to be equal to a reference value g, so that all environmental units evolve in the same way throughout the dynamics, as well as a uniform distribution of the populations in the initial environmental components, namely $p = 1/2$. In particular, we address situations in which ϱ_E in Equation (3) ranges from pure, for $c = \pm 1/2$, to maximally mixed for $c = 0$. The maximally mixed state corresponds in particular to a situation in which the reduced environmental state is unaffected by the interaction with the system. This choice has the advantage of providing a simple parameter characterizing the different considered initial conditions, while, as can be inferred from [33,39], the results are expected to be robust with respect to noise in the initial preparation.

We now consider possible physical manifestations of the difference in the microscopic dynamics and related correlations studying the onset of Darwinistic behaviour and non-Markovianity in various environmental scenarios.

3. Spreading of Correlations

Let us first study the establishment and spread of correlations in the considered scenarios. As discussed in detail in many publications [6,23–25,40–44], this feature might have an impact on the notion of objectivity for a quantum state, in the spirit of so-called quantum Darwinism [3] (see, for example, ref. [7] for a recent review and references therein). We see that it also provides us with interesting insights in the study of quantum non-Markovianity [8,9].

As is clear from Equations (8) and (9), for a uniform coupling, the reduced dynamics has a period of $\pi/2$ in the variable gs, so that we will consider times up to $\pi/(2g)$. In particular, the system is fully decohered for $gs = \pi/4$. This decoherence is connected to the establishment of correlations with the environmental qubits; however, as shown in Figure 1, these correlations (as quantified by the quantum Jensen–Shannon divergence defined in the following subsection) are greater the more environmental qubits we take into account. In particular, for $c = 0$, the reduced system is only correlated at this point of time with the environment as a whole. The overall state according to Equation (5) then reads

$$\rho_{SE}(s) = \frac{1}{2^N} \begin{pmatrix} \rho_{11}(0) \otimes_{k=1}^{N} \begin{pmatrix} 1 & ce^{-i2gs} \\ ce^{i2gs} & 1 \end{pmatrix} & \rho_{10}(0) \otimes_{k=1}^{N} \begin{pmatrix} e^{-i2gs} & c \\ c & e^{i2gs} \end{pmatrix} \\ \rho_{01}(0) \otimes_{k=1}^{N} \begin{pmatrix} e^{i2gs} & c \\ c & e^{-i2gs} \end{pmatrix} & \rho_{00}(0) \otimes_{k=1}^{N} \begin{pmatrix} 1 & ce^{i2gs} \\ ce^{-i2gs} & 1 \end{pmatrix} \end{pmatrix}. \qquad (11)$$

Given that we are considering a dephasing dynamics, a natural choice for the initial condition for the system is a pure state of the form $\rho_S(0) = |+\rangle\langle+|$, with $|+\rangle = (1/\sqrt{2})(|1\rangle + |0\rangle)$, exhibiting the maximum amount of coherence so that $\rho_{ij}(0) = 1/2$ for $i, j = 0, 1$. Starting from this expression one can consider marginals in which less and less environmental units are involved. In particular, we will denote as $\rho_{SE_{fN}}$ the state obtained by tracing over all environmental units not contained in a fraction f of the environment. For the extreme cases f = 0 and f = 1, we recover the reduced and total states, respectively.

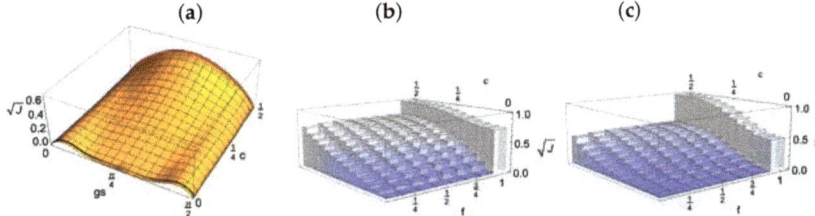

Figure 1. (a) Amount of correlations shared between the system initially in the plus state $|+\rangle = (1/\sqrt{2})(|0\rangle + |1\rangle)$ and one of the environmental qubits, evaluated by considering the QJSD$^{1/2}$, comparing this bipartite state with the product of its marginal as a function of time (in inverse units of the coupling parameter) and of the value c of initial coherence in the environmental states. The quantity is renormalised to the value corresponding to a maximally entangled state. Here and in the following figures, the environment is composed of $N = 8$ units. The black and red lines correspond to $c = 0$ and $c = 1/2$. (b) Distance between total state and product of its marginals at the reference time $gs = \pi/4$ as quantified by the QJSD$^{1/2}$, expressed as a function of the fraction of considered environmental qubits and of the value, c, of coherences in the environmental states. The total state includes the system and a fraction, f, of the environmental qubits. (c) The same quantity obtained considering as the quantifier the relative entropy, thus recovering the mutual information, still keeping the normalisation to the value corresponding to the maximally entangled state. In both figures, we see the emergence of a plateau for $c = 1/2$, which is gradually washed out for smaller values of c, namely when moving from a model in which the environmental units have coherences to a fully diagonal state.

3.1. Quantifiers of Correlations

In order to understand the spreading of correlations in the different models, we are, therefore, interested in their dependence on the considered fraction. In general, given a distinguishability quantifier between quantum states, say D, which is a quantity defined on pairs of quantum states such that $D(\rho, \sigma) \geq 0$ with equality if the states coincide, one can use it as a quantifier of correlations in a bipartite state considering the expression $D(\rho_{SE}, \rho_S \otimes \rho_E)$. For the sake of this study, we consider the square root of the quantum Jensen–Shannon divergence (QJSD$^{1/2}$) and the relative entropy. We use both as quantifiers of bipartite correlations by renormalizing to the value assumed for the case of a maximally entangled state. The choice of the QJSD$^{1/2}$ is motivated by its use in the framework of non-Markovianity [45,46], while the relative entropy is typically used in the framework of quantum Darwinism [7] due to its connection with the mutual information.

The QJSD$^{1/2}$ is defined in terms of the Jensen–Shannon divergence [47] according to

$$\sqrt{J(\rho, \sigma)} = \sqrt{S\left(\frac{\rho + \sigma}{2}\right) - \frac{1}{2}S(\rho) - \frac{1}{2}S(\sigma)}, \qquad (12)$$

where $S(\rho) = -\text{Tr}\,\rho \log \rho$ denotes the von Neumann entropy and logarithms are considered in base 2. This quantity, besides being a well-known distinguishability quantifier, was recently shown to be a distance [48,49]. In particular, when used to evaluate correlations, it takes the form

$$\sqrt{J(\rho_{SE}, \rho_S \otimes \rho_E)} = \sqrt{S\left(\frac{\rho_{SE} + \rho_S \otimes \rho_E}{2}\right) - \frac{1}{2}S(\rho_{SE}) - \frac{1}{2}S(\rho_S) - \frac{1}{2}S(\rho_E)},$$

taking the value $\sqrt{2-(5/8)\log 5} \approx 0.74$ when ρ_{SE} corresponds to the maximally entangled state in $\mathbb{C}^2 \otimes \mathbb{C}^{2N}$. We denote as $\sqrt{J}$ the quantity rescaled by this factor, thus assuming unity for maximally entangled states.

The relative entropy is defined according to [47]

$$S(\rho,\sigma) = \mathrm{Tr}\,\rho\log\rho - \mathrm{Tr}\,\rho\log\sigma, \qquad (13)$$

so that when used to quantify correlations, it leads to the mutual information

$$S(\rho_{SE}, \rho_S \otimes \rho_E) = S(\rho_S) + S(\rho_E) - S(\rho_{SE}), \qquad (14)$$

providing a natural quantifier of both classical and quantum correlations. Considering again logarithms in base 2, it takes the value 2 for the maximally entangled state in $\mathbb{C}^2 \otimes \mathbb{C}^{2N}$, so we denote as S the quantity rescaled by a factor 2.

3.2. Model Dependence of Correlation Formation

The key quantities to be considered in the study of the establishment of correlations between the system and different parts of the environment in the different considered models are, therefore, $\sqrt{J(\rho_{SE_{fN}}, \rho_S \otimes \rho_{E_{fN}})}$ and $S(\rho_{SE_{fN}}, \rho_S \otimes \rho_{E_{fN}})$. Their behaviour is shown in Figure 1b,c, respectively, as a function of the parameter c, which fixes the initial environmental state and therefore the model. As follows from their expressions given in Equations (12) and (14), their determination relies on knowledge of the eigenvalues of $\rho_{SE_{fN}}$, $\rho_S \otimes \rho_{E_{fN}}$ and their average. In turn, these operators depend on the chosen initial state for the system that we have taken to be the pure state $\rho_S(0) = |+\rangle\langle+|$, initially exhibiting the maximum amount of coherence so as to better put into evidence the role of the environment.

For the case $c=0$, one immediately sees from Equation (11) that the environment is left unchanged so that it remains in the maximally mixed state. The eigenvalues of the relevant states can be shown to be

$$\begin{aligned}
\rho_{SE_{fN}}(s) &\to \frac{1}{2^{fN+1}}(1 \pm \cos^{N-fN}(2gs)) \\
\rho_S(s) &\to \frac{1}{2}(1 \pm \cos^N(2gs)) \\
\rho_{E_{fN}}(s) &\to \frac{1}{2^{fN}} \\
\frac{\rho_{SE_{fN}}(s) + \rho_S(s) \otimes \rho_{E_{fN}}(s)}{2} &\to \frac{1}{2^{fN+1}}\left(1 \pm \frac{1}{2}\left|\cos^N(2gs) + \cos^{(1-f)N}(2gs)e^{i2g(\sum_{k=1}^{fN} m_k)s}\right|\right)
\end{aligned} \qquad (15)$$

where the eigenvalues for $\rho_{SE_{fN}}(s)$ and $\rho_{E_{fN}}(s)$ are 2^{fN} degenerate, while the numbers $\{m_k\}$ belong to $\{-1,1\}$ and their value is determined by the associated eigenvector. In terms of these expressions, exploiting the fact that the von Neumann entropy of a state only depends on its eigenvalues,

$$S(\rho) = -\sum_i \rho_i \log \rho_i, \qquad (16)$$

one can analytically determine the relevant expressions for the correlations.

An arbitrary value of the coherences in the initial environmental state calls for a numerical evaluation, whose results are shown in Figure 1b,c at time $gs = \pi/4$, when the system has fully decohered, as can be seen from Equations (8) and (9), thus losing its initial information content. It immediately appears, independently of the chosen correlation quantifier, that for $c = 1/2$, i.e., initially pure environmental units, the system shares an equal amount of correlations with any small fraction of the environment, corresponding to a plateau in the fraction dependence of the correlation quantifiers. This feature is interpreted in the literature as quantum Darwinism [3], namely, a redundant storing of information about the system in different portions of the environment, allowing for a notion of objectivity, in the sense that the same information can be retrieved by different observers accessing distinct parts of the environment. It is to be stressed that the mutual information provides the standard choice of a correlation quantifier in this framework, though others were also considered [40,44]. This notion of objectivity is not uncontroversial; see [7] for a critical discussion and further developments. The formation of the plateau is slowed down with decreasing c, while for $c = 0$, such that the environmental units are maximally mixed, correlations are only established between the system and the environment as a whole. This behaviour, namely, the gradual washing out of Darwinism in the dependence on the state of the environmental units, was already observed in [50], where the von Neumann entropy of the units was used as the figure of merit, which is a monotonic function of the coherence; see also [39,51].

To exemplify the distribution of correlations for the case $c = 0$, let us write the overall state Equation (11) for the case of two environmental qubits, thus obtaining

$$\rho_{SE}(s) = \frac{1}{8}\begin{pmatrix} 1 & e^{-i4gs} \\ e^{i4gs} & 1 \end{pmatrix} \otimes \begin{pmatrix} 1 & 0 & 0 & 0 \\ 0 & 0 & 0 & 0 \\ 0 & 0 & 0 & 0 \\ 0 & 0 & 0 & 0 \end{pmatrix} + \frac{1}{8}\begin{pmatrix} 1 & 1 \\ 1 & 1 \end{pmatrix} \otimes \begin{pmatrix} 0 & 0 & 0 & 0 \\ 0 & 1 & 0 & 0 \\ 0 & 0 & 1 & 0 \\ 0 & 0 & 0 & 0 \end{pmatrix}$$

$$+ \frac{1}{8}\begin{pmatrix} 1 & e^{i4gs} \\ e^{-i4gs} & 1 \end{pmatrix} \otimes \begin{pmatrix} 0 & 0 & 0 & 0 \\ 0 & 0 & 0 & 0 \\ 0 & 0 & 0 & 0 \\ 0 & 0 & 0 & 1 \end{pmatrix}, \quad (17)$$

namely, a classically correlated state, apart from multiples of $gs = \pi/2$, when the factorised initial state is recovered due to periodicity. Tracing out all but one of the environmental qubits, we obtain

$$\rho_{SE_1}(s) = \frac{1}{8}\begin{pmatrix} 2 & 1+e^{-i4gs} \\ 1+e^{i4gs} & 2 \end{pmatrix} \otimes \begin{pmatrix} 1 & 0 \\ 0 & 0 \end{pmatrix} + \frac{1}{8}\begin{pmatrix} 2 & 1+e^{i4gs} \\ 1+e^{-i4gs} & 2 \end{pmatrix} \otimes \begin{pmatrix} 0 & 0 \\ 0 & 1 \end{pmatrix}, \quad (18)$$

which is immediately seen to be factorized for $gs = \pi/4$, i.e., when the system has fully decohered. Accordingly, the information about the reduced system is stored then solely in the global correlations between the system and the environment, and all partial fractions of the environment are not correlated with the reduced system (note that the reduced density matrix of the environment is always maximally mixed). This is exactly the behaviour appearing in Figure 1b,c.

4. Information Backflow

We now want to analyse the features of the different models in the framework of non-Markovianity, which is the study of memory effects in a quantum setting. In this respect, we will make reference to an approach to quantum non-Markovianity focusing on features of the reduced dynamics [8,9], at variance with viewpoints which more closely mimic the classical definition of a non-Markovian process, referring to joint probability distributions [52], thus involving information on intermediate steps necessary in order to extract information from a quantum system [53]. Given that the considered definition of non-Markovian dynamics only involves the reduced dynamics, the whole class of considered initial conditions performs in exactly the same way. Nevertheless, the definition to be considered relies on the information exchange between the system and environment, which manifests differently in the various models.

Let us first briefly formalise the pioneering approach to the non-Markovianity of a quantum dynamics introduced in [54,55]. The basic idea is to consider the evolution in time of the distinguishability between two system states, associating to a non-monotonicity in the time of this quantity the definition of non-Markovian dynamics. The motivation behind this definition is that revivals of distinguishability can be unambiguously associated to information backflow from external degrees of freedom to the system. This approach was initially formulated in terms of the trace distance [9], but is actually amenable to the use of other distinguishability quantifiers, in particular, entropic ones, which come closer to the present treatment focused on the spreading of correlations, as shown in [45,46].

The key quantity to be considered is therefore the distinguishability of two system states evolved from two distinct initial conditions, namely

$$\sqrt{J(\rho_S^1(s), \rho_S^2(s))}, \qquad (19)$$

where, as discussed, we used as the distinguishability quantifier the QJSD$^{1/2}$ as defined in Equation (12). The QJSD$^{1/2}$ is a contraction with respect to the action of any positive trace-preserving map so that $\sqrt{J(\rho_S^1(s), \rho_S^2(s))}$ is monotonically decreasing in the case of a positive divisible evolution. For more general dynamics, this quantity can show revivals in time, pointing to the existence of memory effects. In particular, the revivals from the value at a time s to a value at a later time t can be upper bounded according to

$$\sqrt{J(\rho_S^1(t), \rho_S^2(t))} - \sqrt{J(\rho_S^1(s), \rho_S^2(s))}$$
$$\leqslant \sqrt{J(\rho_E^1(s), \rho_E^2(s))} + \sqrt{J(\rho_{SE}^1(s), \rho_S^1(s) \otimes \rho_E^1(s))} + \sqrt{J(\rho_{SE}^2(s), \rho_S^2(s) \otimes \rho_E^2(s))}, \qquad (20)$$

where $\rho_E^{1,2}(s)$ denote the time-evolved environmental states corresponding to the initial condition $\rho_S^{1,2}(0)$, while $\rho_E^1(0) = \rho_E^2(0)$ is determined as above by fixing the model of interest. Given that all three contributions at the r.h.s. are zero if and only if their arguments are equal, this bound has a clear physical meaning: non-Markovianity as described by revivals in the distinguishability of system states can only take place if correlations have been established between the system and environment, which is captured by the last two terms on the r.h.s of Equation (20) and/or different initial system states have affected, in a different way, the state of the environment, captured by the first term on the r.h.s. of Equation (20). In both cases, some information is stored in degrees of freedom external with respect to the system. The revivals do depend, in general, on the choice of initial system states so that it is natural to consider initial pairs that can be perfectly distinguished, namely, orthogonal states. In our case, given the previously considered choice $\rho_S^1(0) = |+\rangle\langle+|$, this would amount to considering $\rho_S^2(0) = |-\rangle\langle-|$. However, one immediately realises that in analogy to the fact that the reduced system dynamics is only affected by the diagonal matrix elements of the environmental qubits, also the dynamics of the environmental states only depends on the diagonal elements of $\rho_S^{1,2}(0)$ in the σ_z basis. This would automatically imply the vanishing of the first term at the r.h.s. of Equation (20). We therefore consider a more general pair of initial states, namely $\rho_S^1(0) = |+\rangle\langle+|$ and $\rho_S^2(0) = |\theta\rangle\langle\theta|$, with $|\theta\rangle = \cos(\theta/2)|1\rangle - \sin(\theta/2)|0\rangle$, as depicted in Figure 2.

We now want to explore the behaviour of these bounds for the different considered microscopic models, investigating, in particular, what happens when only partial information on the environment can be obtained.

4.1. Model Dependence of Bounds on Distinguishability Revivals

We first analyse the behaviour in time of the bounds, exploring their dependence on the considered model. In particular, we investigate the models arising for the choices $c = 0$ and $c = 1/2$. We recall that the non-Markovianity only depends on the behaviour of the reduced state of the system so that it is exactly the same for all values of c. The revivals of distinguishability for the whole class of initial conditions, expressed by means of the QJSD$^{1/2}$, namely the l.h.s. of Equation (20), are shown in Figure 3 as a function of the rescaled time and the choice of initial system states. As expected, the highest revivals take place for orthogonal initial states, corresponding to $\theta = \pi/2$. The periodicity of the dynamics, due to the uniform coupling, is also apparent. In Figure 4, we show the behaviour of the contributions at the r.h.s. of the bound, which provide information on degrees of freedom, external with respect to the system, so that they are indeed model dependent. We plot the contributions due to established correlations, starting from the initial conditions $\rho_S^1(0)$ and $\rho_S^2(0)$, respectively, together with the distinguishability of the correspondingly evolved environmental states $\rho_E^1(s)$ and $\rho_E^2(s)$, as well as the sum of the three terms, which determines the overall tightness of the bound, Equation (20). The first row shows the result for the model corresponding to $c = 1/2$, in which Darwinism appears, the second for $c = 0$. We see that in the first case, the upper bound is significantly less tight. The main reason is that for $c = 0$, the environmental state does not evolve so that one of the contributions is always zero, while in the other model, changes of the environmental dynamics take place for all choices of the θ parameter different from $\pi/2$, corresponding as discussed above to $\rho_S^2(0) = |-\rangle\langle-|$. The correlations between the second reduced system state and its environment, the only θ-dependent ones, are strongly affected by the parameter fixing this second initial system state but in the opposite manner with larger θ leading to more pronounced correlations. As a result, the upper bound is only weakly θ dependent. Interestingly, the maximum of the upper bound as a function of θ does not correspond to the maximum of the bounded quantity, namely the l.h.s. of Equation (20), shown in Figure 3. In all cases, the dominant contribution is given by the established correlations.

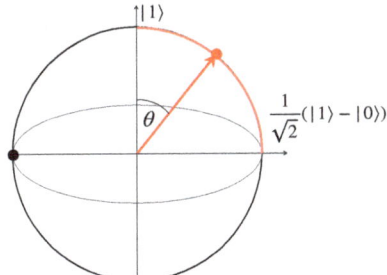

Figure 2. Bloch sphere representation of the considered pair of initial system states. One state is fixed to be the equatorial plus state $|+\rangle = (1/\sqrt{2})(|0\rangle + |1\rangle)$ (black dot), while the other element of the pair belongs to the maximum circle and is characterised by the angle θ (red dot). For $\theta = \pi/2$ it becomes the minus state $|-\rangle = (1/\sqrt{2})(|0\rangle - |1\rangle)$ and one recovers an orthogonal pair of initial states. For $\theta = 0$, it corresponds to the up state $|1\rangle$.

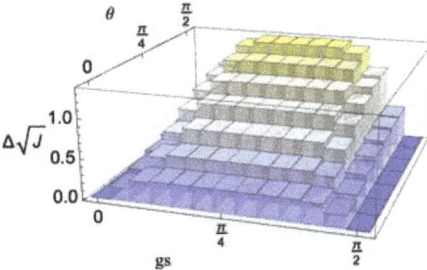

Figure 3. Plot of the l.h.s. of Equation (20) showing the revivals of the QJSD$^{1/2}$ as a function of time and choice of initial system states. The reference time gt is fixed to be $\pi/2$, i.e., after one full period of the evolution, while gs sweeps from 0 to $\pi/2$. The initial pair of system states is given by $\rho_S^1(0) = |+\rangle\langle+|$ and $\rho_S^2(0) = |\theta\rangle\langle\theta|$, as shown in Figure 2, with θ ranging from 0 to $\pi/2$, corresponding to the case of an orthogonal pair and maximizing the revivals.

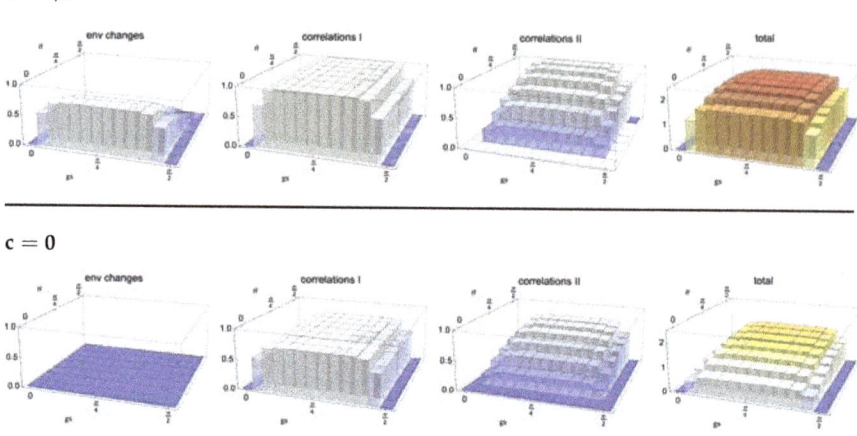

Figure 4. Plot of the different contributions at the r.h.s. of Equation (20), together with their sum, all quantified via the QJSD$^{1/2}$. They are considered as a function of running time gs and initial pair of states fixed by the angle θ. The first row corresponds, as indicated, to the model determined by $c = 1/2$, the second to $c = 0$. For $c = 1/2$, the environmental units have the maximum amount of coherence, while for $c = 0$, they start in a maximally mixed state and the reduced environmental state remains unchanged, so that one of the contributions is equal to zero.

4.2. Fraction Dependence of Bounds on Distinguishability Revivals

In order to understand the role of the spreading of information for the description of non-Markovianity in the different models, we study the behaviour of the quantities at the r.h.s. of Equation (20) when replacing the environment with a smaller one, given by a fraction of the original set of degrees of freedom. To this aim, we fix a reference time taken to be $gs = \pi/4$, corresponding to full decoherence of the reduced system, when quantum Darwinism is typically observed. Since the partial trace is a completely positive trace preserving map, each contribution gets smaller due to contractivity of the QJSD$^{1/2}$ under such maps, a feature shared by all distinguishability quantifiers considered for the description of memory effects. The inequality in Equation (20) is therefore no longer required to hold true since we are lowering the r.h.s. without affecting the l.h.s. The model corresponding to $c = 0$, see last row of Figure 5, is very special in this respect, as no information whatsoever is stored in any fraction of the environment smaller than the total environment so that the bound is immediately violated. For all choices of initial reduced states, correlations are built solely with the total environmental state, while by tracing out any number of environmental qubits, one obtains a factorised state. Additionally, the maximally mixed environmental state is invariant during the evolution for all choices of reduced initial state, a property which is obviously preserved by taking into account only some fraction of environmental degrees of freedom. On the other hand, in the model obtained for $c = 1/2$, such that the initial environmental states are pure, as shown in the first row of Figure 5, the difference in environmental states does not depend on the fraction of the environment we are taking into account. To see the origin of this behaviour, we come back to Equation (11) evaluated at time $gs = \pi/4$ for $c = 1/2$, which, upon taking the partial trace with respect to system and a fraction f of the environment, leads to the state

$$\rho_{E_{fN}}(\pi/(4g)) = \rho_{11}(0)\frac{1}{2^{fN}}\bigotimes_{k=1}^{fN}\begin{pmatrix}1 & -i\\ i & 1\end{pmatrix} + \rho_{00}(0)\frac{1}{2^{fN}}\bigotimes_{k=1}^{fN}\begin{pmatrix}1 & i\\ -i & 1\end{pmatrix}, \qquad (21)$$

whose only non-zero eigenvalues are $\rho_{11}(0)$ and $\rho_{00}(0)$ so that the difference in environmental states is not influenced by the number of environmental units taken into account.

We stress that this is only true for $gs = \pi/4$, the point in time most relevant for the study of quantum Darwinism. This can be seen considering both the dependence on time and fraction as in Figure 6, where both environmental changes and correlations are considered. Remarkably, for this particular model, the occurrence of a plateau as a function of the environmental fraction is not only true for the changes in the environment, but also in the correlations and, consequently, in the sum of these three quantities providing the overall bound. In other words, the information exchange relevant for the onset of non-Markovianity only involves a small portion of the environment, so that the bound holds for any considered fraction. The appearance of these plateaus makes the dynamics indeed compatible with quantum Darwinism, even though it only provides a sufficient condition for the redundant spreading of information.

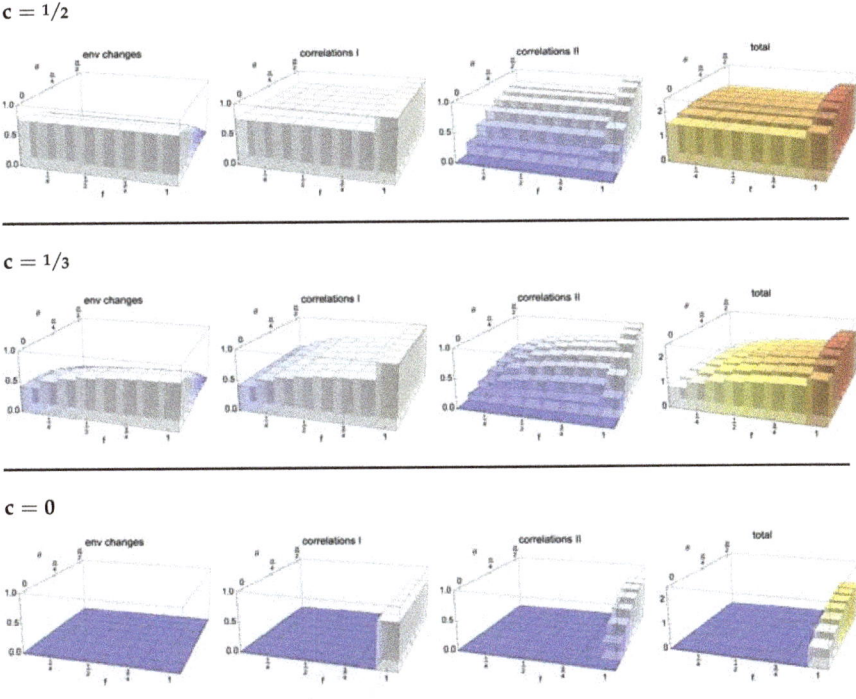

Figure 5. Plot of the different contributions at the r.h.s. of Equation (20), together with their sum, evaluated for the case in which the total state is replaced by a marginal obtained by tracing out some environmental qubits, so that only a fraction f is considered. Additionally, in this case, all quantities are expressed via the QJSD$^{1/2}$. They are considered a function of fraction f and initial pair of states determined by the angle θ for a fixed time $gs = \pi/4$. The first row corresponds, as indicated, to the model determined by $c = 1/2$, the second to $c = 1/3$ and the third to $c = 0$. For $c = 1/2$, plateaus as a function of f are clearly observed, replaced for $c = 1/3$ by a weak dependence. For $c = 0$, a non-zero value is only obtained when including the whole environment since tracing over any environmental units leads to a factorised state.

The occurrence of a very weak dependence with respect to the stepwise inclusions of environmental degrees of freedom is not new; it was indeed already observed in a collisional framework [22]. It reflects the fact that given the size of the system, the correlation with a small portion of the environment is already sufficient to store the information necessary to lead to a revival in distinguishability of the system states. In the present framework, for $c = 1/2$, we are faced with a true plateau, which reflects the pure Darwinistic behaviour exhibited by this model. To better clarify this behaviour, we have also plotted the same quantities for an intermediate choice of the mixing parameter $c = 1/3$; see middle row of Figure 5. In this case, corresponding to a model in which Darwinism is partially washed out [50], a weak dependence on the size of the fraction can be observed, so that a larger part of the environment is necessary to recover the relevant information. For this model, the failure of the upper bound upon tracing out part of the environment can be observed for a small enough fraction and large values of the parameter θ; see Figure 7. While the amount of information flowing back to the open system does not depend on the fraction of the environment taken into account, the capability to trace it back to the established correlations between the system and a portion of the environment, as well as to the changes of the latter, requires now that a large enough portion is considered.

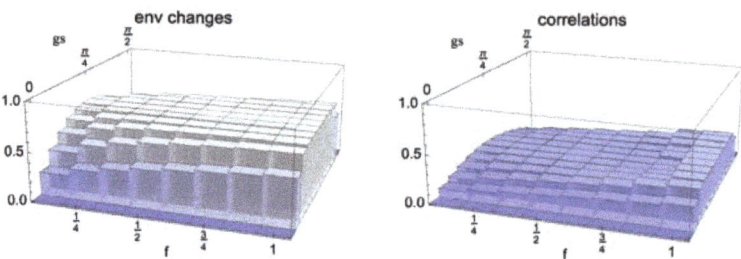

Figure 6. Behaviour of environmental changes and correlations for the model with $c = 1/2$ plotted as a function of both fraction f and time gs. It immediately appears that a plateau as a function of f only takes place for the time $gs = \pi/4$, corresponding to full decoherence of the system.

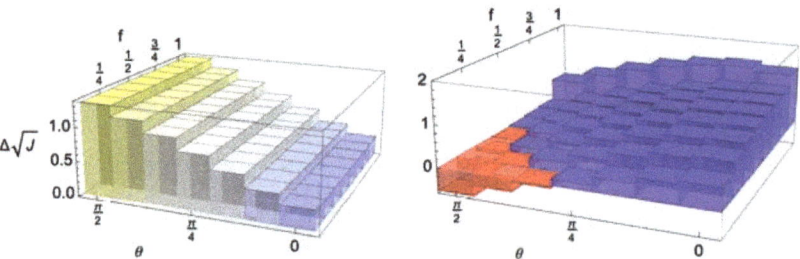

Figure 7. (**Left**) Plot of the l.h.s. of Equation (20) showing the revivals of the QJSD$^{1/2}$ as a function of choice of initial system states for the fixed times $gt = \pi/2$ and $gs = \pi/4$, the latter corresponding to maximal decoherence of the system. The quantity inherently does not depend on f. (**Right**) The difference of the l.h.s. and sum of quantities on the r.h.s. of the inequality given by Equation (20) when taking into account only a fraction f of the environment, for $c = 1/3$ (see Figure 5, last figure of the second row). For the values of environmental fraction f and angle θ (which determines the pair of initial system states) for which the difference is negative (red), the corresponding sum of environmental changes and correlations is no longer an upper bound for the revivals in the reduced dynamics.

5. Conclusions

We have investigated the subtle role that system–environment correlations play in the characterisation of a given dynamics. Through a paradigmatic dephasing model with different initial conditions, which are particularly relevant in exploring the quantum Darwinism framework, we employed tools from the study of non-Markovianity to critically assess the role that these correlations play, revealing that while only a small amount of such correlations are needed for the onset of non-Markovianity, establishing the conditions for classical objectivity necessitates significantly more. Our results indicate that for most microscopical realisations of the reduced dynamics, one can fully capture the non-Markovian characteristics of a given evolution with access to only a small subset of the environmental degrees of freedom, while also revealing that whether the conditions for classical objectivity are satisfied or not is crucially dependent on the precise details of the microscopic model in question, rather than its non-Markovian nature.

Author Contributions: Conceptualisation and formal analysis, N.M. and B.V.; N.M., A.S., S.C. and B.V. contributed to the interpretation and writing. All authors have read and agreed to the published version of the manuscript.

Funding: N.M. was funded by the Alexander von Humboldt Foundation in form of a Feodor-Lynen Fellowship and project ApresSF, supported by the National Science Centre under the QuantERA programme, which has received funding from the European Union's Horizon 2020 research and innovation programme. S.C. gratefully acknowledge the Science Foundation Ireland Starting Investigator Research Grant "SpeedDemon" (No. 18/SIRG/5508) for financial support. A.S. and B.V. acknowledge support from UniMi, via Transition Grant H2020 and PSR-2 2020.

Institutional Review Board Statement: Not applicable.

Informed Consent Statement: Not applicable.

Data Availability Statement: Not applicable.

Conflicts of Interest: The authors declare no conflict of interest.

References

1. Breuer, H.P.; Petruccione, F. *The Theory of Open Quantum Systems*; Oxford University Press: Oxford, UK, 2002.
2. Rivas, A.; Huelga, S.F. *Open Quantum Systems: An Introduction*; Springer: Berlin/Heidelberg, Germany, 2012.
3. Zurek, W.H. Quantum Darwinism. *Nat. Phys.* **2009**, *5*, 181–188. [CrossRef]
4. Horodecki, R.; Korbicz, J.K.; Horodecki, P. Quantum origins of objectivity. *Phys. Rev. A* **2015**, *91*, 032122. [CrossRef]
5. Le, T.P.; Olaya-Castro, A. Objectivity (or lack thereof): Comparison between predictions of quantum Darwinism and spectrum broadcast structure. *Phys. Rev. A* **2018**, *98*, 032103. [CrossRef]
6. Le, T.P.; Olaya-Castro, A. Strong Quantum Darwinism and Strong Independence are Equivalent to Spectrum Broadcast Structure. *Phys. Rev. Lett.* **2019**, *122*, 010403. [CrossRef]
7. Korbicz, J.K. Roads to objectivity: Quantum Darwinism, Spectrum Broadcast Structures, and Strong quantum Darwinism—A review. *Quantum* **2021**, *5*, 571. [CrossRef]
8. Rivas, Á.; Huelga, S.F.; Plenio, M.B. Quantum non-Markovianity: Characterization, quantification and detection. *Rep. Prog. Phys.* **2014**, *77*, 094001. [CrossRef]
9. Breuer, H.P.; Laine, E.M.; Piilo, J.; Vacchini, B. *Colloquium*: Non-Markovian dynamics in open quantum systems. *Rev. Mod. Phys.* **2016**, *88*, 021002. [CrossRef]
10. Ciampini, M.A.; Pinna, G.; Mataloni, P.; Paternostro, M. Experimental signature of quantum Darwinism in photonic cluster states. *Phys. Rev. A* **2018**, *98*, 020101. [CrossRef]
11. Unden, T.K.; Louzon, D.; Zwolak, M.; Zurek, W.H.; Jelezko, F. Revealing the Emergence of Classicality Using Nitrogen-Vacancy Centers. *Phys. Rev. Lett.* **2019**, *123*, 140402. [CrossRef]
12. Chen, M.C.; Zhong, H.S.; Li, Y.; Wu, D.; Wang, X.L.; Li, L.; Liu, N.L.; Lu, C.Y.; Pan, J.W. Emergence of classical objectivity of quantum Darwinism in a photonic quantum simulator. *Sci. Bull.* **2019**, *64*, 580–585. [CrossRef]
13. Chisholm, D.A.; García-Pérez, G.; Rossi, M.A.C.; Maniscalco, S.; Palma, G.M. Witnessing objectivity on a quantum computer. *Quantum Sci. Technol.* **2022**, *7*, 015022. [CrossRef]
14. Liu, B.H.; Li, L.; Huang, Y.F.; Li, C.F.; Guo, G.C.; Laine, E.M.; Breuer, H.P.; Piilo, J. Experimental control of the transition from Markovian to non-Markovian dynamics of open quantum systems. *Nat. Phys.* **2011**, *7*, 931–934. [CrossRef]
15. Rossi, M.A.C.; Benedetti, C.; Tamascelli, D.; Cialdi, S.; Olivares, S.; Vacchini, B.; Paris, M.G.A. Non-Markovianity by undersampling in quantum optical simulators. *Int. J. Quantum Inf.* **2017**, *15*, 1740009. [CrossRef]
16. Liu, Z.D.; Lyyra, H.; Sun, Y.N.; Liu, B.; Li, C.F.; Guo, G.C.; Maniscalco, S.; Piilo, J. Experimental implementation of fully controlled dephasing dynamics and synthetic spectral densities. *Nat. Commun.* **2018**, *9*, 1–7. [CrossRef]
17. Cialdi, S.; Benedetti, C.; Tamascelli, D.; Olivares, S.; Paris, M.G.A.; Vacchini, B. Experimental investigation of the effect of classical noise on quantum non-Markovian dynamics. *Phys. Rev. A* **2019**, *100*, 052104. [CrossRef]
18. White, G.A.L.; Hill, C.D.; Pollock, F.A.; Hollenberg, L.C.L.; Modi, K. Demonstration of non-Markovian process characterisation and control on a quantum processor. *Nat. Commun.* **2020**, *11*, 6301. [CrossRef]
19. Goswami, K.; Giarmatzi, C.; Monterola, C.; Shrapnel, S.; Romero, J.; Costa, F. Experimental characterization of a non-Markovian quantum process. *Phys. Rev. A* **2021**, *104*, 022432. [CrossRef]
20. Lyyra, H.; Siltanen, O.; Piilo, J.; Banerjee, S.; Kuusela, T. Experimental Snapshot Verification of non-Markovianity with Unknown System-Probe Coupling. *arXiv* **2021**, arXiv:2107.07876.

21. Smirne, A.; Megier, N.; Vacchini, B. On the connection between microscopic description and memory effects in open quantum system dynamics. *Quantum* **2021**, *5*, 439. [CrossRef]
22. Campbell, S.; Popovic, M.; Tamascelli, D.; Vacchini, B. Precursors of non-Markovianity. *New J. Phys.* **2019**, *21*, 053036. [CrossRef]
23. Riedel, C.J.; Zurek, W.H.; Zwolak, M. The rise and fall of redundancy in decoherence and quantum Darwinism. *New J. Phys.* **2012**, *14*, 083010. [CrossRef]
24. Roszak, K.; Korbicz, J.K. Entanglement and objectivity in pure dephasing models. *Phys. Rev. A* **2019**, *100*, 062127. [CrossRef]
25. García-Pérez, G.; Chisholm, D.A.; Rossi, M.A.C.; Palma, G.M.; Maniscalco, S. Decoherence without entanglement and quantum Darwinism. *Phys. Rev. Res.* **2020**, *2*, 012061. [CrossRef]
26. Campbell, S.; Ciccarello, F.; Palma, G.M.; Vacchini, B. System-environment correlations and Markovian embedding of quantum non-Markovian dynamics. *Phys. Rev. A* **2018**, *98*, 012142. [CrossRef]
27. Laine, E.M.; Piilo, J.; Breuer, H.P. Witness for initial system-environment correlations in open system dynamics. *EPL* **2010**, *92*, 60010. [CrossRef]
28. Giorgi, G.L.; Galve, F.; Zambrini, R. Quantum Darwinism and non-Markovian dissipative dynamics from quantum phases of the spin-1/2 XX model. *Phys. Rev. A* **2015**, *92*, 022105. [CrossRef]
29. Galve, F.; Zambrini, R.; Maniscalco, S. Non-Markovianity hinders Quantum Darwinism. *Sci. Rep.* **2016**, *6*, 19607. [CrossRef]
30. Pleasance, G.; Garraway, B.M. Application of quantum Darwinism to a structured environment. *Phys. Rev. A* **2017**, *96*, 062105. [CrossRef]
31. Milazzo, N.; Lorenzo, S.; Paternostro, M.; Palma, G.M. Role of information backflow in the emergence of quantum Darwinism. *Phys. Rev. A* **2019**, *100*, 012101. [CrossRef]
32. Lampo, A.; Tuziemski, J.; Lewenstein, M.; Korbicz, J.K. Objectivity in the non-Markovian spin-boson model. *Phys. Rev. A* **2017**, *96*, 012120. [CrossRef]
33. Ryan, E.; Paternostro, M.; Campbell, S. Quantum Darwinism in a structured spin environment. *Phys. Lett. A* **2021**, *416*, 127675. [CrossRef]
34. Martins, W.S.; Soares-Pinto, D.O. Suppressing information storage in a structured thermal bath: Objectivity and non-Markovianity. *arXiv* **2021**, arXiv:2110.03490.
35. Chin, A.W.; Rivas, A.; Huelga, S.F.; Plenio, M.B. Exact mapping between system-reservoir quantum models and semi-infinite discrete chains using orthogonal polynomials. *J. Math. Phys.* **2010**, *51*, 092109. [CrossRef]
36. Martinazzo, R.; Vacchini, B.; Hughes, K.H.; Burghardt, I. Universal Markovian reduction of Brownian particle dynamics. *J. Chem. Phys.* **2011**, *134*, 011101. [CrossRef]
37. Tamascelli, D.; Smirne, A.; Huelga, S.F.; Plenio, M.B. Nonperturbative Treatment of non-Markovian Dynamics of Open Quantum Systems. *Phys. Rev. Lett.* **2018**, *120*, 030402. [CrossRef]
38. Tamascelli, D.; Smirne, A.; Lim, J.; Huelga, S.F.; Plenio, M.B. Efficient Simulation of Finite-Temperature Open Quantum Systems. *Phys. Rev. Lett.* **2019**, *123*, 090402. [CrossRef]
39. Zwolak, M.; Quan, H.T.; Zurek, W.H. Redundant imprinting of information in nonideal environments: Objective reality via a noisy channel. *Phys. Rev. A* **2010**, *81*, 062110. [CrossRef]
40. Zwolak, M.; Zurek, W.H. Complementarity of quantum discord and classically accessible information. *Sci. Rep.* **2013**, *3*, 1729. [CrossRef]
41. Çakmak, B.; Müstecaplıoğlu, Ö.E.; Paternostro, M.; Vacchini, B.; Campbell, S. Quantum Darwinism in a Composite System: Objectivity versus Classicality. *Entropy* **2021**, *23*, 995. [CrossRef]
42. Campbell, S.; Çakmak, B.; Müstecaplıoğlu, O.E.; Paternostro, M.; Vacchini, B. Collisional unfolding of quantum Darwinism. *Phys. Rev. A* **2019**, *99*, 042103. [CrossRef]
43. Mirkin, N.; Wisniacki, D.A. Many-Body Localization and the Emergence of Quantum Darwinism. *Entropy* **2021**, *23*, 1377. [CrossRef] [PubMed]
44. Touil, A.; Yan, B.; Girolami, D.; Deffner, S.; Zurek, W.H. Eavesdropping on the Decohering Environment: Quantum Darwinism, Amplification, and the Origin of Objective Classical Reality. *Phys. Rev. Lett.* **2022**, *128*, 010401. [CrossRef] [PubMed]
45. Megier, N.; Smirne, A.; Vacchini, B. Entropic Bounds on Information Backflow. *Phys. Rev. Lett.* **2021**, *127*, 030401. [CrossRef] [PubMed]
46. Smirne, A.; Megier, N.; Vacchini, B. Holevo skew divergence for the characterization of information backflow. *arXiv* **2022**, arXiv:2201.07812.
47. Bengtsson, I.; Życzkowski, K. *Geometry of Quantum States: An Introduction to Quantum Entanglement*, 2nd ed.; Cambridge University Press: Cambridge, UK, 2017.
48. Sra, S. Metrics induced by Jensen-Shannon and related divergences on positive definite matrices. *Linear Algebra Its Appl.* **2021**, *616*, 125–138. [CrossRef]
49. Virosztek, D. The metric property of the quantum Jensen-Shannon divergence. *Adv. Math.* **2021**, *380*, 107595. [CrossRef]
50. Zwolak, M.; Quan, H.T.; Zurek, W.H. Quantum Darwinism in a Mixed Environment. *Phys. Rev. Lett.* **2009**, *103*, 110402. [CrossRef]
51. Korbicz, J.K.; Horodecki, P.; Horodecki, R. Objectivity in a Noisy Photonic Environment through Quantum State Information Broadcasting. *Phys. Rev. Lett.* **2014**, *112*, 120402. [CrossRef]
52. Pollock, F.A.; Rodriguez-Rosario, C.; Frauenheim, T.; Paternostro, M.; Modi, K. Operational Markov Condition for Quantum Processes. *Phys. Rev. Lett.* **2018**, *120*, 040405. [CrossRef]

53. Vacchini, B.; Smirne, A.; Laine, E.M.; Piilo, J.; Breuer, H.P. Markovianity and non-Markovianity in quantum and classical systems. *New J. Phys.* **2011**, *13*, 093004. [CrossRef]
54. Breuer, H.P.; Laine, E.M.; Piilo, J. Measure for the Degree of Non-Markovian Behavior of Quantum Processes in Open Systems. *Phys. Rev. Lett.* **2009**, *103*, 210401. [CrossRef] [PubMed]
55. Laine, E.M.; Piilo, J.; Breuer, H.P. Measure for the non-Markovianity of quantum processes. *Phys. Rev. A* **2010**, *81*, 062115. [CrossRef]

Article

Non-Markovian Quantum Dynamics in a Squeezed Reservoir

Valentin Link [1,†], Walter T. Strunz [1] and Kimmo Luoma [1,2,*,†]

1. Institut für Theoretische Physik, Technische Universität Dresden, D-01062 Dresden, Germany; valentin.link@tu-dresden.de (V.L.); walter.strunz@tu-dresden.de (W.T.S.)
2. Laboratory of Quantum Optics, Department of Physics and Astronomy, University of Turku, FI-20014 Turun Yliopisto, Finland
* Correspondence: ktluom@utu.fi
† These authors contributed equally to this work.

Abstract: We study non-Markovian dynamics of an open quantum system system interacting with a nonstationary squeezed bosonic reservoir. We derive exact and approximate descriptions for the open system dynamics. Focusing on the spin boson model, we compare exact dynamics with Redfield theory and a quantum optical master equation for both short and long time dynamics and in non-Markovian and Markov regimes. The squeezing of the bath results in asymptotic oscillations in the stationary state, which are captured faithfully by the Redfield master equation in the case of weak coupling. Furthermore, we find that the bath squeezing direction modifies the effective system–environment coupling strength and, thus, the strength of the dissipation.

Keywords: open quantum systems; squeezed states; non-Markovian dynamics

1. Introduction

In 1926 and 1927, two families of quantum states for the quantum harmonic oscillator were proposed by Schrödinger [1] and Kennard [2], respectively. The first family of states included coherent states [3–5] and the second family included squeezed states [6]. These can be distinguished by considering the Heisenberg uncertainty principle:

$$\Delta x^2 \Delta p^2 \geq \frac{\hbar^2}{4},$$

which was discovered also in 1927 [7]. The coherent states saturate this uncertainty principle with equal variances $\Delta x^2 = \Delta p^2 = \hbar/2$ in both quadratures. This makes them the closest to points in phase space; therefore, coherent states are often considered the most classical quantum states. In contrast, for a squeezed state, the variances of one of the quadratures can be smaller that $\hbar/2$. The state is, thus, squeezed along a certain direction in phase space. According to the Heisenberg uncertainty principle, the variance of the other quadrature must then be larger than $\hbar/2$. Often, squeezed states are regarded as nonclassical states [8,9]. In fact, so-called two mode squeezing generates entanglement between two oscillators [10]. In contrast to coherent states, squeezed states are not stationary states of the harmonic oscillator.

Ensembles of harmonic oscillators are commonly considered as quantum environments of open quantum systems. In most applications, these environments are stationary, meaning that the initial state of the reservoir oscillators is a stationary state, for instance, a thermal state (which becomes a coherent state for zero temperature). In a large thermal bath, the system is expected to reach thermal equilibrium [11]. If instead the bath can be prepared in a squeezed state, one directly violates stationarity, resulting in a a breakdown of equilibration.

This can have a drastic impact on the dissipation induced by the bath. In 1986, it was proposed that a nonstationary reservoir consisting of harmonic oscillators prepared in squeezed states can lead to an inhibition of phase decay of an atom [12]. Only in 2013, this prediction was experimentally verified using superconducting qubits [13].

Previous theoretical works on squeezed reservoirs were based on quantum master equations with constant coefficients [14–19]. The validity of these equations requires severe assumptions on the system and bath coupling strength and possibly also a separation of time scales such that a rotating wave approximation can be performed. For this reason, such master equations are unable to capture certain phenomena in an exact manner. For instance, they can predict that the very short time dynamics of an observable is linear in time, whereas the Schrödinger equation actually yields quadratic short time dynamics [20,21].

In this article, we investigate open quantum system dynamics in a non-stationary reservoir consisting of oscillators prepared in two-mode squeezed states (broad band squeezed reservoir) [18]. We derive an exact description of the reduced state dynamics using non-Markovian quantum state diffusion (NMQSD) [22–24]. Then, using NMQSD as a starting point, we derive a Hierarchy of Equations of Motion [25] (HEOM) for the density matrix of the open system based on the Hierarchy of stochastic Pure States (HOPS) [26]. For the example of a single two level system, we compare the short and long time dynamics of the numerically exact HEOM theory with a weak coupling perturbation theory, so-called Redfield theory, and the commonly used standard master equation with time independent coefficients. Our main findings are that, in a parameter regime where a quantum optical master equation would work fine for stationary reservoirs, it can not capture accurately short and long time dynamics. Remarkably, if the bath memory time is short the Redfield theory performs extremely well, matching with exact dynamics and predicting accurate long time dynamics.

2. Model

We consider the following commonly used model for open quantum systems:

$$H = H_S + L\sum_\lambda g_\lambda(a_\lambda + a_\lambda^\dagger) + \sum_\lambda \omega_\lambda a_\lambda^\dagger a_\lambda, \qquad (1)$$

where the environment consists of independent harmonic oscillators (bosonic modes) $[a_\lambda, a_\mu^\dagger] = \delta_{\lambda\mu}$ [19]. The system Hamiltonian H_S and the system coupling operator are left arbitrary, except that we demand $L = L^\dagger$. Moving to an interaction representation with respect to the free bath Hamiltonian, one obtains the following.

$$H(t) = H_S + LB(t), \qquad B(t) = \sum_\lambda g_\lambda(e^{-i\omega_\lambda t}a_\lambda + e^{i\omega_\lambda t}a_\lambda^\dagger) \qquad (2)$$

If the bath's initial state is Gaussian and the coupling of the system to the bath is linear, the response of the bath to the system is fully characterized by the first and second moment of the bath response operator $B(t)$. Typically, and without loss of generality, one considers $\langle B(t)\rangle = 0$. Then, the so-called bath correlation function (BCF) is the only relevant quantity describing the influence of the bath [27]:

$$\alpha(t,s) = \langle B(t)B(s)\rangle, \qquad (3)$$

where the expectation value is with respect to the bath initial state. As an initial condition, for the bath, usually a stationary state of the free bath Hamiltonian is considered. For example, a zero temperature bath is described by vacuum state $|0\rangle$, which is a Gaussian state; hence, it is fully characterized by the following correlations.

$$\begin{aligned}\langle 0|a_\lambda|0\rangle &= 0,\\ \langle 0|a_\lambda a_\mu^\dagger|0\rangle &= \delta_{\lambda\mu},\\ \langle 0|a_\lambda^\dagger a_\mu|0\rangle &= 0,\\ \langle 0|a_\lambda a_\mu|0\rangle &= 0\end{aligned} \qquad (4)$$

This results in a stationary BCF that depends on the time difference only.

$$\alpha(t,s) \equiv \alpha_0(t-s) = \sum_\lambda g_\lambda^2 e^{-i\omega_\lambda(t-s)} \tag{5}$$

An alternative characterization of a stationary bath is given in terms of spectral density:

$$J(\omega) = \frac{1}{\pi} \sum_\lambda g_\lambda^2 \delta(\omega - \omega_\lambda), \tag{6}$$

which is the Fourier transform of the stationary BCF.

In this article, we are interested in the situation where the initial state of the bath is a squeezed vacuum. In particular, we consider two-mode squeezing which is symmetric around a reference frequency ω_0. We denote our squeezed vacuum state by $|\phi\rangle = S|0\rangle$, where S is a unitary squeezing operator. If we order the bath modes according to $\omega_{2\lambda_0-\lambda} = 2\omega_0 - \omega_\lambda$, the state $|\phi\rangle$ is characterized by the following correlations.

$$\begin{aligned}
\langle \phi | a_\lambda | \phi \rangle &= 0, \\
\langle \phi | a_\lambda a_\mu^\dagger | \phi \rangle &= u^2 \delta_{\lambda\mu}, \\
\langle \phi | a_\lambda^\dagger a_\mu | \phi \rangle &= |v|^2 \delta_{\lambda\mu}, \\
\langle \phi | a_\lambda a_\mu | \phi \rangle &= -vu\, \delta_{\mu, 2\lambda_0-\lambda}
\end{aligned} \tag{7}$$

Because S is a unitary operator, the squeezing parameters $u \in \mathbb{R}$ and $v \in \mathbb{C}$ satisfy $u^2 - |v|^2 = 1$. We also have assumed that the two mode squeezing is homogeneous, i.e., u and v are the same for all modes λ. This is often called broadband squeezing. In order to parametrize the squeezing, we introduce real variables r and φ and write

$$u = \cosh(r), \qquad v = \cosh(r)e^{i\varphi}, \tag{8}$$

where r is squeezing strength, and ϕ is the squeezing direction in phase space. $\phi = 0$ corresponds to squeezing the p-quadrature, whereas $\phi = \pi$ corresponds to squeezing the x-quadrature. In case of no squeezing $r = 0$, we recover the vacuum correlations (4). To continue, we further assume that coupling constants g_λ have a symmetry property $g_{2\lambda_0-\lambda} = g_\lambda$, which implies that the spectral density is symmetric around ω_0. From this, we obtain that the bath correlation function has the following structure:

$$\alpha(t,s) = \alpha_0(t-s)(u^2 - vue^{-2i\omega_0 s} - v^* u e^{2i\omega_0 t}) + \alpha_0^*(t-s)|v|^2, \tag{9}$$

where $\alpha_0(t-s)$ is the zero temperature bath correlation function from Equation (5). It is easy to check that this is a valid BCF obeying $\alpha(t,s) = \alpha^*(s,t)$. Note that this function does depend explicitly on both t and s and not only on their difference. This is because the bath initial state is not stationary with respect to the bath Hamiltonian. We assume the following model for the vacuum BCF:

$$\alpha_0(t-s) = \frac{\gamma\Gamma}{2} e^{-\Gamma|t-s| - i\omega_B(t-s)}, \tag{10}$$

which corresponds to a continuous bath with Lorentzian spectral density.

$$J(\omega) = \frac{\gamma}{2} \frac{\Gamma^2}{\Gamma^2 + (\omega_B - \omega)^2} \tag{11}$$

This bath satisfies the required symmetry if $\omega_B = \omega_0$, which we assume in the following. Notably, for such a bath, the white noise limit $\alpha_0(t-s) \to \gamma \delta(t-s)$ exits when $\Gamma \to \infty$.

The non-Markovian open system dynamics of this model can be described with non-Markovian quantum state diffusion (NMQSD) [22,24,28]. NMQSD is a stochastic unraveling of reduced open system dynamics in terms of a Gaussian colored noise process $z(t)$ with statistics $E[z(t)z^*(s)] = \alpha(t,s)$ and $E[z(t)] = E[z(t)z(s)] = 0$. The system state is obtained as the ensemble average of stochastic pure states $|\psi(z^*,t)\rangle$, which depend on this noise process.

$$\rho(t) = E[|\psi(z^*,t)\rangle\langle\psi(z^*,t)|] \tag{12}$$

The stochastic states obey the NMQSD evolution equation.

$$\partial_t |\psi(z^*,t)\rangle = (-iH_S + Lz^*(t))|\psi(z^*,t)\rangle - L\int_0^t ds\, \alpha(t,s) \frac{\delta}{\delta z^*(s)}|\psi(z^*,t)\rangle \tag{13}$$

Different solution strategies for this equation exits, notably the O-operator method [23,29] and the exact HOPS method [26,30,31]. Here, we use NMQSD as a tool to derive perturbative and exact master equations for the squeezed bath problem (9).

Although most results are very general, an example we will consider is the spin boson model. For this model, the system is a simple two level system with the following operators

$$H_S = \frac{\Omega}{2}\sigma_z, \qquad L = \sigma_x. \tag{14}$$

3. Perturbative Master Equations

If the coupling to the bath is weak and/or the BCF decays rapidly, we can make a perturbative approximation to NMQSD. The lowest order perturbative equation is given by the following.

$$\int_0^t ds\, \alpha(t,s)\frac{\delta}{\delta z^*(s)}|\psi(z^*,t)\rangle = \bar{O}(z^*,t)|\psi(z^*,t)\rangle,$$
$$\bar{O}(z^*,t) \approx \int_0^t ds\, \alpha(t,s) e^{-iH_S(t-s)} L e^{iH_S(t-s)}. \tag{15}$$

Because in this approximation the operator $\bar{O}$ does not depend on the stochastic process, a master equation can be directly derived from NMQSD as follows [23].

$$\partial_t \rho(t) = -i[H_S, \rho(t)] + [L, \rho(t)\bar{O}^\dagger(t)] + [\bar{O}(t)\rho(t), L]$$
$$:= \mathcal{L}_t^R(\rho(t)) \tag{16}$$

This is the well known Redfield master equation [32].

Under certain conditions and in a frame rotating with the frequency ω_0, one can derive a master equation with constant coefficients starting from the Redfield equation. The resulting equation is well known from quantum optics textbooks [17,18]. For a derivation, we assume the spin boson model with $L = \sigma_x$ and $H_S = \omega\sigma_z/2$. In particular, we consider the case where $\Omega = \omega_0 + \delta$ and ω_0 defines the fastest timescale $\omega_0 \gg \Gamma \gg \delta$ and $\omega_0 \gg \gamma$. The state in the rotating frame is given by the following.

$$\tilde{\rho}(t) = R(t)\rho(t)R^\dagger(t), \qquad R(t) = \exp\left(i\omega_0 \frac{\sigma_z}{2}t\right) \tag{17}$$

To obtain a master equation with constant coefficients, analogous to the standard quantum optical master equation [32], one explicitly computes the integral in (15) and neglects exponentially decaying terms as well as terms of order δ/Γ. Plugging the result into the Redfield Equation (16) in the rotating frame, one can identify counter-rotating terms that oscillate at frequency $2\omega_0$. Under the above assumptions, these terms can be neglected and one obtains a master equation with time-independent coefficients.

$$\begin{aligned}\partial_t \tilde{\rho}(t) = & -i\frac{\delta}{2}[\sigma_z, \tilde{\rho}(t)] \\ & + \gamma u^2 \left(\sigma_- \tilde{\rho}(t)\sigma_+ - \frac{1}{2}\{\sigma_+, \sigma_-, \tilde{\rho}(t)\}\right) \\ & + \gamma |v|^2 \left(\sigma_+ \tilde{\rho}(t)\sigma_- - \frac{1}{2}\{\sigma_-, \sigma_+, \tilde{\rho}(t)\}\right) \\ & + \gamma uv \sigma_- \tilde{\rho}(t)\sigma_- + \gamma u v^* \sigma_+ \tilde{\rho}(t)\sigma_+ \\ :=& \mathcal{L}^M(\tilde{\rho}(t))\end{aligned} \qquad (18)$$

Note that the coefficients of the last two terms become time dependent if one moves back to the laboratory frame.

In order to assess the validity of these perturbative master equations, we have to compare their predictions with exact results. We discuss in the following how the exact reduced dynamics can be computed using non-Markovian open system methods.

4. Exact Method

We can utilize non-Markovian open system methods to compute the exact reduced dynamics in the squeezed reservoir. In particular, due to the exponential form of the bath correlation function, we can easily generalize hierarchical methods for the squeezed bath. To this aim, we decompose the BCF in the following manner:

$$\alpha(t,s) = \alpha_1(t,s) + \alpha_2(t,s) \qquad (19)$$

$$\alpha_1(t,s) = \frac{\gamma \Gamma}{2}(u^2 - vu e^{-2i\omega_0 s})e^{-i\omega_0(t-s) - \Gamma|t-s|} \qquad (20)$$

$$\alpha_2(t,s) = \frac{\gamma \Gamma}{2}(|v|^2 - v^* u e^{2i\omega_0 s})e^{i\omega_0(t-s) - \Gamma|t-s|} \qquad (21)$$

To solve the linear NMQSD Equation (13), we further define the corresponding functional differential operators:

$$\mathcal{D}_j = \int_0^t ds\, \alpha_j(t,s) \frac{\delta}{\delta z_s^*}, \qquad j = 1, 2, \qquad (22)$$

so that (13) becomes the following.

$$\partial_t |\psi\rangle = -iH|\psi\rangle + L z_t^* |\psi\rangle - L \sum_{j=1,2} \mathcal{D}_j |\psi\rangle \qquad (23)$$

Because of the exponential form of the kernels (20), we can compute the time derivative of the functional differential operators.

$$\partial_t \mathcal{D}_j = -W_j \mathcal{D}_j + \alpha_j(t,t) \frac{\delta}{\delta z_t^*}, \qquad W_1 = W_2^* = i\omega_0 + \Gamma \qquad (24)$$

This allows employing the hierarchy of pure states (HOPS) scheme to solve NMQSD. In particular, one defines an 'auxiliary state' for every double-index $n \in \mathbb{N}_0^2$.

$$|\psi^n\rangle = (\mathcal{D}_1)^{n_1} (\mathcal{D}_2)^{n_2} |\psi\rangle \qquad (25)$$

These states obey the hierarchy of pure states equation of motion.

$$\partial_t |\psi^n\rangle = \left(-iH_S + Lz_t^* - \sum_{j=1,2} n_j W_j\right)|\psi^n\rangle - L\sum_{j=1,2}|\psi^{n+e_j}\rangle + L\sum_{j=1,2}\alpha_j(t,t)n_j|\psi^{n-e_j}\rangle \quad (26)$$

In this equation, we set $(e_j)_i = \delta_{ij}$. The exact NMQSD solution is simply the 'root' state of the hierarchy $|\psi\rangle = |\psi^{(0)}\rangle$. Truncating the hierarchy at a finite depth yields a closed set of equations, which can be numerically integrated. Typically, for a weak coupling, only a few auxiliary states have to be taken into account to achieve convergence. There also exists a hierarchy of operators complementary to HOPS, which is known as the hierarchy of equations of motions (HEOM) [25,30]. We define auxilliary operators with two multiindices (n, m) as follows.

$$\rho^{(n,m)} = E\left[|\psi^{(n)}\rangle\langle\psi^{(m)}|\right] \quad (27)$$

Upon employing the HOPS Equation (26) with relation $E[z_t \ldots] = E\left[\sum_j \mathcal{D}_j \ldots\right]$, we find the hierarchical equations of motion:

$$\begin{aligned}\partial_t \rho^{(n,m)} = &-i[H, \rho^{(n,m)}] - \sum_{j=1,2}(n_j W_j + m_j W_j^*)\rho^{(n,m)} \\ &+ \sum_{j=1,2}\left(n_j \alpha_j(t,t)L\rho^{(n-e_j,m)} + m_j \alpha_j^*(t,t)\rho^{(n,m-e_j)}L\right) \\ &+ \sum_{j=1,2}\left([\rho^{(n+e_j,m)}, L] + [L, \rho^{(n,m+e_j)}]\right),\end{aligned} \quad (28)$$

where the reduced state of the system is simply given by $\rho(t) = \rho^{(0,0)}(t)$. We can use a truncated hierarchy to accurately describe the non-Markovian open system dynamics of the model, even for strong coupling (large γ) and long memory time (small Γ).

5. Dynamics

The fidelity $F_t = |\langle\psi_0|\rho(t)|\psi_0\rangle|^2$ of time-evolved state $\rho(t)$ with an initial pure system state $|\psi_0\rangle$ can be used to investigate how master equations capture short time dynamics. In general, the fidelity behaves for short times as [20]:

$$F_t^F = 1 - (\Delta H_S^2 + \Gamma_F)t^2, \quad (29)$$

where $\Gamma_F = 2\alpha(0,0)$ and $\Delta X^2 = \langle X^2\rangle - \langle X\rangle^2$ are the variances of operator X.

A quantum optical master equation that has constant coefficients, such as Equation (18), instead, leads to a linear short time behavior for the fidelity of the state of the system alone [21]:

$$F_t^M = 1 - \Gamma_M t + \mathcal{O}(t^2), \quad (30)$$

where $\Gamma_M = \sum_\mu c_\mu(\langle R_\mu L_\mu\rangle - \langle R_\mu\rangle\langle L_\mu\rangle)$. Here, operators L_μ, R_μ are the operators, which act on the left or on the right, respectively, in the sandwich term of the master equation.

The quadratic short time behavior is captured exactly by the Redfield theory, which is the lowest order perturbation theory.

$$F_t^R = 1 - (\Delta H_S^2 + \Gamma_F)t^2 \quad (31)$$

In Figure 1, we compare the short time linear rate Γ_M computed for master Equation (18) and the quadratic rate Γ_F for the full system. We observe that the full rate has a maximum at $\varphi = \pi$, which corresponds to squeezing along the x-direction. The two-level system is coupled to the x-quadrature of the bath, and squeezing in this direction increases the coupling strength which should lead to faster decay. In contrast, the master equation predicts a minimum for $\phi = \pi$, which is not in line with the microscopic theory.

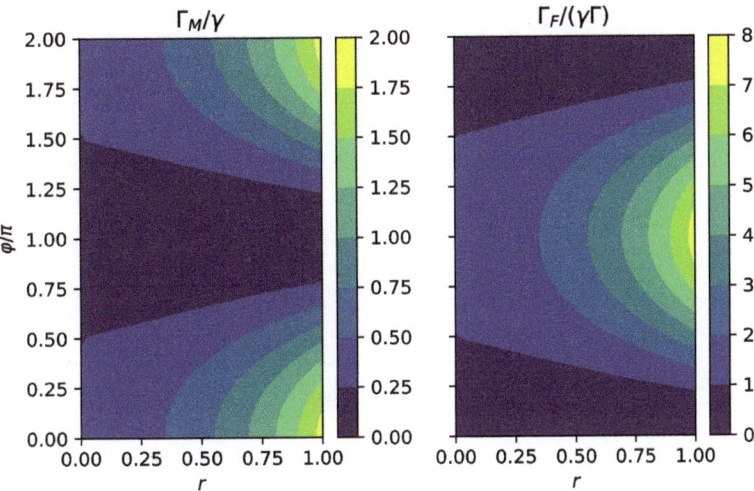

Figure 1. (**Left**): Linear rate Γ_M for short time dynamics due to the Markov master equation divided by the overall coupling strength γ. (**Right**): Quadratic rate for short time dynamics for the total system Γ_F divided by $\gamma\Gamma$, where Γ is the inverse bath correlation time scale. Γ_F is proportional to $|u - v|^2$, which has a maximum when $\varphi = \pi$. Γ_M is proportional to $u(v + v^*)$, which has a minimum at $\varphi = \pi$. Here, we consider the spin boson model (14) in a squeezed bath (9) with $u = \cosh(r)$ and $v = \sinh(r)e^{i\varphi}$ and initial state $|\psi_0\rangle = |+\rangle := \frac{1}{\sqrt{2}}(|0\rangle + |1\rangle)$, where $|0\rangle$ and $|1\rangle$ are the eigenstates of σ_z. We have chosen the following parameters: $r = 1/2$, $\Gamma = 5\gamma$, and $\Omega = \omega_B = \omega_0 = \gamma$.

In Figure 2, we compare the logarithm of the fidelity computed using the HEOM (28), the Redfield theory (16), and the master equation (18) with quadratic short time estimates (29), (31) and the linear estimate (30).

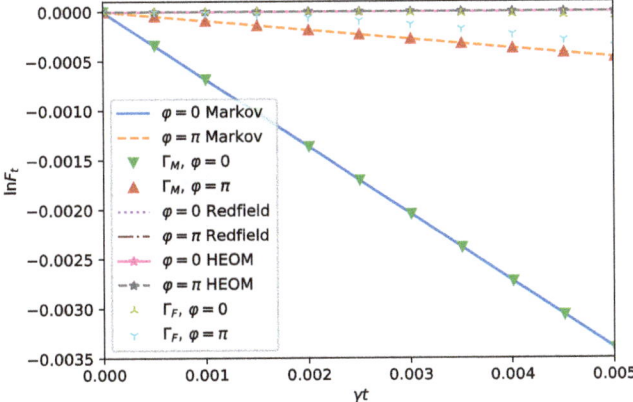

Figure 2. Short time dynamics of the spin boson model (14) in the squeezed bath (9) with $\Gamma = 5\gamma$, $\Omega = \omega_B = \omega_0 = \gamma$, $r = 0.5$, and $|\psi_0\rangle = |+\rangle$. The logarithm of the fidelity F_t is displayed for short times within different approximate and exact descriptions. The quadratic short time dynamics holds up to $\gamma t = 0.002$ for $\varphi = \pi$ as the HEOM and the Redfield theory start to deviate from the short time expansion. For $\varphi = 0$, the quadratic short time dynamics, HEOM, and the Redfield agree well in the range of the plot. This is explained by the effectively strong system environment coupling for $\varphi = \pi$, which sets a different regime of validity for the short time expansion. The parameters are chosen as in Figure 1.

The quadratic estimates; the HEOM and the Redfield curves are in line with each other for both squeezing directions $\varphi = 0$ and $\varphi = \pi$. The linear prediction and the master equation curves also are on top of each other but show a different behavior for different ϕ. For $\varphi = 0$, the decay of the fidelity is faster than for $\varphi = \pi$, as expected from Figure 1.

For longer times, the fidelity is still captured correctly by the Redfield equation, while the Markovian equation becomes valid only asymptoically, as seen in Figure 3.

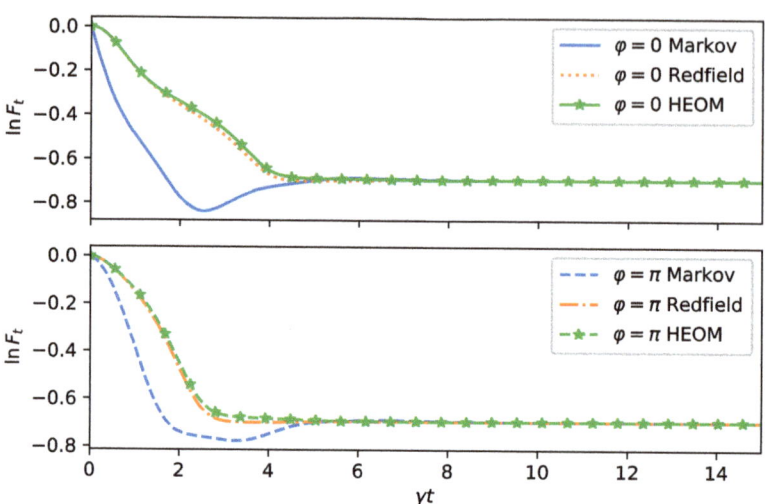

Figure 3. Dynamics of the fidelity as in Figure 2 but for long times and for two squeezing directions $\varphi = 0$ (**top**) and for $\varphi = \pi$ (**bottom**). The decay of the fidelity is faster for $\varphi = \pi$ for HEOM and Redfield as expected from the microscopic model. Predictions from the quantum optical master equation (Markov) show an opposite behavior and the fidelity even has a positive slope at intermediate times.

We now turn to the long time dynamics, which reveals the steady state properties. In Figure 4, we compare the time evolution computed from HEOM, Redfield, and master equation for $\varphi = 0$. We do the same for $\varphi = \pi$ in Figure 5. The same conclusions hold as before: For $\varphi = \pi$, the decay is faster, as can be observed from HEOM and Redfield curves. The steady state prediction of the master equation is far-off from the Refield and HEOM computations, which both agree exptremely well for the choosen parameters. This is because the memory time of the bath $1/\Gamma$ is chosen to be very short. As expected for a spin boson model, the steady state reaches a finite $\langle \sigma_z \rangle$ value. However, due to the non-stationary bath, some residual oscillations remain indefinitely in long time dynamics.

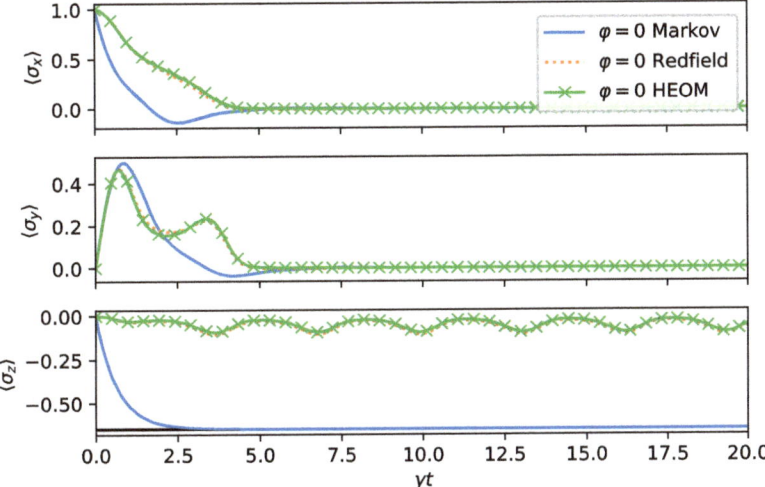

Figure 4. Long time dynamics of the spin boson model (14) in the squeezed bath (9) as in Figure 2 with $\varphi = 0$. Both approximate methods describe correctly that the x and y Bloch sphere components decay to zero. The σ_z expectation value asymptotically acquires a finite value modulated by weak oscillations which are captured properly in the Redfield theory.

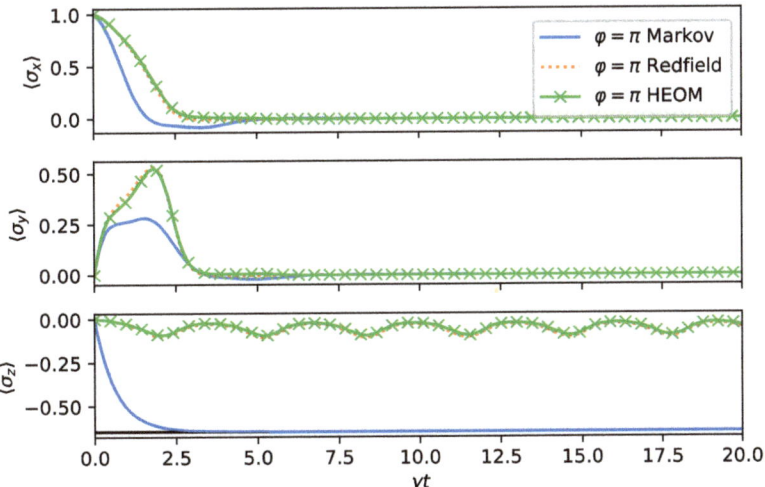

Figure 5. Long time dynamics as in Figure 4, except $\varphi = \pi$.

Next, we investigate the Markov limit where we expect the master Equation (18) to be applicable. We chose $\Omega = \omega_0 = 10\gamma$, $\Gamma = 3\gamma$, which is in a regime where the assumptions for the rotating wave approximation are satisfied. Moreover, since $\Gamma/\gamma = 3$, the BCF decays faster than the time scale set for system bath interaction by γ. As we can observe from Figure 6, the master equation, the Redfield theory, and HEOM are in good qualitative agreement. The rapid oscillations present in HEOM and Redfield solutions are removed by the secular approximation behind the Markovian master equation.

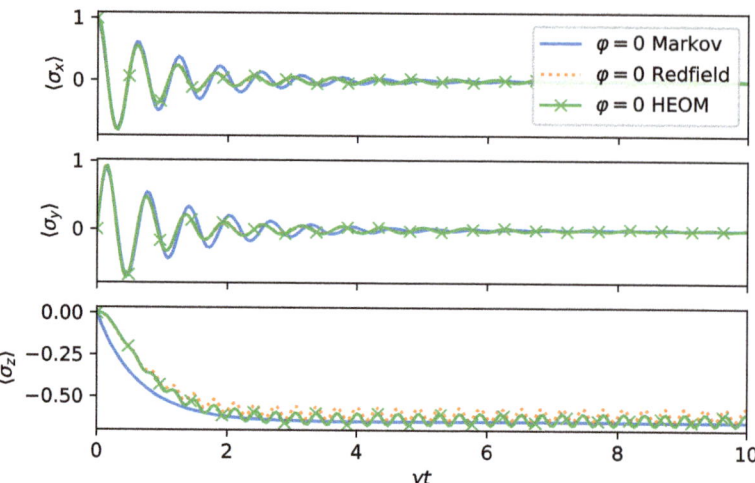

Figure 6. Dynamics of the spin boson model (14) in the squeezed bath (9) with $\Gamma = 3\gamma$, $\Omega = 10\gamma$, $\omega_0 = \Omega$, $r = 0.5$, $\varphi = 0$, and initial state $|\psi_0\rangle = |+\rangle$. The Markovian master Equation (18) agrees well with the exact dynamics but does not capture small asymptotic oscillations.

When we change the direction of the squeezing to $\varphi = \pi$, hence effectively coupling the system and the environment more strongly, the agreement is not as good, as shown in Figure 7. This in particularly visible for the expectation value $\langle \sigma_y \rangle$. The asymptotic values are, however, captured accurately.

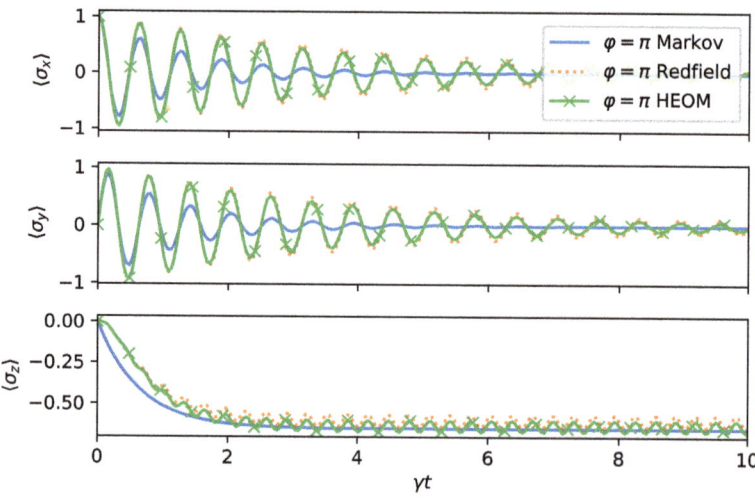

Figure 7. Dynamics of the spin boson model as in Figure 6, except $\varphi = \pi$.

Lastly, we investigate a regime for non-Markovian dynamics. The Redfield theory is a weak system–environment coupling theory. We expect it to fail when the bath correlation function decays on a slower time scale than the system environment interactions; that is, when $\Gamma < \gamma$. For short times, the Redfield theory agrees with the exact results. We confirm these statements in Figure 8, where one observes that the Redfield and the quantum optical master equation are both far-off from the exact solution. In fact, in this regime, the solution of the Redfield equation ceases to be positive, as can be observed from $\langle \sigma_z \rangle < -1$. To compute the exact dynamics, we have estimated convergence of HEOM by increasing the hierarchy depth until the relative change in the solution is less than 10^{-2}.

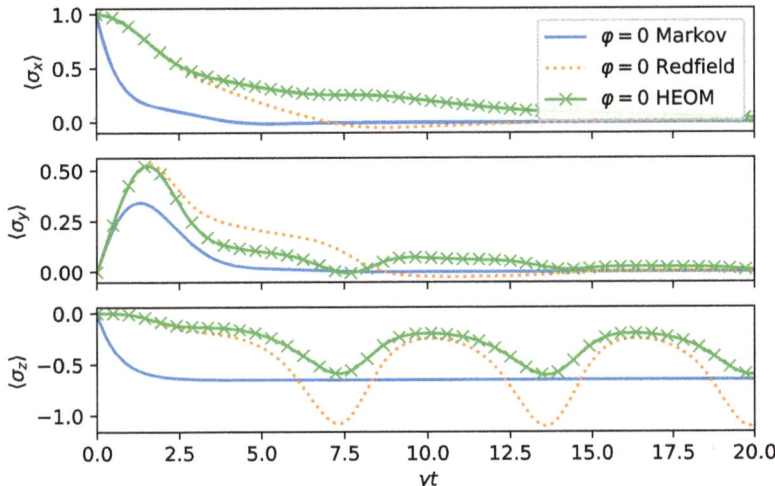

Figure 8. Highly non-Markovian dynamics in the spin boson model. We have chosen $|\psi_0\rangle = |+\rangle$, $\Gamma = \gamma/2$, $\Omega = \omega_B = \omega_0 = \gamma/2$, and $\varphi = 0$. We are in the strong system–envinronment coupling regime since $\gamma > \Gamma$. This means that system–environment dynamics occurs on a faster time scale than the bath correlation function decay time. The failure of weak coupling master equations is expected.

6. Conclusions

In this article, we have revisited an old quantum optical model, namely, the decay to a squeezed reservoir [12]. This model has been realized experimentally using superconducting qubits [13] and is an interesting example of non-stationary open system dynamics. We investigated the short and long time dynamics of the model using textbook master equations [17–19], perturbative Redfield theory [32], and exact hierarchical methods [25,26], which we generalize to treat our non-Markovian squeezed bath model. Assuming broadband two mode squeezing, a model for the bath correlation function can be proposed where the bath memory time can be easily controlled by a single parameter Γ. This corresponds to a Lorentzian spectral density, which yields an exponentially decaying bath correlation function. We showed how in the limit where $\Gamma \gg \gamma$, where γ is the overall system environment coupling, the Redfield theory performs extremely well. However, the dynamics is far from a regime where a usual "quantum optical master equation" is valid. This is due to the fact that there are other time scales involved which need to satisfy a strict hierarchical order so that the Markov approximation can be justified. These timescales are determined by the free system evolution (Ω) and the bath resonance (ω_0). The quantum optical master equation is valid only in a regime where ω_0 is by far the fastest time-scale. All in all, the Redfield theory, which is based on weak coupling approximation only, produces the correct short and long time dynamics in a wide parameter range and is conceptually and numerically much simpler then more advanced methods such as HEOM. To those concerned about the possible positivity violations when using the Redfield theory, we would like to point out that this should be seen merely as a symptom of the breakdown of the weak coupling perturbation theory [32].

Author Contributions: V.L. and K.L. contributed equally to this work. W.T.S. contributed to the development of the concept and initial ideas behind this project. All authors have read and agreed to the published version of the manuscript.

Funding: This research received no external funding.

Institutional Review Board Statement: Not applicable.

Informed Consent Statement: Not applicable.

Data Availability Statement: Not applicable.

Conflicts of Interest: The authors declare no conflict of interest.

Abbreviations

The following abbreviations are used in this manuscript:

NMQSD	Non-Markovian quantum state diffusion;
HEOM	Hierarchical equations Of motion;
HOPS	Hierarchy of pure states;
BCF	Bath correlation function.

References

1. Schrödinger, E. Der stetige Übergang von der Mikro- zur Makromechanik. *Naturwissenschaften* **1926**, *14*, 664–666. https://doi.org/10.1007/BF01507634. [CrossRef]
2. Kennard, E.H. Zur Quantenmechanik einfacher Bewegungstypen. *Z. Phys.* **1927**, *44*, 326–352. doi: [CrossRef]
3. Klauder, J.R. The action option and a Feynman quantization of spinor fields in terms of ordinary c-numbers. *Ann. Phys.* **1960**, *11*, 123–168. doi: [CrossRef]
4. Glauber, R.J. Coherent and Incoherent States of the Radiation Field. *Phys. Rev.* **1963**, *131*, 2766–2788. PhysRev.131.2766. [CrossRef]
5. Sudarshan, E.C.G. Equivalence of Semiclassical and Quantum Mechanical Descriptions of Statistical Light Beams. *Phys. Rev. Lett.* **1963**, *10*, 277–279. doi: [CrossRef]
6. Plebanski, J. Wave Functions of a Harmonic Oscillator. *Phys. Rev.* **1956**, *101*, 1825–1826. doi: [CrossRef]
7. Heisenberg, W. Über den anschaulichen Inhalt der quantentheoretischen Kinematik und Mechanik. *Z. Phys.* **1927**, *43*, 172–198. doi: [CrossRef]
8. Mandel, L.; Wolf, E. *Optical Coherence and Quantum Optics*; Cambridge University Press: Cambridge, UK, 1995. 10.1017/CBO9781139644105. [CrossRef]
9. Dodonov, V.; Man'ko, V. *Theory of Nonclassical States of Light*; Taylor & Francis: London, UK, 2003.
10. Adesso, G.; Illuminati, F. Entanglement in continuous-variable systems: Recent advances and current perspectives. *J. Phys. A Math. Theor.* **2007**, *40*, 7821–7880. doi: [CrossRef]
11. Bach, V.; Fröhlich, J.; Sigal, I.M. Return to equilibrium. *J. Math. Phys.* **2000**, *41*, 3985–4060. doi: [CrossRef]
12. Gardiner, C.W. Inhibition of Atomic Phase Decays by Squeezed Light: A Direct Effect of Squeezing. *Phys. Rev. Lett.* **1986**, *56*, 1917–1920. doi: [CrossRef]
13. Murch, K.W.; Weber, S.J.; Beck, K.M.; Ginossar, E.; Siddiqi, I. Reduction of the radiative decay of atomic coherence in squeezed vacuum. *Nature* **2013**, *499*, 62–65. doi: [CrossRef] [PubMed]
14. Gorini, V.; Kossakowski, A.; Sudarshan, E.C.G. Completely positive dynamical semigroups of N-level systems. *J. Math. Phys.* **1976**, *17*, 821–825. doi: [CrossRef]
15. Lindblad, G. On the generators of quantum dynamical semigroups. *Commun. Math. Phys.* **1976**, *48*, 119–130. 10.1007/BF01608499. doi: [CrossRef]
16. Dum, R.; Parkins, A.S.; Zoller, P.; Gardiner, C.W. Monte Carlo simulation of master equations in quantum optics for vacuum, thermal, and squeezed reservoirs. *Phys. Rev. A* **1992**, *46*, 4382–4396. doi: [CrossRef] [PubMed]
17. Scully, M.O.; Zubairy, M.S. *Quantum Optics*; Cambridge University Press: Cambridge, UK, 1997. CBO9780511813993. [CrossRef]
18. Walls, D.; Milburn, G. *Quantum Optics*; Springer: Berlin/Heidelberg, Germany, 2008.
19. Breuer, H.; Petruccione, F. *The Theory of Open Quantum Systems*; Oxford University Press: Oxford, UK, 2002.
20. Braun, D.; Haake, F.; Strunz, W.T. Universality of Decoherence. *Phys. Rev. Lett.* **2001**, *86*, 2913–2917. PhysRevLett.86.2913. doi: [CrossRef] [PubMed]
21. Beau, M.; Kiukas, J.; Egusquiza, I.L.; del Campo, A. Nonexponential Quantum Decay under Environmental Decoherence. *Phys. Rev. Lett.* **2017**, *119*, 130401. doi: [CrossRef] [PubMed]
22. Strunz, W.T. Linear quantum state diffusion for non-Markovian open quantum systems. *Phys. Lett. A* **1996**, *224*, 25–30. doi: [CrossRef]

23. Strunz, W.T.; Yu, T. Convolutionless Non-Markovian master equations and quantum trajectories: Brownian motion. *Phys. Rev. A* **2004**, *69*, 052115. doi: [CrossRef]
24. Megier, N.; Strunz, W.T.; Viviescas, C.; Luoma, K. Parametrization and Optimization of Gaussian Non-Markovian Unravelings for Open Quantum Dynamics. *Phys. Rev. Lett.* **2018**, *120*, 150402. doi: [CrossRef]
25. Tanimura, Y. Numerically "exact" approach to open quantum dynamics: The hierarchical equations of motion (HEOM). *J. Chem. Phys.* **2020**, *153*, 020901. doi: [CrossRef]
26. Suess, D.; Eisfeld, A.; Strunz, W.T. Hierarchy of Stochastic Pure States for Open Quantum System Dynamics. *Phys. Rev. Lett.* **2014**, *113*, 150403. doi: [CrossRef] [PubMed]
27. Mascherpa, F.; Smirne, A.; Somoza, A.D.; Fernández-Acebal, P.; Donadi, S.; Tamascelli, D.; Huelga, S.F.; Plenio, M.B. Optimized auxiliary oscillators for the simulation of general open quantum systems. *Phys. Rev. A* **2020**, *101*, 052108. doi: [CrossRef]
28. Diósi, L.; Gisin, N.; Strunz, W.T. Non-Markovian quantum state diffusion. *Phys. Rev. A* **1998**, *58*, 1699–1712. doi: [CrossRef]
29. Roden, J.; Strunz, W.T.; Eisfeld, A. Non-Markovian quantum state diffusion for absorption spectra of molecular aggregates. *J. Chem. Phys.* **2011**, *134*, 034902. doi: [CrossRef] [PubMed]
30. Suess, D.; Strunz, W.T.; Eisfeld, A. Hierarchical Equations for Open System Dynamics in Fermionic and Bosonic Environments. *J. Stat. Phys.* **2015**, *159*, 1408–1423. doi: [CrossRef]
31. Hartmann, R.; Strunz, W.T. Exact Open Quantum System Dynamics Using the Hierarchy of Pure States (HOPS). *J. Chem. Theory Comput.* **2017**, *13*, 5834–5845. doi: [CrossRef]
32. Hartmann, R.; Strunz, W.T. Accuracy assessment of perturbative master equations: Embracing nonpositivity. *Phys. Rev. A* **2020**, *101*, 012103. doi: [CrossRef]

Article

Memory Effects in High-Dimensional Systems Faithfully Identified by Hilbert–Schmidt Speed-Based Witness

Kobra Mahdavipour [1,2], Mahshid Khazaei Shadfar [1,2], Hossein Rangani Jahromi [3,*], Roberto Morandotti [2] and Rosario Lo Franco [1,*]

1. Dipartimento di Ingegneria, Università di Palermo, Viale delle Scienze, 90128 Palermo, Italy; kobra.mahdavipour@unipa.it (K.M.); mahshid.khazaeishadfar@unipa.it (M.K.S.)
2. INRS-EMT, 1650 Boulevard Lionel-Boulet, Varennes, QC J3X 1S2, Canada; roberto.morandotti@inrs.ca
3. Physics Department, Faculty of Sciences, Jahrom University, Jahrom P.O. Box 74135111, Iran
* Correspondence: h.ranganijahromi@jahromu.ac.ir (H.R.J.); rosario.lofranco@unipa.it (R.L.F.)

Abstract: A witness of non-Markovianity based on the Hilbert–Schmidt speed (HSS), a special type of quantum statistical speed, has been recently introduced for low-dimensional quantum systems. Such a non-Markovianity witness is particularly useful, being easily computable since no diagonalization of the system density matrix is required. We investigate the sensitivity of this HSS-based witness to detect non-Markovianity in various high-dimensional and multipartite open quantum systems with finite Hilbert spaces. We find that the time behaviors of the HSS-based witness are always in agreement with those of quantum negativity or quantum correlation measure. These results show that the HSS-based witness is a faithful identifier of the memory effects appearing in the quantum evolution of a high-dimensional system with a finite Hilbert space.

Keywords: non-Markovianity; Hilbert–Schmidt speed; high-dimensional system; multipartite open quantum systems; memory effects

1. Introduction

The unavoidable interaction of quantum systems with their environments induces decoherence and dissipation of energy. Recently, because of important developments in both theoretical and experimental branches of quantum information theory, studies of memory effects (non-Markovianity) during the evolution of quantum systems have attracted much attention (see Refs. [1–3] for some reviews). Some approaches used for a quantitative description of non-Markovian processes are either related to the presence of information backflows [4] or to the indivisibility of the dynamical map [5]. However, while well-defined for classical evolution, the notion of non-Markovianity appears to still lack a unique definition in the quantum scenario [6].

Non-Markovian processes, exhibiting quantum memory effects, have been characterized and observed in various realistic systems such as quantum optical systems [7–12], superconducting qubits [13,14], photonic crystals [15–17], light-harvesting complexes [18], and chemical compounds [19,20]. Moreover, it is known that non-Markovianity can be a resource for quantum information tasks [21–25]. Accordingly, various witnesses have been proposed to identify non-Markovianity based on, for example, distinguishability between evolved quantum states of the system [4], fidelity [26–28], quantum relative entropies [29,30], quantum Fisher information [31], capacity measure [32–34] and Bloch volume measure [35–37].

It has been shown that the nonmonotonic behavior of quantum resources such as entanglement [5], quantum coherence [38–41] and quantum mutual information [42] can be interpreted as a witness of quantum non-Markovianity. Using entanglement to witness non-Markovianity was first proposed in Ref. [5]. This proposal has been theoretically investigated for qubits coupled to bosonic environments [43–45], for a damped harmonic

oscillator [46], and for random unitary dynamics and classical noise models [47–49]. It is also shown that entanglement cannot capture all the quantumness of correlations because there are some separable mixed states with vanishing entanglement, which can nevertheless have have nonzero quantum correlations [50]. Therefore, quantum correlations are more robust than entanglement [51–54], while entanglement may suffer sudden death [55,56]. Consequently, many methods to quantify quantum correlations have been provided, among which quantum discord [57,58] and measurement-induced disturbance [59] are proper for any bipartite state.

Recently, Hilbert–Schmidt speed (HSS) [60], a measure of quantum statistical speed which has the advantage of avoiding diagonalization of the evolved density matrix, has been proposed and employed as a faithful witness of non-Markovianity in Hermitian systems [61–64] and an efficient tool in quantum metrology [65,66]. These studies are so far especially limited to low-dimensional systems, while high-dimensional ones have not been investigated in detail. We know that high-dimensional systems play a crucial role in increasing the security in quantum cryptography [67,68], as well as in enhancing quantum logic gates, fault-tolerant quantum computation and quantum error correction [69]. This motivates us to check the sensitivity of HSS-based witness to detect non-Markovianity in high-dimensional and multipartite open quantum systems.

In this work, we analyze the validity of our HSS-based witness in various examples of high-dimensional open quantum systems with finite Hilbert spaces, such as qudits and hybrid qubit–qutrit systems. In particular, we consider a single qudit (spin-S systems) subject to a squeezed vacuum reservoir [70], and hybrid qubit–qutrit system coupled to quantum as well as classical noises [71]. We observe that the HSS-based witness is consistent with established non-Markovianity quantifiers based on dynamical breakdown of monotonicity for the quantum information resources.

The paper is organized as follows: In Section 2, we briefly review the definition of quantifiers. In Section 3, the sensitivity of HSS-based witness in high-dimensional and multipartite open quantum systems with finite Hilbert spaces through various examples is studied. Finally, Section 4 summarizes the main results and prospects.

2. Preliminaries

In this section, we briefly review the relevant quantifiers and concepts employed in this paper.

2.1. Non-Markovinity Definition

A classical *Markov process* is described by a family of random variables $\{X(t), t \in I \subset \mathbb{R}\}$, for which the probability that X takes a value x_n at any arbitrary time $t_n \in I$, provided that it took value x_{n-1} at some previous time $t_{n-1} < t_n$, can be determined uniquely and may not be influenced by the possible values of X at times prior to t_{n-1}. It can be formulated in terms of conditional probabilities as follows: $\mathbb{P}(x_n, t_n | x_{n-1}, t_{n-1}; \ldots; x_0, t_0) = \mathbb{P}(x_n, t_n | x_{n-1}, t_{n-1})$ for all $\{t_n \geq t_{n-1} \geq \ldots \geq t_0\} \subset I$. Roughly speaking, its concept is connected with the memorylessness of the process and informally encapsulated by the statement that "a Markov process has no memory of the history of past values of X, i.e., the future of the process is independent of its history".

To achieve a similar formulation in the quantum scenario we should find a way to define $\mathbb{P}(x_n, t_n | x_{n-1}, t_{n-1}; \ldots; x_0, t_0)$ for quantum systems. In the classical realm, we may sample a stochastic variable without affecting its posterior statistics. However, 'sampling' a quantum system requires measuring process, and hence disturbs the state of the system, affecting the subsequent outcomes. Therefore, $\mathbb{P}(x_n, t_n | x_{n-1}, t_{n-1}; \ldots; x_0, t_0)$ depends on not only the dynamics but also the measurement process. Since in such a case the Markovian character of a quantum dynamical system is dependent on the the measurement scheme, chosen to obtain $\mathbb{P}(x_n, t_n | x_{n-1}, t_{n-1}; \ldots; x_0, t_0)$, a definition of quantum Markovianity in terms of which is a challenging task. In fact, a reliable definition of quantum Markovianity should be independent of what is required to verify it.

The aforesaid problem may be solved by adopting a different approach focusing on studying one-time probabilities $\mathbb{P}(x,t)$. For these, in *linear* quantum evolutions, the definition of Markovianity reduces to the concept of *divisibility* defined without any explicit reference to measurement processes in the quantum scenario [1]. To introduce the divisibility concept, let us assume that the inverse of a quantum dynamical map $\mathcal{E}_t$ exists for all times $t \geq 0$. Then it is possible to define a two-parameter family of maps by means of $\mathcal{E}_{t,s} = \mathcal{E}_t \mathcal{E}_s^{-1}$ ($t \geq s \geq 0$) such that $\mathcal{E}_{t,0} = \mathcal{E}_t$ and $\mathcal{E}_{t,0} = \mathcal{E}_{t,s}\mathcal{E}_{s,0}$. It should be noted that the existence of the inverse for all positive times guarantees the possibility of introducing the notion of divisibility, while $\mathcal{E}_{t,0}$ and $\mathcal{E}_{s,0}$ are required to be completely positive by construction, the map $\mathcal{E}_{t,s}$ need not be completely positive and not even positive. It stems from the fact that the inverse $\mathcal{E}_s^{-1}$ of a completely positive map $\mathcal{E}_s$ need not be positive. The family of dynamical maps is called (C)P divisible when $\mathcal{E}_{t,s}$ is (completely) positive for all $t \geq s \geq 0$.

The trace norm given by $\| \rho \| = \text{Tr}\sqrt{\rho^\dagger \rho} = \sum_k \sqrt{a_k}$, in which a_k's represent the eigenvalues of $\rho^\dagger \rho$, leads to an important measure called *trace distance*, $D(\rho^1, \rho^2) = \frac{1}{2} \| \rho^1 - \rho^2 \|$, for the distance between two quantum states ρ^1 and ρ^2. The trace distance $D(\rho^1, \rho^2)$ is interpreted as the *distinguishability* between states ρ^1 and ρ^2. Moreover, it is *contractive* for any completely positive and trace preserving (CPTP) map $\mathcal{E}$ affecting two arbitrary quantum states $\rho^{1,2}$, i.e., $D(\mathcal{E}(\rho^1), \mathcal{E}(\rho^2)) \leq D(\rho^1, \rho^2)$ [3]. Because the dynamics of an open quantum system is described by a CPTP map $\mathcal{E}_t$, the trace distance between the initial states is always larger than the trace distance between the time-evolved quantum states. Nevertheless, this fact does *not* mean that $D(\rho^1(t), \rho^2(t))$, in which $\rho^{1,2}(t) \equiv \mathcal{E}_t(\rho^{1,2}(0))$, exhibits a monotonically decreasing function versus time [72].

There are various ways to define and detect non-Markovianity or memory effects in quantum mechanics (see [1] for a review). In Refs. [4,29], Breuer–Laine–Piilo (BLP) proposed one of the most well-known approaches, based on the variation in distinguishability of quantum states, to characterize the non-Markovian feature of the system dynamics. This is the non-Markovianity definition which we mention in our paper. According to BLP measure, for a Markovian process, the distinguishability between any two initial states of the open system, continuously diminishes over time. In other words, a quantum evolution, mathematically described by a quantum dynamical map $\mathcal{E}_t$, is called Markovian if, for any arbitrary pair of initial quantum states $\rho^1(0)$ and $\rho^2(0)$, the evolved trace distance $D(\rho^1(t), \rho^2(t))$ monotonically decreases with time. Hence, quantum Markovian dynamics exhibits a continuous loss of information from the open system to the environment. Consequently, a non-Markovian evolution is defined as a process in which, for certain time intervals, $\text{d}D(\rho^1(t), \rho^2(t))/\text{d}t > 0$, usually interpreted as the information flowing back into the system temporarily. Provided that $\mathcal{E}_t$ is invertible, one can show that the quantum process is BLP Markovian if and only if $\mathcal{E}_t$ is P-divisible [3,73].

2.2. HSS-Based Witness of Non-Markovianity

Considering the distance measure [60]

$$[d(p,q)]^2 = \frac{1}{2} \sum_x |p_x - q_x|^2, \tag{1}$$

where $p = \{p_x\}_x$ and $q = \{q_x\}_x$ denote the probability distributions, one can quantify the distance between infinitesimally close distributions taken from a one-parameter family $p_x(\phi)$ and then define the classical statistical speed as

$$s[p(\phi_0)] = \frac{d}{d\phi} d(p(\phi_0 + \phi), p(\phi_0)). \tag{2}$$

These classical notions can be generalized to the quantum case by taking a pair of quantum states ρ and σ, and writing $p_x = \text{Tr}\{E_x \rho\}$ and $q_x = \text{Tr}\{E_x \sigma\}$ which represent the measurement probabilities corresponding to the positive-operator-valued measure (POVM) defined by $\{E_x \geq 0\}$ satisfying $\sum_x E_x = \mathbb{I}$.

The associated quantum distance, which is called Hilbert–Schmidt distance [74], can be achieved by maximizing the classical distance over all possible choices of POVMs [75]

$$D(\rho, \sigma) \equiv \max_{\{E_x\}} d(p, q) = \sqrt{\frac{1}{2}\text{Tr}\left[(\rho - \sigma)^2\right]}. \quad (3)$$

Consequently the HSS, i.e. the corresponding quantum statistical speed, is defined as follows:

$$HSS(\rho_\phi) \equiv HSS_\phi \equiv \max_{\{E_x\}} s[p(\phi)] = \sqrt{\frac{1}{2}\text{Tr}\left[\left(\frac{d\rho_\phi}{d\phi}\right)^2\right]}, \quad (4)$$

which can be easily computed without the diagonalization of $d\rho_\phi/d\phi$.

The recently proposed protocol, completely consistent with the BLP witness and used to detect non-Markovianity based on the HSS, is now briefly recalled [61]. We consider an n-dimensional quantum system whose initial state is given by

$$|\psi_0\rangle = \frac{1}{\sqrt{n}}(e^{i\phi}|\psi_1\rangle + \ldots + |\psi_n\rangle), \quad (5)$$

where ϕ is an unknown phase shift and $\{|\psi_1\rangle, \ldots, |\psi_n\rangle\}$ denotes a complete and orthonormal set (basis) for the corresponding Hilbert space $\mathcal{H}$. Given this initial state, the HSS-based witness of non-Markovianity is defined by

$$\text{Non-Markovianity Witness}: \chi(t) \equiv \frac{dHSS(\rho_\phi(t))}{dt} > 0, \quad (6)$$

in which $\rho_\phi(t)$ is the evolved state of the system.

2.3. Quantum Entanglement Measure

Quantum entanglement is a kind of quantum correlations which, from an operational point of view, can be defined as those correlations between different subsystems which cannot be generated by local operations and classical communication (LOCC) procedures. We use negativity [76] to quantify the quantum entanglement of the state, which is a reliable measure of entanglement in the case of qubit–qubit and qubit–qutrit systems [77].

For any bipartite state, ρ_{AB}, the negativity is defined as

$$\mathcal{N}(\rho_{AB}) = \sum_i |\lambda_i|, \quad (7)$$

where λ_i is the negative eigenvalue of ρ^{T_k}, with ρ^{T_k} denoting the partial transpose of the density matrix ρ_{AB} with respect to subsystem $k = A, B$. Negativity can also be computed by the formula [78]

$$\mathcal{N}(\rho_{AB}) = \frac{1}{2}\left(\left\|\rho^{T_k}\right\| - 1\right), \quad (8)$$

in which the trace norm of ρ^{T_k} is equal to the sum of the absolute values of its eigenvalues [79], that is

$$\left\|\rho^{T_k}\right\| = \sum_i |\mu_i|, \quad (9)$$

where the spectral decomposition of ρ^{T_k} is given by $\sum_i \mu_i |i\rangle\langle i|$.

2.4. Quantum Correlation Quantifier: Measurement-Induced Disturbance

We use measurement-induced disturbance MID [59] as an alternative nonclassicality indicator for quantifying the quantum correlations of the bipartite quantum systems. It is defined as the minimum disturbance caused by local projective measurements leaving the reduced states invariant.

Considering the spectral resolutions of the reduced density states $\rho_A = \sum_i p_i^A \Pi_i^A$ and $\rho_B = \sum_j p_j^B \Pi_i^B$, one can compute the MID as follows:

$$\mathcal{M}(\rho_{AB}) = \mathcal{I}\rho_{AB} - \mathcal{I}(\Pi(\rho_{AB})), \tag{10}$$

where $\mathcal{I}$ is the mutual quantum information given by

$$\mathcal{I}(\rho_{AB}) = S(\rho_A) + S(\rho_B) - S(\rho_{AB}), \tag{11}$$

in which $S(\rho) = -\mathrm{tr}\rho \log(\rho)$ denotes the von Neumann entropy and

$$\Pi(\rho_{AB}) = \sum_{i,j} \left(\Pi_i^A \otimes \Pi_j^B \right) \rho_{AB} \left(\Pi_i^A \otimes \Pi_j^B \right). \tag{12}$$

3. Analyzing the Efficiency of the HSS Witness in High-Dimensional Systems with Finite Hilbert Spaces

In this section, we check the sanity of HSS-based witness through several paradigmatic high-dimensional quantum systems with finite Hilbert spaces. The analyses are based on the fact that for systems in which the corresponding subsystems are coupled to independent environments, the oscillations of quantum correlations with time are associated with the non-Markovian evolution of the system [12,47,80], resulting in the transfer of correlations back and forth among the various parts of the total system. Moreover, by comparing the results presented in Refs. [10,61,81,82], we can demonstrate that the BLP measure of non-Markovianity can be used as a valid definition of non-Markovianity, when we intend to detect non-Markovianity by revivals of quantum correlations.

In particular, we consider a single qudit subject to a quantum environment, and a hybrid qubit-qutrit system coupled to independent as well as common quantum and classical noises. We show that the oscillation of the HSS-based witness is in qualitative agreement with nonmonotonic variations of the quantum resources, and hence it can be introduced as a faithful identifier of non-Markovianity in such high-dimensional systems with finite Hilbert spaces.

It should be noted that the efficiency of the HSS-based witness in detecting the non-Markovian nature of the dynamics directly depends on adopting the correct parametrization of the initial state of Equation (5), as discussed in Ref. [61]. However, often choosing the computational basis as the complete orthonormal set $\{|\psi_1\rangle, \dots, |\psi_n\rangle\}$ is enough to capture the non-Markovianity, as shown in this paper. In all examples discussed below, the HSS is computed for the pure initial states while the quantum correlations may be calculated for mixed ones to illustrate the general efficiency off the HSS-based witness.

3.1. Single-Qudit Interacting with a Quantum Environment

3.1.1. Coupling to a Thermal Reservoir

Let consider the spin-S systems interacting with a thermal reservoir modeled by an infinite chain of quantum harmonic oscillators with ω_k, b_k, and $b_k^\dagger$ being, respectively, the frequency, annihilation, and creation operators for the k-th oscillator. The total Hamiltonian of the system is given by

$$H = \omega_0 S_z + \sum_k \omega_k b_k^\dagger b_k + \sum S_z(g_k b_k^\dagger + g_k^* b_k), \tag{13}$$

in which ω_0 denote the transition frequency between any neighboring energy states of the spin, and S_z, the z component of spin operator, can be represented by a diagonal matrix

$S_z = \text{diag}[s, s-1, \ldots, -s]$ in the eigen-basis $\{|i\rangle, i = s, \ldots, -s\}$. In the interaction picture Equation (13) into is expressed as

$$H_I = \sum S_z (g_k b_k^\dagger e^{i\omega_k t} + g_k^* b_k e^{-i\omega_k t}), \tag{14}$$

where g_k denotes the coupling strength between the spin and the environment through the dephasing interaction. Up to an overall phase factor, the corresponding unitary propagator is obtained as

$$V(t) = \exp\left[\frac{1}{2} S_z \sum_k \left(\alpha_k b_k^\dagger - \alpha^* b_k\right)\right], \tag{15}$$

where $\alpha_k = 2g_k(1 - e^{i\omega_k t})/\omega_k$.

It is assumed that the initial state of the spin-bath system is in a product state $\rho_T(0) = \rho(0) \otimes \rho_B$ in which $\rho(0)$ denotes the initial state of spin, and

$$\rho_B = \frac{1}{Z_B} e^{-\beta \sum_k \omega_k b_k^\dagger b_k} \tag{16}$$

represents the thermal equilibrium state of the bath with partition function Z_B and inverse temperature $\beta = \frac{1}{k_B T}$. The evolved state of the system can be calculated by [83]

$$\rho_{nm}(t) = \rho_{nm}(0) \exp\left[-(n-m)^2 \Gamma(t)\right], \tag{17}$$

where $n, m = -s, -s+1, \ldots, 0, \ldots, s-1, s$ and, in the continuum-mode limit, the decoherence function is given by

$$\Gamma(t) = \int_0^\infty J(\omega) \coth\left(\frac{\omega}{2k_b T}\right) \frac{1 - \cos(\omega t)}{\omega^2} d\omega, \tag{18}$$

with spectral density $J(\omega) = \sum_k |g_k|^2 \delta(\omega - \omega_k)$.

The $\Gamma(t)$ behavior closely depends on the characteristics of the environment. Here we consider the Ohmic-like reservoirs with spectral density

$$J(\omega) = \alpha \frac{\omega^s}{\omega_c^{s-1}} \exp\left(\frac{-\omega}{\omega_c}\right), \tag{19}$$

where α represents a dimensionless coupling strength, and ω_c denotes the cutoff frequency of the bath. Changing the Ohmic parameter s, one can obtain sub-Ohmic ($0 < s < 1$), Ohmic ($s = 1$) and super-Ohmic ($s > 1$) reservoirs.

3.1.2. Coupling to a Squeezed Vacuum Reservoir

In the case that the spin system is coupled to a squeezed vacuum reservoir, the reduced density-matrix elements are similar to the ones presented in Equation (17) when the decoherence function $\Gamma(t)$ is replaced by

$$\gamma(t) = \int_0^\infty J(\omega) \frac{(1 - \cos(\omega t))}{\omega^2} [\cosh(2r) - \sinh(2r) \cos(\omega t - \theta)] d\omega, \tag{20}$$

where r is the squeezed amplitude parameter, and θ denotes the squeezed angle.

Because the structures of the density matrices are the same in both scenarios (coupling to thermal and squeezed vacuum reservoirs), we only focus on the interaction of the system with the squeezed vacuum reservoir, noting that the general results also holds for the thermal reservoir.

We take the qudit in the pure initial state

$$|\psi\rangle = \frac{1}{\sqrt{2s+1}} (e^{i\phi}|s\rangle + |s-1\rangle + |s-2\rangle + \cdots + |-s\rangle), \tag{21}$$

which leads to the evolved state $\rho(t)$ given by

$$\rho(t) = \frac{1}{2s+1}\begin{pmatrix} 1 & e^{-\gamma(t)}e^{i\phi} & \cdots & e^{-(2s)^2\gamma(t)}e^{i\phi} \\ e^{-\gamma(t)}e^{-i\phi} & 1 & \cdots & e^{-(2s-1)^2\gamma(t)} \\ e^{-4\gamma(t)}e^{-i\phi} & e^{-\gamma(t)} & \cdots & e^{-(2s-2)^2\gamma(t)} \\ \vdots & & 1 & \ddots \\ e^{-(2s)^2\gamma(t)}e^{-i\phi} & e^{-(2s-1)^2\gamma(t)} & \cdots & 1 \end{pmatrix}. \quad (22)$$

Therefore, the time derivative of the HSS-based witness is obtained as

$$\chi(t) = -\frac{1}{2s+1}\frac{\partial\gamma(t)}{\partial t}\frac{\sum_{k=1}^{2s} k^2 e^{-2k^2\gamma(t)}}{\sum_{k=1}^{2s} e^{-2k^2\gamma(t)}}. \quad (23)$$

The HSS-based witness $\chi(t) > 0$ tells us that the process is non-Markovian whenever $\frac{\partial\gamma(t)}{\partial t} < 0$, which corresponds to time intervals in which the decoherence function decreases, leading to the re-coherence phenomenon. As known, in this system the non-Markovian effects, originating from the non-divisible maps, appear when the decoherence function temporarily decays with time [84]. Therefore, our witness correctly predicts the intervals at which the memory effects arise in this single-qudit system. Moreover, when $\gamma(t)$ is a monotonous increasing function of time, the dynamics is Markovian because the coherence decays monotonously with time.

3.2. Hybrid Qubit–Qutrit System Interacting with Various Quantum and Classical Environments

The composite hybrid qubit(A)–qutrit(B) system consists of a spin–$\frac{1}{2}$ subsystem (qubit A) and a spin-1 subsystem (qutrit B). In the following, we study the interaction of this composite system with local non-Markovian environments A and B, or with a common environment C modeling quantum or classical noises. The theoretical schematic of this system is depicted in Figure 1.

3.2.1. Coupling to Independent Squeezed Vacuum Reservoirs

Now we investigate the scenario in which each of the subsystems, i.e., the qubit A ($s_A = \frac{1}{2}$) and qutrit B ($s_B = 1$), interacts independently with its local squeezed vacuum reservoir. For simplicity we assume that the characteristics of the reservoirs are similar. Equation (17), with the decoherence factor introduced in Equation (20), gives the reduced density matrices of the subsystems. Computing them and applying the method presented in [81], one can obtain the elements of the evolved density matrix of the composite system as [85]

$$\rho_{AB_{nm}}(t) = \rho_{AB_{nm}}(0)\exp\left[-(n_A - m_A)^2 - (n_B - m_B)^2\right]\gamma(t), \quad (24)$$

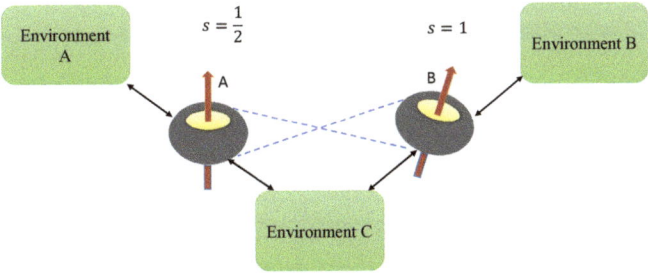

Figure 1. Illustration of the composite qubit(A)-qutrit(B) system; Blue dashed lines represent entanglement between the subsystems. The bipartite system can interact either with independent local environments E_A, E_B or with a common environment E_C.

where $n_A, m_A = -s_A, \ldots, s_A$ and $n_B, m_B = -s_B, \ldots, s_B$.

Pure initial state. We take the hybrid qubit–qutrit system initially in a pure state given by [61]

$$|\psi\rangle = \frac{1}{\sqrt{6}}\left(e^{i\phi}|00\rangle + |01\rangle + |02\rangle + |10\rangle + |11\rangle + |12\rangle\right), \qquad (25)$$

which leads to a dynamics of the system described by the evolved reduced density matrix $\rho(t)$ whose elements are presented in Appendix A.1. Then, the HSS is obtained as

$$\text{HSS} = \frac{1}{6}\sqrt{2e^{-2\gamma(t)} + e^{-4\gamma(t)} + e^{-8\gamma(t)} + e^{-10\gamma(t)}}. \qquad (26)$$

The dynamics of negativity, MID and HSS computed by the evolved state of the system are plotted in Figure 2. We find that each of the measures initially decreases with time, then starts to increase, and finally remains approximately constant over time, a behavior known as the freezing phenomenon [86–92]. As discussed, the revival of the quantum correlation measures can be attributed to the non-Markovian evolution of the system [47]. We see that the behaviors of the HSS, negativity and quantum correlation exhibit an excellent qualitative agreement. Consequently, the HSS-based witness can precisely capture the non-Markovian dynamics of the composite system.

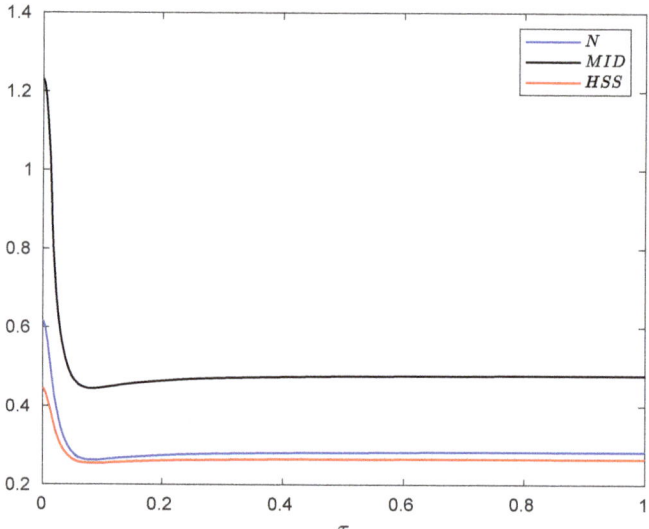

Figure 2. Evolution of the negativity, MID and HSS as a function of dimensionless time $\tau = \omega_0 t$ when each subsystem of the hybrid qubit–qutrit system, starting from the initial pure state, is independently subject to a squeezed vacuum reservoir. The values of the other parameters are $\alpha = 0.1$, $\omega_c = 20\omega_0$, $r = 0.3$, $\phi = \pi$ and $s = 3$.

Mixed initial state. The non-Markovianity of the system, as faithfully individuated by quantum correlation measures, may in general depend on the initial state. It is thus important to investigate whether the HSS witness, obtained from the initial pure state of Equation (25) by definition, is capable to identify the non-Markovian character of the system dynamics also when the system starts from a mixed state. We shall study this aspect here and in all the other environmental conditions considered hereafter (see sections below devoted to a mixed initial state).

We consider the one-parameter mixed entangled state as the initial state of the hybrid qubit–qutrit system [93]

$$\rho_0(p) = \frac{p}{2}(|01\rangle\langle 01| + |11\rangle\langle 11|) + p|\psi^+\rangle\langle\psi^+| + (1-2p)|\psi^-\rangle\langle\psi^-|, \quad (27)$$

where

$$|\psi^+\rangle = \frac{1}{\sqrt{2}}(|00\rangle + |12\rangle),$$
$$|\psi^-\rangle = \frac{1}{\sqrt{2}}(|02\rangle + |10\rangle), \quad (28)$$

in which the entanglement parameter p varies from 0 to 1 such that $\rho(p)$ is entangled except for $p = \frac{1}{3}$. We point out that such a state is taken as the initial state of the system for the dynamics of the quantum correlation quantifiers, namely negativity and MID. We find that Equation (27) leads to the evolved state of the system

$$\rho(t) = \begin{pmatrix} \frac{p}{2} & 0 & 0 & 0 & 0 & \frac{p}{2}\mathcal{F} \\ 0 & \frac{p}{2} & 0 & 0 & 0 & 0 \\ 0 & 0 & \frac{1-2p}{2} & \frac{1-2p}{2}\mathcal{F} & 0 & 0 \\ 0 & 0 & \frac{1-2p}{2}\mathcal{F} & \frac{1-2p}{2} & 0 & 0 \\ 0 & 0 & 0 & 0 & \frac{p}{2} & 0 \\ \frac{p}{2}\mathcal{F} & 0 & 0 & 0 & 0 & \frac{p}{2} \end{pmatrix}, \quad (29)$$

where $\mathcal{F} = e^{-5\gamma(t)}$. Then, the negativity is given by [71]

$$\mathcal{N} = \frac{(p-1)}{2} + \frac{1}{4}|p + (1-p)\mathcal{F}| + \frac{1}{4}|p - (1-p)\mathcal{F}| + \frac{1}{4}|p - (1-2p)\mathcal{F}| + \frac{1}{4}|p + (1-2p)\mathcal{F}|. \quad (30)$$

Moreover, using Equation (10) we can compute the MID as

$$\mathcal{M} = \frac{(1-p)}{2}[(1+\mathcal{F})\log(1+\mathcal{F}) + (1-\mathcal{F})\log(1-\mathcal{F})]. \quad (31)$$

In Figure 3, we compare the evolution of HSS, obtained from the initial pure state of Equation (25), with the dynamics of negativity and MID, computed for the mixed initial state of Equation (15), for different values of p. The dynamics of the HSS is again in perfect agreement with that observed for the entanglement and quantum correlations as quantified by the negativity and MID, respectively. Therefore, the HSS-based witness, computed versus the phase parameter encoded into an initial pure state of the system, can efficiently detect the non-Markovian dynamics even in the case when the initial state of our high-dimensional system is not pure. It should be noted that in the presence of sudden death of entanglement, which occurs for some values of the entanglement parameter (for example, for $p = 0.4$), only the HSS and MID show the same dynamics. Hence, the negativity cannot be used as a faithful witness of non-Markovianity when it exhibits the sudden death phenomenon.

In the case of initially entangled noninteracting qubits in independent non-Markovian quantum environments, entanglement or quantum correlation revivals can be explained in terms of transfer of correlations back and forth from the composite system to the various parts of the total system. This is due to the back-action via the environment on the system, which creates correlations between qubits and environments and between the environments themselves. Accordingly, in this case the non-Markovianity is defined as backflow of information from the environment(s) to the system(s).

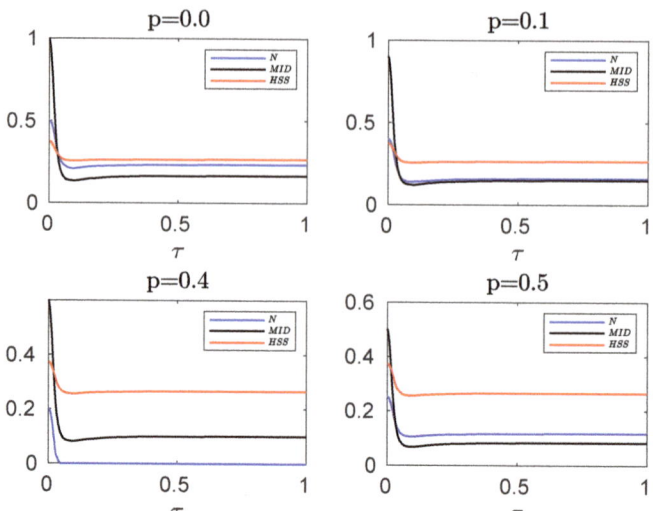

Figure 3. Comparing the evolution of negativity and MID computed for the initial mixed state of the hybrid qubit–qutrit system, when each subsystem is independently coupled to a squeezed vacuum reservoir, with HSS (obtained from the initial pure state) for different values of the entanglement parameter p. In all plots the remaining parameters are $\alpha = 0.1$, $s = 3$, $\omega_c = 20\,\omega_0$, $r = 0.3$.

3.2.2. Coupling to Classical Environments

Here we assume that the hybrid qubit-qutrit system is affected by a classical environment implemented by random telegraph noise (RTN) with a Lorentzian spectrum. It is a famous class of non-Gaussian noises used to generate the low-frequency $\frac{1}{f^\alpha}$ noise both theoretically and experimentally. It is also responsible for coherent dynamics in quantum solid-state nanodevices [94–96]. Physically, the RTN may result from one of the following scenarios: (i) charges flipping between two locations in space (charge noise); (ii) electrons trapping in shallow subgap formed at the boundary between a superconductor and an insulator (noise of critical current); and (iii) spin diffusion on a superconductor surface generated by the exchange mediated by the conduction electrons (flux noise) [97,98]. The Hamiltonian of the qubit–qutrit system under the RTN is given by

$$\mathcal{H}(t) = \mathcal{H}_0 + \mathcal{H}_I$$
$$\mathcal{H}_0 = \sum_{k=A,B} \epsilon_k S_k^Z, \mathcal{H}_I = \sum_{k=A,B} [J_k L_k(t) + J_c C(t)] S_z^k, \quad (32)$$

where ϵ_k denote the energy of an isolated qubit (qutrit), $S_z^A = \sigma_z$ and S_z^B represent the spin operators of, respectively, the qubit and the qutrit in the z-direction. Moreover, J_k and J_c represent the coupling strengths of each marginal system to the local and non-local RTN, such that we consider two types of system-environment interactions, namely

(1) Local or independent environments (ie): $J_k = \nu \neq 0$ and $J_c = 0$;
(2) Non-local or common environments (ce): $J_k = 0$ and $J_c = \nu \neq 0$.

Furthermore, $L_k(t)$ and $C(t)$ denote the random variables used to introduce the stochastic processes. They are used to describe the different conditions under which the subsystems undergo decoherence due to the environment. Here, they represent classical random fluctuating fields such as bistable fluctuators flipping between two fixed values $\pm m$ at rates γ_k and γ, respectively. For simplicity, we assume that $\gamma_k = \gamma$. For the *autocorrelation function* of the random variable $\eta(t) = \{L_k(t); C(t)\}$ we have $\langle \delta\eta(t)\delta\eta(t')\rangle = \exp[-2\gamma|t-t'|]$ with a Lorentzian power spectrum $S(\omega) = \frac{4\gamma}{\omega^2+\gamma^2}$. Defining the parameter $q = \frac{\gamma}{\nu}$, we can identify two regimes for the dynamics of quantum correlations: the Markovian regime ($q \gg 1$: fast RTN), and the non-Markovian regime ($q \ll 1$: slow RTN). The time-evolving state of the system under the influence of the RTN is given by

$$\rho(\{\eta\}, t) = U(\{\eta\}, t)\rho(0)U^\dagger(\{\eta\}, t). \tag{33}$$

in which the time-evolution operator $U(\{\eta\}, t)$ called the stochastic unitary operator in the interaction picture is given by

$$U(\{\eta\}, t) = \exp\left[-i\int_0^t \mathcal{H}_I(t')dt'\right]. \tag{34}$$

where $\eta(t) = \{L_k(t); C(t)\}$ stands for the different realizations of the stochastic process. Because $U(\{\eta\}, t)$ depends on the noise, we should perform the ensemble average over the noise fields to obtain the reduced density matrix of the open system, i.e.,

$$\rho_{ie(ce)} = \langle \rho(\{\eta\}, t) \rangle_{\eta(t)}. \tag{35}$$

The evolved state of the system in the presence of independent environments (ie) and collective environments (ce) is obtained as

$$\begin{aligned}\rho_{ie}(t) &= \langle\langle \rho(\theta_A(t), \theta_B(t), t) \rangle_{\theta_A}\rangle_{\theta_B} \\ \rho_{ce}(t) &= \langle \rho(\theta(t), t) \rangle_\theta,\end{aligned} \tag{36}$$

where $\theta_k(t) = \nu \int_0^t L_k(t')dt'$ ($k = A, B$) and $\theta(t) = \nu \int_0^t C(t')dt$. Calculation of the above terms requires the computation of averaged terms of the type $\langle e^{\pm in\theta} \rangle$ ($n \in \mathbb{N}$) given by [99]

$$\begin{aligned}\langle e^{in\theta} \rangle &= D_n(\tau) = \langle \cos(n\theta) \rangle \pm i\langle \sin(n\theta) \rangle, \\ \langle \sin(n\theta) \rangle &= 0,\end{aligned} \tag{37}$$

$$\langle \cos(n\theta) \rangle = \begin{cases} e^{-q\tau}\left[\cosh(\xi_{qn}\tau) + \frac{q}{\xi_{qn}}\sinh(\xi_{qn}\tau)\right], & q > n \\ e^{-q\tau}\left[\cos(\xi_{nq}\tau) + \frac{q}{\xi_{nq}}\sin(\xi_{nq}\tau)\right], & q < n \end{cases}$$

where $\xi_{ab} = \sqrt{a^2 - b^2}$ ($(a, b) = n, q$), and $\tau = \nu t$ denotes the scaled (dimensionless) time [71].

Pure initial state in the presence of independent classical environments. Here, we assume that each of the qubits and qutrits interact locally with local RTN, while the composite system starts with the pure initial state in Equation (25). For this case, the elements of evolved density matrix are given in Appendix A.2. Then the HSS is obtained as

$$HSS = \frac{1}{6}\sqrt{D_1^2(\tau) + 2D_2^2(\tau) + D_2^2(\tau)D_1^2(\tau) + D_2^4(\tau)}. \tag{38}$$

In Figure 4, we illustrate the time behaviors of the negativity, MID and HSS in the non-Markovian regime as a function of the dimensionless time. It is clear that when the entanglement sudden death occurs, the HSS and MID synchronously oscillate with time as they are suppressed to the minimum value and then rise. Moreover, at the first revival of the measures, the minimum point of the HSS exactly coincides with that of the negativity. After that moment we see that maximum (minimum) points of the HSS are in complete coincidence with maximum (minimum) points of the negativity as well as MID. This perfect qualitative agreement between HSS and entanglement or quantum correlations is evidence that the HSS-based witness can precisely detect non-Markovianity in the presence of classical noises.

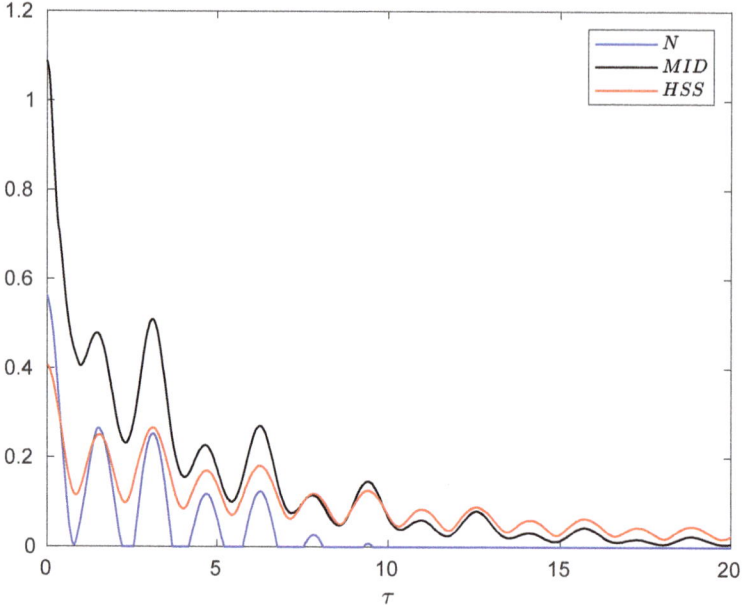

Figure 4. Evolution of negativity, MID and HSS as a function of dimensionless time $\tau = \nu t$ when each subsystem of the hybrid qubit–qutrit system, starting from the initial pure state, is independently subject to a random telegraph noise in non-Markovian regime $q = 0.1$.

Mixed initial state in the presence of independent classical environments. Now we compare the dynamics of the HSS, obtained from the initial pure state of Equation (25), with the evolution of the negativity and quantum correlation computed for the initial mixed state of Equation (27). The evolved density matrix, the corresponding negativity and quantum correlation are obtained from, respectively, Equations (29)–(31) replacing $\mathcal{F}$ with $D_2(\tau)^2$.

Figure 5 exhibits this comparison for different values of the entanglement parameter p. Not considering the periods when the sudden death of the entanglement occurs, we observe that the maximum and minimum points of the measures are very close to each other and small deviations originate from the fact that the initial state, used for computation of the HSS-based measure, should be optimized over all possible parametrizations. Therefore, the HSS-based measure remains as a valid non-Markovianity identifier in the presence of the classical noises.

Mixed initial state in the presence of a common classical environment. Let us now compare the dynamics of the HSS, obtained as usual from the initial pure state of Equation (25) by definition, with the evolution of the negativity and quantum correlation computed for the initial mixed state of Equation (27), when both the qubit and the qutrit are embedded into a common RTN source in the non-Markovian regime. The elements of the evolved dynamical density matrix are given in Appendix A.3. Then, one can easily determine the HSS as

$$HSS = \frac{1}{6}\sqrt{D_1(\tau)^2 + 2D_2(\tau)^2 + D_3(\tau)^2 + D_4(\tau)^2}. \quad (39)$$

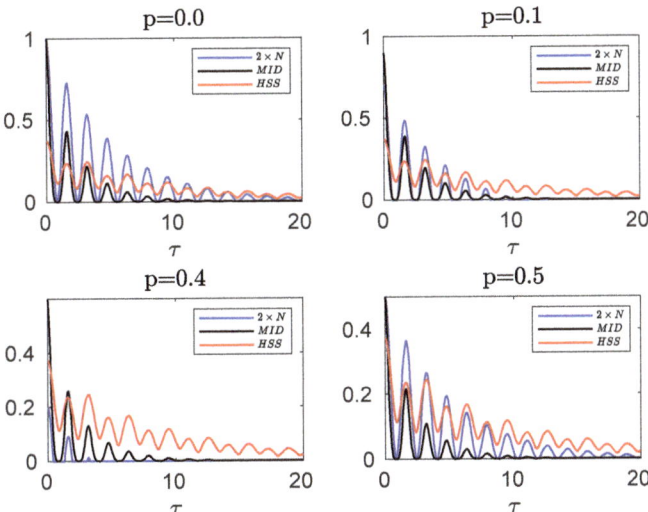

Figure 5. Comparing the evolution of negativity and MID computed for the initial mixed state of the hybrid qubit–qutrit system, when each subsystem is independently coupled to a random telegraph noise, with HSS (obtained from the initial pure state) for different values of the entanglement parameter p in the non-Markovian regime: $q = 0.1$.

Moreover, the evolved density matrix of the hybrid qubit–qutrit system for the initial mixed state of Equation (27) is obtained as

$$\rho(t) = \begin{pmatrix} \frac{p}{2} & 0 & 0 & 0 & 0 & \frac{p}{2}\mathcal{F}e^{i\phi} \\ 0 & \frac{p}{2} & 0 & 0 & 0 & 0 \\ 0 & 0 & \frac{1-2p}{2} & \frac{1-2p}{2} & 0 & 0 \\ 0 & 0 & \frac{1-2p}{2} & \frac{1-2p}{2} & 0 & 0 \\ 0 & 0 & 0 & 0 & \frac{p}{2} & 0 \\ \frac{p}{2}\mathcal{F}e^{-i\phi} & 0 & 0 & 0 & 0 & \frac{p}{2} \end{pmatrix}, \quad (40)$$

where $\mathcal{F} = D_4(\tau)$.

As a consequence, we find that the negativity and MID are, respectively,

$$\mathcal{N} = \frac{1}{4}[(p-1) + |3p-1| + |(1-2p) - p\mathcal{F}| + |(1-2p) + p\mathcal{F}|], \quad (41)$$

$$\mathcal{M} = (1-2p) + \frac{p}{2}(1+\mathcal{F})\log(1+\mathcal{F}) + \frac{p}{2}(1-\mathcal{F})\log(1-\mathcal{F}). \quad (42)$$

For common environments, we know that mutual interaction between subsystems, induced by the common environment, may lead to the preservation of correlations or even result in creation of quantum correlations between the subsystems [82,100–102]. Therefore, revivals of the quantum correlations cannot be necessarily linked to pure non-Markovianity effects and hence we do not expect complete consistency between the HSS and quantum correlations behaviors (see Figure 6 demonstrating this feature of common environments causing the MID to fail in detecting non-Markovianity). Except for these situations, we see that the maximum (minimum) points of the HSS computed for the initial pure state are very close to those of the MID calculated for the initial mixed state.

It should be noted that the classical environments cannot store any quantum correlations on their own, and hence they do not become entangled with their respective quantum systems. Accordingly, common interpretation of non-Markovianity in accordance with inflow (outflow) of information to (from) the system may be problematic in the presence of the RTN and other similar classical noises [47,103]. In other words, it is somewhat misleading to talk about information flow from the system(s) to the environment(s) or information backflow from the environment(s) to the system(s). The better interpretation is to say that the quantum system has a recording memory of the events affecting its dynamics. When the quantum memory starts remembering, the information about the past events becomes accessible, leading to revival of the quantum correlations and hence to the appearance of quantum non-Markovianity [104].

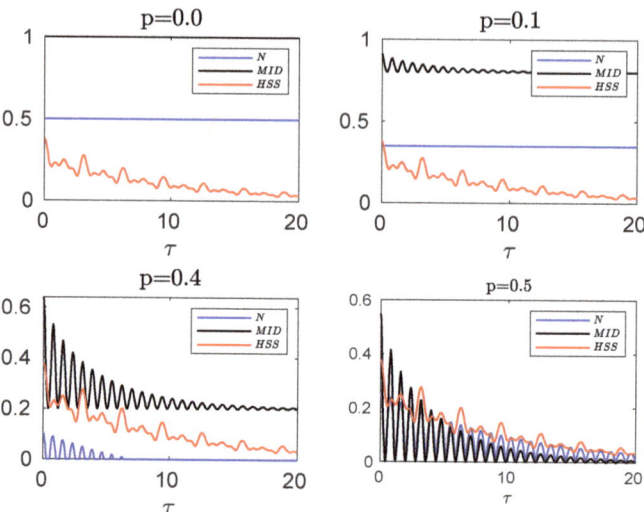

Figure 6. Comparing the evolution of negativity and MID computed for the initial mixed state of the hybrid qubit–qutrit system, when its subsystems are subject to a common RTN source, with HSS (obtained from the initial pure state) for different values of the entanglement parameter p in the non-Markovian regime: $q = 0.1$.

3.2.3. Composite Classical-Quantum Environments

Here we investigate a hybrid system formed by a qubit subjected to a random telegraph noise and a qutrit independently subjected to a squeezed vacuum reservoir. The Hamiltonian of such a system can be written as

$$\mathcal{H} = \mathcal{H}_{qb}(t) \otimes \mathcal{I}_{qt} + \mathcal{I}_{qb} \otimes \mathcal{H}_{qt}(t). \tag{43}$$

where $\mathcal{I}_{qb(qt)}$ denotes the identity operator acting on the subspace of the qubit (qutrit). Moreover, the Hamiltonians of the local interaction of the qubit and qutrit, $\mathcal{H}_{qb}(t)$ and $\mathcal{H}_{qt}(t)$, as well as their corresponding evolution operators, $\mathcal{U}_{qb}(\theta,t)$ and $\mathcal{U}_{qt}(\theta,t)$ can be extracted from Sections 3.2.2 and 3.1. In addition, one can consider the unitary evolution operator of the system as $\mathcal{U} = \mathcal{U}_{qb}(\theta,t) \otimes \mathcal{U}_{qt}(t)$. Then, the evolved density matrix of the this system can then be obtained by averaging the unitary evolved density matrix over the stochastic process induced by the RTN.

Pure initial state. The elements of the evolved density matrix when starting from the pure state of Equation (25) are given in Appendix A.4, leading to the following expression for the HSS:

$$HSS = \frac{1}{6}\sqrt{\left(e^{-2\gamma(t)} + e^{-8\gamma(t)}\right)\left(1 + D_2(\tau)^2\right) + D_2(\tau)^2}. \tag{44}$$

The time behaviors of negativity, MID and HSS are shown in Figure 7 illustrating that all measures exhibit simultaneous oscillations with time such that their maximum and minimum points exactly coincide. This excellent agreement confirms the faithfulness of the HSS-based measure to detect memory effects.

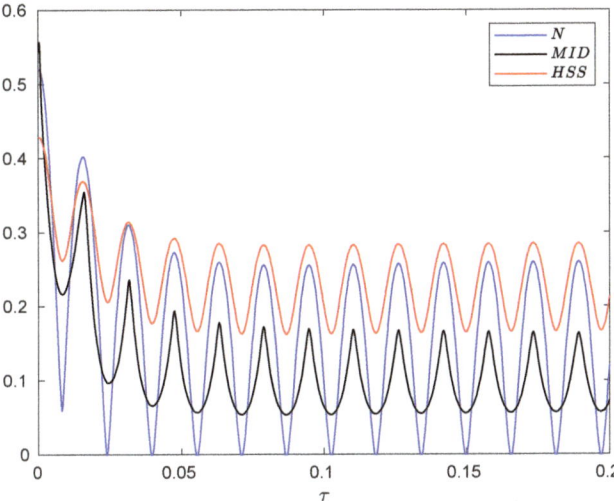

Figure 7. Evolution of negativity, MID and HSS as a function of dimensionless time τ when the subsystems of the hybrid qubit–qutrit system, starting from the initial pure state, are independently subject to composite classical-quantum environments. The values of the other parameters are given by $\alpha = 0.1$, $\omega_c = 20\, \omega_0$, $r = 0.3$, and $\nu = 100$.

Mixed initial state. Using Equation (27) as the initial state and computing the evolved state of the system (see Appendix B.4), we find that the the negativity and MID, respectively, are in the form of Equations (30) and (31) with $\mathcal{F} = D_2(\tau)e^{-4\gamma(t)}$. In Figure 8, the dynamics of negativity and MID, obtained for the initial mixed state, has been compared with that of the HSS (computed for the initial pure state) in the non-Markovian regime.

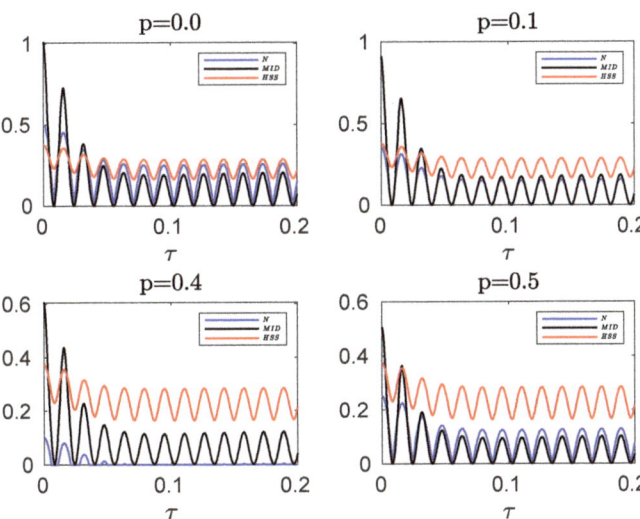

Figure 8. Comparing the evolution of the negativity and MID, computed for the initial mixed state of the hybrid qubit–qutrit system, when the subsystems are independently subject to composite classical-quantum environments, with the HSS obtained from the initial pure state for different values of the entanglement parameter p in the non-Markovian regime: $q = 0.1$. The values of the other parameters are given by $\alpha = 0.1$, $s = 3$, $\omega_c = 20\, \omega_0$, $p = 0$ and $\nu = 100$.

The related analyses are similar to those in the above discussed scenarios, showing that the HSS-based witness may be a proper non-Markovianity identifier even if the initial state of high-dimensional systems is not pure.

4. Conclusions

Recently, the HSS-based witness, a quantifier of quantum statistical speed which has the advantage of avoiding the diagonalization of the evolved density matrix, has been introduced as a trustful witness of non-Markovianity in low-dimensional systems [61]. In this work, we have generalized this result showing that the proposed witness is a bona-fide identifier of non-Markovianity for high-dimensional and multipartite open quantum systems with finite Hilbert spaces. This result stems from the observation that the HSS-based witness is in perfect agreement with established non-Markovianity identifiers based on the dynamical breakdown of monotonicity for quantum information resources, such as negativity and measurement-induced disturbance. We have found that, despite the common interpretation of non-Markovianity in terms of backflow of information from the environment to the system may be problematic [6], the HSS-based witness is capable to detect memory effects of the evolved quantum system.

In order to construct a non-Markovianity measure on the basis of a geometric distance between two quantum states, one of desirable properties is that the distance is contractive, i.e., nonincreasing under any completely positive trace preserving (CPTP) map. It has been shown that the HSS is contractive under CPTP maps in low-dimensional Hermitian systems [61]. Checking all of the dynamical cases presented here, we have found that the contractivity of the HSS holds not only in low dimensional systems but also in finite high-dimensional ones. Recently, an HSS-like measure has been used to analyze the quantum speed limit for continuous-variable systems following Gaussian preserving dynamics [105]. Therefore, our results also motivate further studies about HSS applications in detecting non-Markovianity in continuous variable systems.

By definition, the HSS-based witness of memory effects is obtained by maximizing the speed of a classical distance measure between the probability distributions, over all quantum measurements. This, as a prospect, may induce the idea of the the possibility to use classical-like description of density matrix properties in probability representation of quantum mechanics.

Recently, K. Goswami et al. [106] have reported a quantum-optics experimental setup to implement a non-Markovian process—specifically, a process with initial classical correlations between system and environment. It should be noted that in all systems investigated in this paper we have adopted the usual assumption that the system and its environment are initially uncorrelated. It would be interesting to generalize the application of the HSS-based non-Markovianity witness to scenarios in which initial correlations between the system and environment rise. This will be studied in detail in our future work.

Author Contributions: Conceptualization, H.R.J.; methodology, K.M., M.K.S., H.R.J. and R.L.F.; formal analysis, K.M. and M.K.S.; investigation, K.M., M.K.S., H.R.J. and R.L.F.; writing—original draft preparation, K.M.; writing—review and editing, H.R.J., R.M. and R.L.F.; supervision, R.M. and R.L.F. All authors have read and agreed to the published version of the manuscript.

Funding: R.M. acknowledges support from NSERC, MEI and the CRC program in Canada. R.L.F. acknowledges support from "Sistema di Incentivazione, Sostegno e Premialità della Ricerca Dipartimentale" of the Department of Engineering, University of Palermo.

Institutional Review Board Statement: Not applicable.

Informed Consent Statement: Not applicable.

Data Availability Statement: Not applicable.

Conflicts of Interest: The authors declare no conflict of interest.

Appendix A. Pure Hybrid Qubit–Qutrit Evolved Density Matrix

This appendix presents the elements of the evolved density matrix of hybrid qubit–qutrit system, starting from the initial pure state of Equation (25), in the presence of quantum and classical noises. This evolved state is required for the assessment of non-Markovianity via the HSS-based witness.

Appendix A.1. Squeezed Vacuum Reservoirs

The elements of the evolved density matrix, when each subsystem of the hybrid qubit–qutrit system is independently subject to a squeezed vacuum reservoir, in the computational basis $|00\rangle, |01\rangle, |02\rangle, |10\rangle, |11\rangle, |12\rangle$ are given by

$$\rho_{11}(t) = \rho_{22}(t) = \rho_{33}(t) = \rho_{44}(t) = \rho_{55}(t) = \rho_{66}(t) = \frac{1}{6},$$

$$\rho_{12}(t) = \rho_{14}(t) = \rho_{21}^*(t) = \rho_{41}^*(t) = \frac{1}{6}e^{i\phi}e^{-\gamma(t)},$$

$$\rho_{13}(t) = \rho_{31}^*(t) = \frac{1}{6}e^{i\phi}e^{-4\gamma(t)}, \quad \rho_{15}(t) = \rho_{51}^*(t) = \frac{1}{6}e^{-2\gamma(t)},$$

$$\rho_{16}(t) = \rho_{61}^*(t) = e^{i\phi}e^{-5\gamma(t)},$$

$$\rho_{23}(t) = \rho_{25}(t) = \rho_{32}(t) = \rho_{36}(t) = \rho_{45}(t) = \rho_{52}(t) = \rho_{54}(t) = \rho_{56}(t) \qquad \text{(A1)}$$

$$= \rho_{63}(t) = \rho_{65}(t) = \frac{1}{6}e^{-\gamma(t)},$$

$$\rho_{46}(t) = \rho_{64}(t) = \frac{1}{6}e^{-4\gamma(t)},$$

$$\rho_{24}(t) = \rho_{26}(t) = \rho_{35}(t) = \rho_{42}(t) = \rho_{53}(t) = \rho_{62}(t) = \frac{1}{6}e^{-2\gamma(t)},$$

$$\rho_{34}(t) = \rho_{43}(t) = \frac{1}{6}e^{-5\gamma(t)}.$$

Appendix A.2. Independent Random Telegraph Noise

The elements of the evolved density matrix, when each subsystem of the hybrid qubit–qutrit system is independently subject to the classical random telegraph noise, can be obtained as

$$\rho_{11}(t) = \rho_{22}(t) = \rho_{33}(t) = \rho_{44}(t) = \rho_{55}(t) = \rho_{66}(t) = \frac{1}{6}$$

$$\rho_{12}(t) = \rho_{21}^*(t) = \frac{1}{6}e^{i\phi}D_1(\tau)$$

$$\rho_{23}(t) = \rho_{32}(t) = \rho_{45}(t) = \rho_{54}(t) = \rho_{56}(t) = \rho_{65}(t) = \frac{1}{6}D_1(\tau)$$

$$\rho_{13}(t) = \rho_{14}(t) = \rho_{31}^*(t) = \rho_{41}^*(t) = \frac{1}{6}e^{i\phi}D_2(\tau)$$

$$\rho_{25}(t) = \rho_{36}(t) = \rho_{46}(t) = \rho_{52}(t) = \rho_{63}(t) = \rho_{64}(t) = \frac{1}{6}D_2(\tau) \qquad \text{(A2)}$$

$$\rho_{15}(t) = \rho_{51}^*(t) = \frac{1}{6}e^{i\phi}D_2(\tau)D_1(\tau)$$

$$\rho_{24}(t) = \rho_{26}(t) = \rho_{35}(t) = \rho_{42}(t) = \rho_{53}(t) = \rho_{62}(t) = \frac{1}{6}D_2(\tau)D_1(\tau)$$

$$\rho_{16}(t) = \rho_{61}^*(t) = \frac{1}{6}e^{i\phi}D_2^2(\tau)$$

$$\rho_{34}(t) = \rho_{43}(t) = \frac{1}{6}D_2^2(\tau).$$

Appendix A.3. Common Random Telegraph Noise

The elements of the evolved density matrix, when the qubit and qutrit are subject to a common RTN source, are given by

$$\rho_{11}(t) = \rho_{22}(t) = \rho_{33}(t) = \rho_{44}(t) = \rho_{55}(t) = \rho_{66}(t) = \frac{1}{6}$$

$$\rho_{12}(t) = \rho_{21}^*(t) = \frac{1}{6}e^{i\phi}D_1(\tau)$$

$$\rho_{23}(t) = \rho_{32}(t) = \rho_{24}(t) = \rho_{42}(t) = \rho_{35}(t) = \rho_{53}(t) =$$

$$\rho_{45}(t) = \rho_{54}(t) = \rho_{56}(t) = \rho_{65}(t) = \frac{1}{6}D_1(\tau)$$

$$\rho_{13}(t) = \rho_{14}(t) = \rho_{31}^*(t) = \rho_{41}^*(t) = \frac{1}{6}e^{i\phi}D_2(\tau)$$

$$\rho_{25}(t) = \rho_{36}(t) = \rho_{46}(t) = \rho_{52}(t) = \rho_{63}(t) = \rho_{64}(t) = \frac{1}{6}D_2(\tau) \quad (A3)$$

$$\rho_{15}(t) = \rho_{51}^*(t) = \frac{1}{6}e^{i\phi}D_3(\tau)$$

$$\rho_{24}(t) = \rho_{26}(t) = \rho_{35}(t) = \rho_{42}(t) = \rho_{53}(t) = \rho_{62}(t) = \frac{1}{6}D_2(\tau)D_1(\tau)$$

$$\rho_{16}(t) = \rho_{61}^*(t) = \frac{1}{6}e^{i\phi}D_4(\tau)$$

$$\rho_{34}(t) = \rho_{43}(t) = \frac{1}{6}.$$

Appendix A.4. Composite Classical-Quantum Environments

The elements of the evolved density matrix, when the qubit and qutrit are independently subject to, respectively, random telegraph noise channel and squeezed vacuum reservoirs, can be obtained as

$$\rho_{11}(t) = \rho_{22}(t) = \rho_{33}(t) = \rho_{44}(t) = \rho_{55}(t) = \rho_{66}(t) = \frac{1}{6}$$

$$\rho_{12} = \rho_{21}^* = \frac{1}{6}e^{i\phi}e^{-\gamma(t)}$$

$$\rho_{23}(t) = \rho_{32}(t) = \rho_{45}(t) = \rho_{54}(t) = \rho_{56}(t) = \rho_{65}(t) = \frac{1}{6}e^{-\gamma(t)}$$

$$\rho_{13}(t) = \rho_{31}^*(t) = \frac{1}{6}e^{i\phi}e^{-4\gamma(t)}$$

$$\rho_{14}(t) = \rho_{41}^*(t) = \frac{1}{6}e^{i\phi}D_2(\tau)$$

$$\rho_{15}(t) = \rho_{51}^*(t) = \frac{1}{6}e^{i\phi}D_2(\tau)e^{-\gamma(t)} \quad (A4)$$

$$\rho_{16}(t) = \rho_{61}^*(t) = \frac{1}{6}e^{i\phi}D_2(\tau)e^{-4\gamma(t)}$$

$$\rho_{25}(t) = \rho_{36}(t) = \rho_{52}(t) = \rho_{63}(t) = \frac{1}{6}D_2(\tau)$$

$$\rho_{24}(t) = \rho_{26}(t) = \rho_{35}(t) = \rho_{42}(t) = \rho_{53}(t) = \rho_{62}(t) = \frac{1}{6}D_2(\tau)e^{-\gamma(t)}$$

$$\rho_{34}(t) = \rho_{43}(t) = \frac{1}{6}D_2(\tau)e^{-4\gamma(t)}$$

$$\rho_{46}(t) = \rho_{64}(t) = \frac{1}{6}e^{-4\gamma(t)}.$$

Appendix B. Mixed Hybrid Qubit–Qutrit Evolved Density Matrix

This appendix presents the elements of the evolved density matrix of hybrid qubit–qutrit system, starting from the initial mixed state of Equation (27), in the presence of quantum and classical noises.

Appendix B.1. Squeezed Vacuum Reservoirs

The elements of the evolved density matrix, when each subsystem of the hybrid qubit–qutrit system is independently subject to a squeezed vacuum reservoir, are given by

$$\rho(t) = \begin{pmatrix} \frac{p}{2} & 0 & 0 & 0 & 0 & \frac{p}{2}\mathcal{F} \\ 0 & \frac{p}{2} & 0 & 0 & 0 & 0 \\ 0 & 0 & \frac{1-2p}{2} & \frac{1-2p}{2}\mathcal{F} & 0 & 0 \\ 0 & 0 & \frac{1-2p}{2}\mathcal{F} & \frac{1-2p}{2} & 0 & 0 \\ 0 & 0 & 0 & 0 & \frac{p}{2} & 0 \\ \frac{p}{2}\mathcal{F} & 0 & 0 & 0 & 0 & \frac{p}{2} \end{pmatrix}, \quad (A5)$$

and the partial transpose with respect to the subsystem A is

$$\left(\rho(t)^{AB}\right)^{T_A} = \begin{pmatrix} \frac{p}{2} & 0 & 0 & 0 & 0 & \frac{1-2p}{2}\mathcal{F} \\ 0 & \frac{p}{2} & 0 & 0 & 0 & 0 \\ 0 & 0 & \frac{1-2p}{2} & \frac{p}{2}\mathcal{F} & 0 & 0 \\ 0 & 0 & \frac{p}{2}\mathcal{F} & \frac{1-2p}{2} & 0 & 0 \\ 0 & 0 & 0 & 0 & \frac{p}{2} & 0 \\ \frac{1-2p}{2}\mathcal{F} & 0 & 0 & 0 & 0 & \frac{p}{2} \end{pmatrix}, \quad (A6)$$

where the $\mathcal{F} = e^{-5\gamma((t))}$.

Appendix B.2. Independent Random Telegraph Noise

The elements of the evolved density matrix, when each subsystem of the hybrid qubit–qutrit system is independently subject to the classical random telegraph noise, are given by Equation (A5) with $\mathcal{F} = D_2(\tau)^2$.

Appendix B.3. Common Random Telegraph Noise

The evolved density matrix, when the qubit and qutrit are subject to a common RTN source, is given by

$$\rho(t) = \begin{pmatrix} \frac{p}{2} & 0 & 0 & 0 & 0 & \frac{p}{2}\mathcal{F} \\ 0 & \frac{p}{2} & 0 & 0 & 0 & 0 \\ 0 & 0 & \frac{1-2p}{2} & \frac{1-2p}{2} & 0 & 0 \\ 0 & 0 & \frac{1-2p}{2} & \frac{1-2p}{2} & 0 & 0 \\ 0 & 0 & 0 & 0 & \frac{p}{2} & 0 \\ \frac{p}{2}\mathcal{F} & 0 & 0 & 0 & 0 & \frac{p}{2} \end{pmatrix}, \quad (A7)$$

where $\mathcal{F} = D_4(\tau)$.

Appendix B.4. Composite Classical-Quantum Environments

The elements of the evolved density matrix, when the qubit and qutrit are independently subject to, respectively, random telegraph noise channel and squeezed vacuum reservoirs, are given by Equation (A5) with $\mathcal{F} = D_2(\tau)e^{-4\gamma(t)}$.

References

1. Rivas, Á.; Huelga, S.F.; Plenio, M.B. Quantum non-Markovianity: Characterization, quantification and detection. *Rep. Prog. Phys.* **2014**, *77*, 094001. [CrossRef] [PubMed]
2. De Vega, I.; Alonso, D. Dynamics of non-Markovian open quantum systems. *Rev. Mod. Phys.* **2017**, *89*, 015001. [CrossRef]
3. Breuer, H.P.; Laine, E.M.; Piilo, J.; Vacchini, B. Colloquium: Non-Markovian dynamics in open quantum systems. *Rev. Mod. Phys.* **2016**, *88*, 021002. [CrossRef]
4. Breuer, H.P.; Laine, E.M.; Piilo, J. Measure for the Degree of Non-Markovian Behavior of Quantum Processes in Open Systems. *Phys. Rev. Lett.* **2009**, *103*, 210401. [CrossRef] [PubMed]
5. Rivas, A.; Huelga, S.F.; Plenio, M.B. Entanglement and Non-Markovianity of Quantum Evolutions. *Phys. Rev. Lett.* **2010**, *105*, 050403. [CrossRef]
6. Banacki, M.; Marciniak, M.; Horodecki, K.; Horodecki, P. Information backflow may not indicate quantum memory. *arXiv* **2020**, arXiv:2008.12638.
7. Tang, J.S.; Li, C.F.; Li, Y.L.; Zou, X.B.; Guo, G.C.; Breuer, H.P.; Laine, E.M.; Piilo, J. Measuring non-Markovianity of processes with controllable system-environment interaction. *EPL (Europhys. Lett.)* **2012**, *97*, 10002. [CrossRef]
8. Liu, B.H.; Cao, D.Y.; Huang, Y.F.; Li, C.F.; Guo, G.C.; Laine, E.M.; Breuer, H.P.; Piilo, J. Photonic realization of nonlocal memory effects and non-Markovian quantum probes. *Sci. Rep.* **2013**, *3*, 1781. [CrossRef]
9. Liu, B.H.; Li, L.; Huang, Y.F.; Li, C.F.; Guo, G.C.; Laine, E.M.; Breuer, H.P.; Piilo, J. Experimental control of the transition from Markovian to non-Markovian dynamics of open quantum systems. *Nat. Phys.* **2011**, *7*, 931–934. [CrossRef]
10. Xu, J.S.; Sun, K.; Li, C.F.; Xu, X.Y.; Guo, G.C.; Andersson, E.; Lo Franco, R.; Compagno, G. Experimental recovery of quantum correlations in absence of system-environment back-action. *Nat. Commun.* **2013**, *4*, 2851. [CrossRef]
11. Chiuri, A.; Greganti, C.; Mazzola, L.; Paternostro, M.; Mataloni, P. Linear Optics Simulation of Quantum Non-Markovian Dynamics. *Sci. Rep.* **2012**, *2*, 968. [CrossRef] [PubMed]
12. Orieux, A.; Ferranti, G.; D'Arrigo, A.; Lo Franco, R.; Benenti, G.; Paladino, E.; Falci, G.; Sciarrino, F.; Mataloni, P. Experimental on-demand recovery of quantum entanglement by local operations within non-Markovian dynamics. *Sci. Rep.* **2015**, *5*, 8575. [CrossRef] [PubMed]
13. White, G.A.L.; Hill, C.D.; Pollock, F.A.; Hollenberg, L.C.L.; Modi, K. Demonstration of non-Markovian process characterisation and control on a quantum processor. *Nat. Commun.* **2020**, *11*, 6301. [CrossRef] [PubMed]
14. Ferreira, V.S.; Banker, J.; Sipahigil, A.; Matheny, M.H.; Keller, A.J.; Kim, E.; Mirhosseini, M.; Painter, O. Collapse and Revival of an Artificial Atom Coupled to a Structured Photonic Reservoir. *Phys. Rev. X* **2021**, *11*, 041043. [CrossRef]
15. Bellomo, B.; Lo Franco, R.; Maniscalco, S.; Compagno, G. Entanglement trapping in structured environments. *Phys. Rev. A* **2008**, *78*, 060302. [CrossRef]
16. Hoeppe, U.; Wolff, C.; Küchenmeister, J.; Niegemann, J.; Drescher, M.; Benner, H.; Busch, K. Direct Observation of Non-Markovian Radiation Dynamics in 3D Bulk Photonic Crystals. *Phys. Rev. Lett.* **2012**, *108*, 043603. [CrossRef] [PubMed]
17. Burgess, A.; Florescu, M. Modelling non-Markovian dynamics in photonic crystals with recurrent neural networks. *Opt. Mater. Express* **2021**, *11*, 2037–2048. [CrossRef]
18. Chin, A.W.; Datta, A.; Caruso, F.; Huelga, S.F.; Plenio, M.B. Noise-assisted energy transfer in quantum networks and light-harvesting complexes. *New J. Phys.* **2010**, *12*, 065002. [CrossRef]
19. Shao, J. Decoupling quantum dissipation interaction via stochastic fields. *J. Chem. Phys.* **2004**, *120*, 5053–5056. [CrossRef]
20. Pomyalov, A.; Tannor, D.J. The non-Markovian quantum master equation in the collective-mode representation: Application to barrier crossing in the intermediate friction regime. *J. Chem. Phys.* **2005**, *123*, 204111. [CrossRef]
21. Huelga, S.F.; Rivas, A.; Plenio, M.B. Non-Markovianity-Assisted Steady State Entanglement. *Phys. Rev. Lett.* **2012**, *108*, 160402. [CrossRef] [PubMed]
22. Vasile, R.; Olivares, S.; Paris, M.A.; Maniscalco, S. Continuous-variable quantum key distribution in non-Markovian channels. *Phys. Rev. A* **2011**, *83*, 042321. [CrossRef]
23. Chin, A.W.; Huelga, S.F.; Plenio, M.B. Quantum Metrology in Non-Markovian Environments. *Phys. Rev. Lett.* **2012**, *109*, 233601. [CrossRef] [PubMed]
24. Laine, E.M.; Breuer, H.P.; Piilo, J. Nonlocal memory effects allow perfect teleportation with mixed states. *Sci. Rep.* **2014**, *4*, 4620. [CrossRef] [PubMed]
25. Dong, Y.; Zheng, Y.; Li, S.; Li, C.C.; Chen, X.D.; Guo, G.C.; Sun, F.W. Non-Markovianity-assisted high-fidelity Deutsch–Jozsa algorithm in diamond. *npj Quantum Inf.* **2018**, *4*, 3. [CrossRef]
26. Vasile, R.; Maniscalco, S.; Paris, M.G.A.; Breuer, H.P.; Piilo, J. Quantifying non-Markovianity of continuous-variable Gaussian dynamical maps. *Phys. Rev. A* **2011**, *84*, 052118. [CrossRef]
27. Rajagopal, A.K.; Usha Devi, A.R.; Rendell, R.W. Kraus representation of quantum evolution and fidelity as manifestations of Markovian and non-Markovian forms. *Phys. Rev. A* **2010**, *82*, 042107. [CrossRef]
28. Jahromi, H.R.; Amini, M.; Ghanaatian, M. Multiparameter estimation, lower bound on quantum Fisher information, and non-Markovianity witnesses of noisy two-qubit systems. *Quantum Inf. Process.* **2019**, *18*, 338. [CrossRef]
29. Laine, E.M.; Piilo, J.; Breuer, H.P. Measure for the non-Markovianity of quantum processes. *Phys. Rev. A* **2010**, *81*, 062115. [CrossRef]

30. Usha Devi, A.R.; Rajagopal, A.K.; Sudha. Open-system quantum dynamics with correlated initial states, not completely positive maps, and non-Markovianity. *Phys. Rev. A* **2011**, *83*, 022109. [CrossRef]
31. Lu, X.M.; Wang, X.; Sun, C.P. Quantum Fisher information flow and non-Markovian processes of open systems. *Phys. Rev. A* **2010**, *82*, 042103. [CrossRef]
32. Bylicka, B.; Chruściński, D.; Maniscalco, S. Non-Markovianity as a resource for quantum technologies. *arXiv* **2013**, arXiv:1301.2585.
33. Benedetti, C.; Paris, M.G.A.; Maniscalco, S. Non-Markovianity of colored noisy channels. *Phys. Rev. A* **2014**, *89*, 012114. [CrossRef]
34. Addis, C.; Brebner, G.; Haikka, P.; Maniscalco, S. Coherence trapping and information backflow in dephasing qubits. *Phys. Rev. A* **2014**, *89*, 024101. [CrossRef]
35. Lorenzo, S.; Plastina, F.; Paternostro, M. Geometrical characterization of non-Markovianity. *Phys. Rev. A* **2013**, *88*, 020102. [CrossRef]
36. Tufarelli, T.; Kim, M.S.; Ciccarello, F. Non-Markovianity of a quantum emitter in front of a mirror. *Phys. Rev. A* **2014**, *90*, 012113. [CrossRef]
37. Apollaro, T.J.G.; Lorenzo, S.; Di Franco, C.; Plastina, F.; Paternostro, M. Competition between memory-keeping and memory-erasing decoherence channels. *Phys. Rev. A* **2014**, *90*, 012310. [CrossRef]
38. Baumgratz, T.; Cramer, M.; Plenio, M.B. Quantifying Coherence. *Phys. Rev. Lett.* **2014**, *113*, 140401. [CrossRef]
39. Winter, A.; Yang, D. Operational Resource Theory of Coherence. *Phys. Rev. Lett.* **2016**, *116*, 120404. [CrossRef]
40. Chitambar, E.; Streltsov, A.; Rana, S.; Bera, M.N.; Adesso, G.; Lewenstein, M. Assisted Distillation of Quantum Coherence. *Phys. Rev. Lett.* **2016**, *116*, 070402. [CrossRef]
41. Streltsov, A.; Adesso, G.; Plenio, M.B. Colloquium: Quantum coherence as a resource. *Rev. Mod. Phys.* **2017**, *89*, 041003. [CrossRef]
42. Luo, S.; Fu, S.; Song, H. Quantifying non-Markovianity via correlations. *Phys. Rev. A* **2012**, *86*, 044101. [CrossRef]
43. Zeng, H.S.; Tang, N.; Zheng, Y.P.; Wang, G.Y. Equivalence of the measures of non-Markovianity for open two-level systems. *Phys. Rev. A* **2011**, *84*, 032118. [CrossRef]
44. Uchiyama, C. Exploring initial correlations in a Gibbs state by application of external field. *Phys. Rev. A* **2012**, *85*, 052104. [CrossRef]
45. Lorenzo, S.; Plastina, F.; Paternostro, M. Role of environmental correlations in the non-Markovian dynamics of a spin system. *Phys. Rev. A* **2011**, *84*, 032124. [CrossRef]
46. Vasile, R.; Galve, F.; Zambrini, R. Spectral origin of non-Markovian open-system dynamics: A finite harmonic model without approximations. *Phys. Rev. A* **2014**, *89*, 022109. [CrossRef]
47. Lo Franco, R.; Bellomo, B.; Andersson, E.; Compagno, G. Revival of quantum correlations without system-environment back-action. *Phys. Rev. A* **2012**, *85*, 032318. [CrossRef]
48. D'Arrigo, A.; Lo Franco, R.; Benenti, G.; Paladino, E.; Falci, G. Recovering entanglement by local operations. *Ann. Phys.* **2014**, *350*, 211–224. [CrossRef]
49. D'Arrigo, A.; Benenti, G.; Lo Franco, R.; Falci, G.; Paladino, E. Hidden entanglement, system-environment information flow and non-Markovianity. *Int. J. Quant. Infor.* **2014**, *12*, 1461005. [CrossRef]
50. Datta, A.; Shaji, A.; Caves, C.M. Quantum Discord and the Power of One Qubit. *Phys. Rev. Lett.* **2008**, *100*, 050502. [CrossRef]
51. Streltsov, A.; Kampermann, H.; Bruß, D. Behavior of Quantum Correlations under Local Noise. *Phys. Rev. Lett.* **2011**, *107*, 170502. [CrossRef] [PubMed]
52. Ciccarello, F.; Giovannetti, V. Creating quantum correlations through local nonunitary memoryless channels. *Phys. Rev. A* **2012**, *85*, 010102. [CrossRef]
53. Maziero, J.; Céleri, L.C.; Serra, R.M.; Vedral, V. Classical and quantum correlations under decoherence. *Phys. Rev. A* **2009**, *80*, 044102. [CrossRef]
54. Bellomo, B.; Compagno, G.; Lo Franco, R.; Ridolfo, A.; Savasta, S. Dynamics and extraction of quantum discord in a multipartite open system. *Int. J. Quant. Infor.* **2011**, *9*, 1665–1676. [CrossRef]
55. Yu, T.; Eberly, J. Sudden death of entanglement. *Science* **2009**, *323*, 598–601. [CrossRef]
56. Almeida, M.P.; de Melo, F.; Hor-Meyll, M.; Salles, A.; Walborn, S.; Ribeiro, P.S.; Davidovich, L. Environment-induced sudden death of entanglement. *Science* **2007**, *316*, 579–582. [CrossRef] [PubMed]
57. Ollivier, H.; Zurek, W.H. Quantum discord: A measure of the quantumness of correlations. *Phys. Rev. Lett.* **2001**, *88*, 017901. [CrossRef]
58. Henderson, L.; Vedral, V. Classical, quantum and total correlations. *J. Phys. A Math. Gen.* **2001**, *34*, 6899. [CrossRef]
59. Luo, S. Using measurement-induced disturbance to characterize correlations as classical or quantum. *Phys. Rev. A* **2008**, *77*, 022301. [CrossRef]
60. Gessner, M.; Smerzi, A. Statistical speed of quantum states: Generalized quantum Fisher information and Schatten speed. *Phys. Rev. A* **2018**, *97*, 022109. [CrossRef]
61. Rangani Jahromi, H.; Mahdavipour, K.; Khazaei Shadfar, M.; Lo Franco, R. Witnessing non-Markovian effects of quantum processes through Hilbert-Schmidt speed. *Phys. Rev. A* **2020**, *102*, 022221. [CrossRef]
62. Rangani Jahromi, H.; Lo Franco, R. Searching for exceptional points and inspecting non-contractivity of trace distance in (anti-)PT-symmetric systems. *arXiv* **2021**, arXiv:2101.04663.
63. Rangani Jahromi, H. Remote sensing and faithful quantum teleportation through non-localized qubits. *Phys. Lett.* **2022**, *424*, 127850. [CrossRef]

64. Rangani Jahromi, H.; Haseli, S. Quantum memory and quantum correlations of Majorana qubits used for magnetometry. *Quant. Inf. Comput.* **2020**, *20*, 935. [CrossRef]
65. Rangani Jahromi, H.; Lo Franco, R. Hilbert–Schmidt speed as an efficient figure of merit for quantum estimation of phase encoded into the initial state of open n-qubit systems. *Sci. Rep.* **2021**, *11*, 7128. [CrossRef]
66. Rangani Jahromi, H.; Radgohar, R.; Hosseiny, S.M.; Amniat-Talab, M. Estimating energy levels of a three-level atom in single and multi-parameter metrological schemes. *arXiv* **2021**, arXiv:2110.10256.
67. Bruß, D.; Macchiavello, C. Optimal Eavesdropping in Cryptography with Three-Dimensional Quantum States. *Phys. Rev. Lett.* **2002**, *88*, 127901. [CrossRef] [PubMed]
68. Cerf, N.J.; Bourennane, M.; Karlsson, A.; Gisin, N. Security of Quantum Key Distribution Using d-Level Systems. *Phys. Rev. Lett.* **2002**, *88*, 127902. [CrossRef] [PubMed]
69. Gottesman, D. Fault-Tolerant Quantum Computation with Higher-Dimensional Systems. In *Quantum Computing and Quantum Communications*; Williams, C.P., Ed.; Springer: Berlin/Heidelberg, Germany, 1999; pp. 302–313.
70. Ji, Y.; Hu, J. Control of quantum correlation of high dimensional system in squeezed vacuum reservoir. *Optik* **2020**, *208*, 164088. [CrossRef]
71. Tchoffo, M.; Tsokeng, A.T.; Tiokang, O.M.; Nganyo, P.N.; Fai, L.C. Frozen entanglement and quantum correlations of one-parameter qubit-qutrit states under classical noise effects. *Phys. Lett.* **2019**, *383*, 1856–1864. [CrossRef]
72. Breuer, H.P. Foundations and measures of quantum non-Markovianity. *J. Phys.* **2012**, *45*, 154001. [CrossRef]
73. Wißmann, S.; Breuer, H.P.; Vacchini, B. Generalized trace-distance measure connecting quantum and classical non-Markovianity. *Phys. Rev. A* **2015**, *92*, 042108. [CrossRef]
74. Ozawa, M. Entanglement measures and the Hilbert–Schmidt distance. *Phys. Lett.* **2000**, *268*, 158–160. [CrossRef]
75. Luo, S.; Zhang, Q. Informational distance on quantum-state space. *Phys. Rev. A* **2004**, *69*, 032106. [CrossRef]
76. Plenio, M.B. Logarithmic negativity: A full entanglement monotone that is not convex. *Phys. Rev. Lett.* **2005**, *95*, 090503. [CrossRef] [PubMed]
77. Nakahara, M. *Quantum Computing: From Linear Algebra to Physical Realizations*; CRC Press: Boca Raton, FL, USA, 2008.
78. Jaeger, G. *Quantum Information*; Springer: Berlin/Heidelberg, Germany, 2007.
79. Wilde, M.M. *Quantum Information Theory*; Cambridge University Press: Cambridge, UK, 2013.
80. Tong, Q.J.; An, J.H.; Luo, H.G.; Oh, C.H. Mechanism of entanglement preservation. *Phys. Rev. A* **2010**, *81*, 052330. [CrossRef]
81. Bellomo, B.; Lo Franco, R.; Compagno, G. Non-Markovian Effects on the Dynamics of Entanglement. *Phys. Rev. Lett.* **2007**, *99*, 160502. [CrossRef] [PubMed]
82. Lo Franco, R.; Bellomo, B.; Maniscalco, S.; Compagno, G. Dynamics of quantum correlations in two-qubit systems within non-Markovian environments. *Int. J. Mod. Phys.* **2013**, *27*, 1345053. [CrossRef]
83. Fan, Z.L.; Tian, J.; Zeng, H.S. Entanglement and non-Markovianity of a spin-S system in a dephasing environment. *Chin. Phys.* **2014**, *23*, 060303. [CrossRef]
84. Fanchini, F.F.; de Oliveira Soares-Pinto, D.; Adesso, G. *Lectures on General Quantum Correlations and Their Applications*; Springer: Berlin/Heidelberg, Germany, 2017.
85. Ji, Y.; Ke, Q.; Hu, J. Quantum correlation of high dimensional system in a dephasing environment. *Phys. Low-Dimens. Syst. Nanostruct.* **2018**, *99*, 139–144. [CrossRef]
86. Mazzola, L.; Piilo, J.; Maniscalco, S. Sudden Transition between Classical and Quantum Decoherence. *Phys. Rev. Lett.* **2010**, *104*, 200401. [CrossRef] [PubMed]
87. Bromley, T.R.; Cianciaruso, M.; Adesso, G. Frozen Quantum Coherence. *Phys. Rev. Lett.* **2015**, *114*, 210401. [CrossRef] [PubMed]
88. Aaronson, B.; Lo Franco, R.; Adesso, G. Comparative investigation of the freezing phenomena for quantum correlations under nondissipative decoherence. *Phys. Rev. A* **2013**, *88*, 012120. [CrossRef]
89. Aaronson, B.; Lo Franco, R.; Compagno, G.; Adesso, G. Hierarchy and dynamics of trace distance correlations. *New J. Phys.* **2013**, *15*, 093022. [CrossRef]
90. Cianciaruso, M.; Bromley, T.R.; Roga, W.; Lo Franco, R.; Adesso, G. Universal freezing of quantum correlations within the geometric approach. *Sci. Rep.* **2015**, *5*, 10177. [CrossRef] [PubMed]
91. Haikka, P.; Johnson, T.H.; Maniscalco, S. Non-Markovianity of local dephasing channels and time-invariant discord. *Phys. Rev. A* **2013**, *87*, 010103. [CrossRef]
92. Lo Franco, R. Nonlocality threshold for entanglement under general dephasing evolutions: A case study. *Quant. Inf. Proc.* **2016**, *15*, 2393–2404. [CrossRef]
93. Karpat, G.; Gedik, Z. Correlation dynamics of qubit–qutrit systems in a classical dephasing environment. *Phys. Lett.* **2011**, *375*, 4166–4171. [CrossRef]
94. Galperin, Y.M.; Altshuler, B.L.; Bergli, J.; Shantsev, D.V. Non–Gaussian Low-Frequency Noise as a Source of Qubit Decoherence. *Phys. Rev. Lett.* **2006**, *96*, 097009. [CrossRef]
95. Burkard, G. Non-Markovian qubit dynamics in the presence of $1/f$ noise. *Phys. Rev. B* **2009**, *79*, 125317. [CrossRef]
96. Benedetti, C.; Buscemi, F.; Bordone, P.; Paris, M.G.A. Dynamics of quantum correlations in colored-noise environments. *Phys. Rev. A* **2013**, *87*, 052328. [CrossRef]
97. Faoro, L.; Ioffe, L.B. Microscopic Origin of Low-Frequency Flux Noise in Josephson Circuits. *Phys. Rev. Lett.* **2008**, *100*, 227005. [CrossRef] [PubMed]

98. Yoshihara, F.; Harrabi, K.; Niskanen, A.O.; Nakamura, Y.; Tsai, J.S. Decoherence of Flux Qubits due to $1/f$ Flux Noise. *Phys. Rev. Lett.* **2006**, *97*, 167001. [CrossRef] [PubMed]
99. Tsokeng, A.T.; Tchoffo, M.; Fai, L.C. Quantum correlations and decoherence dynamics for a qutrit-qutrit system under random telegraph noise. *Quant. Inf. Proc.* **2017**, *16*, 191. [CrossRef]
100. Mazzola, L.; Maniscalco, S.; Piilo, J.; Suominen, K.A.; Garraway, B.M. Sudden death and sudden birth of entanglement in common structured reservoirs. *Phys. Rev. A* **2009**, *79*, 042302. [CrossRef]
101. Benatti, F.; Floreanini, R.; Piani, M. Environment Induced Entanglement in Markovian Dissipative Dynamics. *Phys. Rev. Lett.* **2003**, *91*, 070402. [CrossRef] [PubMed]
102. Braun, D. Creation of Entanglement by Interaction with a Common Heat Bath. *Phys. Rev. Lett.* **2002**, *89*, 277901. [CrossRef]
103. Lo Franco, R.; Compagno, G. Overview on the phenomenon of two-qubit entanglement revivals in classical environments. In *Lectures on General Quantum Correlations and Their Applications*; Springer: Berlin/Heidelberg, Germany, 2017; pp. 367–391.
104. Rangani Jahromi, H.; Amniat-Talab, M. Precision of estimation and entropy as witnesses of non-Markovianity in the presence of random classical noises. *Ann. Phys.* **2015**, *360*, 446–461. [CrossRef]
105. Poggi, P.M.; Campbell, S.; Deffner, S. Diverging Quantum Speed Limits: A Herald of Classicality. *PRX Quantum* **2021**, *2*, 040349. [CrossRef]
106. Goswami, K.; Giarmatzi, C.; Monterola, C.; Shrapnel, S.; Romero, J.; Costa, F. Experimental characterization of a non-Markovian quantum process. *Phys. Rev. A* **2021**, *104*, 022432. [CrossRef]

Article

Effect of Quantum Coherence on Landauer's Principle

Kazunari Hashimoto *,† and Chikako Uchiyama *,†

Faculty of Engineering, University of Yamanashi, 4-3-11 Takeda, Kofu 400-8511, Yamanashi, Japan
* Correspondence: hashimotok@yamanashi.ac.jp (K.H.); hchikako@yamanashi.ac.jp (C.U.)
† These authors contributed equally to this work.

Abstract: Landauer's principle provides a fundamental lower bound for energy dissipation occurring with information erasure in the quantum regime. While most studies have related the entropy reduction incorporated with the erasure to the lower bound (entropic bound), recent efforts have also provided another lower bound associated with the thermal fluctuation of the dissipated energy (thermodynamic bound). The coexistence of the two bounds has stimulated comparative studies of their properties; however, these studies were performed for systems where the time-evolution of diagonal (population) and off-diagonal (coherence) elements of the density matrix are decoupled. In this paper, we aimed to broaden the comparative study to include the influence of quantum coherence induced by the tilted system–reservoir interaction direction. By examining their dependence on the initial state of the information-bearing system, we find that the following properties of the bounds are generically held regardless of whether the influence of the coherence is present or not: the entropic bound serves as the tighter bound for a sufficiently mixed initial state, while the thermodynamic bound is tighter when the purity of the initial state is sufficiently high. The exception is the case where the system dynamics involve only phase relaxation; in this case, the two bounds coincide when the initial coherence is zero; otherwise, the thermodynamic bound serves the tighter bound. We also find the quantum information erasure inevitably accompanies constant energy dissipation caused by the creation of system–reservoir correlation, which may cause an additional source of energetic cost for the erasure.

Keywords: Landauer's principle; quantum coherence; energy dissipation

1. Introduction

Information processing accompanies inevitable energy dissipation. According to Landauer's principle [1], the ultimate source of energy dissipation is information erasure, and it is bounded from below by the corresponding reduction in informational entropy. The principle establishes a fundamental link between information theory and thermodynamics [2–5]. In the classical regime, its validity has been proven for a wide range of systems, both theoretically [6,7] and experimentally [8–11]. In recent years, rapid developments in quantum technologies stimulate generalizations of the principle to the quantum regime [7,12,13]. Remarkably, in Ref. [13], Reeb and Wolf provided a clear framework for quantum information erasure and successfully derived a quantum version of Landauer's principle, which states that the energy dissipation occurred with the quantum information erasure is lower-bounded by the corresponding reduction of the von Neumann entropy of the information-bearing system. Since energy dissipation is ubiquitous in quantum operations, its clear understanding is intrinsically important both from fundamental and practical viewpoints. In this regard, several studies have examined the lower bound for the energy dissipation in quantum information processing [14–19] or operation of quantum heat engine [20,21].

Despite the conventional Landauer's principle being rooted in the information theory, recent studies in quantum thermodynamics provide another lower bound related to the thermal fluctuation of the dissipated energy [22,23]. Because of its completely different physical origin from the entropic lower bound, subsequent comparative studies on the relative tightness of the two bounds have been stimulated [22–25]. In these studies, the two bounds are compared for systems where a single two-level system transversally contacts with finite [22–24] or infinite [25] reservoirs. For the transversal interaction, the dynamics of the population and the coherence are decoupled. Under the assumption, they clarified the following generic features: for the systematically changed initial state of the system, the thermodynamic bound depends only on the initial population, whereas the entropic bound is relevant to the initial coherence. Since the interplay between the population and the coherence is one of the most significant aspects of quantum operations, it is highly desirable to extend the studies to a more generic system–reservoir interaction. Indeed, a number of recent studies [26,27] address the influence of quantum coherence on energy dissipation by evaluating the entropic bound in the presence of longitudinal system–reservoir interaction. Our main aim in the present paper is to proceed in this direction to the comparative study of the two bounds.

In this paper, we provide a systematic study of the relative tightness of the bounds for the spin–boson model consisting of a single spin-1/2 and an infinitely large bosonic reservoir with a tilted system–reservoir interaction direction. By adjusting the angle of the interaction direction, we control the coupling between the population and the coherence. Our analysis is based on the full-counting statistics (FCS) formalism of the bounds [23] with the time-convolutionless type quantum master equation, which is time-local even beyond the Markov approximation [25,28–30]. With this formalism, we show that the above-summarized trends of the bounds reported in Ref. [25] hold even under the influence of quantum coherence. We also point out that Reeb and Wolf's quantum information erasure protocol inevitably accompanies constant energy dissipation caused by the creation of system–reservoir correlation, which may cause an additional source of energetic cost for the erasure.

2. Thermal Quantum Information Erasure

In the original work Ref. [1], R. Landauer argued to "erase" or "reset" a classical bit by interacting it with a "thermal reservoir" or "energy sink", and bringing it to a "definite" state. In the quantum regime, a general framework of the information erasure was formulated in Ref. [13], which satisfies the following prerequisites:

1. the protocol involves an information-bearing system S and a thermal reservoir R, both described by certain Hamiltonians, denoted H_S and H_R, respectively,
2. the reservoir R is initially in the thermal equilibrium with a certain inverse temperature β, $\rho_R(0) = \rho_R^{eq} \equiv \exp(-\beta H_R)/\mathrm{Tr}_R[\exp(-\beta H_R)]$, where $\rho_R(t)$ is the reduced density operator of R,
3. the system S and the reservoir R are initially uncorrelated, $\rho_{\mathrm{tot}}(0) = \rho_S(0) \otimes \rho_R^{eq}$, where $\rho_{\mathrm{tot}}(0)$ is the total density operator of S+R and $\rho_S(t)$ is the reduced density operator of S,
4. the erasure process itself proceeds by a unitary evolution generated by the total Hamiltonian $H = H_S + H_R + H_{SR}$, where H_{SR} is an interaction between S and R.

Following the above framework, we consider a specific protocol of a quantum information erasure: we erase an information content of a spin S by interacting it with an infinite bosonic reservoir R until it reaches a steady-state satisfying $d\rho_S(t)/dt = 0$.

3. Lower Bounds for the Energy Dissipation

The above-formulated information erasure accompanies unavoidable energy exchange, or "energy dissipation", between the system and the reservoir. The actual amount of the dissipated energy can be evaluated as

$$\langle \Delta Q \rangle = \mathrm{Tr}_R[H_R(\rho_R(t) - \rho_R(0))]. \tag{1}$$

Landauer's principle claims that the dissipated energy has a lower bound, meaning that the information erasure requires a specific energetic cost, and it may not be zero. In the present paper, we systematically compare two lower bounds with different physical origins: (a) the entropic bound defined by the entropy change during the erasure process and (b) the thermodynamic bound defined by the thermal fluctuation of the dissipated energy. Let us briefly review each bound in the rest of the present section.

3.1. Entropic Bound

In Ref. [13,31], an equality for the dissipated energy $\langle \Delta Q \rangle$ was derived

$$\beta \langle \Delta Q \rangle = \Delta S + I(S';R') + D(\rho_R(t) || \rho_R(0)), \tag{2}$$

where $\Delta S \equiv S(\rho_S(0)) - S(\rho_S(t))$, with von Neumann entropy $S(\rho_S) \equiv -\text{Tr}_S[\rho \ln \rho_S]$, is the entropy decrease in the system, $I(S';R') \equiv S(\rho_S(t)) + S(\rho_R(t)) - S(\rho_{\text{tot}}(t))$ is the mutual information between S and R, quantifying the correlation building up between S and R, and $D(\rho_R(t)||\rho_R(0)) \equiv \text{Tr}_E[\rho_R(t) \ln \rho_R(t)] - \text{Tr}_R[\rho_R(t) \ln \rho_R(0)]$ is the relative entropy in R representing the increase in free energy in the environment [31]. Because any deviation from the initial preparation of the total system, the second and third prerequisites, creates a system–reservoir correlation or free energy in the environment, both $I(S';R')$ and $D(\rho_R(t)||\rho_E(0))$ are positive in the quantum information erasure process [13,31]. The equality thus provides the quantum version of Landauer's inequality

$$\beta \langle \Delta Q \rangle \geq \Delta S, \tag{3}$$

which states that the dissipated energy (Equation (1)) is bounded from below by the corresponding reduction of the von Neumann entropy

$$\mathcal{B}_E \equiv \frac{1}{\beta} \Delta S, \tag{4}$$

We thus refer to (4) as the *entropic bound*.

3.2. Thermodynamic Bound

Recently, growing interest in the thermodynamics of quantum systems has induced a closer examination of the relation between the dissipated energy and its fluctuation in the quantum information erasure process [22]. By considering the probability distribution function (pdf) $P(\Delta Q)$ for the net energy dissipation during the erasure process, the positiveness of the pdf and the convexity of the Boltzmann factor for the dissipated energy, $\partial^2 e^{-\beta \Delta Q}/\partial (\Delta Q)^2 \geq 0$, allow using the well-known Jensen's inequality to have the relation

$$\beta \langle \Delta Q \rangle \geq -\ln \langle e^{-\beta \Delta Q} \rangle, \tag{5}$$

where the statistical average is taken over the pdf as $\langle e^{-\beta \Delta Q} \rangle = \int_{-\infty}^{\infty} d\Delta Q\, e^{-\beta \Delta Q} P(\Delta Q)$. The inequality implies that the dissipated energy is bounded from below by the quantity

$$\mathcal{B}_T \equiv -\frac{1}{\beta} \ln \langle e^{-\beta \Delta Q} \rangle. \tag{6}$$

We thus refer to (6) as the *thermodynamic bound*.

4. Full-Counting Statistics Formalism

The dissipated energy $\langle \Delta Q \rangle$ and the thermodynamic bound $\mathcal{B}_T$ can be evaluated by using the full counting statistics (FCS) based on a two-point projective measurement of the reservoir energy H_R [23,30,32]. The measurement scheme is summarized as follows: first, at $\tau = 0$, we measure H_R to obtain an outcome E_0, secondly, during $0 \leq \tau \leq t$, the system undergoes a time evolution brought by the system–reservoir coupling, finally, at $\tau = t$, we measure H_R once again to obtain another outcome E_t. The net amount of dissipated energy during the time interval t is therefore given by $\Delta Q = E_t - E_0$, where its sign is chosen to be positive when the energy is transferred from the system to the environment. The statistics of ΔQ are summarized in its probability distribution function

$$P(\Delta Q, t) \equiv \sum_{E_t, E_0} \delta[\Delta Q - (E_t - E_0)] P[E_t, E_0], \tag{7}$$

with the joint probabilities obtainning the measurement outcomes

$$P[E_t, E_0] \equiv \text{Tr}[P_{E_t} U(t,0) P_{E_0} W(0) P_{E_0} U^\dagger(t,0) P_{E_t}], \tag{8}$$

where P_{E_τ} represents the eigenprojector of H_R associated with the eigenvalue E_τ, $U(t,0)$ represents the unitary time evolution of the total system, and $W(0)$ is the initial state of the total system. Cumulants of ΔQ are provided by the cumulant generating function (cgf)

$$\Theta(\chi, t) \equiv \ln \int_{-\infty}^{\infty} d\Delta Q P(\Delta Q, t) e^{-\chi \Delta Q}, \tag{9}$$

where χ is the *counting field* associated with ΔQ, e.g., the mean value is given by the first derivative of cgf as

$$\langle \Delta Q \rangle = \left. \frac{\partial \Theta(\chi, t)}{\partial(-\chi)} \right|_{\chi=0}. \tag{10}$$

Despite the usual definition of the cgf employing the mean value of $e^{i\chi \Delta Q}$ [32], here we employ $e^{-\chi \Delta Q}$. This change enables us to make a direct connection between the cgf and the mean value of the Boltzmann factor in Equation (6) as

$$\Theta(\beta, t) = \ln \int_{-\infty}^{\infty} d\Delta Q P(\Delta Q, t) e^{-\beta \Delta Q} = \ln \langle e^{-\beta \Delta Q} \rangle. \tag{11}$$

Thus, the thermodynamic bound is directly obtained from the cgf as

$$\mathcal{B}_T(t) = -\frac{1}{\beta} \Theta(\beta, t). \tag{12}$$

The full-counting statistics provides a systematic procedure to evaluate the cgf [32]. By using Equations (7) and (8), and introducing the evolution operator modified to include the counting field χ by $U^{(\chi)}(t,0) \equiv e^{-\chi H_R/2} U(t,0) e^{+\chi H_R/2}$ with $\bar{W}(0) \equiv \sum_{E_0} P_{E_0} W(0) P_{E_0}$, we have

$$\Theta(\chi, t) = \ln \text{Tr}_S[\rho^{(\chi)}(t)], \tag{13}$$

where $\rho^{(\chi)}(t) \equiv \text{Tr}_R[U^{(\chi)}(t,0) \bar{W}(0) U^{(-\chi)-1}(t,0)]$ is the density operator including the counting field. Note that for $\chi = 0$, $\rho^{(\chi)}(t)$ reduces to the usual reduced density operator for the system S as $\rho^{(0)}(t) = \text{Tr}_R[W(t)]$. Under the factorized intial condition assumed in the quantum information erasure, the time evolution of the density operator can be described by the time-convolutionless type quantum master equation [28,33–41]

$$\frac{d}{dt} \rho^{(\chi)}(t) = \xi^{(\chi)}(t) \rho^{(\chi)}(t). \tag{14}$$

The superoperator $\xi^{(\chi)}(t)$ generates time evolution of $\rho^{(\chi)}(t)$. Taking up to the second order in its cumulant expansion with respect to the system–reservoir interaction H_{SR} [40], the superoperator is given by

$$\xi^{(\chi)}(t) \rho_S = -\frac{i}{\hbar}[H_S, \rho_S] + K_2^{(\chi)}(t) \rho_S, \tag{15}$$

with

$$K_2^{(\chi)}(t)\rho_S \equiv -\frac{1}{\hbar^2}\int_0^t d\tau \, \mathrm{Tr}_R[H_{SR},[H_{SR}(-\tau),\rho_S\otimes\rho_R^{\mathrm{eq}}]_\chi]_\chi, \quad (16)$$

where $H_{SR}(t) \equiv e^{i(H_S+H_R)t/\hbar} H_{SR} e^{-i(H_S+H_R)t/\hbar}$, and $[X,Y]_\chi \equiv X^{(\chi)}Y - YX^{(-\chi)}$ with $X^{(\chi)} \equiv e^{-\chi H_R/2} X e^{+\chi H_R/2}$. We note that the familiar master equation describing the time evolution of the usual density operator is recovered by taking $\chi = 0$ on Equation (14).

With these formalisms, the mean value of the dissipated energy $\langle \Delta Q \rangle$, the entropic bound $\mathcal{B}_E$, and the thermodynamic bound $\mathcal{B}_T$ are respectively expressed as

$$\langle \Delta Q \rangle = \int_0^t \mathrm{Tr}_S\left[\left.\frac{\partial \xi^{(\chi)}(\tau)}{\partial(-\chi)}\right|_{\chi=0} \rho_S^{(0)}(\tau)\right] d\tau, \quad (17)$$

(see Ref. [28] for details)

$$\mathcal{B}_E(t) = \frac{1}{\beta}(S(\rho_S^{(0)}(0)) - S(\rho_S^{(0)}(t))), \quad (18)$$

and

$$\mathcal{B}_T(t) = -\frac{1}{\beta}\Theta(\beta,t) = -\frac{1}{\beta}\ln \mathrm{Tr}_S[\rho_S^{(\beta)}(t)]. \quad (19)$$

5. Spin—Boson Model

5.1. Model

For simplicity, we hereafter use units with $\hbar = 1$. As a working model, we consider a spin–boson model consisting of a single spin-1/2 system (S) and an infinitely large bosonic reservoir (R). The Hamiltonian for the system consists of three terms $H = H_S + H_R + H_{SR}$, with

$$H_S = \frac{\omega_0}{2}\sigma_z, \quad H_R = \sum_k \omega_k b_k^\dagger b_k \quad (20)$$

where $\sigma_{z,x}$ denote the Pauli matrices, ω_0 denotes the energy difference between the excited state and the ground state of the spin, ω_k is energy of the k-th bosonic mode of the reservoir and b_k ($b_k^\dagger$) annihilation (creation) operator for the boson. The bosonic reservoir is bilinearly coupled to the spin, and the interaction direction is tilted $\theta \in [0,\pi]$ from the x-axis

$$H_{SR} = (\cos\theta \sigma_x + \sin\theta \sigma_z) \otimes B_R, \quad (21)$$

with $B_R \equiv \sum_k(g_k b_k^\dagger + g_k^* b_k)$, where g_k is the coupling strength between the system and the k-th bosonic mode. By adjusting the parameter θ, we can control the direction of the system–reservoir interaction. For $\theta = 0$, π, the system–reservoir interaction is transversal, thus the dynamics of the population and the coherence is decoupled as in the case of the previous study [25]. For $\theta = \pi/2$, the system Hamiltonian H_S commutes with the interaction Hamiltonian H_{SR}, thus the system energy is invariant. In the sense that the dynamics include only phase relaxation, this case corresponds to pure dephasing.

We note that the above-presented model is equivalent to a system consisting of a single spin subjected to a tilted magnetic field and the bosonic reservoir as shown in Appendix B. Even adjusting the system–reservoir interaction is challenging to realize experimentally, applying the tilted magnetic field to the spin may be much easier.

5.2. The Bloch Vector Representation

By assuming a sufficiently weak system–reservoir coupling, we employ the second-order TCL master equation (Equations (14)–(16)) to describe the thermalization process of the system. In this paper, we focus on the interplay between the dynamics of the population and the coherence. For this purpose, it is convenient to introduce the Bloch vector representation of the density operator because its x, y- and z-components respectively represent coherence and population.

In the presence of the counting field, the density operator of the spin $\rho_S^{(\chi)}(t)$ is represented by the Bloch vector including the counting field $v^{(\chi)}(t) = (v_x^{(\chi)}(t), v_y^{(\chi)}(t), v_z^{(\chi)}(t), v_0^{(\chi)}(t))^\mathrm{T}$ with $v_\mu^{(\chi)}(t) \equiv \mathrm{Tr}_S[\sigma_\mu \rho_S^{(\chi)}(t)]$ ($\mu = x, y, z, 0$), where $\sigma_0 \equiv I$ is the identity operator. The fourth component is required because the unity of the trace of $\rho_S^{(\chi)}(t)$ is not held for $\chi \neq 0$. Because the density operator $\rho_S^{(\chi)}(t)$ is reduced to the ordinary density operator for $\chi = 0$, the Bloch vector is also reduced to the ordinary Bloch vector as $v^{(0)}(t) = (v_x^{(0)}(t), v_y^{(0)}(t), v_z^{(0)}(t), 1)^\mathrm{T}$.

Using the Bloch vector representation, the master equation (Equation (14)) is cast into the form as

$$\frac{d}{dt} v^{(\chi)}(t) = G(t) v^{(\chi)}(t), \qquad (22)$$

with the 4 × 4 matrix

$$G^{(\chi)}(t) = \begin{pmatrix} A_{11}^{(\chi)}(t) & A_{12}^{(\chi)}(t) \\ A_{21}^{(\chi)}(t) & A_{22}^{(\chi)}(t) \end{pmatrix}, \qquad (23)$$

where $A_{ij}^{(\chi)}(t)$ ($i, j = 1, 2$) are 2 × 2 block matrices, whose lengthy expressions are summarized in Appendix A. Among the four blocks, the diagonal blocks $A_{11}^{(\chi)}(t)$ and $A_{22}^{(\chi)}(t)$ describe time-evolution of coherence and population, respectively. The off-diagonal blocks $A_{12}^{(\chi)}(t)$ and $A_{21}^{(\chi)}(t)$ describe coupling between the coherence and the population. Importantly, the off-diagonal blocks $A_{12}^{(\chi)}$ and $A_{21}^{(\chi)}$ (Equations (A2) and (A3)) are proportional to $\sin 2\theta$, thus they vanish for $\theta = 0, \pi$ as well as for $\theta = \pi/2$. In this case, the time evolutions of the population and the coherence are decoupled. Otherwise, for $\theta \neq 0, \pi/2, \pi$, the quantum coherence influences the population dynamics. We also note that, for $\theta = \pi/2$, the diagonal block $A_{22}^{(\chi)}(t)$ vanishes for $\chi = 0$, β indicating invariance of $v_z^{(0)}(t), v_z^{(\beta)}(t)$ and $v_0^{(\beta)}(t)$, (see Equations (A11) and (A12) in Appendix A). Physically, the dynamics involve only dephasing but no population (energy) relaxation.

In terms of the Bloch vector, the bounds are formally expressed as

$$\begin{aligned} \mathcal{B}_E(t) = & -\ln\sqrt{1-|v(0)|^2} - |v(0)|\mathrm{artanh}|v(0)| \\ & + \ln\sqrt{1-|v(t)|^2} + |v(t)|\mathrm{artanh}|v(t)|, \end{aligned} \qquad (24)$$

with $|v(t)| \equiv \sqrt{(v_x^{(0)}(t))^2 + (v_y^{(0)}(t))^2 + (v_z^{(0)}(t))^2}$, and

$$\mathcal{B}_T(t) = -\ln(v_0^{(\beta)}(t)). \qquad (25)$$

Since the cumulant generating function is expressed as $\Theta(\eta, t) = \ln v_0^{(\eta)}(t)$, the mean dissipated energy, Equation (17), is rewritten as

$$\langle \Delta Q \rangle = \left. \frac{\partial v_0^{(\chi)}(t)}{\partial (-\chi)} \right|_{\chi=0}. \qquad (26)$$

From these formal expressions, we find that both the thermodynamic bound $\mathcal{B}_T(t)$ and the mean dissipated energy $\langle \Delta Q \rangle$ are associated with $v_0^{(\chi)}(t)$. In contrast, the entropic bound depends on the components $v_{x,y,z}^{(\chi)}(t)$.

6. Relative Tightness of the Bounds

We examine the relative tightness of the bound $\mathcal{B}_{T,E}$ against the dissipated energy $\langle \Delta Q \rangle$ in the presence of quantum coherence. Here, we regard a bound as tighter if the bound takes a closer value to the dissipated energy. For this purpose, we numerically evaluate the bounds and the dissipated energy using the expressions Equations (24)–(26).

In the following numerical calculations, the time interval t was taken sufficiently long as the system reached the steady-state. To describe the system–reservoir coupling, we use the Ohmic spectral density with the exponential cutoff $J(\omega) \equiv \sum_k |g_k|^2 \delta(\omega - \omega_k) = \lambda \omega \exp[-\omega/\Omega]$, where λ is the coupling strength and Ω is the cutoff frequency. We choose ω_0 as the frequency unit for the numerical calculations.

6.1. Dependence on Initial State

Let us first examine the initial state dependence of the relative tightness in the case where the time evolutions of the population and the coherence are coupled. In Figure 1, we set $\theta = \pi/4$ and plot values of the bounds and the dissipated energy for systematically changed initial states. In panel (a), we show a 3D plot of the dissipated energy $\langle \Delta Q \rangle$ (orange surface), the thermodynamic bound $\mathcal{B}_T$ (blue surface), and the entropic bound $\mathcal{B}_E$ (red surface) with respect to $v_z^{(0)}(0)$ and $v_x^{(0)}(0)$ while setting $v_y^{(0)}(0) = 0$. Panels (b) and (c) show cross-sections of the panel (a) at $v_x^{(0)}(0) = 0$ and at $v_z^{(0)}(0) = 0$, respectively. The figures show that both bounds are always located below the dissipated energy, meaning that both quantities properly bind from below the dissipated energy.

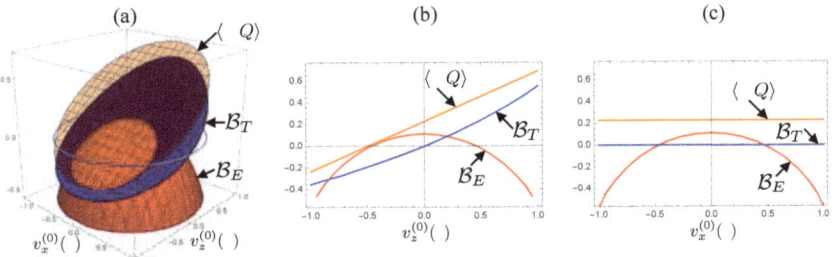

Figure 1. Dependences of the energy $\langle \Delta Q \rangle$ and the bounds $\mathcal{B}_{T,E}$ on the initial state of the system for $\theta = \pi/4$. The initial condition is chosen by changing $v_x^{(0)}(0)$ and $v_z^{(0)}(0)$ while fixing $v_y(0) = 0$. (**a**) 3D plot of $\langle \Delta Q \rangle$ (orange surface), $\mathcal{B}_T$ (blue surface) and $\mathcal{B}_E$ (red surface) with respect to $v_x(0)$ and $v_z(0)$. The purple circle indicates the surface of Bloch sphere with $v_y^{(0)}(0) = 0$. (**b**) cross-section of the 3D plot at $v_x^{(0)}(0) = 0$ plotted with respect to $v_z^{(0)}(0)$. (**c**) cross-section at $v_z^{(0)}(0) = 0$ plotted with respect to $v_x^{(0)}(0)$. For the numerical calculations, we set the parameters to $\lambda = 0.01$, $\Omega = 1$, and $\beta = 1$.

In the figures, we see the following difference: the dissipated energy $\langle \Delta Q \rangle$ and the thermodynamic bound $\mathcal{B}_T$ monotonically decrease as $v_z(0)$ decreases but they are independent of $v_x^{(0)}(0)$, while the entropic bound $\mathcal{B}_E$ depends isotropically on both $v_x^{(0)}(0)$ and $v_z^{(0)}(0)$ and decreases for growing $|v(0)|$. Because of the difference, the relative tightness of the bounds exhibits a clear boundary where the tightness switches; see the region where the red surface intersects with the blue surface. As a consequence, the entropic bound serves as the tighter bound if the initial state is sufficiently mixed as it is located near the center of the Bloch sphere; in contrast, the thermodynamic bound is tighter if the purity of the initial state is sufficiently high as it is located near the surface of the Bloch sphere. These qualitative features of the bounds are in agreement with the case for $\theta = 0$, where the time evolutions of the population and the coherence are decoupled, studied in the previous study in Ref. [25], indicating that the above-summarized dependencies of the bounds on the initial state generically hold regardless of whether the dynamics are influenced by the quantum coherence or not.

The only exception is the pure-dephasing case, $\theta = \pi/2$, presented in Figure 2. In this case, both of the dissipated energy $\langle \Delta Q \rangle$ and the thermodynamic bound $\mathcal{B}_T$ are constant for arbitrary $v_x^{(0)}(0)$ and $v_z^{(0)}(0)$, while the entropic bound $\mathcal{B}_E$ coincides with $\mathcal{B}_T$ on $v_z^{(0)}(0)$ axis and it decreases as $|v_x^{(0)}(0)|$ increases. We also see that the dissipated energy takes a non-zero (≈0.02) positive value, indicating that a certain amount of energy dissipation to the reservoir occurs regardless of the initial state.

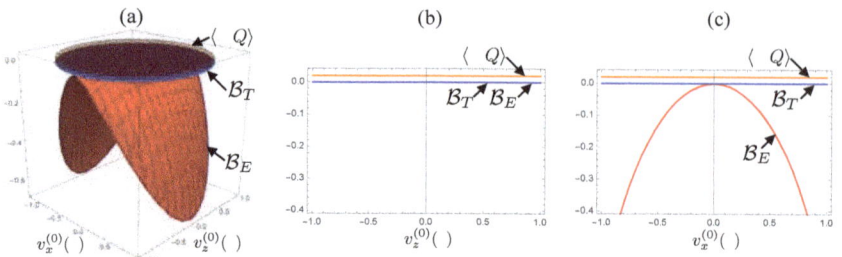

Figure 2. Dependences of the energy $\langle \Delta Q \rangle$ and the bounds $\mathcal{B}_{T,E}$ on the initial state of the system for $\theta = \pi/2$. (**a**) 3D plot of $\langle \Delta Q \rangle$ (orange surface), $\mathcal{B}_T$ (blue surface), and $\mathcal{B}_E$ (red surface) with respect to $v_x(0)$ and $v_z(0)$. (**b**) cross-section of the 3D plot at $v_x^{(0)}(0) = 0$ plotted with respect to $v_z^{(0)}(0) = 0$. (**c**) cross-section at $v_z^{(0)}(0) = 0$ plotted with respect to $v_x^{(0)}(0) = 0$. For the numerical calculations, we set the parameters to $\lambda = 0.01$, $\Omega = 1$, and $\beta = 1$ (same as in Figure 1).

The constant energy dissipation can be understood from the uncorrelated initial state $\rho_{\text{tot}}(0) = \rho_S(0) \otimes \rho_R^{\text{eq}}$ (see the third prerequisite of the quantum information erasure protocol in Section 2) and the invariance of the system energy. Since the total system is prepared in the uncorrelated state, the exchange of energy driven by the interaction $\mathcal{H}_{SR}$ creates a system–reservoir correlation, which results in an attractive force. The creation of the attractive force corresponds to the withdrawal of certain energy from the system–reservoir interaction, and the energy dissipates to the reservoir because the system energy is invariant in the pure-dephasing case.

The thermodynamics bound is constantly zero. It is a direct consequence of the invariance of the trace $v_0^{(\beta)}(t)$; because the density operator initially coincides with the ordinary density operator $\rho_S^{(\beta)}(0) = \rho_S^{(0)}(0)$, unity of the trace hold for arbitrary $t > 0$. The behavior of the entropic bound can be understood from the pure-dephasing character of the system dynamics; since the dynamic involves only dephasing, the states located on the $v_z^{(0)}(0)$ axis are invariant over time, and the states with $v_x^{(0)}(0) \neq 0$ suffer dephasing. Regarding the relative tightness, both bounds coincide for initial states with $v_x^{(0)}(0) = 0$, while the thermodynamic bound serves as a tighter bound for arbitrary initial states with $v_x^{(0)}(0) \neq 0$.

6.2. Dependence on Quantum Coherence

Let us now examine the dependences of the bounds on the strength of the coherence–population coupling, controlled by the parameter θ. In Figure 3, we plot values of the bounds and the dissipated energy for systematically changed coherence parameter θ and the initial population $v_z^{(0)}(0)$ with setting $v_x^{(0)}(0) = v_y^{(0)}(0) = 0$. In panel (a), we provide a 3D plot of the dissipated energy $\langle \Delta Q \rangle$ (orange surface), the thermodynamic bound $\mathcal{B}_T$ (blue surface) and the entropic bound $\mathcal{B}_E$ (red surface) with respect to θ and $v_z^{(0)}(0)$. Panels (b)–(e) show cross-sections of the 3D plot for two pure states with (b) $v_z^{(0)} = 1$ and (c) $v_z^{(0)} = -1$ as well as for two thermal mixed states, whose population is represented by $v_z^{(0)}(0) = (\exp[-\beta_S \omega_0/2] - \exp[+\beta_S \omega_0/2])/(\exp[-\beta_S \omega_0/2] + \exp[+\beta_S \omega_0/2])$ with an effective inverse temperature β_S, with (d) $\beta_S = 0$ and (e) $\beta_S = 1(= \beta)$.

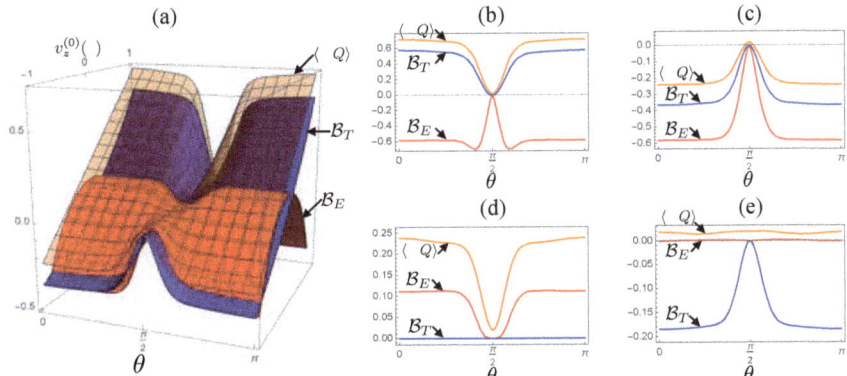

Figure 3. Dependences of the energy $\langle \Delta Q \rangle$ and the bounds $\mathcal{B}_{T,E}$ on the coherence parameter θ and the initial population $v_z^{(0)}(0)$ with setting $v_x^{(0)}(0) = v_y^{(0)}(0) = 0$. Panel (**a**) shows a 3D plot of $\langle \Delta Q \rangle$ (orange surface), $\mathcal{B}_T$ (blue surface) and $\mathcal{B}_E$ (red surface). Panels (**b**) and (**c**): cross-sections of the 3D plot for two pure initial states (**b**) $v_z^{(0)}(0) = 1$ and (**c**) $v_z^{(0)}(0) = -1$. Panels (**d**) and (**e**): cross-sections of the 3D plot corresponding to thermal initial states $\rho_S^{(0)}(0) = \exp[-\beta_S H_S]/\text{Tr}_S[\exp[-\beta_S H_S]]$ with (**d**) $\beta_S = 0$ (high temperature limit) and (**e**) $\beta_S = 1(=\beta)$. For the numerical calculations, we set the parameters to $\lambda = 0.01$, $\Omega = 1$, and $\beta = 1$ (same as in Figure 1).

From the figures, we find that the dissipated energy and the bounds are insensitive to θ except for $\theta \approx \pi/2$. Regarding the relative tightness of the bounds, the entropic bound serves as a tighter bound for most thermal initial states with positive effective temperatures, corresponding to the region with $v_z^{(0)}(0) < 0$, while the thermodynamic bound is tighter for pure initial states, $v_z^{(0)}(0) = +1$ (panel (**b**)) and $v_z^{(0)}(0) = -1$ (panel (**c**)), or most states with negative temperatures $\beta_S < 0$, corresponding to the region with $v_z^{(0)}(0) > 0$. The drastic changes in the quantities in the vicinity of $\theta = \pi/2$ are caused by the pure-dephasing character of the system dynamics. In the region, the system dynamics are dominated by dephasing and the population relaxation only gives a minor contribution, thus the quantities rapidly change to recover their behavior at $\theta = \pi/2$ presented in Figure 2.

7. Conclusions and Discussions

In the present paper, we have examined the properties of two lower bounds for energy dissipation associated with Reeb and Wolf's quantum information erasure under the influence of quantum coherence. As a working model, we considered a single spin-1/2 and a bosonic reservoir with a tilted system–reservoir interaction direction, where we could control the coupling between the dynamics of the population and the coherence by adjusting the angle of the interaction direction θ.

By setting the angle to be switching on the population–coherence coupling, we found that the bounds show the following trends: the entropic bound serves as the tighter bound if the initial state is sufficiently mixed; while, if the purity of the initial state is sufficiently high, the thermodynamic bound is tighter. These trends are in agreement with the case in which the population and the coherence are decoupled [25]. It indicates that these dependencies of the bounds on the initial state generically hold regardless of whether the influence of the quantum coherence is present or not. Indeed, we showed that the bounds and the dissipated energy are insensitive to changing the angle for most values of θ.

The only exception is the case where the angle of the interaction direction is set to $\theta = \pi/2$. In this case, the dynamics involve only dephasing, but no energy relaxation occurs. As a result, both dissipated energy and the thermodynamic bound are independent of the initial state, while the entropic bound decreases as the initial coherence increases.

Regarding the relative tightness, the two bounds coincide when the initial coherence is zero; otherwise, the thermodynamic bound serves as the tighter bound.

Apart from the quantum coherence between the ground state and the excited state of the spin, the constant energy dissipation caused by the system–reservoir interaction (see Figure 2 and its explanations in the main text) indicates that the coherence between the system and the reservoir is also a non-negligible source of energetic cost in quantum information erasure. Even it clearly appears in the pure-dephasing case, the energy dissipation due to the system–reservoir interaction always occurs within Reeb and Wolf's framework of erasure. This is because the creation of the system–reservoir correlation in the course of the erasure process is inevitable for the factorized initial state assumed in its third prerequisite. Indeed, in Ref. [42], the authors showed that the system–reservoir interaction gives a non-negligible influence on the performance of a quantum Otto engine, especially in the non-Markovian scenario. The inclusion of the energetic cost for erasure caused by the interaction needs further investigation.

In this paper, we have studied the quantum information erasure stored in the single spin system by contacting a bosonic reservoir and bringing the spin to its steady state. Even though such a setup is universally found in energy dissipation in open systems, it is rather minor as the information erasure protocol in quantum information processing. Indeed, recent studies [26,27] focus on the erasure by externally controlling the spin and bringing it to the ground state. Particularly, in Ref. [27], it is shown that the external driving creates quantum coherence and it inevitably causes additional energetic cost, thus it may affect the relative performance of the bounds. Extension of this work to include the effect of the external driving is also left for future investigations.

While we have considered in this paper the spin-1/2 interacting with the infinite bosonic reservoir describing the surrounding radiation field or phonon field, another important source of dissipation is the coupling with surrounding spins [43–47]. Indeed, in actual implementations of the qubit, such as the semiconductor quantum dot [48–50] or the nitrogen-vacancy center in diamond [51,52], coupling with surrounding nuclear spins causes energy dissipation and decoherence. In some studies [49,50], it is pointed out that an electron spin interacting with the collective spin reservoir shows a strong non-Markovian feature and long-lived quantum coherence. Since these features of the spin reservoir affect the quantum information erasure, there are several efforts to study the erasure via a finite spin reservoir [53,54]. Thus, it is worthwhile to extend the present study to the spin reservoir case.

Appendix A. The Bloch Equation Including the Counting Field

The block matrixes $A_{ij}^{(\chi)}(t)$ in the Bloch vector representation of the master equation, Equation (22), are expressed as

$$A_{11}^{(\chi)}(t) = \begin{pmatrix} a_{-}^{+(\chi)}(t)\cos^2\theta + c_{+}^{+(\chi)}\sin^2\theta & -\omega_0 + b_{-}^{+(\chi)}(t)\cos^2\theta \\ \omega_0 - b_{+}^{+(\chi)}(t)\cos^2\theta & a_{+}^{+(\chi)}(t)\cos^2\theta + c_{+}^{+(\chi)}(t)\sin^2\theta \end{pmatrix}, \quad (A1)$$

$$A_{12}^{(\chi)}(t) = \frac{1}{2}\sin 2\theta \begin{pmatrix} c_{-}^{+(\chi)}(t) - a_{+}^{-(\chi)}(t) & -ib_{+}^{-(\chi)}(t) \\ -b_{+}^{+(\chi)}(t) & i(a_{+}^{-(\chi)}(t) - c_{+}^{-(\chi)}(t)) \end{pmatrix}, \quad (A2)$$

$$A_{21}^{(\chi)}(t) = \frac{1}{2}\sin 2\theta \begin{pmatrix} a_{-}^{+(\chi)}(t) - c_{+}^{+(\chi)}(t) & b_{+}^{+(\chi)}(t) \\ -ib_{-}^{-(\chi)}(t) & i(a_{-}^{-(\chi)}(t) - c_{-}^{-(\chi)}(t)) \end{pmatrix}, \quad (A3)$$

and

$$A_{22}^{(\chi)}(t) = \begin{pmatrix} a_{+}^{+(\chi)}(t)\cos^2\theta + c_{-}^{+(\chi)}(t)\sin^2\theta & ib_{+}^{-(\chi)}(t)\cos^2\theta \\ ib_{-}^{-(\chi)}(t)\cos^2\theta & a_{-}^{+(\chi)}(t)\cos^2\theta + c_{-}^{+(\chi)}(t)\sin^2\theta \end{pmatrix}. \quad (A4)$$

The matrix elements involve the autocorrelation function of a reservoir operator

$$\langle B_R^{(\chi)} B_R^{(\chi)}(-\tau) \rangle \equiv \text{Tr}_R[B_R^{(\chi)} B_R^{(\chi)}(-\tau) \rho_R^{eq}], \qquad (A5)$$

where $B_R^{(\chi)} \equiv e^{-\chi H_R/2} B_R e^{+\chi H_R/2}$ and $B_R^{(\chi)}(-\tau) \equiv e^{-iH_R\tau} B_R^{(\chi)} e^{+iH_R\tau}$, as

$$a_{+(-)}^{\pm(\chi)}(t) \equiv -\int_0^t d\tau [h_{+(-)}^{(\chi)}(\tau) \pm h_{+(-)}^{(-\chi)*}(\tau)] \cos(\omega_0 \tau), \qquad (A6)$$

$$b_{+(-)}^{\pm(\chi)}(t) \equiv -\int_0^t d\tau [h_{+(-)}^{(\chi)}(\tau) \pm h_{+(-)}^{(-\chi)*}(\tau)] \sin(\omega_0 \tau), \qquad (A7)$$

$$c_{+(-)}^{\pm(\chi)}(t) \equiv -\int_0^t d\tau [h_{+(-)}^{(\chi)}(\tau) \pm h_{+(-)}^{(-\chi)*}(\tau)], \qquad (A8)$$

with

$$h_\pm^{(\eta)}(\tau) \equiv \langle B_R^{(\chi)} B_R^{(\chi)}(-\tau) \rangle \pm \langle B_R^{(-\chi)} B_R^{(\chi)}(-\tau) \rangle. \qquad (A9)$$

By setting $\theta = \pi/2$, the diagonal block $A_{22}^\chi(t)$ becomes

$$A_{22}^{(\chi)}(t) = \begin{pmatrix} c_-^{+(\chi)}(t) & 0 \\ 0 & c_-^{+(\chi)}(t) \end{pmatrix}. \qquad (A10)$$

For $\chi = 0$, we have $h_-^{(0)}(\tau) = 0$ leading to $c_-^{+(0)}(t) = 0$, thus the block vanishes as

$$A_{22}^{(0)}(t) = \begin{pmatrix} 0 & 0 \\ 0 & 0 \end{pmatrix}. \qquad (A11)$$

For $\chi = \beta$, we have the equality $\text{Tr}_R[b_k^\dagger b_k \rho_R^{eq}] e^{\beta \omega_k} = \text{Tr}_R[b_k b_k^\dagger \rho_R^{eq}]$ leading to the relations $\langle B_R^{(-\beta)}(-\tau) B_R^{(\beta)} \rangle = \langle B_R^{(\beta)} B_R^{(\beta)}(-\tau) \rangle$ and $\langle B_R^{(-\beta)} B_R^{(\beta)}(-\tau) \rangle = \langle B_R^{(-\beta)}(-\tau) B_R^{(-\beta)} \rangle$. These relations leads to $c_-^{+(0)}(t) = 0$, thus the block vanishes as

$$A_{22}^{(\beta)}(t) = \begin{pmatrix} 0 & 0 \\ 0 & 0 \end{pmatrix}. \qquad (A12)$$

Appendix B. A Single Spin Subjected to a Tilted Magnetic Field

The working model described by Equations (20) and (21) is equivalent to the system consisting of a single spin subjected to a tilted magnetic field and the bosonic reservoir. The equivalence can be shown by applying the unitary transformation

$$U_S \equiv \begin{pmatrix} \cos\frac{\theta}{2} & \sin\frac{\theta}{2} \\ -\sin\frac{\theta}{2} & \cos\frac{\theta}{2} \end{pmatrix}, \qquad (A13)$$

to H_S and H_{SR} as

$$\tilde{H}_S = \frac{\omega_0}{2} \begin{pmatrix} \cos\theta & \sin\theta \\ \sin\theta & -\cos\theta \end{pmatrix} \equiv \frac{\omega_0}{2} (\cos\theta \tilde{\sigma}_z + \sin\theta \tilde{\sigma}_x), \qquad (A14)$$

and

$$\tilde{H}_{SR} = \tilde{\sigma}_x \otimes B_R. \qquad (A15)$$

In this view, ω_0 represents energy splitting due to the magnetic field, and θ represents the angle of the magnetic field with respect to the z-axis.

Author Contributions: Conceptualization, C.U.; Formal analysis, K.H.; Writing—original draft, K.H.; Writing—review & editing, C.U. All authors have read and agreed to the published version of the manuscript.

Funding: This research was funded by Japan Society for the Promotion of Science, grant number 19K14611; Grant-in-Aid for Scientific Research on Innovative Areas, Science of Hy- brid Quantum Systems, grant number 18H04290.

Institutional Review Board Statement: Not applicable

Informed Consent Statement: Not applicable

Conflicts of Interest: The authors declare no conflict of interest

References

1. Landauer, R. Irreversibility and Heat Generation in the Computing Process. *IBM J. Res. Dev.* **1961**, *5*, 183. [CrossRef]
2. Penrose, O. *Foundations of Statistical Mechanics: A Deductive Treatment*; Pergamon: New York, NY, USA, 1970.
3. Bennet, C.H. Logical Reversibility of Computation. *IBM J. Res. Dev.* **1973**, *17*, 525. [CrossRef]
4. Landauer, R. Information is Physical. *Phys. Today* **1991**, *44*, 23. [CrossRef]
5. Plenio, M.B.; Vitelli, V. The physics of forgetting: Landauer's erasure principle and information theory. *Contemp. Phys.* **2001**, *42*, 25. [CrossRef]
6. Shizume, K. Heat generation required by information erasure. *Phys. Rev. E* **1995**, *52*, 3495. [CrossRef]
7. Piechocinska, B. Information erasure. *Phys. Rev. A* **2000**, *61*, 062314. [CrossRef]
8. Toyabe, S.; Sagawa, T.; Ueda, M.; Muneyuki, E.; Sano, M. Experimental demonstration of information-to-energy conversion and validation of the generalized Jarzynski equality. *Nat. Phys.* **2010**, *6*, 988. [CrossRef]
9. Orlov, A.O.; Lent, C.S.; Thorpe, C.C.; Boechler, G.P.; Snider, G.L. Experimental Test of Landauer's Principle at the Sub-$k_B T$ Level. *Jpn. J. Appl. Phys.* **2012**, *51*, 06FE10. [CrossRef]
10. Bérut, A.; Arakelyan, A.; Petrosyan, A.; Ciliberto, S.; Dillenschneider, R.; Lutz, E. Experimental verification of Landauer's principle linking information and thermodynamics. *Nature* **2012**, *483*, 187. [CrossRef]
11. Jun, Y.; Gavrilov, M.; Bechhoefer, J. High-Precision Test of Landauer's Principle in a Feedback Trap. *Phys. Rev. Lett.* **2014**, *113*, 190601. [CrossRef]
12. Hilt, S.; Shabbir, S.; Anders, J.; Lutz, E. Landauer's principle in the quantum regime. *Phys. Rev. E* **2011**, *83*, 030102. [CrossRef] [PubMed]
13. Reeb, D.; Wolf, M.M. An improved Landauer principle with finite-size corrections. *New J. Phys.* **2014**, *16*, 103011. [CrossRef]
14. Sagawa, T.; Ueda, M. Minimal Energy Cost for Thermodynamic Information Processing: Measurement and Information Erasure. *Phys. Rev. Lett.* **2009**, *102*, 250602. [CrossRef]
15. Faist, P.; Dupuis, F.; Oppenheim, J.; Renner, R. The minimal work cost of information processing. *Nat. Commun.* **2015**, *6*, 7669. [CrossRef] [PubMed]
16. Mohammady, M.H.; Mohseni, M.; Omar, Y. Minimising the heat dissipation of quantum information erasure. *New J. Phys.* **2016**, *18*, 015011. [CrossRef]
17. Bedingham, D.J.; Maroney, O.J.E. The thermodynamic cost of quantum operations. *New J. Phys.* **2016**, *18*, 113050. [CrossRef]
18. Peterson, J.P.S.; Sarthour, R.S.; Souza, A.M.; Oliveira, I.S.; Goold, J.; Modi, K.; Soares-Pinto, D.O.; Céleri, L.C. Experimental demonstration of information to energy conversion in a quantum system at the Landauer limit. *Proc. R. Soc. A* **2016**, *472*, 20150813. [CrossRef]
19. Chitambar, E.; Gour, G. Quantum resource theories. *Rev. Mod. Phys.* **2019**, *91*, 025001. [CrossRef]
20. Goold, J.; Huber, M.; Riera, A.; del Rio, L.; Skrzypczyk, P. The role of quantum information in thermodynamics—A topical review. *J. Phys. A Math. Theor.* **2016**, *49*, 143001. [CrossRef]
21. Millen, J.; Xuereb, A. Perspective on quantum thermodynamics. *New J. Phys.* **2016**, *18*, 011002. [CrossRef]
22. Goold, J.; Paternostro, M.; Modi, K. Nonequilibrium Quantum Landauer Principle. *Phys. Rev. Lett.* **2015**, *114*, 060602. [CrossRef] [PubMed]
23. Guarnieri, G.; Campbell, S.; Goold, J.; Pigeon, S.; Vacchini, B.; Paternostro, M. Full counting statistics approach to the quantum non-equilibrium Landauer bound. *New J. Phys.* **2017**, *19*, 103038. [CrossRef]
24. Campbell, S.; Guarnieri, G.; Paternostro, M.; Vacchini, B. Nonequilibrium quantum bounds to Landauer's principle: Tightness and effectiveness. *Phys. Rev. A* **2017**, *96*, 042109. [CrossRef]
25. Hashimoto, K.; Vacchini, B.; Uchiyama, C. Lower bounds for the mean dissipated heat in an open quantum system. *Phys. Rev. A* **2020**, *101*, 052114. [CrossRef]
26. Miller, H.J.D.; Guarnieri, G.; Mitchison, M.T.; Gould, J. Quantum Fluctuations Hinder Finite-Time Information Erasure near the Landauer Limit. *Phys. Rev. Lett.* **2020**, *125*, 160602. [CrossRef] [PubMed]
27. Vu, T.V.; Saito, S. Finite-Time Quantum Landauer Principle and Quantum Coherence. *Phys. Rev. Lett.* **2022**, *128*, 010602.
28. Uchiyama, C. Nonadiabatic effect on the quantum heat flux control. *Phys. Rev. E* **2014**, *89*, 052108. [CrossRef]
29. Guarnieri, G.; Uchiyama, C.; Vacchini, B. Energy backflow and non-Markovian dynamics. *Phys. Rev. A* **2016**, *93*, 012118. [CrossRef]
30. Hashimoto, K.; Uchiyama, C. Nonadiabaticity in Quantum Pumping Phenomena under Relaxation. *Entropy* **2019**, *21*, 842. [CrossRef]

31. Esposito, M.; Lindenberg, K.; Van den Broeck, C. Entropy production as correlation between system and reservoir. *New J. Phys.* **2010**, *12*, 013013. [CrossRef]
32. Esposito, M.; Harbola, U.; Mukamel, S. Nonequilibrium fluctuations, fluctuation theorems, and counting statistics in quantum systems. *Rev. Mod. Phys.* **2009**, *81*, 1665. [CrossRef]
33. Kubo, R. Stochastic Liouville Equations. *J. Math. Phys.* **1963**, *4*, 174. [CrossRef]
34. Van Kampen, N.G. A cumulant expansion for stochastic linear differential equations. I. *Physica* **1974**, *74*, 215. [CrossRef]
35. Van Kampen, N.G. A cumulant expansion for stochastic linear differential equations. II. *Physica* **1974**, *74*, 239. [CrossRef]
36. Hashitsume, N.; Shibata, F.; Shingu, M. Quantal master equation valid for any time scale. *J. Stat. Phys.* **1977**, *17*, 155. [CrossRef]
37. Shibata, F.; Takahashi, Y.; Hashitsume, N. A generalized stochastic liouville equation. Non-Markovian versus memoryless master equations. *J. Stat. Phys.* **1977**, *17*, 171. [CrossRef]
38. Chaturvedi, S.; Shibata, F. Time-convolutionless projection operator formalism for elimination of fast variables. Applications to Brownian motion. *Z. Phys. B Condens. Matter* **1979**, *35*, 297. [CrossRef]
39. Shibata, F.; Arimitsu, T. Expansion Formulas in Nonequilibrium Statistical Mechanics. *J. Phys. Soc. Jpn.* **1980**, *49*, 891. [CrossRef]
40. Uchiyama, C.; Shibata, F. Unified projection operator formalism in nonequilibrium statistical mechanics. *Phys. Rev. E* **1999**, *60*, 2636. [CrossRef]
41. Breuer, H.-P.; Petruccione, F. *The Theory of Open Quantum Systems*; Oxford University Press: Oxford, UK, 2002.
42. Shirai, Y.; Hashimoto, K.; Tezuka, R.; Uchiyama, C.; Hatano, N. Non-Markovian effect on quantum Otto engine: Role of system-reservoir interaction. *Phys. Rev. Res.* **2021**, *3*, 023078. [CrossRef]
43. Breuer, H.-.; Burgarth, D.; Petruccione, F. Non-Markovian dynamics in a spin star system: Exact solution and approximation techniques. *Phys. Rev. B* **2004**, *70*, 045323. [CrossRef]
44. Cucchietti, F.M.; Paz, J.P.; Zurek, W.H. Decoherence from spin environments. *Phys. Rev. A* **2005**, *72*, 052113. [CrossRef]
45. Camalet, S.; Chitra, R. Effect of random interactions in spin baths on decoherence. *Phys. Rev. B* **2007**, *75*, 094434. [CrossRef]
46. Segal, D. Two-level system in spin baths: Non-adiabatic dynamics and heat transport. *J. Chem. Phys.* **2014**, *140*, 164110. [CrossRef] [PubMed]
47. Mirza, A.R.; Zia, M.; Chaudhry, A.Z. Master equation incorporating the system-environment correlations present in the joint equilibrium state. *Phys. Rev. A* **2021**, *104*, 042205. [CrossRef]
48. Taylor, J.M.; Marcus, C.M.; Lukin, M.D. Long-Lived Memory for Mesoscopic Quantum Bits. *Phys. Rev. Lett.* **2003**, *90*, 206803. [CrossRef]
49. Wu, L.-A. Dressed qubits in nuclear spin baths. *Phys. Rev. A* **2010**, *81*, 044305. [CrossRef]
50. Jing, J.; Wu, L.-A. Decoherence and control of a qubit in spin baths: an exact master equation study. *Sci. Rep.* **2018**, *8*, 1471. [CrossRef]
51. Ivády, V. Longitudinal spin relaxation model applied to point-defect qubit systems. *Phys. Rev. B* **2020**, *101*, 155203. [CrossRef]
52. Kwiatkowski, D.; Szańkowski, P.; Cywiński, Ł. Influence of nuclear spin polarization on the spin-echo signal of an NV-center qubit. *Phys. Rev. B* **2020**, *101*, 155412. [CrossRef]
53. Vaccaro, J.A.; Barnett, S.M. Information erasure without an energy cost. *Proc. R. Soc. A* **2011**, *467*, 1770. [CrossRef]
54. Croucher, T.; Vaccaro, J.A. Thermodynamics of memory erasure via a spin reservoir. *Phys. Rev. E* **2021**, *103*, 042140. [CrossRef] [PubMed]

Article

Quantum Non-Markovian Environment-to-System Backflows of Information: Nonoperational vs. Operational Approaches

Adrián A. Budini [1,2]

[1] Consejo Nacional de Investigaciones Científicas y Técnicas (CONICET), Centro Atómico Bariloche, Avenida E. Bustillo Km 9.5, Bariloche 8400, Argentina
[2] Universidad Tecnológica Nacional (UTN-FRBA), Fanny Newbery 111, Bariloche 8400, Argentina

Abstract: Quantum memory effects can be qualitatively understood as a consequence of an environment-to-system backflow of information. Here, we analyze and compare how this concept is interpreted and implemented in different approaches to quantum non-Markovianity. We study a nonoperational approach, defined by the distinguishability between two system states characterized by different initial conditions, and an operational approach, which is defined by the correlation between different outcomes associated to successive measurement processes performed over the system of interest. The differences, limitations, and vantages of each approach are characterized in detail by considering diverse system–environment models and dynamics. As a specific example, we study a non-Markovian depolarizing map induced by the interaction of the system of interest with an environment characterized by incoherent and coherent self-dynamics.

Keywords: open quantum systems; quantum non-Markovianity

Citation: Budini, A.A. Quantum Non-Markovian Environment-to-System Backflows of Information: Nonoperational vs. Operational Approaches. *Entropy* **2022**, *24*, 649. https://doi.org/10.3390/e24050649

Academic Editors: Bassano Vacchini, Andrea Smirne and Nina Megier

Received: 7 March 2022
Accepted: 29 April 2022
Published: 5 May 2022

Publisher's Note: MDPI stays neutral with regard to jurisdictional claims in published maps and institutional affiliations.

Copyright: © 2022 by the author. Licensee MDPI, Basel, Switzerland. This article is an open access article distributed under the terms and conditions of the Creative Commons Attribution (CC BY) license (https://creativecommons.org/licenses/by/4.0/).

1. Introduction

The time-evolution of both classical and quantum systems may develop memory effects [1–4]. Nevertheless, the characterization and definition of these effects is quite different in both regimes [5–7]. As is well known, in a classical regime memory effects can be rigorously defined in a probabilistic approach. The independence or dependence of conditional probabilities on the previous system history define, respectively, the (memoryless) Markovian and non-Markovian regimes [1].

In a quantum regime, one is immediately confronted with an extra aspect. In fact, the state of a quantum system (and consequently its history) can only be determined by performing a measurement process, which intrinsically implies a perturbation to its (originally unperturbed) dynamics. Therefore, the definition of memory effects and quantum non-Markovianity can be tackled from two intrinsically different approaches. In *nonoperational approaches*, memory effects are defined by taking solely into account the properties of the unperturbed open system dynamics (its propagator). In *operational approaches*, memory effects are defined by the statistical properties of different outcomes associated to system measurement processes and transformations (such as unitary ones).

A wide variety of measures and memory witnesses have been utilized in the context of nonoperational approaches (see reviews [5–7]). The first proposals correspond to deviations of the system propagator from divisibility [8,9] and a nonmonotonous behavior of the trace distance (TD) between two distinct system states [10,11]. In this context, memory effects were associated to an *environment-to-system backflow of information*: information stored in the initial system state is transferred to the environmental degrees of freedom; their influence on the system at later times implies a backflow of information that leads to memory effects. In spite of this clear and well-motivated interpretation [12–14], the precise assessment of this concept is still under debate [15–23].

The basic idea of operational approaches is to appeal to the standard definition of memory effects in terms of probabilities [1]. Hence, the (quantum) system must be subjected to a set of measurement processes such that their statistical properties determine the presence or absence of memory effects [24–27]. The study and understanding of this approach was performed in the recent literature [28–34], including alternative definitions and analysis of information flows [35,36].

The main goal of this paper is to analyze and to compare how the concept of environment-to-system backflow of information is interpreted and implemented in operational and nonoperational approaches. As a nonoperational memory witness, we take the TD between two different systems' initial states [10,11], also taking into account the bounds on its revival behavior that have been characterized recently [22,23]. As an operational memory witness, we consider a conditional past–future (CPF) correlation [26,27], both in deterministic and random schemes [36]. The comparison is performed by considering different system–environment models and analyzing in each case the information flows from the two perspectives. We consider statistical mixtures of Markovian system evolutions and systems coupled to incoherent [16] and coherent casual bystander environments [37], which are characterized by a self-dynamics that is independent of the system degrees of freedom. In addition, we consider (standard) unitary system–environment models [2]. As a specific model, we study a depolarizing map induced by the interaction of a system with a finite set of incoherent degrees of freedom. In this regime, as well as in a quantum coherent one, we explain how and why both approaches lead to different notions of quantum non-Markovianity and environment-to-system backflows of information.

The paper is outlined as follows. In Section 2 we review the definition and main properties of the considered nonoperational [10,11,22,23] and operational [26,27,36] approaches. In Section 3 we study both approaches by considering different system–environment models. In Section 4, we study the depolarizing map. In Section 5, we provide the conclusions.

2. Quantum Non-Markovianity

Here, we briefly review the main characteristics of the different approaches to quantum non-Markovianity.

2.1. Nonoperational Approach

If the open system is not affected or perturbed during its evolution, the unique object that allows defining the presence or absence of memory effects is its (unperturbed) density matrix propagator. The rigorous theory of quantum dynamical semigroups [38] motivate associating the (memoryless) quantum Markovian regime with propagators whose time-evolution obey a Lindblad equation (or Gorini–Kossakowski–Sudarshan–Lindblad equation). Consequently, any (scalar) measure or property that quantifies departures of the system propagator from a Lindblad equation can be taken as a witness of quantum memory effects.

Lindblad equations lead to completely positive propagators between two arbitrary times [38]. As is well known, completely positive transformations lead to very specific contractive properties for different distance measures and entropic quantities [39]. For example, the TD between two arbitrary density matrices ρ and σ, defined as $\mathbf{D}(\rho, \sigma) \equiv (1/2)\mathrm{Tr}|\rho - \sigma|$, under a completely positive transformation Φ, fulfills the inequality $\mathbf{D}(\Phi[\rho], \Phi[\sigma]) \leq \mathbf{D}(\rho, \sigma)$. Consequently, it is possible to *define* quantum Markovianity by the condition [10,11]

$$\mathbf{D}(\rho^s_{t+\tau}, \sigma^s_{t+\tau}) \leq \mathbf{D}(\rho^s_t, \sigma^s_t), \tag{1}$$

where ρ^s_t and σ^s_t are two arbitrary evolved system states that differ in their initial conditions, $\rho^s_0 \neq \sigma^s_0$. Alternatively, one can interpret that quantum memory effects are present whenever this inequality is not fulfilled for a set of two arbitrary time intervals $t \geq 0$ and $\tau > 0$.

In spite of the simplicity and efficacy of the previous theoretical frame, in general, it is not possible to know or infer which physical processes are involved when the contractive condition (1) is not fulfilled. A remarkable advance in this direction was recently obtained in Refs. [22,23] by establishing the inequality

$$\mathbf{D}(\rho^s_{t+\tau}, \sigma^s_{t+\tau}) \leq \mathbf{D}(\rho^s_t, \sigma^s_t) + \mathbf{D}(\rho^e_t, \sigma^e_t) \qquad (2)$$
$$+ \mathbf{D}(\rho^{se}_t, \rho^s_t \otimes \rho^e_t) + \mathbf{D}(\sigma^{se}_t, \sigma^s_t \otimes \sigma^e_t).$$

Here, ρ^{se}_t and σ^{se}_t are the evolved system–environment states with initial conditions $\rho^{se}_0 = \rho^s_0 \otimes \rho^e_0$ and $\sigma^{se}_0 = \sigma^s_0 \otimes \sigma^e_0$. As usual, the system and bath states follow from partial trace operations, $\rho^s_t = \mathrm{Tr}_e[\rho^{se}_t]$ and $\rho^e_t = \mathrm{Tr}_s[\rho^{se}_t]$. The asymmetry between system and environment ($s \leftrightarrow e$) is introduced by taking in both cases the same initial environmental state, $\rho^e_0 = \sigma^e_0$.

The result (2) only relies on the triangle inequality fulfilled by the TD. Thus, it is valid for arbitrary system–environment models. In addition, this expression allows to bounding the environment-to-system backflow of information *defined* by the "revivals"

$$\mathbf{D}(\rho^s_{t+\tau}, \sigma^s_{t+\tau}) - \mathbf{D}(\rho^s_t, \sigma^s_t) > 0. \qquad (3)$$

The remaining (bounding) contributions in the rhs of Equation (2) have a *clear physical interpretation*. One can relate the contribution $\mathbf{D}(\rho^e_t, \sigma^e_t)$ to changes in the environmental state, while the terms $\mathbf{D}(\rho^{se}_t, \rho^s_t \otimes \rho^e_t) + \mathbf{D}(\sigma^{se}_t, \sigma^s_t \otimes \sigma^e_t)$ measure the correlations established between the system and the environment [22,23]. Nevertheless, it is important to realize that these physical processes do not guarantee the developing of revivals. The right conclusion is that *given* that there exists revivals, their origin can related to changes in the environmental state or to the establishing of system–environment correlations.

It was also proven that the inequality (2) remains valid when the TD is replaced by a telescopic relative entropy and the square root of a quantum Jensen–Shannon divergence [22,23]. Thus, the interpretation of the bounds remains the same when using these entropic quantities.

2.2. Operational Approach

In a probabilistic frame, given a sequence of system states $x \to y \to z$ with joint probability $P(z, y, x)$, Markovianity is defined by the condition

$$P(z, y, x) = P(z|y)P(y|x)P(x), \qquad (4)$$

where $P(b|a)$ denotes in general the conditional probability of b given a. By Bayes rule, the equality (4) implies the (memoryless) condition $P(z|y, x) = P(z|y)$. Similar constraints emerge when considering higher joint probabilities involving an arbitrary number of events [1].

For quantum systems, the definition of Markovianity in terms of probabilities unavoidably implies performing a set of system measurement processes. In Refs. [24,25], by means of a process tensor formalism, the Markovian condition is taken into account for arbitrary (higher order) joint probabilities. Nevertheless, for *quantum* systems coupled to standard environment models (standard classical noises and/or unitary system–environment interaction models), only three measurement events are enough for detecting departures from a (probabilistic) Markovian regime [26,27]. In such a case, the condition (4) can be conveniently rewritten as a CPF independence,

$$P(z, x|y) = P(z|y)P(x|y). \qquad (5)$$

This result follows straightforwardly by using $P(z, x|y) = P(z, y, x)/P(y)$, where $P(y) = \sum_{z,x} P(z, y, x)$.

The CPF independence (5) implies that any (conditional) correlation between past and future events witnesses memory effects. Correspondingly, a CPF correlation is defined as [26,27]

$$C_{pf}(t, \tau)|_{\breve{y}} \stackrel{d/r}{=} \sum_{z,x} zx[P(z, x|\breve{y}) - P(z|\breve{y})P(x|\breve{y})], \qquad (6)$$

where $\{x\}$ and $\{z\}$ are the (past and future) measurement outcomes. The time dependence (t,τ) emerges because the past, present, and future measurements are performed at the initial time $t=0$, at time t, and $t+\tau$, respectively. Evidently, $C_{pf}(t,\tau)|_{\check{y}}$ vanishes in a (probabilistic) Markovian regime (Equation (5)).

In Equation (6), the change $y \to \check{y}$ was introduced, which is stretchy related with the definition of memory effects and information flows in this approach. Two different measurement schemes are necessary [36]. In a deterministic scheme (denoted with the supra d), after the intermediate measurement (whose outcome defines the conditional property) no change is introduced. Hence, $\check{y} = y$. In a random scheme (denoted with the supra r), after the intermediate measurement, the system state is randomly chosen ($y \to \check{y}$) over the set of possible states associated to the outcomes $\{y\}$. The CPF correlation is defined with this renewed conditional state.

In the deterministic scheme, the CPF correlation $[C_{pf}(t,\tau)|_{\check{y}} \stackrel{d}{\neq} 0]$ detects memory effects (departures with respect to Equation (4), or equivalently, Equation (5)) independently of the specific system–environment model. In the random scheme, a nonvanishing CPF correlation $[C_{pf}(t,\tau)|_{\check{y}} \stackrel{r}{\neq} 0]$, by *definition*, detects the presence of environment-to-system backflows of information (or bidirectional system–environment information flows). This relation is motivated by the complementary case $C_{pf}(t,\tau)|_{\check{y}} \stackrel{r}{=} 0$ that applies when the environment (which induces the memory effects $C_{pf}(t,\tau)|_{\check{y}} \stackrel{d}{\neq} 0$) is unperturbed by its coupling with the system [36].

The previous characteristics of the deterministic and random schemes can be easily understood from the properties of projective measurements performed over bipartite systems [37]. Interestingly, the formalism remains the same and is also valid for purely (classically) incoherent system–environment arrangements.

2.3. Bipartite Propagator vs. Single Propagator

Before comparing both approaches (next section), here, we clarify which dynamical objects determine each one. In the nonoperational approach, the presence of memory effects (TD revivals defined by Equation (3)) can be determined after knowing solely the system (single) propagator. In contrast, for determining the bound defined by Equation (2), it is necessary to know the bipartite system–environment propagator specified for a given initial bath state.

In contrast, the operational approach can only be characterized by knowing (exact or approximate) the bipartite propagator for different initial bath states (the initial one and the bath state after the intermediate measurement). As a matter of fact, the CPF correlation (6) can be written as a function of the joint probability $P(z,\check{y},x)$. Assuming that the three measurements are projective ones, in the deterministic scheme it reads [36]

$$\frac{P(z,\check{y},x)}{P(x)} \stackrel{d}{=} \mathrm{Tr}_{se}(E_z \mathcal{G}^{se}_{t+\tau,t}[\rho_{\check{y}} \otimes \mathrm{Tr}_s(E_{\check{y}} \mathcal{G}^{se}_{t,0}[\rho^{se}_x])]), \tag{7}$$

while in the random scheme it is [36]

$$\frac{P(z,\check{y},x)}{P(x)} \stackrel{r}{=} \mathrm{Tr}_{se}(E_z \mathcal{G}^{se}_{t+\tau,t}[\rho_{\check{y}} \otimes \mathrm{Tr}_s(\mathcal{G}^{se}_{t,0}[\rho^{se}_x])]) \wp(\check{y}|x). \tag{8}$$

In these expressions, $\mathcal{G}^{se}_{t+\tau,t}$ is the *bipartite propagator* between t and $t+\tau$. In addition, $E_m \equiv |m\rangle\langle m|$ and $\rho_m \equiv |m\rangle\langle m|$ $[m=z,\check{y},x]$ represent the (positive) effect measurement operators and postmeasurement states, respectively. The sets $\{|m\rangle\}$ $[m=z,\check{y},x]$ are the eigenstates of each measured observable. Furthermore, $\rho^{se}_x \equiv \rho_x \otimes \rho^e_0$ and $P(x) = \langle x|\rho^s_0|x\rangle$. The random scheme is parameterized by an arbitrary conditional probability $\wp(\check{y}|x)$ that defines the change in the system state ($y \to \check{y}$) after the intermediate measurement.

The different dependence of both approaches on the bipartite propagator leads to strong different conclusions about memory effects and information flows, which are analyzed in the next section.

3. Comparing Both Approaches

In order to perform a systematic comparison we consider different system–environment models and approximations. In general, we assume that the bipartite system–environment state ρ_t^{se} evolves as

$$\frac{d}{dt}\rho_t^{se} = (\mathcal{L}_s + \mathcal{L}_e + \mathcal{L}_{se})[\rho_t^{se}], \tag{9}$$

where $\mathcal{L}_s$ and $\mathcal{L}_e$ define the self-dynamics of the system and the environment, respectively, while $\mathcal{L}_{se}$ defines their mutual interaction. This interaction term may be unitary or include dissipative couplings.

3.1. Born–Markov Approximation

For systems weakly coupled to their environments, the Born–Markov approximation [2] allows to write the bipartite state as

$$\rho_t^{se} \simeq \rho_t^s \otimes \rho_0^e, \tag{10}$$

where ρ_t^s is the system state, while ρ_0^e is the (almost) unperturbed environment state.

When this approximation is valid, in the *nonoperational approach*, it is simple to check that Equation (2) reduces to Equation (1). In fact, $\mathbf{D}(\rho_t^e, \sigma_t^e) = \mathbf{D}(\rho_t^{se}, \rho_t^s \otimes \rho_t^e) = \mathbf{D}(\sigma_t^{se}, \sigma_t^s \otimes \sigma_t^e) = 0$. Furthermore, ρ_t^s can be well approximated by a Lindblad equation, which guarantees the absence of any revival in $\mathbf{D}(\rho_t^s, \sigma_t^s)$. Thus, the dynamics is Markovian.

In the *operational approach*, by introducing the approximation (10) into Equations (7) and (8) straightforwardly, it follows that $C_{pf}(t,\tau)|_y \stackrel{d/r}{=} 0$ (Equation (6)). These results are independent of which observables are measured. Thus, the dynamics is Markovian.

In this case (Equation (10)), both approaches coincide. Strong differences appear in the cases studied below.

3.2. Casual Bystander Environments

A wide class of "non-Markovian" dynamics can be derived by assuming that the system interacts with a "casual bystander" environment. These baths are defined by the independence of their marginal states $\rho_t^e = \text{Tr}_s[\rho_t^{se}]$ of any degree of freedom of the system. Alternatively, the time evolution of ρ_t^e can be written in the environment Hilbert space without involving any operator or state of the system. These properties must be valid for arbitrary system and environment (separable) initial conditions.

For fulfilling the previous properties, the interaction term $\mathcal{L}_{se}$ in the general evolution (9) must be restricted such that

$$\text{Tr}_s(\mathcal{L}_{se}[\rho_t^{se}]) = \mathcal{A}[\rho_t^e], \tag{11}$$

where $\mathcal{A}$ is an arbitrary superoperator acting on ρ_t^e that does not have any dependence on the system degrees of freedom. In general, this constraint can only be satisfied by dissipative (nonunitary) system–environment couplings. On the other hand, the bath dynamics can be quantum [37] or a classical (incoherent) one [16].

In the *nonoperational approach*, the independence of the environment state on the system degrees of freedom cannot be translated to any restriction on the inequality defined by Equation (2). In fact, under the constraint (11), the TD may or not present revivals, *property that can only be cheeked for each specific model*. Thus, some dynamics are classified as Markovian and other as non-Markovian. The unique simplification that can be introduced is to assume that the environment state does not evolve in time, $\rho_t^e = \rho_0^e$, that is, the environment begins in its stationary state. In this case, Equation (2) reduces to

$$\mathbf{D}(\rho_{t+\tau}^s, \sigma_{t+\tau}^s) - \mathbf{D}(\rho_t^s, \sigma_t^s) \leq \mathbf{D}(\rho_t^{se}, \rho_t^s \otimes \rho_0^e) \\ + \mathbf{D}(\sigma_t^{se}, \sigma_t^s \otimes \rho_0^e). \quad (12)$$

Even in this case ($\rho_t^e = \rho_0^e$), the TD may or may not present revivals, that is, depending on the model, the system may be classified as Markovian or non-Markovian.

In Equation (12), any environment-to-system backflow of information can be related to the establishing of the correlations $\mathbf{D}(\rho_t^{se}, \rho_t^s \otimes \rho_0^e) + \mathbf{D}(\sigma_t^{se}, \sigma_t^s \otimes \rho_0^e)$. Certainly, the system–environment correlations (always) changes in time. Nevertheless, even when there are no revivals in the TD system–environment, correlations are established. This feature represents a central problem for the interpretation of this approach. In addition, here, the environment state is completely independent of the system (and even of time). Thus, the revivals of the TD must be taken as a (mathematical) model-dependent property whose origin cannot be related to any physical process that implies a *physical* transfer of information from the environment to the system.

A different perspective emerges in the *operational approach*. By using the independence of the environment state $[\rho_t^e = \mathrm{Tr}_s(\rho_t^{se})]$ of any degree of freedom of the system, it is possible to check that the joint probability (7) of the deterministic scheme *does not fulfill* the Markov property (4). In contrast, it is simple to check that the joint probability (8) of the random scheme *fulfills* the Markov property (4). Consequently, a casual bystander environment leads to the CPF correlations (Equation (6))

$$C_{pf}(t,\tau)|_{\tilde{y}} \stackrel{d}{\neq} 0, \qquad C_{pf}(t,\tau)|_{\tilde{y}} \stackrel{r}{=} 0. \quad (13)$$

In this approach, the property $C_{pf}(t,\tau)|_{\tilde{y}} \stackrel{d}{\neq} 0$, valid for any model under the constraint (11), implies that the system dynamics is non-Markovian. Its origin can be related to the establishing of (arbitrary) system–environment correlations. On the other hand, the property $C_{pf}(t,\tau)|_{\tilde{y}} \stackrel{r}{=} 0$, which is valid for arbitrary measurement processes and specific models, is read as the *absence* of bidirectional system–environment information flows. In fact, given that the environment is characterized by a self-dynamics that is completely independent of the system, any environment-to-system backflow of information (as detected in the nonoperational approach) does not rely on any physical process that affects the environment state or its dynamics.

The meaning of the previous analysis is clarified by specifying different bipartite models that fulfill the evolution (9) and the constraint (11).

3.2.1. Classical Mixture of Quantum Markovian Dynamics

Given a set of *different* system Lindblad superoperators $\{\mathcal{L}_s^c\}$, which may include both unitary and dissipative contributions, and given a set of normalized positive weights $\{p_c\}$, $\sum_c p_c = 1$, a classical statistical mixture of Markovian dynamics is defined by the bipartite state

$$\rho_t^{se} = \sum_c \exp(t\mathcal{L}_s^c)[\rho_0^s] \otimes p_c |c\rangle\langle c|. \quad (14)$$

Here, $\{|c\rangle\langle c|\}$ is a set of projectors associated to the environment space. The marginal system and environment states read

$$\rho_t^s = \sum_c p_c \exp(t\mathcal{L}_s^c)[\rho_0^s], \qquad \rho_t^e = \sum_c p_c |c\rangle\langle c|. \quad (15)$$

Memory effects in this kind of non-Markovian system dynamics have been explored in the literature [40–44]. Notice that the environment does not have any dynamics. Even more, the system dynamics can be performed by mixing in a random way (with weight p_c) each of the evolved Markovian system states $\exp(t\mathcal{L}_s^c)[\rho_0^s]$. Thus, the detection of an environment-to-system backflow of information via Equation (3) seems to have a formal mathematical interpretation rather than a physical one. On the other hand, in the operational approach, this case is characterized by Equation (13), which guarantees the presence of memory effects $C_{pf}(t,\tau)|_{\tilde{y}} \stackrel{d}{\neq} 0$ but not any bidirectional information flow, $C_{pf}(t,\tau)|_{\tilde{y}} \stackrel{r}{=} 0$.

3.2.2. Interaction with Stochastic Classical Degrees of Freedom

When the system interacts with stochastic classical degrees of freedom, the bipartite state can be written as

$$\rho_t^{se} = \sum_c \rho_t^c \otimes p_c(t)|c\rangle\langle c|. \tag{16}$$

In contrast to the previous case (Equation (14)), the weights $\{p_c(t)\}$ are time-dependent and the evolution of the states $\{\rho_t^c\}$ may involve coupling between all of them. In fact, under the constraint (11), the more general evolution can be written as [16]

$$\frac{d\tilde{\rho}_t^c}{dt} = \mathcal{L}_s^c[\tilde{\rho}_t^c] - \sum_{c'} \gamma_{c'c} \tilde{\rho}_t^c + \sum_{c'} \gamma_{cc'} \mathbb{S}_{cc'}[\tilde{\rho}_t^{c'}]. \tag{17}$$

Here, $\tilde{\rho}_t^c \equiv p_c(t)\rho_t^c$. Thus, $p_c(t) = \text{Tr}_s(\tilde{\rho}_t^c)$. Furthermore, $\{\mathbb{S}_{cc'}\}$ are arbitrarily completely positive system transformations, which are trace preserving $\text{Tr}_s(\mathbb{S}_{cc'}[\rho]) = \text{Tr}_s(\rho)$. Consequently, the environment probabilities $\{p_c(t)\}$ obey a classical master equation

$$\frac{dp_c(t)}{dt} = -\sum_{c'} \gamma_{c'c} p_c(t) + \sum_{c'} \gamma_{cc'} p_{c'}(t), \tag{18}$$

which in turn shows the role played by the coupling rates $\{\gamma_{c'c}\}$. In contrast, the system dynamics depart from a Markovian (Lindblad) evolution. From some specific models, it is possible to recover some phenomenological non-Markovian master equations (see, for example, [45–47]).

In the nonoperational approach, it is very difficult to predict if a given dynamics (Equation (16)) leads or not to revivals in the TD. If the incoherent degrees of freedom begin in their stationary state, $p_c(0) = \lim_{t\to\infty} p_c(t)$, one is confronted with the bounds defined by Equation (12). Even in this case, one cannot predict when there exists or not an environment-to-system backflow of information.

Interestingly, the origin of the contributions $\mathbf{D}(\rho_t^{se}, \rho_t^s \otimes \rho_0^e) + \mathbf{D}(\sigma_t^{se}, \sigma_t^s \otimes \rho_0^e)$ in Equation (12) (or in general in Equation (2)) can be easily read from the evolution (17). In fact, this equation shows that the system evolution is *totally conditioned* to the environment dynamics. The contributions $\mathcal{L}_s^c$ are "active" whenever the environment is in the state $|c\rangle\langle c|$. Furthermore, the system suffers the transformation $\rho \to \mathbb{S}_{c'c}[\rho]$ whenever the environment "jumps" between the states $c \to c'$. This is the physical mechanism that leads to the system–environment correlations, which in turn does not imply any system-dependent change in the environment state or dynamics. Thus, the interpretation of revivals in the TD as environment-to-system backflow of information is again controversial.

Independently of the Lindblad contributions $\{\mathcal{L}_s^c\}$, the superoperators $\{\mathbb{S}_{cc'}\}$, and rates $\{\gamma_{c'c}\}$, the operational approach is characterized by Equation (13), that is, the dynamics is non-Markovian $[C_{pf}(t,\tau)|_{\tilde{y}} \stackrel{d}{\neq} 0]$ without the development of any bidirectional system–environment information flow $[C_{pf}(t,\tau)|_{\tilde{y}} \stackrel{r}{=} 0]$.

3.2.3. Environmental Quantum Degrees of Freedom

The condition Equation (11) can be satisfied even when the environment is a quantum one, that is, it develops coherent behaviors. In this case, the bipartite state can be written as

$$\rho_t^{se} = \sum \rho_t^c \otimes p_c(t)|c_t\rangle\langle c_t|. \tag{19}$$

In contrast to Equation (16), due to the quantum nature of the environment, the projectors $\{|c_t\rangle\langle c_t|\}$ are time-dependent. In fact, they define the base in which the environment density matrix ρ_t^e is diagonal. The more general bipartite evolution (9) under the constraint (11), in its diagonal representation, is given by [37]

$$\frac{d}{dt}\rho_t^{se} = (\mathcal{L}_s + \mathcal{L}_e)[\rho_t^{se}] + \sum_\alpha \Gamma_\alpha\, B_\alpha \mathbb{S}_\alpha[\rho_t^{se}] B_\alpha^\dagger$$
$$-\frac{1}{2}\sum_\alpha \Gamma_\alpha \{B_\alpha^\dagger B_\alpha, \rho_t^{se}\}_+, \qquad (20)$$

where $\{\cdot,\cdot\}_+$ is an anticommutator operation. Furthermore, $\{B_\alpha\}$ are arbitrary environment operators, while $\mathbb{S}_\alpha$ are completely positive trace-preserving system superoperators. The rates $\{\Gamma_\alpha\}$ set the environment dynamics. In fact,

$$\frac{d}{dt}\rho_t^e = \mathcal{L}_e[\rho_t^e] + \sum_\alpha \Gamma_\alpha \left(B_\alpha \rho_t^e B_\alpha^\dagger - \frac{1}{2}\{B_\alpha^\dagger B_\alpha, \rho_t^e\}_+ \right), \qquad (21)$$

which is a Lindblad dynamics completely independent of the system degrees of freedom. These evolutions recover, as particular cases, some phenomenological collisional models introduced in the literature (see, for example, [48–50]).

The physical interpretation of the evolution (20) is quite similar to that of Equation (17). In fact, here, the application of the system superoperators $\mathbb{S}_\alpha$ occurs whenever the environment suffers a transition associated to the operators B_α. This (unidirectional) mechanism defines how the system–environment correlations are built up.

In the nonoperational approach, even when the environment begins in its stationary state $\rho_0^e = \lim_{t\to\infty} \rho_t^e$ (where ρ_t^e obeys Equation (21)), it is not possible to infer for an arbitrary model the presence or absence of revivals in the TD (Equation (3)). In contrast, the operational approach is still characterized by Equation (13).

3.3. Unitary System–Environment Interactions

Independently of the specific models, the correlation between the system and the casual bystander environments introduced previously does not involve quantum entanglement [51] (see the separable states Equations (14), (16) and (19)). In contrast, quantum entanglement may emerge when considering Hamiltonian (time-reversible) system–environment interactions. In fact, solely for special system–environment initial conditions, a bipartite unitary dynamics does not induce quantum entanglement [52–54].

The total Hamiltonian is written as

$$H_T = H_s + H_e + H_I. \qquad (22)$$

Each contribution corresponds to the system, environment, and interaction Hamiltonians, respectively. The bipartite propagator is

$$\mathcal{G}_{t,t_0}^{se}[\bullet] = \exp[-i(t-t_0)H_T] \bullet \exp[+i(t-t_0)H_T]. \qquad (23)$$

In the *nonoperational approach*, each contribution in the rhs of Equation (2) makes complete sense in this context. In fact, almost all unitary interactions lead to a change in the environment state and also induce the development of (arbitrary) system–environment correlations. When revivals in the TD develop, Equation (2) defines a bound with a clear physical meaning. Nevertheless, in general, it is not possible to infer which kind of dynamics develop or do not develop revivals in the TD. Even for a given (Hamiltonian) model, depending on the underlying parameters, the system dynamics may be Markovian or not. Consequently, it is not clear which physical property defines the boundary between Markovian and non-Markovian dynamics.

In the *operational approach*, given that the state and dynamics of the environment are in general modified by a unitary interaction, instead of Equation (13), here, it follows

$$C_{pf}(t,\tau)|_{\tilde{y}} \stackrel{d}{\neq} 0, \qquad C_{pf}(t,\tau)|_{\tilde{y}} \stackrel{r}{\neq} 0. \tag{24}$$

Both inequalities can be supported by performing a perturbation theory based on projector techniques [31]. Consistently, it has been shown that even close to the validity of a Born–Markov approximation, the operational approach can detect memory effects [34].

The inequality $C_{pf}(t,\tau)|_{\tilde{y}} \stackrel{d}{\neq} 0$ implies that the system dynamics is non-Markovian (system–environment correlations are developed during the evolution), while $C_{pf}(t,\tau)|_{\tilde{y}} \stackrel{r}{\neq} 0$ detects the presence of bidirectional information flows. In fact, here, the environment state and evolution always depend on the system degrees of freedom.

There exists a unique exception to Equation (24), which reduces to Equation (13). Hence, even when the environment state is modified, for any system observables, one obtains $C_{pf}(t,\tau)|_{\tilde{y}} \stackrel{r}{=} 0$. While this property is certainly *undesirable*, this case has a clear physical interpretation. It emerges when, in a given environmental base $\{|e\rangle\}$, the diagonal part of the bipartite propagator (23) can be written as

$$\langle e|\mathcal{G}^{se}_{t,0}[\bullet]|e\rangle = \mathcal{T}^{(e)}_{t,0}\langle e|\bullet|e\rangle, \tag{25}$$

where $\mathcal{T}^{(e)}_{t,0}$ is a *system* (density matrix) propagator that parametrically depends on each environmental state $\{|e\rangle\}$. The condition (25) is fulfilled, *for example*, when the environment and interaction Hamiltonians commutate

$$[H_e, H_I] = 0. \tag{26}$$

Introducing the condition (25) into Equations (7) and (8), it is possible to check that $C_{pf}(t,\tau)|_{\tilde{y}} \stackrel{d}{\neq} 0$, and $C_{pf}(t,\tau)|_{\tilde{y}} \stackrel{r}{=} 0$. This last equality *does not imply* that the environment in not affected. It emerges because the system state assumes the structure

$$\rho^s_t = \text{Tr}_e(\mathcal{G}^{se}_{t,0}[\rho^s_0 \otimes \rho^e_0]) = \sum_e \langle e|\rho^e_0|e\rangle \mathcal{T}^{(e)}_{t,0}[\rho^s_0]. \tag{27}$$

Therefore, the system evolution can be written as a statistical superposition of unitary maps, quite similar to Equation (15). Consequently, for unitary system–environment models, the condition $C_{pf}(t,\tau)|_{\tilde{y}} \stackrel{r}{=} 0$ allows to detect when the system dynamics (even between measurements) can be represented by a *Hamiltonian ensemble*, a property that has been of interest in the recent literature [55].

4. Example

In this section, we consider an explicit example of the dynamics discussed previously. The quantum system (s), taken for simplicity as a two-level system, interacts with an incoherent environment (e) (see Section 3.2.2), which here is defined by four discrete states, denoted as $\{|1\rangle, |2\rangle, |3\rangle, |4\rangle\}$. Correspondingly, the bipartite system–environment state is written as

$$\rho^{se}_t = \sum_{k=1,2,3,4} \tilde{\rho}_k(t) \otimes |k\rangle\langle k|. \tag{28}$$

The system and environment states then read

$$\rho^s_t = \sum_{k=1,2,3,4} \tilde{\rho}_k(t), \qquad \rho^e_t = \sum_{k=1,2,3,4} p_k(t)|k\rangle\langle k|, \tag{29}$$

where $p_k(t) = \text{Tr}_s[\tilde{\rho}_k(t)]$. The evolution of the unnormalized system states $\{\tilde{\rho}_k(t)\}_{k=1}^{k=4}$ is taken as

$$\frac{d\tilde{\rho}_4(t)}{dt} = -\gamma\tilde{\rho}_4(t) + \phi \sum_{k=1,2,3} \sigma_k \tilde{\rho}_k(t) \sigma_k, \tag{30a}$$

$$\frac{d\tilde{\rho}_k(t)}{dt} = -\phi\tilde{\rho}_k(t) + \left(\frac{\gamma}{3}\right) \sigma_k \tilde{\rho}_4(t) \sigma_k, \quad k = 1,2,3. \tag{30b}$$

In this expression, γ and ϕ are characteristic coupling rates. Furthermore, the set of Pauli matrices is denoted as $(\sigma_x, \sigma_y, \sigma_z, I) \leftrightarrow (\sigma_1, \sigma_2, \sigma_3, \sigma_4)$, where I is the identity matrix in the two-dimensional system Hilbert space. From Equations (30a) and (30b), the evolution of the environment populations is defined by the following classical master equation

$$\frac{dp_4(t)}{dt} = -\gamma p_4(t) + \phi \sum_{k=1,2,3} p_k(t), \tag{31a}$$

$$\frac{dp_k(t)}{dt} = -\phi p_k(t) + \left(\frac{\gamma}{3}\right) p_4(t), \quad k = 1,2,3. \tag{31b}$$

This equation is completely independent of the system degrees of freedom. Thus, the evolution ((30a) and (30b)) has a simple interpretation. When the environment suffers the transition $|4\rangle \xrightarrow{\gamma/3} |k\rangle$ or the transition $|k\rangle \xrightarrow{\phi} |4\rangle$ ($k = 1,2,3$), the transformation $\sigma_k \bullet \sigma_k$ is *conditionally* applied over the open quantum system.

Equations (30a) and (30b) can be solved after specifying the bipartite initial conditions. We consider a separable state, $\rho_0^{se} = \rho_0^s \otimes \rho_0^e$, which implies $\tilde{\rho}_k(0) = \rho_0^s p_k(0)$. In general, each auxiliary state $\tilde{\rho}_k(t)$ can be written as a superposition of the Pauli channels acting on the initial system state ρ_0^s, that is,

$$\tilde{\rho}_k(t) = \sum_{j=1,2,3,4} g_k^j(t) \sigma_j \rho_0^s \sigma_j, \tag{32}$$

where $\{g_k^j(t)\}$ are (sixteen) scalar functions that depend on time. Their initial conditions are $g_k^4(0) = p_k(0)$ and $g_k^j(0) = 0$, with $j = 1,2,3$, and $k = 1,2,3,4$. The evolution of the set $\{g_k^j(t)\}$ follows after inserting the previous expression for $\tilde{\rho}_k(t)$ into Equations (30a) and (30b). Consistent with their definition, $p_k(t) = \text{Tr}_s[\tilde{\rho}_k(t)]$, the environment populations are recovered as

$$p_k(t) = \sum_{j=1,2,3,4} g_k^j(t). \tag{33}$$

4.1. Depolarizing Dynamics

The evolution of the auxiliary states Equations (30a) and (30b) is (structurally) the same for the states $\{\tilde{\rho}_1(t), \tilde{\rho}_2(t), \tilde{\rho}_3(t)\}$. Thus, if we consider environment initial conditions where $p_1(0) = p_2(0) = p_3(0)$, from Equations (29) and (32), it follows that the solution map $\rho_0^s \to \rho_t^s$ must be a depolarizing channel [39], that is,

$$\rho_t^s = w(t)\rho_0^s + \frac{1-w(t)}{3} \sum_{k=1,2,3} \sigma_k \rho_0^s \sigma_k, \tag{34}$$

where the positive weight $w(t)$, from Equation (32), follows as

$$w(t) = \sum_{k=1,2,3,4} g_k^4(t). \tag{35}$$

Consistently, $[1 - w(t)]/3 = \sum_{k=1,2,3,4} g_k^j(t)$, with $j = 1, 2, 3$.

The more natural initial conditions for the environment are their stationary populations $p_k^\infty \equiv \lim_{t\to\infty} p_k(t)$, where $p_k(t)$ is defined by Equations (31a) and (31b). Straightforwardly, we obtain

$$p_4^\infty = \frac{\phi}{\gamma+\phi}, \qquad p_k^\infty = \frac{1}{3}\frac{\gamma}{\gamma+\phi} \qquad (k=1,2,3). \tag{36}$$

Under the assumption $p_k(0) = p_k^\infty$, after obtaining the set $\{g_k^j(t)\}$ in an explicit analytical way, the function $w(t)$ that characterizes the depolarizing channel Equation (34) can be written as

$$w(t) = \frac{(\gamma^2+3\phi^2)}{3(\gamma+\phi)^2} + \frac{4\gamma\phi}{3(\gamma+\phi)^2}e^{-(\gamma+\phi)t} + \frac{2\gamma}{3(\gamma+\phi)}e^{-\phi t}, \tag{37}$$

which consistently satisfies $w(0) = 1$. Furthermore, $\lim_{t\to\infty} w(t) \neq 0$. On the hand, the environment dynamics is stationary, that is, $p_k(t) = p_k(0) = p_k^\infty$ (Equation (36)).

4.2. Operational vs. Nonoperational Quantum Non-Markovianity

In the *nonoperational approach*, quantum non-Markovianity is defined by the revivals in the trace distance between two different initial states, Equation (3). By using that $(I/2) = (\rho + \sum_{k=1,2,3}\sigma_k\rho\sigma_k)/4$ [39], the depolarizing map (34) can be rewritten as $\rho_t^s = w(t)\rho_0^s + (1/3)[1 - w(t)](2I - \rho_0^s)$. Thus, the trace distance straightforwardly can be written as

$$D[\rho_t^s, \sigma_t^s] = \left|\frac{4w(t)-1}{3}\right| D[\rho_0^s, \sigma_0^s] \equiv d(t) D[\rho_0^s, \sigma_0^s] \tag{38}$$

where $D[\rho_0^s, \sigma_0^s]$ is the trace distance between the two initial states ρ_0^s and σ_0^s. Notice that the decay of the trace distance does not depend on the initial states, being dictated by the function $d(t)$.

In Figure 1a, we plot the function $d(t)$ for different values of the characteristic parameter ϕ/γ. As expected from Equation (37), $D[\rho_t^s, \sigma_t^s]$ decays in a monotonous way without developing any revival. Thus, under the trace distance criteria, the dynamics is *Markovian*, and there is not any environment-to-system backflow of information. Nevertheless, notice that for any value of ϕ/γ, system–environment correlations are built up during the dynamics [see Equation (28)]. This feature, which is irrelevant for the TD decay behavior, is relevant for the CPF correlation.

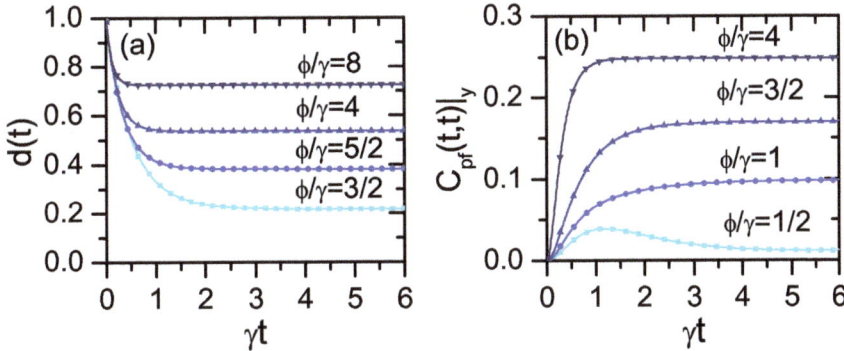

Figure 1. (a) Decay of the trace distance $d(t)$ (Equation (38)) corresponding to the model ((31a) and (31b)). (b) Time dependence of the CPF correlation $C_{pf}(t,t)|_{\bar{y}}$ in the deterministic scheme [56] corresponding to the same model. The value of the quotient ϕ/γ is indicated in each plot.

In the *operational approach*, the presence of memory effects is witnessed by the CPF correlation (Equation (6)) in the deterministic scheme. We assume that the three measurements are projective ones, all of them being performed in the z-direction of the Bloch sphere. Furthermore, the initial condition of the system is taken as $\rho_0^s = |\psi\rangle\langle\psi|$, where $|\psi\rangle$ is an eigenstate of the x-Pauli matrix. Explicit general expression for $C_{pf}(t,\tau)|_{\bar{y}}$ in terms of the coefficients $\{g_k^j(t)\}$ can be found in Ref. [57] (see corresponding Appendix D). Under the previous assumptions, the CPF correlation can be obtained in an analytical way, which is written in [56]. Simple expressions are obtained for specific values of the decay rates. For example, for $\phi = \gamma$, it follows

$$C_{pf}(t,\tau)|_{\tilde{y}} \stackrel{d}{=} \frac{4}{81}(1 - e^{-\gamma t})(1 - e^{-\gamma \tau}) \qquad (39)$$
$$\times (2 + e^{-\gamma t} + e^{-\gamma \tau} + 5e^{-\gamma(t+\tau)}).$$

Due to the symmetry of the problem, in all cases $C_{pf}(t,\tau)|_{\tilde{y}}$ does not depend on the value of the conditional $\tilde{y} = \pm 1$.

In Figure 1b, we plot the CPF correlation at equal times $C_{pf}(t,t)|_{\tilde{y}}$ for different values of ϕ/γ. In contrast to the nonoperational approach, here, for all possible values of the characteristic parameter ϕ/γ it is fulfilled $C_{pf}(t,\tau)|_{\tilde{y}} \stackrel{d}{\neq} 0$, which indicates a *non-Markovian* regime. In fact, the system is strongly correlated with the environment (Equation (28)).

The system–environment correlations emerge due to a unidirectional dependence of the system dynamics on the environment transitions (Equations (30a) and (30b)). In fact, the environment populations do not depend on the system degrees of freedom (see Equations (31a) and (31b)). These properties are relevant in the random scheme and imply that $C_{pf}(t,\tau)|_{\tilde{y}} \stackrel{r}{=} 0$ (Equation (13)). This result is valid for arbitrary measurement processes, indicating in the operational approach the absence of any environment-to-system backflow of information.

4.3. Environment-to-System Backflow of Information

In the previous section, we concluded that both approaches differ in the classification of the dynamics (Markovian vs. non-Markovian), but (due to different reasons) agree in the absence of any environment-to-system backflow of information. Here, we show that in general, both approaches also differ in this last aspect. Different mechanisms can be proposed for obtaining a revival in the trace distance Equation (38).

4.3.1. Slow Modulation of the Stationary Environment State

First, we consider the same model (Equations (30a) and (30b)), but in addition, it is assumed that the characteristic rates are time-dependent, $\gamma \to \gamma(t)$, $\phi \to \phi(t)$, with

$$\gamma(t) = \gamma[1 + b(t)] > 0, \quad \phi(t) = \phi[1 - b(t)] > 0. \qquad (40)$$

Here, $b(t)$ is an arbitrary function of time that fulfills the constraint $-1 < b(t) < 1$. The previous structure is chosen for simplifying the argument and calculus. Nevertheless, we remark that similar dependences can be implemented in different experimental situations (see for example Ref. [58]). The more relevant aspect is that the assumption (40) can be implemented by affecting solely the environmental degrees of freedom (see Equations (31a) and (31b)).

In addition, in Equation (40), it is assumed that

$$\left|\frac{d}{dt}b(t)\right| \ll \gamma, \quad \left|\frac{d}{dt}b(t)\right| \ll \phi. \qquad (41)$$

Hence, the time dependence of $b(t)$ can be considered slow with respect to the decay times $(1/\gamma)$ and $(1/\phi)$. Consequently, the full dynamics can be described in an adiabatic approximation, where the full bipartite system in the long time regime ($\gamma t \gg 1$, $\phi t \gg 1$) rapidly adjusts to the instantaneous values of $\gamma(t)$ and $\phi(t)$. In particular, in this regime, the environment populations from Equation (36) can be written as

$$p_4^\infty(t) \simeq \frac{\phi}{\gamma + \phi}[1 - b(t)], \quad p_k^\infty(t) \simeq \frac{1}{3}\frac{\gamma}{\gamma + \phi}[1 + b(t)], \qquad (42)$$

where $k = 1, 2, 3$. For simplicity, we assumed that $(\gamma - \phi) \ll (\gamma + \phi)$, which allows to approximate $\gamma(t) + \phi(t) = (\gamma + \phi) + b(t)(\gamma - \phi) \simeq (\gamma + \phi)$.

In the long time regime, the *nonoperational approach* is characterized by the value $\lim_{t\to\infty} w(t) \neq 0$ (see Equations (37) and (38)). For time-independent rates, this quantity can be written in terms of the stationary populations $\{p_k^\infty\}_{k=1}^{k=4}$ (Equation (36)) as $\lim_{t\to\infty} w(t) = [p_4^\infty]^2 + \sum_{k=1,2,3}[p_k^\infty]^2$. Given that in the slow modulation regime (Equation (41)) these values become time dependent, $p_k^\infty \longrightarrow p_k^\infty(t)$ (Equation (42)), it follows that

$$w(t) \stackrel{slow}{\simeq} [p_4^\infty(t)]^2 + \sum_{k=1,2,3}[p_k^\infty(t)]^2, \quad \gamma t \gg 1, \ \phi t \gg 1. \tag{43}$$

Therefore, under the previous hypothesis, the stationary values of the TD in Figure 1a [$d(t) = |4w(t) - 1|/3$] become proportional to the arbitrary function $b(t)$. This result implies that one can obtain *arbitrary revivals in the trace distance* (Equation (38)) by choosing different time dependences of the function $b(t)$. Alternatively, an *arbitrary environment-to-system backflow of information can be produced* by changing solely in a slow way the ("stationary") environment populations. Nevertheless, we remark that the full dynamics is essentially the same as in the static-rate case. While one can associate the revivals in the TD to the system–environment correlations, these correlations have the same origin and structure as in the absence of revivals, such as in Figure 1a (static case) and when $b(t)$ does not lead to revivals.

In the deterministic scheme, the *operational approach* is characterized by the stationary value [56]

$$\lim_{\substack{t\to\infty \\ \tau\to\infty}} C_{pf}(t,\tau)|_{\bar{y}} \stackrel{d}{=} \frac{8\gamma(\gamma - 3\phi)^2(\gamma + 3\phi)}{81(\gamma + \phi)^4}, \tag{44}$$

which can also be written in terms of $\{p_k^\infty\}_{k=1}^{k=4}$ (Equation (36)). Thus, under the same conditions that guarantee the slow modulation regime (Equations (41) and (42)), the stationary values of $C_{pf}(t,t)|_{\bar{y}}$ plotted in Figure 1b also become proportional to the function $b(t)$. Nevertheless, in this approach, this property does not imply the presence of any backflow of information. In fact, given that the environment state does not depend at all on the system degrees of freedom, even in the slow modulation regime, it follows that $C_{pf}(t,\tau)|_{\bar{y}} \stackrel{r}{=} 0$ (Equation (13)). In this way, it is clear that both the nonoperational and operational approaches also strongly disagree in this aspect.

4.3.2. Quantum Coherent Contributions in the Environment Dynamics

The system–environment dynamics associated to the depolarizing channel (Equations (30a) and (30b)) can alternatively be represented through a Lindblad equation. In fact, the evolution of the bipartite state ρ_t^{se} can be written as

$$\begin{aligned}
\frac{d\rho_t^{se}}{dt} &= +\frac{\gamma}{3}\sum_{k=1,2,3}(B_k\sigma_k[\rho_t^{se}]\sigma_k B_k^\dagger - \frac{1}{2}\{B_k^\dagger B_k, \rho_t^{se}\}_+) \\
&\quad + \phi \sum_{k=1,2,3}(B_k^\dagger \sigma_k[\rho_t^{se}]\sigma_k B_k - \frac{1}{2}\{B_k B_k^\dagger, \rho_t^{se}\}_+) \\
&\quad - i[H_e, \rho_t^{se}],
\end{aligned} \tag{45}$$

where the bath operators are $B_k \equiv |k\rangle\langle 4|$, $k = 1, 2, 3$. As before, $\{|1\rangle, |2\rangle, |3\rangle, |4\rangle\}$ are the environment base. Defining the states $\tilde{\rho}_k \equiv \langle k|\rho_t^{se}|k\rangle$, it is simple to check that the first two lines of the previous Lindblad dynamics recover the time evolution introduced in Equations (30a) and (30b).

From Equation (45), it is simple to check that the bath state ($\rho_t^e = \text{Tr}_s[\rho_t^{se}]$) obeys a Lindblad equation that, even with the extra contribution $-i[H_e, \rho_t^{se}]$, is independent of the system degrees of freedom. Thus, the environment is still a casual bystander one (see Equations (20) and (21)). In order to obtain a (system) depolarizing channel (Equation (34)), the symmetry between the bath states $\{|1\rangle, |2\rangle, |3\rangle\}$ must be granted. For example, the Hamiltonian

$$H_e = \frac{\Omega}{2} \sum_{k=1,2,3} (|k\rangle\langle 4| + |4\rangle\langle k|) \tag{46}$$

fulfills this property.

In consistence with the solution defined by Equations (28) and (32), here, the bipartite state is written as
$$\rho_t^{se} = \sum_{k=1,2,3,4} (\sigma_k \rho_0^s \sigma_k) \otimes \varrho_t^k, \qquad (47)$$
where $\{\varrho_t^k\}$ are states in the environment Hilbert space. In order to obtain analytically treatable solutions, we assume the bipartite initial condition
$$\rho_0^{se} = \rho_0^s \otimes \rho_0^e = \rho_0^s \otimes |4\rangle\langle 4|. \qquad (48)$$
Under this assumption ($\rho_0^e = |4\rangle\langle 4|$), given that the underlying system stochastic dynamics associated to Equation (45) is the same as in the incoherent case (Equation (30)), it follows that the system state goes back to the initial condition ρ_0^s whenever the environment goes back to the state $|4\rangle$. This property straightforwardly follows from $\sigma_k^2 = I$. Therefore, under the assumption (48), here, the depolarizing map Equation (34) is defined with the function
$$w(t) = \mathrm{Tr}_e[\varrho_t^4] = \langle 4|\rho_t^e|4\rangle, \qquad (49)$$
where ρ_t^e is the density matrix of the environment. Consistently, $[1 - w(t)]/3 = \mathrm{Tr}_e[\varrho_t^k] = \langle k|\rho_t^e|k\rangle$, with $k = 1, 2, 3$. Consequently, the decay of the trace distance is proportional to the bath population $\langle 4|\rho_t^e|4\rangle$. Its explicit analytical expression is rather complex and noninformative [59].

In this alternative situation, it is clear that H_e induces intrinsic quantum coherent oscillations in the environment dynamics, which in turn may lead to oscillations in the trace distance (Equation (38)). In Figure 2, we plot the TD decay $d(t) = |4w(t) - 1|/3$ taking $\phi = \gamma$ and for different values of Ω/γ. When $\Omega/\gamma < 1$, a monotonous decay is observed. Nevertheless, for $\Omega/\gamma > 1$, *revivals* in the TD are observed.

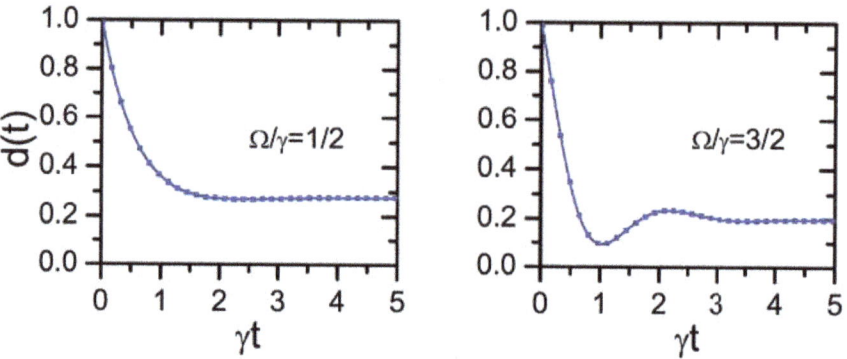

Figure 2. Decay of the trace distance $d(t)$ (Equations (38) and (49)) corresponding to the model (45) with $\phi = \gamma$ for different values of the Hamiltonian frequency Ω/γ.

The CPF correlation in the deterministic scheme cannot be calculated in an analytical way. Nevertheless, given that the system dynamics is still controlled by the environment (self) transitions, it follows that $C_{pf}(t,\tau)|_{\bar{y}} \overset{d}{\neq} 0$. Thus, the dynamics become non-Markovian in both approaches ($\Omega/\gamma > 1$). Nevertheless, given that the environment is a casual bystander one, in the random scheme it is valid that $C_{pf}(t,\tau)|_{\bar{y}} \overset{r}{=} 0$ (Equation (13)) for any value of Ω/γ. Consequently, in the same way as in the previous model (Equation (40)), the nonoperational and operational approaches give different results about the presence of environment-to-system backflows of information.

5. Summary and Conclusions

The interpretation of quantum memory effects in terms of an environment-to-system backflow of information is still under vivid debate. In this contribution, we presented a partial view of this problem by comparing how this concept is introduced and interpreted in nonoperational and operational approaches to quantum non-Markovianity.

Our main contribution is a comparison between both formalisms for different environment models. We considered casual bystander environments, which are characterized by a density matrix that does not depend on the system degrees of freedom. This class covers classical statistical mixtures of Markovian dynamics (Equation (14)), interactions with stochastic classical degrees of freedom (Equation (16)), and environmental quantum degrees of freedom (Equation (19)). In addition, we considered unitary system–environment models (Equation (22)).

As a nonoperational approach, we used the TD between two system states with different initial conditions. This formalism is characterized by the bound Equation (2). We have argued that, in general, it is not possible to predict if for a given model the TD presents or does not present revivals in its time behavior. This property is valid for all environmental models. In the case of casual bystander ones, the previous feature represents an obstacle for giving a consistent physical interpretation of any environment-to-system backflow of information defined as revivals in the TD (Equation (3)). In fact, for these dynamics, the system–environment correlations emerge due to the unidirectional dependence of the system dynamics in the state of the environment and its transitions. In particular, for stationary environments, it is not possible to know when the system–environment correlations lead to the presence or absence of backflows of information. The possibility of obtaining monotonous decay behaviors of the TD for unitary interaction models also represents an undesirable property because, in general, the environment state is modified by its interaction with the system.

As an operational approach, we used a CPF correlation (Equation (6)), which is defined by three consecutive system measurement processes. Both deterministic and random schemes were considered (with associated joint probabilities Equations (7) and (8)). In the case of casual bystander environments, the CPF correlation in the deterministic scheme does not vanish, while in the random scheme it vanishes identically for any chosen measurement observables (Equation (13)). Thus, in this approach, any casual bystander environment leads to a non-Markovian system dynamics but not any bidirectional information flow is detected. In the case of Hamiltonian models, in general, in both schemes the CPF correlation does not vanish, indicating non-Markovian system dynamics and the presence of bidirectional information flows (Equation (24)). An undesirable exception to this last property emerges when the system dynamics can equivalently be represented by a random unitary map (Equations (25) and (27)).

As a specific example, we considered a system coupled to an environment able to induce depolarizing dynamics (Equations (30a), (30b), (40) and (45)). We found that both approaches differ in the Markovian and non-Markovian regimes, as well in the presence or absence of environment-to-system backflows of information.

In general, both operational and nonoperational approaches to quantum non-Markovianity provide necessary and complementary points of view for defining and understanding memory effects in open quantum systems. The present results shed light on some conceptual differences and properties of these approaches. They may be useful for extending the application of these formalisms for the understanding of memory effects induced by structured or spatially extended environments.

Funding: This research received no external funding.

Institutional Review Board Statement: Not applicable.

Informed Consent Statement: Not applicable.

Data Availability Statement: Not applicable.

Acknowledgments: This paper was supported by Consejo Nacional de Investigaciones Científicas y Técnicas (CONICET), Argentina.

Conflicts of Interest: The author declares no conflict of interest.

References and Notes

1. van Kampen, N.G. *Stochastic Processes in Physics and Chemistry*; North-Holland: Amsterdam, The Netherlands, 1992.
2. Breuer, H.P.; Petruccione, F. *The Theory of Open Quantum Systems*; Oxford University Press: Oxford, UK, 2002.
3. de Vega, I.; Alonso, D. Dynamics of non-Markovian open quantum systems. *Rev. Mod. Phys.* **2017**, *89*, 015001. [CrossRef]
4. Li, L.; Hall, M.J.W.; Wiseman, H.M. Concepts of quantum non-Markovianity: A hierarchy. *Phys. Rep.* **2018**, *759*, 1–51. [CrossRef]
5. Breuer, H.P.; Laine, E.M.; Piilo, J.; Vacchini, V. Colloquium: Non-Markovian dynamics in open quantum systems. *Rev. Mod. Phys.* **2016**, *88*, 021002. [CrossRef]
6. Breuer, H.P. Foundations and measures of quantum non-Markovianity. *J. Phys. B* **2012**, *45*, 154001. [CrossRef]
7. Rivas, A.; Huelga, S.F.; Plenio, M.B. Quantum non-Markovianity: Characterization, quantification and detection. *Rep. Prog. Phys.* **2014**, *77*, 094001. [CrossRef]
8. Wolf, M.M.; Eisert, J.; Cubitt, T.S.; Cirac, J.I. Assessing Non-Markovian Quantum Dynamics. *Phys. Rev. Lett.* **2008**, *101*, 150402. [CrossRef]
9. Rivas, A.; Huelga, S.F.; Plenio, M.B. Entanglement and Non-Markovianity of Quantum Evolutions. *Phys. Rev. Lett.* **2010**, *105*, 050403. [CrossRef]
10. Breuer, H.P.; Laine, E.M.; Piilo, J. Measure for the Degree of Non-Markovian Behavior of Quantum Processes in Open Systems. *Phys. Rev. Lett.* **2009**, *103*, 210401. [CrossRef]
11. Laine, E.M.; Piilo, J.; Breuer, H. Measure for the non-Markovianity of quantum processes. *Phys. Rev. A* **2010**, *81*, 062115. [CrossRef]
12. Guarnieri, G.; Uchiyama, C.; Vacchini, B. Energy backflow and non-Markovian dynamics. *Phys. Rev. A* **2016**, *93*, 012118. [CrossRef]
13. Guarnieri, G.; Nokkala, J.; Schmidt, R.; Maniscalco, S.; Vacchini, B. Energy backflow in strongly coupled non-Markovian continuous-variable systems. *Phys. Rev. A* **2016**, *94*, 062101. [CrossRef]
14. Schmidt, R.; Maniscalco, S.; Ala-Nissila, T. Heat flux and information backflow in cold environments. *Phys. Rev. A* **2016**, *94*, 010101. [CrossRef]
15. Megier, N.; Chruściński, D.; Piilo, J.; Strunz, W.T. Eternal non-Markovianity: From random unitary to Markov chain realisations. *Sci. Rep.* **2017**, *7*, 6379. [CrossRef] [PubMed]
16. Budini, A.A. Maximally non-Markovian quantum dynamics without environment-to-system backflow of information. *Phys. Rev. A* **2018**, *97*, 052133. [CrossRef]
17. Wudarski, F.A.; Petruccione, F. Exchange of information between system and environment: Facts and myths. *Euro Phys. Lett.* **2016**, *113*, 50001. [CrossRef]
18. Breuer, H.P.; Amato, G.; Vacchini, B. Mixing-induced quantum non-Markovianity and information flow. *New J. Phys.* **2018**, *20*, 043007. [CrossRef]
19. De Santis, D.; Johansson, M. Equivalence between non-Markovian dynamics and correlation backflows. *New J. Phys.* **2020**, *22*, 093034. [CrossRef]
20. De Santis, D.; Johansson, M.; Bylicka, B.; Bernardes, N.K.; Acín, A. Witnessing non-Markovian dynamics through correlations. *Phys. Rev. A* **2020**, *102*, 012214. [CrossRef]
21. Banacki, M.; Marciniak, M.; Horodecki, K.; Horodecki, P. Information backflow may not indicate quantum memory. *arXiv* 2008, arXiv:2008.12638.
22. Megier, N.; Smirne, A.; Vacchini, B. Entropic Bounds on Information Backflow. *Phys. Rev. Lett.* **2021**, *127*, 030401. [CrossRef]
23. Campbell, S.; Popovic, M.; Tamascelli, D.; Vacchini, B. Precursors of non-Markovianity. *New J. Phys.* **2019**, *21*, 053036. [CrossRef]
24. Pollock, F.A.; Rodríguez-Rosario, C.; Frauenheim, T.; Paternostro, M.; Modi, K. Operational Markov Condition for Quantum Processes. *Phys. Rev. Lett.* **2018**, *120*, 040405. [CrossRef] [PubMed]
25. Pollock, F.A.; Rodríguez-Rosario, C.; Frauenheim, T.; Paternostro, M.; Modi, K. Non-Markovian quantum processes: Complete framework and efficient characterization. *Phys. Rev. A* **2018**, *97*, 012127. [CrossRef]
26. Budini, A.A. Quantum Non-Markovian Processes Break Conditional Past-Future Independence. *Phys. Rev. Lett.* **2018**, *121*, 240401. [CrossRef] [PubMed]
27. Budini, A.A. Conditional past-future correlation induced by non-Markovian dephasing reservoirs. *Phys. Rev. A* **2019**, *99*, 052125. [CrossRef]

28. Taranto, P.; Pollock, F.A.; Milz, S.; Tomamichel, M.; Modi, K. Quantum Markov Order. *Phys. Rev. Lett.* **2019**, *122*, 140401. [CrossRef]
29. Taranto, P.; Milz, S.; Pollock, F.A.; Modi, K. Structure of quantum stochastic processes with finite Markov order. *Phys. Rev. A* **2019**, *99*, 042108. [CrossRef]
30. Jørgensen, M.R.; Pollock, F.A. Exploiting the Causal Tensor Network Structure of Quantum Processes to Efficiently Simulate Non-Markovian Path Integrals. *Phys. Rev. Lett.* **2019**, *123*, 240602. [CrossRef]
31. Bonifacio, M.; Budini, A.A. Perturbation theory for operational quantum non-Markovianity. *Phys. Rev. A* **2020**, *102*, 022216. [CrossRef]
32. Han, L.; Zou, J.; Li, H.; Shao, B. Non-Markovianity of A Central Spin Interacting with a Lipkin–Meshkov–Glick Bath via a Conditional Past–Future Correlation. *Entropy* **2020**, *22*, 895. [CrossRef]
33. Ban, M. Operational non-Markovianity in a statistical mixture of two environments. *Phys. Lett. A* **2021**, *397*, 127246. [CrossRef]
34. de Lima Silva, T.; Walborn, S.P.; Santos, M.F.; Aguilar, G.H.; Budini, A.A. Detection of quantum non-Markovianity close to the Born-Markov approximation. *Phys. Rev. A* **2020**, *101*, 042120. [CrossRef]
35. Hsieh, Y.-Y.; Su, Z.-Y.; Goan, H.-S. Non-Markovianity, information backflow, and system–environment correlation for open-quantum-system processes. *Phys. Rev. A* **2019**, *100*, 012120. [CrossRef]
36. Budini, A.A. Detection of bidirectional system–environment information exchanges. *Phys. Rev. A* **2021**, *103*, 012221. [CrossRef]
37. Budini, A.A. Quantum non-Markovian "casual bystander" environments. *Phys. Rev. A* **2021**, *104*, 062216. [CrossRef]
38. Alicki, R.; Lendi, K. *Quantum Dynamical Semigroups and Applications*; Springer: Berlin/Heidelberg, Germany, 2007.
39. Nielsen, M.A.; Chuang, I.L. *Quantum Computation and Quantum Information*; Cambridge University Press: Cambridge, UK, 2000.
40. Chruscinski, D.; Wudarski, F.A. Non-Markovian random unitary qubit dynamics. *Phys. Lett. A* **2013**, *377*, 1425. [CrossRef]
41. Non-Markovianity degree for random unitary evolution. *Phys. Rev. A* **2015**, *91*, 012104. [CrossRef]
42. Wudarski, F.A.; Nalezyty, P.; Sarbicki, G.; Chruscinski, D. Admissible memory kernels for random unitary qubit evolution. *Phys. Rev. A* **2015**, *91*, 042105. [CrossRef]
43. Wudarski, F.A.; Chruscinski, D. Markovian semigroup from non-Markovian evolutions. *Phys. Rev. A* **2016**, *93*, 042120. [CrossRef]
44. Siudzinska, K.; Chruscinski, D. Memory kernel approach to generalized Pauli channels: Markovian, semi-Markov, and beyond. *Phys. Rev. A* **2017**, *96*, 022129. [CrossRef]
45. Sutherland, C.; Brun, T.A.; Lidar, D.A. Non-Markovianity of the post-Markovian master equation. *Phys. Rev. A* **2018**, *98*, 042119. [CrossRef]
46. Shabani, A.; Lidar, D.A. Completely positive post-Markovian master equation via a measurement approach. *Phys. Rev. A* **2005**, *71*, 020101. [CrossRef]
47. Budini, A.A. Post-Markovian quantum master equations from classical environment fluctuations. *Phys. Rev. E* **2014**, *89*, 012147. [CrossRef]
48. Vacchini, B. Non-Markovian master equations from piecewise dynamics. *Phys. Rev. A* **2013**, *87*, 030101. [CrossRef]
49. Budini, A.A. Embedding non-Markovian quantum collisional models into bipartite Markovian dynamics. *Phys. Rev. A* **2013**, *88*, 032115. [CrossRef]
50. Budini, A.A.; Grigolini, P. Non-Markovian nonstationary completely positive open-quantum-system dynamics. *Phys. Rev. A* **2009**, *80*, 022103. [CrossRef]
51. Horodecki, R.; Horodecki, P.; Horodecki, M.; Horodecki, K. Quantum entanglement. *Rev. Mod. Phys.* **2009**, *81*, 865. [CrossRef]
52. Roszak, K.; Cywiński, Ł. Characterization and measurement of qubit-environment-entanglement generation during pure dephasing. *Phys. Rev. A* **2015**, *92*, 032310. [CrossRef]
53. Roszak, K.; Cywiński, Ł. Equivalence of qubit-environment entanglement and discord generation via pure dephasing interactions and the resulting consequences. *Phys. Rev. A* **2018**, *97*, 012306. [CrossRef]
54. Roszak, K. Criteria for system–environment entanglement generation for systems of any size in pure-dephasing evolutions. *Phys. Rev. A* **2018**, *98*, 052344. [CrossRef]
55. Chen, H.-B.; Gneiting, C.; Lo, P.-Y.; Chen, Y.-N.; Nori, F. Simulating Open Quantum Systems with Hamiltonian Ensembles and the Nonclassicality of the Dynamics. *Phys. Rev. Lett.* **2018**, *120*, 030403. [CrossRef] [PubMed]
56. $C_{pf}(t,\tau)|_{\tilde{y}} \stackrel{d}{=} \frac{8}{81(\gamma+\phi)^4} e^{-2t\gamma-\tau\gamma-3t\phi-2\tau\phi}\gamma\,((-2e^{(t+\tau)(\gamma+2\phi)}(\gamma-3\phi)^2\phi - 2e^{2t\gamma+3t\phi+\tau\phi}(\gamma-3\phi)^2\phi - e^{2t\gamma+\tau\gamma+3t\phi+\tau\phi}(\gamma-3\phi)^2(\gamma+\phi) - e^{2t(\gamma+\phi)+\tau(\gamma+2\phi)}(\gamma-3\phi)^2(\gamma+\phi) - 16e^{\tau\phi+2t(\gamma+\phi)}\gamma\phi(\gamma+\phi) - 16e^{\tau(\gamma+\phi)+t(\gamma+2\phi)}\gamma\phi(\gamma+\phi) + e^{2t\gamma+\tau\gamma+3t\phi+2\tau\phi}(\gamma-3\phi)^2(\gamma+3\phi)) + e^{(2t+\tau)(\gamma+\phi)}(\gamma+\phi)^2(\gamma+9\phi) + 2e^{t\gamma+2t\phi+\tau\phi}\phi(9\gamma^2+2\gamma\phi+9\phi^2))$.
57. Budini, A.A.; Garrahan, J.P. Solvable class of non-Markovian quantum multipartite dynamics. *Phys. Rev. A* **2021**, *104*, 032206. [CrossRef]
58. Schuler, S.; Speck, T.; Tietz, C.; Wrachtrup, J.; Seifert, U. Experimental Test of the Fluctuation Theorem for a Driven Two-Level System with Time-Dependent Rates. *Phys. Rev. Lett.* **2005**, *94*, 180602. [CrossRef] [PubMed]
59. In the Laplace domain, $f(u) = \int_0^\infty dt\, e^{-ut} f(t)$, it reads $\langle 4|\rho_u^e|4\rangle = A(u)/B(u)$, where $A(u) = \gamma(u+\phi)(2u+\gamma+\phi) + (3(u+\phi)+2\gamma)\Omega^2$ and $B(u) = 3u(u+\phi)(u+\gamma+\phi)(2u+\gamma+\phi) + 6u(3(u+\phi)+\gamma)\Omega^2$.

Article

Disentanglement Dynamics in Nonequilibrium Environments

Mingli Chen, Haonan Chen, Tao Han and Xiangji Cai *

School of Science, Shandong Jianzhu University, Jinan 250101, China
* Correspondence: xiangjicai@foxmail.com

Abstract: We theoretically study the non-Markovian disentanglement dynamics of a two-qubit system coupled to nonequilibrium environments with nonstationary and non-Markovian random telegraph noise statistical properties. The reduced density matrix of the two-qubit system can be expressed as the Kraus representation in terms of the tensor products of the single qubit Kraus operators. We derive the relation between the entanglement and nonlocality of the two-qubit system which are both closely associated with the decoherence function. We identify the threshold values of the decoherence function to ensure the existences of the concurrence and nonlocal quantum correlations for an arbitrary evolution time when the two-qubit system is initially prepared in the composite Bell states and the Werner states, respectively. It is shown that the environmental nonequilibrium feature can suppress the disentanglement dynamics and reduce the entanglement revivals in non-Markovian dynamics regime. In addition, the environmental nonequilibrium feature can enhance the nonlocality of the two-qubit system. Moreover, the entanglement sudden death and rebirth phenomena and the transition between quantum and classical nonlocalities closely depend on the parameters of the initial states and the environmental parameters in nonequilibrium environments.

Keywords: open quantum system; decoherence; disentanglement

Citation: Chen, M.; Chen, H.; Han, T.; Cai, X. Disentanglement Dynamics in Nonequilibrium Environments. *Entropy* **2022**, *24*, 1330. https://doi.org/10.3390/e24101330

Academic Editors: Bassano Vacchini, Nina Megier and Andrea Smirne

Received: 17 August 2022
Accepted: 17 September 2022
Published: 21 September 2022

Publisher's Note: MDPI stays neutral with regard to jurisdictional claims in published maps and institutional affiliations.

Copyright: © 2022 by the authors. Licensee MDPI, Basel, Switzerland. This article is an open access article distributed under the terms and conditions of the Creative Commons Attribution (CC BY) license (https://creativecommons.org/licenses/by/4.0/).

1. Introduction

Coherence and entanglement are two basic quantum features of nonclassical systems, which play vital roles in quantum mechanical community as specific resources ranging from fundamental questions to wide applications in quantum computing, quantum metrology and quantum information science [1–6]. It is known that any quantum system loses quantum features during time evolution resulting from the unavoidable couplings between the system and the environments. The loss of quantum features induced by the environments is considered as a fundamental obstacle to the construction of quantum information processors and the realization of ultrafast quantum computation. The study of decoherence and disentanglement dynamics of open quantum systems can help us further expand the understanding of the environmental effects on the dynamical evolution of the quantum systems and the real origins of the loss of quantum features and quantum-classical transition, which has potential applications in preserving quantum features against the environmental noise and in realizing quantum manipulation and control and quantum measurement [7–22].

During the last few decades, the dynamics of open quantum systems is usually investigated within Markov approximation, i.e., when we neglect the memory effect of the dynamical evolution and the higher-order environmental correlations, described by a formally solvable Lindblad type master equation. With the development of the experimental technique, it has been observed accurately that the dynamical evolution of open quantum systems is closely associated with a flow of information from the environments back into the system. For instance, the electronic energy transfer processes in photosynthesis and the dynamical decoherence in quantum bit systems exhibit strong non-Markovian behavior [23–28]. In recent decades, increasing attention has been attracted to theoretically studying the dynamics of open quantum systems beyond the framework of Markovian approximation [29–38], and there have been well established theoretical approaches to study the non-Markovian dynamics of open quantum systems within the framework of classical and quantum treatments [39–63]. Meanwhile, the coherence and entanglement revivals and entanglement sudden death and rebirth phenomena have been extensively studied theoretically and observed experimentally in the presence of the non-Markovian behavior in the quantum dynamics [64–70].

Recently, the nonequilibrium feature of the environments in many crucial dynamical processes has been experimentally observed. In these processes, the environmental initial states caused by the interaction with the quantum systems cannot become stationary in time, which corresponds to the environments around the quantum systems being out of equilibrium [71–74]. Random telegraph noise (RTN) is an important classical non-Gaussian noise, which has theoretically simulated the environmental influences on open quantum systems, such as single molecule fluorescence [75,76], disentanglement, decoherence and frequency modulation processes in the presence of low-frequency $1/f^\alpha$ noise [77–83]. Furthermore, the quantum dynamics that are stochastically driven by the classical fluctuating field displaying random telegraph fluctuations have been investigated experimentally [84,85]. The previous investigations usually assumed that the RTN displays stationary and Markovian properties. As a matter of fact, the stationary and Markovian assumption is only an idealization of both real internal fluctuations and external disturbances, and the real properties of the fluctuations and disturbances induced by the environments are neither stationary nor Markovian. Based on this fact, the stationary non-Markovian RTN and the nonstationary non-Markovian RTN with an exponential memory kernel have been successively put forward and discussed [86,87], and the latter has been widely used to study the relevant issues on the dynamics of open quantum systems in nonequilibrium environments [87–93]. Studying the environmental nonequilibrium effects on quantum coherence due to the significant role in the dynamical evolution of the open quantum systems has increasingly drawn much attention, and the theoretical results demonstrate that nonequilibrium environments cause the energy levels shift of the quantum system and delay the transition critical time of decoherence from classical to quantum [87,88,92,93]. To the best of our knowledge, the disentanglement dynamics in nonequilibrium environments has not been studied yet. Meanwhile, some other important physical questions arise naturally and should be further addressed: Can we find the close relations between the local decoherence and nonlocal entanglement and quantum nonlocality of open quantum systems in nonequilibrium environments? How do the environmental nonequilibrium feature influence the disentanglement dynamics and quantum nonlocality of open quantum systems? Are there the entanglement sudden death and rebirth phenomena or the transition between quantum and classical nonlocalities in nonequilibrium environments?

In this paper, we theoretically study the non-Markovian dynamics of a two-qubit system interacting with nonequilibrium environments, which display nonstationary and non-Markovian RTN statistical properties. The two-qubit system consists of two noncoupling identical single qubits independently interacting with its local nonequilibrium environment, of which the reduced density matrix can be expressed as the Kraus representation in terms of the tensor products of the single qubit Kraus operators. We derive the relations between the decoherence function and the entanglement quantified by the concurrence and the nonlocality characterized by the Bell function. We identify the threshold values of the decoherence function to ensure the existences of the concurrence and nonlocal quantum correlations at an arbitrary evolution time for the two-qubit system prepared initially in the composite Bell states and the Werner states, respectively. It is demonstrated that the environmental nonequilibrium feature can suppress both the decoherence and disentanglement dynamics and that it can reduce the coherence and entanglement revivals in non-Markovian dynamics regime. In addition, the environmental nonequilibrium feature can enhance the nonlocality of the two-qubit system. Moreover, the phenomena of entanglement sudden death and rebirth and the transition between quantum and classical nonlocalities are closely dependent on the parameters of the initial states in nonequilibrium environments.

This paper is organized as follows. In Section 2, we introduce the theoretical framework of non-Markovian disentanglement dynamics in nonequilibrium environments. We employ the non-Markovianity, concurrence and Bell function to describe the non-Markovian two-qubit disentanglement dynamics in nonequilibrium environments. In Section 3, we discuss the numerical results of the non-Markovian two noninteracting qubit disentanglement dynamics in nonequilibrium environments with nonstationary and non-Markovian RTN statistical properties. In Section 4, we present the conclusions from the present study.

2. Theoretical Framework

2.1. Non-Markovian Disentanglement Dynamics of a Two-Qubit System

We consider a two-qubit system T consisting of two noninteracting identical single qubits A and B independently interacting with its nonequilibrium environment exhibiting nonstationary and non-Markovian RTN statistical properties, respectively. The single qubit S ($S = A, B$) can be characterized as a two-level system with the states $|1\rangle$ and $|0\rangle$. The environmental effects lead to the stochastic fluctuations in the Hamiltonian of the two-qubit system as

$$H_T(t) = H_S(t) \otimes I + I \otimes H_S(t), \tag{1}$$

where I denotes the identity matrix and $H_S(t)$ is the stochastic Hamiltonian of the single qubit system S coupled to its local nonequilibrium environment E, written as

$$H_S(t) = \frac{\hbar}{2}[\omega_0 + \xi(t)]\sigma_z, \tag{2}$$

with ω_0 denoting the frequency difference of the single qubit system, $\sigma_z = |1\rangle\langle 1| - |0\rangle\langle 0|$ being the Pauli matrix in the single qubit basis $\mathscr{B}_S = \{|1\rangle, |0\rangle\}$ and the environmental noise $\xi(t)$ subject to a generalized RTN stochastic process.

Due to the fact that the two single qubits of the system do not interact with each other initially, the dynamics of the two-qubit system can be obtained from that of a singe qubit system by means of the Kraus representation [40,94]. Thus, to derive the dynamics of the two-qubit system, we first consider that of the single qubit system. Because the environmental effects lead to the stochastic fluctuations in the frequency difference between the states $|1\rangle$ and $|0\rangle$, the single qubit system undergoes pure decoherence during its dynamical evolution. By taking an average over the environmental noise $\xi(t)$, we can express the reduced density matrix of the single qubit system in the Kraus representation as

$$\rho_S(t) = \sum_{\mu=1}^{2} K_{S\mu}(t)\rho_S(0)K_{S\mu}^{\dagger}(t), \tag{3}$$

with the single qubit Kraus operators $K_{S\mu}$

$$K_{S1}(t) = \begin{pmatrix} 1 & 0 \\ 0 & e^{i\omega_0 t}F(t) \end{pmatrix}, K_{S2}(t) = \begin{pmatrix} 0 & 0 \\ 0 & \sqrt{1-|F(t)|^2} \end{pmatrix}, \tag{4}$$

where $F(t) = \langle \exp[i\int_0^t dt'\xi(t')]\rangle$ denotes the decoherence function with $\langle \cdots \rangle$ being the average taken over the environmental noise $\xi(t)$. The diagonal elements of the reduced density matrix of the single qubit system are time independent and the off diagonal elements evolve with time

$$\begin{aligned} \rho_{00}(t) &= \rho_{00}(0), \\ \rho_{11}(t) &= 1 - \rho_{00}(t), \\ \rho_{01}(t) &= \rho_{10}^*(t) = \rho_{01}(0)e^{i\omega_0 t}F(t). \end{aligned} \tag{5}$$

Because of the nonstationary statistical property of the environmental noise, the decoherence function is complex. The dynamical evolution of the single qubit system is closely associated with the decoherence rate $\gamma(t) = -\text{Re}[(d/dt)F(t)/F(t)]$ and the frequency shift $s(t) = -\text{Im}[(d/dt)F(t)/F(t)]$ [87,88].

In the presence of the standard RTN, the amplitude of the environmental noise jumps randomly with the switching rate λ between the values $\pm \nu$. The ratio ν/λ describes the environmental coupling and there are two important dynamic regimes identified: the weak coupling regime $\nu/\lambda < 1$ and the strong coupling regime $\nu/\lambda > 1$. The statistical properties of the standard RTN is time-homogeneous, Markovian and stationary. Physically, the statistical properties of the generalized RTN can be extracted from that of the standard RTN based on classical probability theory [95]. In the following, we introduce a class of time-homogeneous, non-Markovian and nonstationary RTN (see Appendix A).

For the time-homogeneous generalized RTN process, the environmental non-Markovian property is described by a generalized master equation for the time evolution of the conditional probability [86]

$$\frac{\partial}{\partial t}\mathbb{P}(\xi, t|\xi', t') = \int_{t'}^{t} K(t-\tau)\lambda \mathbb{T}\mathbb{P}(\xi, \tau|\xi', t')d\tau, \qquad (6)$$

where $K(t-\tau)$ is the memory kernel of the environmental noise, and the conditional probability $\mathbb{P}(\xi, t|\xi', t')$ and transition matrix $\mathbb{T}$ are respectively expressed as

$$\mathbb{P}(\xi, t|\xi', t') = \begin{pmatrix} P(+\nu, t|\xi', t') \\ P(-\nu, t|\xi', t') \end{pmatrix}, \mathbb{T} = \begin{pmatrix} -1 & 1 \\ 1 & -1 \end{pmatrix}. \qquad (7)$$

Physically, the extraction of a subensemble non-Markovian processes with the memory effect taken into account means that the statistical properties of the environmental noise depend on previous history. When the environmental noise is memoryless, i.e., $K(t-\tau) = \delta(t-\tau)$, the non-Markovian RTN recovers the Markovian one and its memory effect vanishes. By means of the Laplace transformation $\tilde{\mathbb{P}}(\xi, s|\xi', t') = \int_0^\infty \mathbb{P}(\xi, t|\xi', t')e^{-st}dt$, the conditional probability in Equation (6) can be analytically expressed as

$$\mathbb{P}(\xi, t|\xi', t') = \left[I + \frac{1-\mathcal{P}(t-t')}{2}\mathbb{T}\right]\mathbb{P}(\xi, t'|\xi', t'), \qquad (8)$$

where the auxiliary probability function $\mathcal{P}(t-t') = \mathscr{L}^{-1}[e^{-st'}\tilde{\mathcal{P}}(s)]$ with $\tilde{\mathcal{P}}(s) = 1/[s+2\lambda \tilde{K}(s)]$ and $\mathscr{L}^{-1}$ denotes the inverse Laplace transform. Due to the fact that the memory kernel in the conditional probability depends on the time difference, the environmental noise is subject to an homogeneous stochastic process.

The environmental nonstationary property arises from the initial distribution

$$P(\xi_0, 0) = \frac{1}{2}(1+a)\delta_{\xi_0,\nu} + \frac{1}{2}(1-a)\delta_{\xi_0,-\nu}, \qquad (9)$$

where a is the nonstationary parameter and $-1 \leq a \leq 1$. Correspondingly, the nonstationary one-point probability distribution satisfies

$$P(\xi, t) = \sum_{\xi_0} P(\xi, t|\xi_0, 0)P(\xi_0, 0) = \frac{1}{2}[1+a\mathcal{P}(t)]\delta_{\xi,\nu} + \frac{1}{2}[1-a\mathcal{P}(t)]\delta_{\xi,-\nu}. \qquad (10)$$

Physically, the extraction of a subensemble nonstatioanry processes with initial nonstationary distribution means that the statistical property of the environmental noise is time dependent initially, which corresponds to the environment being in a certain initial nonequilibrum state [95]. For the case $a = 0$, the environmental noise only displays stationary property corresponding to that the environment is in equilibrium [87,88].

According to the non-Markovian and nonstationary properties described above, the statistical characteristics of the environmental noise $\xi(t)$ are described by the first and second-order moments

$$\langle \xi(t) \rangle = a\nu \mathcal{P}(t),$$
$$\langle \xi(t)\xi(t') \rangle = \nu^2 \mathcal{P}(t-t'). \tag{11}$$

where $\mathscr{L}^{-1}$ denotes the inverse Laplace transform. According to the Bayes' theorem, the environmental higher odd- and even-order moments satisfy the factorization

$$\begin{aligned}\langle \xi(t_1)\xi(t_2)\cdots\xi(t_{2n-1})\rangle &= \langle \xi(t_1)\xi(t_2)\rangle\langle \xi(t_3)\xi(t_4)\rangle\cdots\langle \xi(t_{2n-1})\rangle \\ &= a\nu^{2n-1}\mathcal{P}(t_1-t_2)\cdots\mathcal{P}(t_{2n-1}), \\ \langle \xi(t_1)\xi(t_2)\cdots\xi(t_{2n})\rangle &= \langle \xi(t_1)\xi(t_2)\rangle\langle \xi(t_3)\xi(t_4)\rangle\cdots\langle \xi(t_{2n-1})\xi(t_{2n})\rangle \\ &= \nu^{2n}\mathcal{P}(t_1-t_2)\cdots\mathcal{P}(t_{2n-1}-t_{2n}),\end{aligned} \tag{12}$$

for the order of the time instants $t_1 > \cdots > t_{2n}$ ($n \geq 2$). This factorization relation for the higher-order correlation functions recovers to the case that the RTN process exhibits only stationary property due to the vanishing of the odd moments of the environmental noise [86,96]. It is worth mentioning that nonstationary property of the environmental noise only influences the odd-order moments due to our extraction of the subensemble time-homogeneous nonstatioanry processes made above. If the environmental noise $\xi(t)$ exhibits stationary statistical property, namely, $a = 0$, the odd-order moments in its statistical characteristics will vanish [86,96].

We consider the case that the environmental memory kernel is of an exponential form as $K(t-\tau) = \kappa e^{-\kappa(t-\tau)}$ with κ denoting the memory decay rate. The smaller is the decay rate κ, the stronger is the environmental non-Markovian property. For the case $\kappa \to +\infty$, namely, the memoryless case $K(t-\tau) = \delta(t-\tau)$, the environmental noise only exhibits Markovian property. Based on the exponential form of the memory kernel, each order moment of the environmental noise obeys the closed second-order differential relation

$$\frac{d^2}{dt^2}\langle \xi(t)\cdots\xi(t_n)\rangle + \kappa\frac{d}{dt}\langle \xi(t)\cdots\xi(t_n)\rangle + 2\kappa\lambda\langle \xi(t)\cdots\xi(t_n)\rangle = 0. \tag{13}$$

In terms of Equation (13) and the generalized Dyson expansion for the decoherence function

$$F(t) = 1 + \sum_{n=1}^{\infty} i^n \int_0^t dt_1 \cdots \int_0^{t_{n-1}} dt_n \langle \xi(t_1)\cdots\xi(t_n)\rangle, \tag{14}$$

for all the time instants $t > t_1 > \cdots > t_n > 0$, we obtain a closed third-order differential equation for the decoherence function in the single qubit system

$$\frac{d^3}{dt^3}F(t) + \kappa\frac{d^2}{dt^2}F(t) + (2\kappa\lambda + \nu^2)\frac{d}{dt}F(t) + \kappa\nu^2 F(t) = 0, \tag{15}$$

with the initial conditions $F(0) = 1$, $(d/dt)F(0) = ia\nu$ and $(d^2/dt^2)F(0) = -\nu^2$. Correspondingly, the decoherence function for the single qubit system can be exactly expressed as [88]

$$F(t) = \mathscr{L}^{-1}[\mathcal{F}(s)], \quad \mathcal{F}(s) = \frac{s^2 + \kappa s + 2\kappa\lambda + ia\nu(s+\kappa)}{s^3 + \kappa s^2 + (2\kappa\lambda + \nu^2)s + \kappa\nu^2}. \tag{16}$$

We now construct the reduced density matrix of the two-qubit system in the standard product basis $\mathscr{B}_T = \{|1\rangle = |11\rangle, |2\rangle = |10\rangle, |3\rangle = |01\rangle, |4\rangle = |00\rangle\}$. Based on the two-qubit basis and by taking an average over the environmental noise, we express the reduced density matrix of the two-qubit system in the Kraus representation as

$$\rho_T(t) = \sum_{\mu=1}^{4} K_{T\mu}(t)\rho_T(0)K_{T\mu}^{\dagger}(t), \qquad (17)$$

where the two-qubit Kraus operators $K_{T\mu}(t) = K_{S\nu}(t) \otimes K_{S\upsilon}(t)(\nu, \upsilon = 1, 2)$ are the tensor products of the single qubit Kraus operators

$$\begin{aligned}
K_{T1}(t) &= \begin{pmatrix} 1 & 0 \\ 0 & e^{i\omega_0 t}F(t) \end{pmatrix} \otimes \begin{pmatrix} 1 & 0 \\ 0 & e^{i\omega_0 t}F(t) \end{pmatrix}, \\
K_{T2}(t) &= \begin{pmatrix} 1 & 0 \\ 0 & e^{i\omega_0 t}F(t) \end{pmatrix} \otimes \begin{pmatrix} 1 & 0 \\ 0 & \sqrt{1-|F(t)|^2} \end{pmatrix}, \\
K_{T3}(t) &= \begin{pmatrix} 0 & 0 \\ 0 & \sqrt{1-|F(t)|^2} \end{pmatrix} \otimes \begin{pmatrix} 1 & 0 \\ 0 & e^{i\omega_0 t}F(t) \end{pmatrix}, \\
K_{T4}(t) &= \begin{pmatrix} 0 & 0 \\ 0 & \sqrt{1-|F(t)|^2} \end{pmatrix} \otimes \begin{pmatrix} 0 & 0 \\ 0 & \sqrt{1-|F(t)|^2} \end{pmatrix}.
\end{aligned} \qquad (18)$$

Due to the pure decoherence, the diagonal elements of the reduced density matrix are time-independent and the off-diagonal elements decay with time monotonously (Markovian behavior) or non-monotonously (non-Markovian behavior). According to the two-qubit Kraus operators expression for the reduced density matrix in Equation (17), the diagonal elements do not evolve with time

$$\begin{aligned}
\rho_{11}(t) &= \rho_{11}(0), \\
\rho_{22}(t) &= \rho_{22}(0), \\
\rho_{33}(t) &= \rho_{33}(0), \\
\rho_{44}(t) &= 1 - [\rho_{11}(0) + \rho_{22}(0) + \rho_{33}(0)],
\end{aligned} \qquad (19)$$

and time-dependent off diagonal elements can be written as

$$\begin{aligned}
\rho_{21}(t) &= \rho_{12}^*(t) = \rho_{21}(0)e^{i\omega_0 t}F(t), \\
\rho_{31}(t) &= \rho_{13}^*(t) = \rho_{31}(0)e^{i\omega_0 t}F(t), \\
\rho_{32}(t) &= \rho_{23}^*(t) = \rho_{32}(0)|F(t)|^2, \\
\rho_{41}(t) &= \rho_{14}^*(t) = \rho_{41}(0)e^{i(2\omega_0)t}F^2(t), \\
\rho_{42}(t) &= \rho_{24}^*(t) = \rho_{42}(0)e^{i\omega_0 t}F(t), \\
\rho_{43}(t) &= \rho_{34}^*(t) = \rho_{43}(0)e^{i\omega_0 t}F(t).
\end{aligned} \qquad (20)$$

By taking the optimization over all pairs of initial states, the non-Markovianity quantifying the flow of information exchange between the two-qubit system and environment can be expressed as [30,97]

$$\mathcal{N}_T = \max_{\rho_T^{1,2}(0)} \int_{\frac{d\mathcal{D}}{dt}>0} \frac{d}{dt}\mathcal{D}(\rho_T^1(t), \rho_T^2(t))dt = -2\int_{\gamma(t)<0} \gamma(t)|F(t)|^2 dt, \qquad (21)$$

where $\mathcal{D}(\rho_T^1, \rho_T^2) = \frac{1}{2}\mathrm{tr}|\rho_T^1 - \rho_T^2|$ denotes the trace distance between the two-qubit states ρ_T^1 and ρ_T^2 and the optimal pair of initial states can be chosen as the maximally entangled states of super-decoherent Bell states $|\psi_{\pm}(0)\rangle = (|00\rangle \pm |11\rangle)/\sqrt{2}$ or sub-decoherent Bell states $|\varphi_{\pm}(0)\rangle = (|01\rangle \pm |10\rangle)/\sqrt{2}$ [98,99]. The two-qubit dynamics display non-Markovian behavior if the decoherence rate $\gamma(t)$ takes negative values in some time intervals.

2.2. Relations between Local Decoherence and Nonlocal Entanglement and Quantum Nonlocality

Due to the environmental effects on its evolution, the two-qubit system undergoes dynamical disentanglement. Since the two single qubits of the system do not interact with each other, the dynamics of the two-qubit system can be obtained from that of a singe qubit system, as we derived above. Thus, the local decoherence described by the decoherence function $F(t)$ plays an important role in the dynamics of the two-qubit system as that in a single qubit system [100,101]. Can we find the close relations between the local decoherence and nonlocal entanglement and quantum nonlocality of the two-qubit sytem in nonequilibrium environments? Are there the entanglement sudden death and rebirth phenomena or the transition between quantum and classical nonlocalities of the two-qubit system in nonequilibrium environments? To further study the effects of the local decoherence on the nonlocal entanglement and quantum nonlocality of the two-qubit sytem, we use the concurrence $C(t)$ and the Clauser-Horne-Shimony-Holt (CHSH) form of Bell function $B(t)$ to quantify the entanglement and quantum nonlocality of the two-qubit system (see Appendix B), respectively [94,102,103].

In the following, we derive the relations between the decoherence function and the entanglement quantified by the concurrence and the nonlocality characterized by the Bell function for the two-qubit system initially prepared in the composite Bell states and Werner states with an X structure density matrix, respectively [104,105]. In contrast to the previous investigations [82,100] that only discussed the threshold values of the initial state parameters for the existences of the concurrence and quantum nonlocality initially, we not only discuss the initial threshold values of the state parameters but also discuss the threshold values of the decoherence function for the existences of the concurrence and quantum nonlocality at an arbitrary time t.

We first focus on the initial states of the system in the composite Bell states of the form [106]

$$\rho(0) = \frac{1+c}{2}|\psi_\pm(0)\rangle\langle\psi_\pm(0)| + \frac{1-c}{2}|\varphi_\pm(0)\rangle\langle\varphi_\pm(0)|, \tag{22}$$

where the initial state parameter c is real and satisfies $-1 \leq c \leq 1$. It has, by studying the quantum mutual information, quantum discord and classical correlations of the dynamics, which demonstrates that for the initial states in Equation (22) there is a sudden transition from classical to quantum decoherence for the two-qubit system coupled to a nonequilibrium environment exhibiting generalized RTN property, and the nonequilibrium feature of the environment can delay the critical time of the transition of decoherence from classical to quantum [92]. The concurrence at time t for the two-qubit system prepared in the initial states of Equation (22) can be reduced to

$$C(t) = \max\left\{0, \frac{1+|c|}{2}|F(t)|^2 - \frac{1-|c|}{2}\right\}. \tag{23}$$

The initial concurrence of the two-qubit system prepared in the composite Bell states in Equation (22) can be expressed as $C(0) = |c|$, since the initial value of the decoherence function satisfies $F(0) = 1$. Therefore, the entanglement of the two-qubit system exists except for the special case $c = 0$. For the case $-1 \leq c < 0$, the concurrence at time t exists if the threshold value of the decoherence function satisfies $|F(t)| > |F_{th}^C| = \sqrt{(1+c)/(1-c)}$, whereas if it exists at time t for the case $0 < c \leq 1$, the threshold value of the decoherence function satisfies $|F(t)| > |F_{th}^C| = \sqrt{(1-c)/(1+c)}$. In both Markovian and non-Markovian dynamics regimes, there are no entanglement sudden death and rebirth phenomena for the case $|c| = 1$, whereas for the case $0 < |c| < 1$, the entanglement sudden death phenomenon occurs, and in the non-Markovian dynamics regime, the entanglement rebirth phenomenon can occur if the secondary maximum of the decoherence function is larger than the threshold value $|F_{th}^C|$.

The time dependent maximum CHSH-Bell function $B(t)$ for the initial states of the two-qubit system of Equation (22) can be reduced to

$$\mathcal{B}(t) = 2\sqrt{|F(t)|^4 + c^2}. \tag{24}$$

The presence of entanglement $\mathcal{C}(t) > 0$, namely, $c \neq 0$, is a necessary condition to achieve nonlocality. The initial CHSH-Bell function $\mathcal{B}(0) = 2\sqrt{1+c^2} > 2$ corresponds to the fact that the two-qubit system always initially displays the quantum nonlocality. In a long time limit $t \to +\infty$, for the case $|c| = 1$, $\mathcal{B}(+\infty) = 2$, and thus the two-qubit system always displays quantum nonlocality. For the case $0 < |c| < 1$ the threshold value of the decoherence function should satisfy $|F(t)| > |F_{\text{th}}^{\mathcal{B}}| = \sqrt[4]{1-c^2}$ to ensure that the CHSH-Bell function $\mathcal{B}(t)$ is larger than the classical threshold $\mathcal{B}_{\text{th}}$ and the nolocality of the two-qubit system undergoes the transition from quantum to classical.

The close relation between $\mathcal{B}(t)$ and $\mathcal{C}(t)$ for the two-qubit system prepared in the initial composite Bell states of Equation (22) can be expressed as

$$\mathcal{B}(t) = \begin{cases} \frac{2}{1-c}\sqrt{[2\mathcal{C}(t)+1+c]^2 + c^2(1-c)^2}, & -1 \leq c < 0, \\ \frac{2}{1+c}\sqrt{[2\mathcal{C}(t)+1-c]^2 + c^2(1+c)^2}, & 0 < c \leq 1. \end{cases} \tag{25}$$

For the case $-1 \leq c < 0$, the classical threshold $\mathcal{C}_{\text{th}}$, which corresponds to the Bell function $\mathcal{B}(t) > \mathcal{B}_{\text{th}} = 2$ only exists for $-1 < c < 0$ and can be expressed as $\mathcal{C}_{\text{th}} = (1-c)\sqrt{1-c^2}/2 - (1+c)/2$, whereas for $c = -1$, the maximum CHSH-Bell function $\mathcal{B}(t)$ is always larger than the threshold $\mathcal{B}_{\text{th}} = 2$. Similarly, for the case $0 < c \leq 1$, the threshold $\mathcal{C}_{\text{th}}$ for the Bell function larger than the threshold $\mathcal{B}_{\text{th}} = 2$ exists for $0 < c < 1$ and can be expressed as $\mathcal{C}_{\text{th}} = (1+c)\sqrt{1-c^2}/2 - (1-c)/2$, while the maximum CHSH-Bell function $\mathcal{B}(t)$ is always larger than the threshold $\mathcal{B}_{\text{th}} = 2$ for $c = 1$.

We now focus on the case that the two-qubit system is prepared for in a subclass of Bell-diagonal states, namely, the Werner states [1,107]

$$\begin{aligned} \rho_\psi(0) &= r|\psi_\pm(0)\rangle\langle\psi_\pm(0)| + \frac{1-r}{4}I_4, \\ \rho_\varphi(0) &= r|\varphi_\pm(0)\rangle\langle\varphi_\pm(0)| + \frac{1-r}{4}I_4, \end{aligned} \tag{26}$$

where $0 \leq r \leq 1$ denotes the purity parameter of the initial states, and I_4 is the 4×4 identity matrix. The concurrence for the two-qubit system prepared in the Werner states initially of Equation (26) can be reduced to

$$\mathcal{C}^\psi(t) = \mathcal{C}^\varphi(t) = \max\left\{0, r|F(t)|^2 - \frac{1}{2}(1-r)\right\}. \tag{27}$$

The entanglement of the two-qubit system exists if the initial value of concurrence $\mathcal{C}(0)$ in the Werner states is larger than zero, correspondingly $1/3 < r \leq 1$. The concurrence exists at time t if the threshold value of the decoherence function satisfies $|F(t)| > |F_{\text{th}}^{\mathcal{C}}| = \sqrt{(1-r)/(2r)}$. The entanglement sudden death and rebirth phenomena only occur in non-Markovian dynamics regimes for the case $r = 1$, whereas for the case $1/3 < r < 1$, the entanglement sudden death phenomenon occurs in both Markovian and non-Markovian dynamics regimes. The entanglement rebirth phenomenon can occur if the secondary maximum of the decoherence function is larger than the threshold value $|F_{\text{th}}^{\mathcal{C}}|$ in the non-Markovian dynamics regime.

The time dependent maximum CHSH-Bell function $\mathcal{B}(t)$ for the initial Werner states of Equation (26) can be reduced to

$$\mathcal{B}(t) = 2r\sqrt{|F(t)|^4 + 1}. \tag{28}$$

In the presence of entanglement $\mathcal{C}(t) > 0$, namely $1/3 < r| \leq 1$, if the initial CHSH-Bell function $\mathcal{B}(0) = 2\sqrt{2}r > 2$, namely $\sqrt{2}/2 < r \leq 1$, the two-qubit system displays quantum nonlocality initially. For the case $r = 1$, $\mathcal{B}(+\infty) = 2$ in long time limit $t \to +\infty$, and the two-qubit system always displays quantum nonlocality, whereas the two-qubit system exhibits the transition from quantum to classical nolocalities for the case $\sqrt{2}/2 < r < 1$, and the threshold value of the decoherence function satisfies $|F(t)| > |F_{\text{th}}^{\mathcal{B}}| = \sqrt[4]{1/r^2 - 1}$, provided that the CHSH-Bell function $\mathcal{B}(t)$ is larger than the classical threshold $\mathcal{B}_{\text{th}}$. The initial CHSH-Bell function $\mathcal{B}(0) \leq 2$ and the two-qubit system always displays classical nonlocality for the case $1/3 < r \leq \sqrt{2}/2$.

For the two-qubit system prepared initially in the Werner states of Equation (26), the close relation between $\mathcal{B}(t)$ and $\mathcal{C}(t)$ can be expressed as

$$\mathcal{B}(t) = 2\sqrt{\left[\mathcal{C}(t) + \frac{1}{2}(1-r)\right]^2 + r^2}. \tag{29}$$

The classical threshold $\mathcal{C}_{\text{th}}$ corresponding to the Bell function $\mathcal{B}(t) \geq \mathcal{B}_{\text{th}} = 2$ can be expressed as $\mathcal{C}_{\text{th}} = \sqrt{1 - r^2} - (1-r)/2$ which depends only on the purity parameter r of the initial states of Equation (26), and it is a decreasing function of the purity parameter r; for the presence of entanglement $1/3 < r \leq 1$, it satisfies $0 \leq \mathcal{C}_{\text{th}} < (2\sqrt{2} - 1)/3$.

3. Discussion

In this section, we demonstrate the numerical results of the non-Markovian disentanglement dynamics of a two-qubit system consisting of two noninteracting identical single qubits independently coupled to its local nonequilibrium environment. We mainly focus on how the environmental nonstationary and non-Markovian properties influence the non-Markovianity $\mathcal{N}_T$, the entanglement quantified by the concurrence and the nonlocality characterized by the Bell function. The comparisons with the environmental stationary and memoryless cases are also discussed.

Figure 1 shows the non-Markovianity $\mathcal{N}_T$ of a two-qubit system interacting with nonequilibrium environments as a function of the environmental memory decay rate κ and the nonstationary parameter a. Similar to the case of a single qubit system coupled to nonequilibrium environments, for a given value of the environmental memory decay rate κ, the non-Markovianity $\mathcal{N}_T$ shows symmetrical behavior for positive and negative environmental nonstationary parameter a in both weak and strong coupling regimes. As the environmental nonstationary parameter a deviates from zero for a given environmental memory decay rate κ, the non-Markovianity $\mathcal{N}_S$ decreases due to the suppression in the dynamical decoherence induced by the environmental nonequilibrium feature. In both weak and strong coupling regimes, for a given value of the environmental nonstationary parameter a, the non-Markovianity $\mathcal{N}_T$ increases with the decrease in the environmental memory decay rate κ. The non-Markovianity $\mathcal{N}_T$ decreases to zero as the environmental memory decay rate κ increases in the weak coupling regime, as shown in Figure 1a, whereas it does not decrease to zero in the strong coupling regime as displayed in Figure 1b.

Figure 2 displays the time evolution of the concurrence $\mathcal{C}(t)$ and the Bell function $\mathcal{B}(t)$ for different values of the environmental nonstationary parameter a for the two-qubit system prepared initially in the composite Bell states. As shown in Figure 2a, the concurrence $\mathcal{C}(t)$ decays monotonically and there is an entanglement of the sudden death phenomenon in the weak coupling regime for both the nonstationary $a \neq 0$ and stationary $a = 0$ cases. In the strong coupling regime, as the nonstationary parameter $|a|$ increases, the concurrence $\mathcal{C}(t)$ undergoes a transition from monotonical decay to nonmonotonical decay with nonzero entanglement revivals. When the nonstationary parameter $|a|$ is smaller than a certain threshold value $|a_{\text{th}}| = 0.95$, the entanglement only displays sudden death phenomenon and the rebirth phenomenon disappears. In both the weak and strong coupling regimes, the concurrence $\mathcal{C}(t)$ increases as the environmental nonstationary parameter a departs from zero. This indicates that the environmental nonequilibrium feature can suppress the disentanglement dynamics. As displayed in Figure 2b, in the weak coupling regime, the Bell function $\mathcal{B}(t)$ decays monotonically, whereas it shows nonmonotonical decays in the strong coupling regime. In both the weak and strong coupling regimes, the nolocality undergoes a transition from quantum to classical and it increases as the environmental nonstationary parameter a departs from zero. This reflects that the environmental nonequilibrium feature can enhance the quantum nonlocality. In addition, the environmental nonequilibrium feature does not influence the initial values of the concurrence $\mathcal{C}(0)$ and Bell function $\mathcal{B}(0)$ in both the weak and strong coupling regimes for the system prepared in the composite Bell states initially.

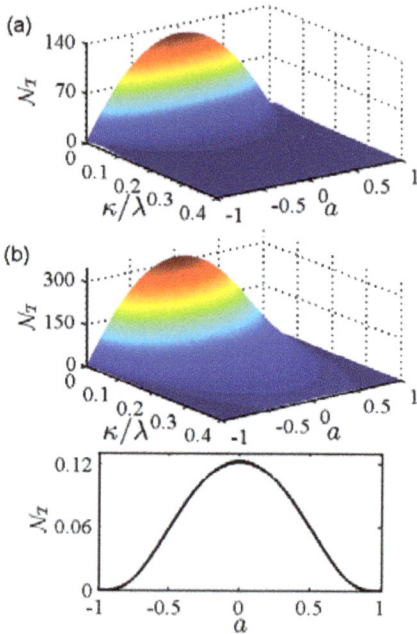

Figure 1. (Color online) Non-Markovianity $\mathcal{N}_T$ of a two-qubit system in nonequilibrium environments as a function of the environmental memory decay rate κ and the nonstationary parameter a in (a) the weak coupling regime with $\nu/\lambda = 0.8$ and (b) the strong coupling regime with $\nu/\lambda = 2$. The bottom panel of (b) is for the memoryless case $\kappa \to +\infty$.

Figure 3 displays the time evolution of the concurrence $\mathcal{C}(t)$ and the Bell function $\mathcal{B}(t)$ for different values of the environmental memory decay rate κ for the two-qubit system prepared initially in the composite Bell states. As shown in Figure 3a, the concurrence $\mathcal{C}(t)$ undergoes a transition from nonmonotonical decay to monotonical decay as the environmental memory decay rate κ increases in both the weak and strong coupling regimes. The entanglement only displays sudden death phenomenon, and the rebirth phenomenon disappears when the environmental memory decay rate κ is larger than the threshold value $\kappa_{th} = 0.27\lambda$ and $\kappa_{th} = 0.87\lambda$ in the weak and strong coupling regimes, respectively. In the presence of entanglement rebirth phenomenon, the entanglement revivals in the concurrence $\mathcal{C}(t)$ become obvious as the environmental memory decay rate κ decreases in both the weak and strong coupling regimes. This indicates that the environmental non-Markovian feature can enhance the entanglement revivals and suppress the disentanglement dynamics. As displayed in Figure 3b, the Bell function $\mathcal{B}(t)$ undergoes a transition from nonmonotonical decay to monotonical decay in the weak coupling regime, whereas in the strong coupling regime, it decays nonmonotonically and it increases as the environmental memory decay rate κ decreases. This reflects that the environmental non-Markovian feature can enhance the quantum nonlocality in the strong coupling regime. In contrast, the decay of the Bell function $\mathcal{B}(t)$ exhibits a transition from nonmonotonical decay to monotonical decay with the increase in the environmental memory decay rate κ in the weak coupling regime.

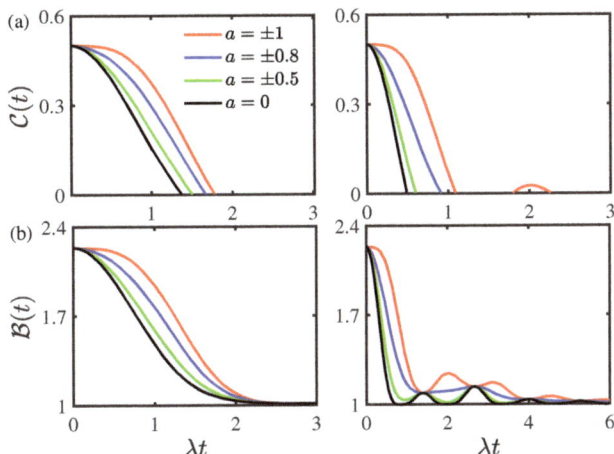

Figure 2. (Color online) Time evolution of (**a**) the concurrence $\mathcal{C}(t)$ and (**b**) the Bell function $\mathcal{B}(t)$ for different values of the environmental nonstationary parameter a for the two-qubit system prepared initially in the composite Bell states with the initial state parameter $|c| = 0.5$. Left panel: the weak coupling regime with $\nu/\lambda = 0.8$. Right panel: the strong coupling regime with $\nu/\lambda = 2$. The environmental memory decay rate is given by $\kappa/\lambda = 1$. The threshold value corresponding to the entanglement rebirth phenomenon in the strong coupling regime in the right panel of (**a**) is $|a_{\text{th}}| = 0.95$.

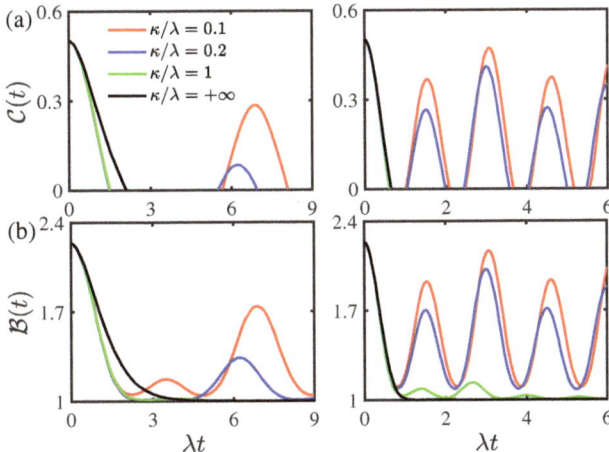

Figure 3. (Color online) Time evolution of (**a**) the concurrence $\mathcal{C}(t)$ and (**b**) the Bell function $\mathcal{B}(t)$ for different values of the environmental memory decay rate κ for the two-qubit system prepared initially in the composite Bell states with the initial state parameter $|c| = 0.5$. Left panel: the weak coupling regime with $\nu/\lambda = 0.8$. Right panel: the strong coupling regime with $\nu/\lambda = 2$. The environmental nonstationary parameter is given by $|a| = 0.5$. The threshold values corresponding to the entanglement rebirth phenomenon in the weak and strong coupling regimes in left and right panel of (**a**) are $\kappa_{\text{th}} = 0.27\lambda$ and $\kappa_{\text{th}} = 0.87\lambda$, respectively.

Figure 4 displays the time evolution of the concurrence $\mathcal{C}(t)$ and the Bell function $\mathcal{B}(t)$ for different values of the initial state parameter c for the two-qubit system prepared initially in the composite Bell states. As shown in Figure 4a, the entanglement displays sudden death phenomenon in the weak couping regime, whereas it displays a transition from sudden death to rebirth for different initial state parameter $|c|$ in the strong coupling regime; as the initial state parameter $|c|$ is smaller than the threshold value $|c_{th}| = 0.57$, the entanglement only displays the sudden death phenomenon, and the rebirth phenomenon disappears. As the initial state parameter $|c|$ increases, the concurrence $\mathcal{C}(t)$ increases in both the weak and strong coupling regimes, and the entanglement revivals in the concurrence $\mathcal{C}(t)$ become obvious in the strong coupling regime. This indicates that the initial state parameter can enhance quantum entanglement. As shown in Figure 4b, the nolocality undergoes a transition from quantum to classical as the initial state parameter $|c|$ decreases from the threshold value $|c_{th}| = 1$ in both the weak and strong coupling regimes. Due to the non-Markovian behavior in the disentanglement dynamics, the Bell function $\mathcal{B}(t)$ decays nonmonotonically. In both the weak and strong coupling regimes, the Bell function $\mathcal{B}(t)$ increases as the initial state parameter $|c|$ increases. This reflects that the initial state parameter can enhance nonlocality. Different from the fact that the environmental nonequilibrium feature does not influence the concurrence and Bell function initially, the initial values of the concurrence $\mathcal{C}(0)$ and Bell function $\mathcal{B}(0)$ depend closely on the initial state parameter $|c|$ and they increase with the increase in the initial state parameter $|c|$ in both the weak and strong coupling regimes. In both the weak and strong coupling regimes, the initial Bell function $\mathcal{B}(0)$ is always larger than the threshold $\mathcal{B}_{th} = 2$ for an arbitrary initial state parameter $|c|$ corresponding to the fact that the two-qubit system always displays quantum nonlocality initially for the two-qubit system prepared in the composite Bell states.

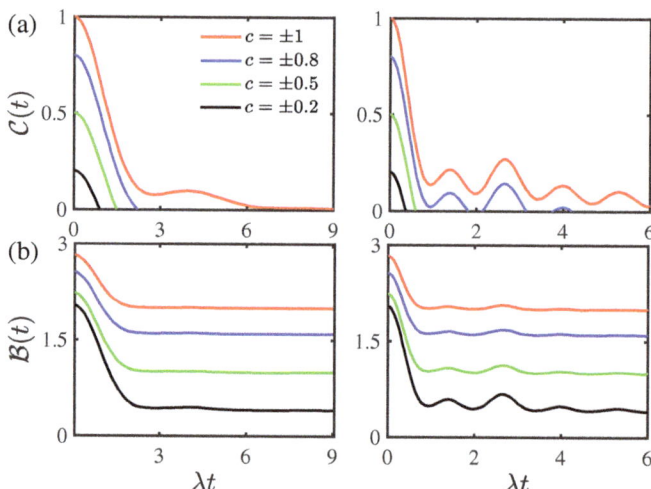

Figure 4. (Color online) Time evolution of (**a**) the concurrence $\mathcal{C}(t)$ and (**b**) the Bell function $\mathcal{B}(t)$ for the two-qubit system prepared initially in the composite Bell states for different values of the initial state parameter c. Left panel: the weak coupling regime with $\nu/\lambda = 0.8$. Right panel: the strong coupling regime with $\nu/\lambda = 2$. The environmental nonstationary parameter is given by $|a| = 0.5$ and the environmental memory decay rate is given by $\kappa/\lambda = 1$. The threshold value corresponding to the entanglement rebirth phenomenon in the strong coupling regime in right panel of (**a**) is $|c_{th}| = 0.57$.

Figure 5 shows the time evolution of the concurrence $\mathcal{C}(t)$ and the Bell function $\mathcal{B}(t)$ for different values of the environmental nonstationary parameter a for the two-qubit system prepared initially in the Werner states. Similar to the case that the two-qubit system initially prepared in the composite Bell states, as displayed in Figure 5a, the concurrence $\mathcal{C}(t)$ decays monotonically, and it exhibits entanglement sudden death phenomenon for both the nonstationary $a \neq 0$ and stationary $a = 0$ cases in the weak coupling regime, whereas there are obvious entanglement sudden death and rebirth phenomena in the strong coupling regime. As shown in Figure 5b, the Bell function $\mathcal{B}(t)$ decays monotonically in the weak coupling regime, while it decays nonmonotonically in the strong coupling regime. It undergoes a transition between quantum and classical nonlocalities in both the weak and strong coupling regimes. As the environmental nonstationary parameter a derivates from zero, the concurrence $\mathcal{C}(t)$ and Bell function $\mathcal{B}(t)$ increase, whereas the initial values of the concurrence $\mathcal{C}(0)$ and Bell function $\mathcal{B}(0)$ do not change in both the weak and strong coupling regimes. This indicates that the environmental nonequilibrium feature can suppress the disentanglement dynamics and enhance the quantum nonlocality but it does not influence the initial concurrence $\mathcal{C}(0)$ and Bell function $\mathcal{B}(0)$. In addition, the influence of the environmental nonequilibrium feature on disentanglement dynamics and quantum nonlocality in the weak coupling regime is more obvious than that in the strong coupling regime.

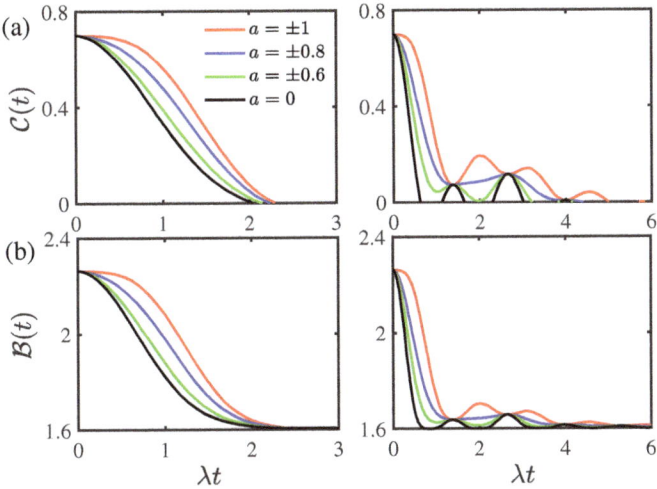

Figure 5. (Color online) Time evolution of (**a**) the concurrence $\mathcal{C}(t)$ and (**b**) the Bell function $\mathcal{B}(t)$ for different values of the environmental nonstationary parameter a for the two-qubit system prepared initially in the Werner states with the initial purity parameter $r = 0.8$. Left panel: the weak coupling regime with $\nu/\lambda = 0.8$. Right panel: the strong coupling regime with $\nu/\lambda = 2$. The environmental memory decay rate is given by $\kappa/\lambda = 1$.

Figure 6 displays the time evolution of the concurrence $\mathcal{C}(t)$ and the Bell function $\mathcal{B}(t)$ for different values of the environmental memory decay rate κ for the two-qubit system prepared initially in the extended Werner states. As displayed in Figure 6a, similar to the case that the two-qubit system initially prepared in the composite Bell states, the concurrence $\mathcal{C}(t)$ exhibits a transition from nonmonotonical decay to monotonical decay in both the weak and strong coupling regimes as the environmental memory decay rate κ increases. The entanglement only displays sudden death phenomenon and the rebirth phenomenon disappears when the environmental memory decay rate κ is larger than the threshold value $\kappa_{\text{th}} = 0.66\lambda$ and $\kappa_{\text{th}} = 1.50\lambda$ in the weak and strong coupling regimes, respectively. In the strong coupling regime, the entanglement revivals in the concurrence $\mathcal{C}(t)$ enhances as the environmental memory decay rate κ decreases. As shown in Figure 6b, the Bell function $\mathcal{B}(t)$ decays nonmonotonically, and for a given time t it decreases with the increase in the environmental memory decay rate κ in the strong coupling regime. In contrast, in the weak coupling regime, the Bell function $\mathcal{B}(t)$ exhibits a transition from nonmonotonical decay to monotonical decay as the environmental memory decay rate κ decreases and the Bell function $\mathcal{B}(t)$ decreases in some time intervals and increases in some other time intervals as the environmental memory decay rate κ decreases.

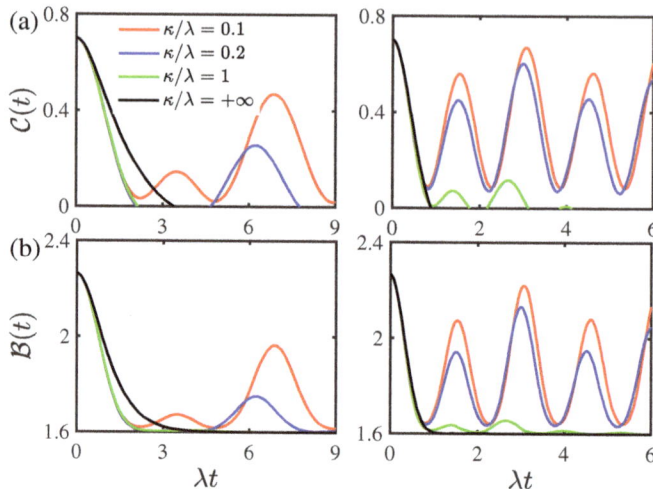

Figure 6. (Color online) Time evolution of (**a**) the concurrence $\mathcal{C}(t)$ and (**b**) the Bell function $\mathcal{B}(t)$ for different values of the environmental memory decay rate κ for the two-qubit system prepared initially in the extended Werner states with the initial purity parameter $r = 0.8$. Left panel: the weak coupling regime with $\nu/\lambda = 0.8$. Right panel: the strong coupling regime with $\nu/\lambda = 2$. The environmental nonstationary parameter is given by $|a| = 0.5$. The threshold values corresponding to the entanglement rebirth phenomenon in the weak and strong coupling regimes in left and right panel of (**a**) are $\kappa_{th} = 0.66\lambda$ and $\kappa_{th} = 1.50\lambda$, respectively.

Figure 7 displays the time evolution of the concurrence $\mathcal{C}(t)$ and Bell function $\mathcal{B}(t)$ for different values of initial purity state parameter r for the two-qubit system prepared initially in the Werner states. As shown in Figure 7a, similar to the case that the two-qubit system initially prepared in the composite Bell states, as the initial purity state parameter r decreases from the threshold value $r_{th} = 1$, the entanglement sudden death phenomenon occurs in the weak coupling regime. In the strong coupling regime, the entanglement displays sudden death and rebirth phenomena, and it only shows sudden death phenomenon; the rebirth phenomenon disappears as the initial purity state parameter r is smaller than the threshold value $r_{th} = 0.65$. With the increase in the initial purity state parameter r, the concurrence $\mathcal{C}(t)$ increases in both the weak and strong coupling regimes and the entanglement revivals in the concurrence $\mathcal{C}(t)$ become obvious in the strong coupling regime. This reflects the fact that the initial purity state parameter r can enhance quantum entanglement. As shown in Figure 7b, the Bell function $\mathcal{B}(t)$ decays monotonically and nonmonotonically in the weak and strong coupling regimes, respectively. In both the weak and strong coupling regimes, the Bell function $\mathcal{B}(t)$ increases as the initial purity state parameter r increases. This indicates that the initial state parameter can enhance nonlocality. As the initial purity state parameter r decreases from the threshold value $r_{th} = 1$, it first undergoes a transition from quantum nonlocality to classical nonlocality and then it only displays classical nonlocality when the initial purity state parameter r is smaller than the threshold value $r_{th} = \sqrt{2}/2$ due to the fact that the initial Bell function $\mathcal{B}(0)$ is not always larger than the threshold $\mathcal{B}_{th} = 2$ for the two-qubit system prepared initially in the Werner states. This is quite different from the case that the two-qubit system prepared initially in the composite Bell states.

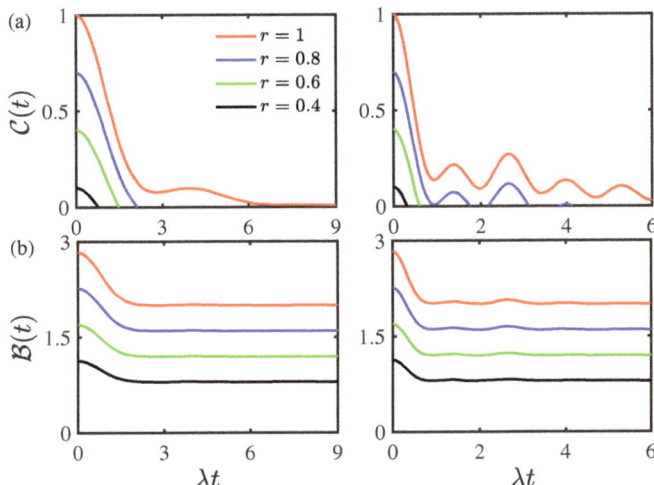

Figure 7. (Color online) Time evolution of (**a**) the concurrence $\mathcal{C}(t)$ and (**b**) the Bell function $\mathcal{B}(t)$ for the two-qubit system prepared initially in the Werner states for different values of the initial purity parameter r. Left panel: the weak coupling regime with $\nu/\lambda = 0.8$. Right panel: the strong coupling regime with $\nu/\lambda = 2$. The environmental nonstationary parameter is given by $|a| = 0.5$ and the environmental memory decay rate is given by $\kappa/\lambda = 1$. The threshold value corresponding to the entanglement rebirth phenomenon in the strong coupling regime in right panel of (a) is $r_{\text{th}} = 0.65$.

Figure 8 shows the time evolution of the concurrence $\mathcal{C}(t)$ and Bell function $\mathcal{B}(t)$ for different values of the coupling strength ν for the two-qubit system prepared initially in the composite Bell states and Werner states, respectively. As displayed in Figure 8a, for the weak coupling case (small ν), the entanglement shows sudden death phenomenon; as the coupling strength ν increases, the entanglement rebirth phenomenon occurs for the two-qubit system initially prepared in the composite Bell states and Werner states. The threshold values corresponding to the entanglement rebirth phenomenon in the composite Bell states and in the Werner states are $\nu_{\text{th}} = 2.2\lambda$ and $\nu_{\text{th}} = 1.47\lambda$, respectively. In addition, as the coupling strength ν increases, the entanglement revivals in the concurrence $\mathcal{C}(t)$ become more obvious. This indicates that the coupling strength can enhance quantum entanglement. As shown in Figure 8b, the Bell function $\mathcal{B}(t)$ undergoes a transition from quantum nonlocality to classical nonlocality for the two-qubit system initially prepared in both the composite Bell states and Werner states. Furthermore, the Bell function $\mathcal{B}(t)$ decays monotonically and nonmonotonically for small and large values of the coupling strength ν, respectively. The Bell function $\mathcal{B}(t)$ decreases as the coupling strength ν increases. This reflects that the coupling strength can suppress nonlocality.

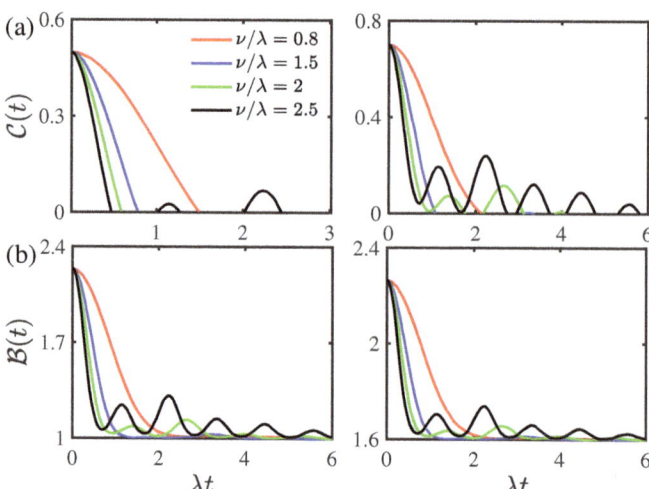

Figure 8. (Color online) Time evolution of (**a**) the concurrence $\mathcal{C}(t)$ and (**b**) the Bell function $\mathcal{B}(t)$ different values of the coupling strength ν. Left panel: for the two-qubit system prepared initially in the composite Bell states with the initial state parameter $|c| = 0.5$. Right panel: for the two-qubit system prepared initially in the Werner states with the initial purity parameter $r = 0.8$. The environmental nonstationary parameter is given by $|a| = 0.5$ and the environmental memory decay rate is given by $\kappa/\lambda = 1$. The threshold values corresponding to the entanglement rebirth phenomenon in the composite Bell states and in the Werner states in left and right panel of (**a**) are $\nu_{th} = 2.2\lambda$ and $\nu_{th} = 1.47\lambda$, respectively.

4. Conclusions

We have theoretically studied the disentanglement dynamics of a two-qubit system in the presence of nonequilibrium environments with nonstationary and non-Markovian RTN statistical properties. The reduced density matrix of the two-qubit system can be expressed in terms of the Kraus representation by means of the tensor products of the single qubit Kraus operators. We have derived the relations between the decoherence function and the entanglement characterized by the concurrence and the nonlocality quantified by the Bell function of the two-qubit system. We have identified the threshold values of the decoherence function to ensure the existences of the concurrence and nonlocal quantum correlations for a given evolution time when the two-qubit system is initially prepared in the composite Bell states and the Werner states, respectively. The results demonstrate that the environmental nonequilibrium feature can suppress the disentanglement of the two-qubit system and reduce the entanglement revivals in the two-qubit disentanglement dynamics. In addition, the environmental nonequilibrium feature can enhance the nonlocality in the two-qubit system. Moreover, the phenomena of entanglement sudden death and rebirth and the transition between quantum and classical nonlocalities closely depend on the parameters of the initial states and the environmental parameters, such as the nonstationary parameter, the memory decay rate and the coupling strength of the environmental noise. Our results are helpful for further understanding the quantum dynamics in nonequilibrium environments.

Author Contributions: Conceptualization, X.C.; Formal analysis, M.C. and T.H.; Writing—original draft preparation, M.C.; Writing—review and editing, H.C. and X.C. All authors have read and agreed to the published version of the manuscript.

Funding: This work was supported by the National Natural Science Foundation of China (Grant Nos. 12005121 and 11947033) and the Natural Science Foundation of Shandong Province (Grant No. ZR2021LL009).

Institutional Review Board Statement: Not applicable.

Informed Consent Statement: Not applicable.

Data Availability Statement: Not applicable.

Conflicts of Interest: The author declares no conflict of interest.

Abbreviations

The following abbreviations are used in this manuscript:
RTN   Random telegraph noise
CHSH   Clauser-Horne-Shimony-Holt
CK   Chapman-Kolmogorov

Appendix A. Generalized RTN Process Based on Classical Probability Theory

Based on the classical probability theory [95], a stochastic process $\xi(t)$ is completely determined by an infinity hierarchy of the multi-point probability distribution

$$\mathcal{P}_n = P(\xi_1, t_1; \cdots ; \xi_n, t_n) = \langle \delta(\xi_1 - \xi(t_1)) \cdots \delta(\xi_n - \xi(t_n)) \rangle, \tag{A1}$$

which represents that the stochastic process $\xi(t)$ takes the valve ξ_1 at time $t_1, \cdots$, and the value ξ_n at time t_n for all ordered sets of time $t_1 > \cdots > t_n$ $(n \geq 1)$. The n-point joint probability $\mathcal{P}_n$ obeys the following four Kolmogorov consistency conditions:

(1) Nonnegative— i.e., $\mathcal{P}_n \geq 0$;
(2) Normalization—i.e., $\sum_{\xi_1} \mathcal{P}_1 = 1$;
(3) Symmetry—i.e., $\mathcal{P}_n$ does not change by interchanging arbitrary pairs (ξ_k, t_k) and (ξ_l, t_l);
(4) Relation between $\mathcal{P}_n$ and $\mathcal{P}_{n-1}$—i.e., $\sum_{\xi_n} \mathcal{P}_n = \mathcal{P}_{n-1}$.

In general, the initial one-point probability distribution $P(\xi_0, 0)$ is given and if we want to obtain $\mathcal{P}_n$, we should also know the conditional probability

$$\mathcal{P}_{1|n-1} = P(\xi_1, t_1 | \xi_2, t_2; \cdots ; \xi_n, t_n) = \langle \delta(\xi_1 - \xi(t_1)) \rangle_{\xi(t_2) = \xi_2, \cdots, \xi(t_n) = \xi_n}, \tag{A2}$$

which is the probability that the stochastic process $\xi(t)$ at time t_1 has the valve ξ_1 under the condition that the stochastic process $\xi(t)$ takes the valve ξ_2 at time $t_2, \cdots$, and the value ξ_n at time t_n. The conditions of nonnegativity and normalization are satisfied

$$\mathcal{P}_{1|n-1} \geq 0, \sum_{\xi_1} \mathcal{P}_{1|1} = 1. \tag{A3}$$

A stochastic process $\xi(t)$ is considered to be stationary if all P_n depend only on the time difference

$$P(\xi_1, t_1 + \tau; \cdots ; \xi_n, t_n + \tau) = P(\xi_1, t_1; \cdots ; \xi_n, t_n). \tag{A4}$$

A necessary but not sufficient condition is that $\mathcal{P}_1$ is independent of time. Equivalently, if there is at least one joint probability, $\mathcal{P}_i$ satisfies

$$P(\xi_1, t_1 + \tau; \cdots ; \xi_i, t_i + \tau) \neq P(\xi_1, t_1; \cdots ; \xi_i, t_i), \tag{A5}$$

the stochastic process $\xi(t)$ is nonstationary. A sufficient but not necessary condition is that $\mathcal{P}_1$ is time-dependent.

A stochastic process $\xi(t)$ is regarded to be Markovian if all $\mathcal{P}_{1|n-1}$ satisfy

$$P(\xi_1, t_1 | \xi_2, t_2; \cdots ; \xi_n, t_n) = P(\xi_1, t_1 | \xi_2, t_2). \tag{A6}$$

That is the probability for the stochastic process $\xi(t)$ at time t_1 to take the valve ξ_1 under the condition that the stochastic process $\xi(t)$ has the valve ξ_2 at time $t_2, \cdots$, and the value

ξ_n at time t_n depends only on the last previous value ξ_2 at time t_2. $\mathcal{P}_{1|1}$ is also called the conditional transition probability. It is remarkable that for a Markovian process, we can reconstruct an arbitrary multi-point probability distribution by means of the initial one-point distribution $P(\xi_0, 0)$ and conditional transition probability $\mathcal{P}_{1|1}$ as

$$P(\xi_1, t_1; \cdots ; \xi_n, t_n) = \prod_{i}^{n-1} P(\xi_i, t_i | \xi_{i+1}, t_{i+1}) P(\xi_n, t_n), \quad (A7)$$

where the one-point probability distribution satisfies

$$P(\xi_1, t_1) = P(\xi_1, t_1 | \xi_0, 0) P(\xi_0, 0). \quad (A8)$$

A necessary but not sufficient condition for a Markov process is that the conditional transition probability obeys the Chapman-Kolmogorov (CK) equation

$$P(\xi_1, t_1 | \xi_3, t_3) = \sum_{\xi_2} P(\xi_1, t_1 | \xi_2, t_2) P(\xi_2, t_2 | \xi_3, t_3). \quad (A9)$$

A stochastic process $\xi(t)$ is non-Markovian if there is at least one conditional probability. $\mathcal{P}_{1|i-1}$ depends not only on the last previous value ξ_{i-1} at time t_{i-1} but on one or more previous values ξ_j at earlier time t_j ($j < i - 1$). A sufficient but not necessary condition is that the CK equation (A9) fails.

The subensemble of non-Markovian and nonstationary homogeneous stochastic processes can be extracted from subensembles of Markovian and stationary stochastic processes [95]. A simple assumption is that $\mathcal{P}_1$ is time-dependent

$$P(\xi, t) = \int P(\xi, t | \xi_0, 0) P(\xi_0, 0) d\xi_0, \quad (A10)$$

with the initial nonstationary distribution $P(\xi_0, 0)$ and the conditional probability $\mathcal{P}_{1|1}$ depends on its previous history

$$\frac{\partial}{\partial t} P(\xi, t | \xi', t') = \int_{t'}^{t} K(t - \tau) \mathcal{M}_\xi P(\xi, \tau | \xi', t') d\tau, \quad (A11)$$

where the initial condition is given by $P(\xi, t' | \xi', t') = \delta(\xi - \xi')$, $K(t - \tau)$ denotes the memory kernel composite environmental noise $\xi(t)$ and $\mathcal{M}_\xi$ is a differential operator only involving derivatives with respect to ξ. Physically, the extraction of a subensemble nonstationary and non-Markovian stochastic processes with memory effect and initial nonstationary distribution taken into account means that the environment is in a certain nonequilibrum state initially and the statistical properties of the environmental noise depend on previous history. For the case $a = 0$, the environmental noise only displays stationary property and the environment is in equilibrium [87,88]. When the environmental noise is memoryless, i.e., $K(t - \tau) = \delta(t - \tau)$, the non-Markovian RTN recovers the Markovian one and its memory effect vanishes.

Appendix B. Entanglement and Quantum Nonlocality of a Two-Qubit System

In this appendix, we introduce the most commonly used measures of the entanglement and quantum nonlocality of a two-qubit system.

For a two-qubit system, all the entanglement measures are compatible, and we can use the concurrence to quantify the entanglement defined as [94,102]

$$\mathcal{C}(t) = \max\left\{0, \sqrt{\lambda_1(t)} - \sqrt{\lambda_2(t)} - \sqrt{\lambda_3(t)} - \sqrt{\lambda_4(t)}\right\}, \quad (A12)$$

where $\lambda_i(t)$ are the eigenvalues of the matrix $\zeta(t) = \rho(t)(\sigma_y \otimes \sigma_y) \rho^*(t)(\sigma_y \otimes \sigma_y)$ arranged in decreasing order with $\rho^*(t)$ denoting the complex conjugation of the two-qubit reduced density matrix $\rho(t)$ in the two-qubit basis $\mathscr{B}_T$. The concurrence $\mathcal{C}(t)$ varies from the maximum 1 for a maximally entangled state to the minimum 0 for a completely disentangled state.

For pure quantum state, the entanglement corresponds to nonlocal correlations, whereas it is not the general case for mixed states due to the fact that the environmental noise gives rise to the decay of nonlocal correlations. The nonlocality can be identified by the violation of the Bell inequalities in the presence of entanglement ($\mathcal{C}(t) > 0$). The Clauser-Horne-Shimony-Holt (CHSH) form of Bell function has been widely used to determine whether there are nonlocal correlations of the entangled system. The maximum Bell function $\mathcal{B}(t)$ for an entangled two-qubit system can be, based on the Horodecki criterion, expressed as [103]

$$\mathcal{B}(t) = 2\sqrt{\max_{j>k}[\mu_j(t) + \mu_k(t)]}, \tag{A13}$$

where the subscripts $j, k = 1, 2, 3$ and $\mu_j(t)$ and $\mu_k(t)$ are functions in terms of the elements of the two-qubit reduced density matrix. If the Bell function $\mathcal{B}(t)$ is larger than the classical threshold $\mathcal{B}_{\text{th}} = 2$, the quantum correlations of the entangled two-qubit system cannot be reproduced by any classical local model.

It is known that the Bell states and Werner mixed states of a two-qubit system play an essential role in quantum computation and quantum information [6]. The two-qubit reduced density matrix expressed in Equation (17) for initial composite Bell states and Werner states has an X structure both initially and during the dynamical evolution. The concurrence $\mathcal{C}(t)$ for an initial X structure reduced density matrix of a two-qubit system can be computed in a particular form as [104]

$$\mathcal{C}_X(t) = \max\{0, \mathcal{C}_1(t), \mathcal{C}_2(t)\}, \tag{A14}$$

where

$$\begin{aligned}\mathcal{C}_1(t) &= 2\left[|\rho_{23}(t)| - \sqrt{\rho_{11}(t)\rho_{44}(t)}\right], \\ \mathcal{C}_2(t) &= 2\left[|\rho_{14}(t)| - \sqrt{\rho_{22}(t)\rho_{33}(t)}\right].\end{aligned} \tag{A15}$$

The time dependent maximum CHSH-Bell function $\mathcal{B}(t)$ for an X structure two-qubit density matrix can be expressed analytically as [105]

$$\mathcal{B}_X(t) = \max\{\mathcal{B}_1(t), \mathcal{B}_2(t)\}, \tag{A16}$$

where $\mathcal{B}_1(t) = 2\sqrt{\mu_1(t) + \mu_2(t)}$ and $\mathcal{B}_2(t) = 2\sqrt{\mu_1(t) + \mu_3(t)}$ with

$$\begin{aligned}\mu_1(t) &= 4[|\rho_{14}(t)| + |\rho_{23}(t)|]^2, \\ \mu_2(t) &= [\rho_{11}(t) + \rho_{44}(t) - \rho_{22}(t) - \rho_{33}(t)]^2, \\ \mu_3(t) &= 4[|\rho_{14}(t)| - |\rho_{23}(t)|]^2.\end{aligned} \tag{A17}$$

References

1. Horodecki, R.; Horodecki, P.; Horodecki, M.; Horodecki, K. Quantum entanglement. *Rev. Mod. Phys.* **2009**, *81*, 865. [CrossRef]
2. Chitambar, E.; Hsieh, M.H. Relating the Resource Theories of Entanglement and Quantum Coherence. *Phys. Rev. Lett.* **2016**, *117*, 020402. [CrossRef] [PubMed]
3. Streltsov, A.; Adesso, G.; Plenio, M.B. *Colloquium*: Quantum coherence as a resource. *Rev. Mod. Phys.* **2017**, *89*, 041003. [CrossRef]
4. Hu, M.L.; Hu, X.; Wang, J.; Peng, Y.; Zhang, Y.R.; Fan, H. Quantum coherence and geometric quantum discord. *Phys. Rep.* **2018**, *762*, 1. [CrossRef]
5. Chitambar, E.; Gour, G. Quantum resource theories. *Rev. Mod. Phys.* **2019**, *91*, 025001. [CrossRef]
6. Nielsen, M.A.; Chuang, I.L. *Quantum Computation and Quantum Information*; Cambridge University Press: Cambridge, UK, 2000.
7. Breuer, H.P.; Petruccione, F. *The Theory of Open Quantum Systems*; Oxford University Press: New York, NY, USA, 2002.
8. Schlosshauer, M. *Decoherence and the Quantum-to-Classical Transition*; Springer: Berlin/Heidelberg, Germany, 2007.
9. Schlosshauer, M. Quantum decoherence. *Phys. Rep.* **2019**, *831*, 1. [CrossRef]
10. Carollo, A.; Valenti, D.; Spagnolo, B. Geometry of quantum phase transitions. *Phys. Rep.* **2020**, *838*, 1. [CrossRef]

11. Yu, T.; Eberly, J.H. Sudden Death of Entanglement. *Science* **2009**, *323*, 598. [CrossRef]
12. Gurvitz, S.A.; Fedichkin, L.; Mozyrsky, D.; Berman, G.P. Relaxation and the Zeno Effect in Qubit Measurements. *Phys. Rev. Lett.* **2003**, *91*, 066801. [CrossRef] [PubMed]
13. Kang, L.; Zhang, Y.; Xu, X.; Tang, X. Quantum measurement of a double quantum dot coupled to two kinds of environment. *Phys. Rev. B* **2017**, *96*, 235417. [CrossRef]
14. Lan, K.; Du, Q.; Kang, L.; Tang, X.; Jiang, L.; Zhang, Y.; Cai, X. Dynamics of an open double quantum dot system via quantum measurement. *Phys. Rev. B* **2020**, *101*, 174302. [CrossRef]
15. Viotti, L.; Lombardo, F.C.; Villar, P.I. Boundary-induced effect encoded in the corrections to the geometric phase acquired by a bipartite two-level system. *Phys. Rev. A* **2020**, *101*, 032337. [CrossRef]
16. Maniscalco, S.; Francica, F.; Zaffino, R.L.; Lo Gullo, N.; Plastina, F. Protecting Entanglement via the Quantum Zeno Effect. *Phys. Rev. Lett.* **2008**, *100*, 090503. [CrossRef] [PubMed]
17. Wu, K.D.; Bäumer, E.; Tang, J.F.; Hovhannisyan, K.V.; Perarnau-Llobet, M.; Xiang, G.Y.; Li, C.F.; Guo, G.C. Minimizing Backaction through Entangled Measurements. *Phys. Rev. Lett.* **2020**, *125*, 210401. [CrossRef] [PubMed]
18. Li, J.; Paraoanu, G.S. Generation and propagation of entanglement in driven coupled-qubit systems. *New J. Phys.* **2009**, *11*, 113020. [CrossRef]
19. Nosrati, F.; Mortezapour, A.; Lo Franco, R. Validating and controlling quantum enhancement against noise by the motion of a qubit. *Phys. Rev. A* **2020**, *101*, 012331. [CrossRef]
20. Nosrati, F.; Castellini, A.; Compagno, G.; Lo Franco, R. Dynamics of spatially indistinguishable particles and quantum entanglement protection. *Phys. Rev. A* **2020**, *102*, 062429. [CrossRef]
21. Czerwinski, A.; Sedziak-Kacprowicz, K.; Kolenderski, P. Phase estimation of time-bin qudits by time-resolved single-photon counting. *Phys. Rev. A* **2021**, *103*, 042402. [CrossRef]
22. Lan, K.; Xie, S.; Cai, X. Geometric quantum speed limits for Markovian dynamics in open quantum systems. *New J. Phys.* **2022**, *24*, 055003. [CrossRef]
23. Collini, E.; Wong, C.Y.; Wilk, K.E.; Curmi, P.M.G.; Brumer, P.; Scholes, G.D. Coherently wired light-harvesting in photosynthetic marine algae at ambient temperature. *Nature* **2010**, *463*, 644. [CrossRef]
24. Panitchayangkoon, G.; Hayes, D.; Fransted, K.A.; Caram, J.R.; Harel, E.; Wen, J.; Blankenship, R.E.; Engel, G.S. Long-lived quantum coherence in photosynthetic complexes at physiological temperature. *Proc. Natl. Acad. Sci. USA* **2010**, *107*, 12766. [CrossRef] [PubMed]
25. Plenio, M.B.; Huelga, S.F. Dephasing-assisted transport: Quantum networks and biomolecules. *New J. Phys.* **2008**, *10*, 113019. [CrossRef]
26. Caruso, F.; Chin, A.W.; Datta, A.; Huelga, S.F.; Plenio, M.B. Highly efficient energy excitation transfer in light-harvesting complexes: The fundamental role of noise-assisted transport. *J. Chem. Phys.* **2009**, *131*, 105106. [CrossRef]
27. Rebentrost, P.; Mohseni, M.; Kassal, I.; Lloyd, S.; Aspuru-Guzik, A. Environment-assisted quantum transport. *New J. Phys.* **2009**, *11*, 033003. [CrossRef]
28. Mohseni, M.; Shabani, A.; Lloyd, S.; Omar, Y.; Rabitz, H. Geometrical effects on energy transfer in disordered open quantum systems. *J. Chem. Phys.* **2013**, *138*, 204309. [CrossRef] [PubMed]
29. Piilo, J.; Maniscalco, S.; Härkönen, K.; Suominen, K.A. Non-Markovian Quantum Jumps. *Phys. Rev. Lett.* **2008**, *100*, 180402. [CrossRef]
30. Breuer, H.; Laine, E.; Piilo, J. Measure for the Degree of Non-Markovian Behavior of Quantum Processes in Open Systems. *Phys. Rev. Lett.* **2009**, *103*, 210401. [CrossRef]
31. Rivas, A.; Huelga, S.F.; Plenio, M.B. Entanglement and Non-Markovianity of Quantum Evolutions. *Phys. Rev. Lett.* **2010**, *105*, 050403. [CrossRef]
32. Zhang, W.M.; Lo, P.Y.; Xiong, H.N.; Tu, M.W.Y.; Nori, F. General Non-Markovian Dynamics of Open Quantum Systems. *Phys. Rev. Lett.* **2012**, *109*, 170402. [CrossRef]
33. Lo Franco, R.; Bellomo, B.; Maniscalco, S.; Compagno, G. Dynamics of quantum correlations in two-qubit systems within non-Markovian environments. *Int. J. Mod. Phys. B* **2013**, *27*, 1345053. [CrossRef]
34. Chruściński, D.; Maniscalco, S. Degree of Non-Markovianity of Quantum Evolution. *Phys. Rev. Lett.* **2014**, *112*, 120404. [CrossRef] [PubMed]
35. Rivas, A.; Huelga, S.F.; Plenio, M.B. Quantum non-Markovianity: Characterization, quantification and detection. *Rep. Prog. Phys.* **2014**, *77*, 094001. [CrossRef] [PubMed]
36. Fanchini, F.F.; Karpat, G.; Çakmak, B.; Castelano, L.K.; Aguilar, G.H.; Farías, O.J.; Walborn, S.P.; Ribeiro, P.H.S.; de Oliveira, M.C. Non-Markovianity through Accessible Information. *Phys. Rev. Lett.* **2014**, *112*, 210402. [CrossRef]
37. Breuer, H.; Laine, E.; Piilo, J.; Vacchini, B. *Colloquium*: Non-Markovian dynamics in open quantum systems. *Rev. Mod. Phys.* **2016**, *88*, 021002. [CrossRef]
38. de Vega, I.; Alonso, D. Dynamics of non-Markovian open quantum systems. *Rev. Mod. Phys.* **2017**, *89*, 015001. [CrossRef]
39. Wang, B.; Xu, Z.Y.; Chen, Z.Q.; Feng, M. Non-Markovian effect on the quantum discord. *Phys. Rev. A* **2010**, *81*, 014101. [CrossRef]
40. Bellomo, B.; Lo Franco, R.; Compagno, G. Non-Markovian Effects on the Dynamics of Entanglement. *Phys. Rev. Lett.* **2007**, *99*, 160502. [CrossRef]

41. Chenu, A.; Beau, M.; Cao, J.; del Campo, A. Quantum Simulation of Generic Many-Body Open System Dynamics Using Classical Noise. *Phys. Rev. Lett.* **2017**, *118*, 140403. [CrossRef] [PubMed]
42. Huelga, S.F.; Rivas, A.; Plenio, M.B. Non-Markovianity-Assisted Steady State Entanglement. *Phys. Rev. Lett.* **2012**, *108*, 160402. [CrossRef]
43. Yan, Y.A.; Shao, J. Equivalence of stochastic formulations and master equations for open systems. *Phys. Rev. A* **2018**, *97*, 042126. [CrossRef]
44. Paladino, E.; Galperin, Y.M.; Falci, G.; Altshuler, B.L. $1/f$ noise: Implications for solid-state quantum information. *Rev. Mod. Phys.* **2014**, *86*, 361. [CrossRef]
45. Addis, C.; Ciccarello, F.; Cascio, M.; Palma, G.; Maniscalco, S. Dynamical decoupling efficiency versus quantum non-Markovianity. *New J. Phys.* **2015**, *17*, 123004. [CrossRef]
46. Lombardo, F.C.; Villar, P.I. Environmentally induced effects on a bipartite two-level system: Geometric phase and entanglement properties. *Phys. Rev. A* **2010**, *81*, 022115. [CrossRef]
47. Ma, J.; Cao, J. Förster resonance energy transfer, absorption and emission spectra in multichromophoric systems. I. Full cumulant expansions and system-bath entanglement. *J. Chem. Phys.* **2015**, *142*, 094106. [CrossRef]
48. Gu, B.; Franco, I. When can quantum decoherence be mimicked by classical noise? *J. Chem. Phys.* **2019**, *151*, 014109. [CrossRef] [PubMed]
49. Poggi, P.M.; Lombardo, F.C.; Wisniacki, D.A. Driving-induced amplification of non-Markovianity in open quantum systems evolution. *Europhys. Lett.* **2017**, *118*, 20005. [CrossRef]
50. Villar, P.I.; Soba, A. Geometric phase accumulated in a driven quantum system coupled to a structured environment. *Phys. Rev. A* **2020**, *101*, 052112. [CrossRef]
51. Czerwinski, A. Open quantum systems integrable by partial commutativity. *Phys. Rev. A* **2020**, *102*, 062423. [CrossRef]
52. Czerwinski, A. Dynamics of Open Quantum Systems-Markovian Semigroups and Beyond. *Symmetry* **2022**, *14*, 1752. [CrossRef]
53. Megier, N.; Smirne, A.; Campbell, S.; Vacchini, B. Correlations, Information Backflow, and Objectivity in a Class of Pure Dephasing Models. *Entropy* **2022**, *24*, 304. [CrossRef]
54. Budini, A.A. Quantum Non-Markovian Processes Break Conditional Past-Future Independence. *Phys. Rev. Lett.* **2018**, *121*, 240401. [CrossRef]
55. Man, Z.X.; Xia, Y.J.; Lo Franco, R. Validity of the Landauer principle and quantum memory effects via collisional models. *Phys. Rev. A* **2019**, *99*, 042106. [CrossRef]
56. Budini, A.A. Conditional past-future correlation induced by non-Markovian dephasing reservoirs. *Phys. Rev. A* **2019**, *99*, 052125. [CrossRef]
57. Budini, A.A. Quantum Non-Markovian Environment-to-System Backflows of Information: Nonoperational vs. Operational Approaches. *Entropy* **2022**, *24*, 649. [CrossRef]
58. Du, P.L.; Wang, Y.; Xu, R.X.; Zhang, H.D.; Yan, Y. System-bath entanglement theorem with Gaussian environments. *J. Chem. Phys.* **2020**, *152*, 034102. [CrossRef]
59. Cai, X. Quantum Dynamics in a Fluctuating Environment. *Entropy* **2019**, *21*, 1040. [CrossRef]
60. Chiang, K.T.; Zhang, W.M. Non-Markovian decoherence dynamics of strong-coupling hybrid quantum systems: A master equation approach. *Phys. Rev. A* **2021**, *103*, 013714. [CrossRef]
61. Zhang, Q.; Man, Z.X.; Xia, Y.J. Non-Markovianity and the Landauer principle in composite thermal environments. *Phys. Rev. A* **2021**, *103*, 032201. [CrossRef]
62. Villar, P.I.; Soba, A. Enhancement of quantum correlations and a geometric phase for a driven bipartite quantum system in a structured environment. *Phys. Rev. A* **2021**, *103*, 032222. [CrossRef]
63. Huang, Y.W.; Zhang, W.M. Exact master equation for generalized quantum Brownian motion with momentum-dependent system-environment couplings. *Phys. Rev. Res.* **2022**, *4*, 033151. [CrossRef]
64. Yu, T.; Eberly, J.H. Quantum Open System Theory: Bipartite Aspects. *Phys. Rev. Lett.* **2006**, *97*, 140403. [CrossRef]
65. López, C.E.; Romero, G.; Lastra, F.; Solano, E.; Retamal, J.C. Sudden Birth versus Sudden Death of Entanglement in Multipartite Systems. *Phys. Rev. Lett.* **2008**, *101*, 080503. [CrossRef]
66. Mazzola, L.; Maniscalco, S.; Piilo, J.; Suominen, K.A. Interplay between entanglement and entropy in two-qubit systems. *J. Phys. B* **2010**, *43*, 085505. [CrossRef]
67. Salles, A.; de Melo, F.; Almeida, M.P.; Hor-Meyll, M.; Walborn, S.P.; Souto Ribeiro, P.H.; Davidovich, L. Experimental investigation of the dynamics of entanglement: Sudden death, complementarity, and continuous monitoring of the environment. *Phys. Rev. A* **2008**, *78*, 022322. [CrossRef]
68. Mazzola, L.; Maniscalco, S.; Piilo, J.; Suominen, K.A.; Garraway, B.M. Sudden death and sudden birth of entanglement in common structured reservoirs. *Phys. Rev. A* **2009**, *79*, 042302. [CrossRef]
69. Chruściński, D.; Kossakowski, A. Non-Markovian Quantum Dynamics: Local versus Nonlocal. *Phys. Rev. Lett.* **2010**, *104*, 070406. [CrossRef]
70. Wang, F.; Hou, P.Y.; Huang, Y.Y.; Zhang, W.G.; Ouyang, X.L.; Wang, X.; Huang, X.Z.; Zhang, H.L.; He, L.; Chang, X.Y.; et al. Observation of entanglement sudden death and rebirth by controlling a solid-state spin bath. *Phys. Rev. B* **2018**, *98*, 064306. [CrossRef]

71. Martens, C.C. Communication: Decoherence in a nonequilibrium environment: An analytically solvable model. *J. Chem. Phys.* **2010**, *133*, 241101. [CrossRef]
72. Martens, C.C. Quantum dephasing of a two-state system by a nonequilibrium harmonic oscillator. *J. Chem. Phys.* **2013**, *139*, 024109. [CrossRef]
73. Lombardo, F.C.; Villar, P.I. Nonunitary geometric phases: A qubit coupled to an environment with random noise. *Phys. Rev. A* **2013**, *87*, 032338. [CrossRef]
74. Lombardo, F.C.; Villar, P.I. Correction to the geometric phase by structured environments: The onset of non-Markovian effects. *Phys. Rev. A* **2015**, *91*, 042111. [CrossRef]
75. Zheng, Y.; Brown, F.L.H. Single-Molecule Photon Counting Statistics via Generalized Optical Bloch Equations. *Phys. Rev. Lett.* **2003**, *90*, 238305. [CrossRef] [PubMed]
76. Brokmann, X.; Hermier, J.P.; Messin, G.; Desbiolles, P.; Bouchaud, J.P.; Dahan, M. Statistical Aging and Nonergodicity in the Fluorescence of Single Nanocrystals. *Phys. Rev. Lett.* **2003**, *90*, 120601. [CrossRef] [PubMed]
77. Burkard, G. Non-Markovian qubit dynamics in the presence of $1/f$ noise. *Phys. Rev. B* **2009**, *79*, 125317. [CrossRef]
78. Rossi, M.A.C.; Paris, M.G.A. Non-Markovian dynamics of single- and two-qubit systems interacting with Gaussian and non-Gaussian fluctuating transverse environments. *J. Chem. Phys.* **2016**, *144*, 024113. [CrossRef]
79. Benedetti, C.; Buscemi, F.; Bordone, P.; Paris, M.G.A. Dynamics of quantum correlations in colored-noise environments. *Phys. Rev. A* **2013**, *87*, 052328. [CrossRef]
80. Benedetti, C.; Paris, M.G.A.; Maniscalco, S. Non-Markovianity of colored noisy channels. *Phys. Rev. A* **2014**, *89*, 012114. [CrossRef]
81. Benedetti, C.; Buscemi, F.; Bordone, P.; Paris, M.G.A. Effects of classical environmental noise on entanglement and quantum discord dynamics. *Int. J. Quantum Inf.* **2012**, *8*, 1241005. [CrossRef]
82. Lo Franco, R.; D'Arrigo, A.; Falci, G.; Compagno, G.; Paladino, E. Entanglement dynamics in superconducting qubits affected by local bistable impurities. *Phys. Scr.* **2012**, *T147*, 014019. [CrossRef]
83. Silveri, M.P.; Tuorila, J.A.; Thuneberg, E.V.; Paraoanu, G.S. Quantum systems under frequency modulation. *Rep. Prog. Phys.* **2017**, *80*, 056002. [CrossRef]
84. Cialdi, S.; Rossi, M.A.C.; Benedetti, C.; Vacchini, B.; Tamascelli, D.; Olivares, S.; Paris, M.G.A. All-optical quantum simulator of qubit noisy channels. *Appl. Phys. Lett.* **2017**, *110*, 081107. [CrossRef]
85. Cialdi, S.; Benedetti, C.; Tamascelli, D.; Olivares, S.; Paris, M.G.A.; Vacchini, B. Experimental investigation of the effect of classical noise on quantum non-Markovian dynamics. *Phys. Rev. A* **2019**, *100*, 052104. [CrossRef]
86. Fuliński, A. Non-Markovian noise. *Phys. Rev. E* **1994**, *50*, 2668. [CrossRef] [PubMed]
87. Cai, X.; Zheng, Y. Non-Markovian decoherence dynamics in nonequilibrium environments. *J. Chem. Phys.* **2018**, *149*, 094107. [CrossRef] [PubMed]
88. Cai, X.; Zheng, Y. Decoherence induced by non-Markovian noise in a nonequilibrium environment. *Phys. Rev. A* **2016**, *94*, 042110. [CrossRef]
89. Cai, X.; Zheng, Y. Quantum dynamical speedup in a nonequilibrium environment. *Phys. Rev. A* **2017**, *95*, 052104. [CrossRef]
90. Lin, D.; Zou, H.M.; Yang, J. Based-nonequilibrium-environment non-Markovianity, quantum Fisher information and quantum coherence. *Phys. Scr.* **2019**, *95*, 015103. [CrossRef]
91. Cai, X.; Meng, R.; Zhang, Y.; Wang, L. Geometry of quantum evolution in a nonequilibrium environment. *Europhys. Lett.* **2019**, *125*, 30007. [CrossRef]
92. Basit, A.; Ali, H.; Badshah, F.; Yang, X.F.; Ge, G.Q. Controlling sudden transition from classical to quantum decoherence via non-equilibrium environments. *New J. Phys.* **2020**, *22*, 033039. [CrossRef]
93. Basit, A.; Ali, H.; Badshah, F.; Yang, X.F.; Ge, G. Nonequilibrium effects on one-norm geometric correlations and the emergence of a pointer-state basis in the weak- and strong-coupling regimes. *Phys. Rev. A* **2021**, *104*, 042417. [CrossRef]
94. Yu, T.; Eberly, J.H. Finite-time Disentanglement via Spontaneous Emission. *Phys. Rev. Lett.* **2004**, *93*, 140404. [CrossRef] [PubMed]
95. van Kampen, N.G. *Stochastic Process in Physics and Chemistry*; North-Holland: Amsterdam, The Netherlands, 1992.
96. Cai, X. Quantum dephasing induced by non-Markovian random telegraph noise. *Sci. Rep.* **2020**, *10*, 88. [CrossRef] [PubMed]
97. Laine, E.M.; Piilo, J.; Breuer, H.P. Measure for the non-Markovianity of quantum processes. *Phys. Rev. A* **2010**, *81*, 062115. [CrossRef]
98. Addis, C.; Haikka, P.; McEndoo, S.; Macchiavello, C.; Maniscalco, S. Two-qubit non-Markovianity induced by a common environment. *Phys. Rev. A* **2013**, *87*, 052109. [CrossRef]
99. Addis, C.; Bylicka, B.; Chruściński, D.; Maniscalco, S. Comparative study of non-Markovianity measures in exactly solvable one- and two-qubit models. *Phys. Rev. A* **2014**, *90*, 052103. [CrossRef]
100. Lo Franco, R.; D'Arrigo, A.; Falci, G.; Compagno, G.; Paladino, E. Preserving entanglement and nonlocality in solid-state qubits by dynamical decoupling. *Phys. Rev. B* **2014**, *90*, 054304. [CrossRef]
101. Lo Franco, R. Nonlocality threshold for entanglement under general dephasing evolutions: A case study. *Quantum Inf. Process.* **2016**, *15*, 2593. [CrossRef]
102. Wootters, W.K. Entanglement of Formation of an Arbitrary State of Two Qubits. *Phys. Rev. Lett.* **1998**, *80*, 2245–2248. [CrossRef]
103. Horodecki, R.; Horodecki, P.; Horodecki, M. Violating Bell inequality by mixed states spin 1/2: Necessary and sufficient condition. *Phys. Lett. A* **1995**, *200*, 340. [CrossRef]
104. Yu, T.; Eberly, J.H. Evolution from entanglement to decoherence of bipartite mixed "X" states. *Quantum Inf. Comput.* **2007**, *7*, 459.

105. Derkacz, L.; Jakóbczyk, L. Clauser-Horne-Shimony-Holt violation and the entropy-concurrence plane. *Phys. Rev. A* **2005**, *72*, 042321. [CrossRef]
106. Mazzola, L.; Piilo, J.; Maniscalco, S. Sudden Transition between Classical and Quantum Decoherence. *Phys. Rev. Lett.* **2010**, *104*, 200401. [CrossRef] [PubMed]
107. Verstraete, F.; Wolf, M.M. Entanglement versus Bell Violations and Their Behavior under Local Filtering Operations. *Phys. Rev. Lett.* **2002**, *89*, 170401. [CrossRef] [PubMed]

Article

Quantum Energy Current Induced Coherence in a Spin Chain under Non-Markovian Environments

Arapat Ablimit [1], Run-Hong He [1], Yang-Yang Xie [1], Lian-Ao Wu [2,3,*] and Zhao-Ming Wang [1,*]

[1] College of Physics and Optoelectronic Engineering, Ocean University of China, Qingdao 266100, China
[2] Ikerbasque, Basque Foundation for Science, 48011 Bilbao, Spain
[3] Department of Physics, University of the Basque Country UPV/EHU, 48080 Bilbao, Spain
* Correspondence: lianao.wu@ehu.es (L.-A.W.); wangzhaoming@ouc.edu.cn (Z.-M.W.)

Abstract: We investigate the time-dependent behaviour of the energy current between a quantum spin chain and its surrounding non-Markovian and finite temperature baths, together with its relationship to the coherence dynamics of the system. To be specific, both the system and the baths are assumed to be initially in thermal equilibrium at temperature T_s and T_b, respectively. This model plays a fundamental role in study of quantum system evolution towards thermal equilibrium in an open system. The non-Markovian quantum state diffusion (NMQSD) equation approach is used to calculate the dynamics of the spin chain. The effects of non-Markovianity, temperature difference and system-bath interaction strength on the energy current and the corresponding coherence in cold and warm baths are analyzed, respectively. We show that the strong non-Markovianity, weak system-bath interaction and low temperature difference will help to maintain the system coherence and correspond to a weaker energy current. Interestingly, the warm baths destroy the coherence while the cold baths help to build coherence. Furthermore, the effects of the Dzyaloshinskii–Moriya (DM) interaction and the external magnetic field on the energy current and coherence are analyzed. Both energy current and coherence will change due to the increase of the system energy induced by the DM interaction and magnetic field. Significantly, the minimal coherence corresponds to the critical magnetic field which causes the first order phase transition.

Keywords: quantum coherence; energy current; non-Markovian dynamics

1. Introduction

Decoherence and dissipation of a quantum system are a consequence of the interaction between the system and its surrounding environment and have been extensively studied in quantum optics, quantum information, or quantum many-body system. Open systems are difficult to deal with due to the complexity of the reservoirs. Born-Markovian approximation has been used to describe the system dynamics, which assumes that the large reservoir is not altered significantly. In this case, the system loses its information into the bath, and these lost information does not play any further role on the system dynamics. At short and intermediate time scales, considering the memory effects of the environment, it may fails to give a correct description of the dynamics. A non-Markovian quantum master equation is therefore required to faithfully reproduce the system dynamics, especially in this era quantum technology in short-time and/or low temperature has been developed thoroughly [1]. In the non-Markovian case, the lost information can flow back to the system from environment within a certain time [2–5]. The key feature of environmental non-Markovianity is the distinguishability between any two states, i.e., strong non-Markovianity corresponds to larger information backflow [6]. The lost information can flow back to the system within a certain time The bath-to-system backflow of information will affect the system dynamics and has been investigated from different perspectives such as regeneration of the coherence [7], energy [8,9], and heat [10,11]. And these phenomena have been observed in different experimental setups [12–14].

Recently, significant efforts have been devoted to non-Markovian dynamics in various aspects of physics, such as quantum chemistry [15], solid state physics [16], and topological physics [17]. Several methods have also been suggested to formally define and quantify the degree of non-Markovianity of the baths [6,18,19]. Global correlation and local information flows in controllable non-Markovian quantum dynamics is recently studied and the quantum Fisher information and quantum mutual information are demonstrated to be capable of measuring the non-Markovianity for a multi-channel open quantum dynamics [20]. Furthermore, in superohmic environment the non-Markovian recovery of the system dynamics and different initial state trace distance non-monotonicity are found using real-time path integral [21]. Nowadays non-Markovianity has been exploited as resource to improve the quantum state transfer fidelity through a spin chain [22], the adiabatic fidelity [23], or quantum communication protocols [24]. Non-Markovian effects from the point view of information backflow is investigated [11], exchange of information and heat in a spin-boson model with a cold reservoir is examined.

In most of these studies, the system is assumed to be initially in a pure state. However the assumption may not be true because of inevitably inaccurate physical operations, environmental temperature and lingering noises. Furthermore, in a multi-qubit quantum system such as nuclear magnetic resonance, it is difficult to manipulate or detect single qubits and prepare pure states [25]. Thus it is of practical significance and necessary to consider initial mixed states in a quantum process in particular qauntum computation [26–28]. In this paper, we consider a general case that the system and the baths are both initially in thermal equilibrium at a certain temperature. We focus on the time evolution of the energy current and coherence of the system in an open system. We use NMQSD approach to investigate the non-Markovian dynamics of the system [29–32]. It determines the quantum dynamics of open systems by solving the non-Markovian diffusive stochastic Schrödinger equation [33,34]. The effects of the environmental (temperature T_b, non-Markovianity γ, interaction strength Γ) and system (DM interaction strength D_z, magnetic field intensity B_z) parameters are analyzed in warm and cold baths, respectively.

2. Formalism

In this section, we review the non-Markovian quantum state diffusion approach (Section 2.1) which will be used in the calculation. We then introduce the spin chain model, the energy current and quantum coherence in Sections 2.2–2.4.

2.1. Non-Markovian Quantum State Diffusion

In open systems, the total Hamiltonian can be written as

$$H_{tot} = H_s + H_b + H_{int}, \quad (1)$$

where H_s, H_b denote the system and bath Hamiltonian, respectively. H_{int} is the interaction Hamiltonian between the system and bath. Suppose the system consists of many qubits. It is reasonable to assume that each qubit is coupled to its own environment. We are thus led to a more complicated model in which the system couples to a collection of independent baths. The Hamiltonian of the bath reads $H_b = \sum_{j=1}^{N} H_b^j$. $H_b^j = \sum_k \omega_k^j b_k^{j\dagger} b_k^j$ (setting $\hbar = 1$) is the Hamiltonian of the jth baths with $b_k^{j\dagger}$, b_k^j being the bosonic creation and annihilation operators of the kth mode with frequency ω_k^j. The system-bath interaction Hamiltonian H_{int} is given by

$$H_{int} = \sum_{j,k} \left(f_k^{j*} L_j^\dagger b_k^j + f_k^j L_j b_k^{j\dagger} \right), \quad (2)$$

where L_j is the Lindblad operator and it characterizes the couplings between the system and the jth bath. f_k^j is the coupling strength between the system and the kth mode of the jth bath. Assume that the jth bath is initially in a thermal equilibrium state at temperature T_j

$$\rho_j(0) = e^{-\beta H_b^j}/Z_j. \tag{3}$$

Here $Z_j = Tr[e^{-\beta H_b^j}]$ is the partition function with $\beta_j = 1/T_j$ (setting $K_B = 1$).

The open system in the bosonic heat bath satisfies the following NMQSD equation [31,33,35]

$$\frac{\partial}{\partial t}|\psi(t)\rangle = [-iH_s + \sum_j (L_j z_j^*(t) + L_j^\dagger w_j^*(t) - L_j^\dagger \overline{O}_{z^*}^{j\dagger}(t) - L_j \overline{O}_{w^*}^j(t))]|\psi(t)\rangle, \tag{4}$$

where $z^*(t), w^*(t)$ are the stochastic environmental noises, and $\overline{O}_\eta^j(t) = \int_0^t \alpha_\eta^j(t,s) O_\eta^j(t,s,z_j^*,w_j^*)$. The O operator is an operator defined by an *ansatz* $O_\eta^j(t,s,z_j^*,w_j^*)|\psi(t)\rangle = \frac{\delta}{\delta\eta(s)}|\psi(t)\rangle$ (for details, see [33]). It has memory kernel and depends on the nature of noise as well as the form of the coupling between the system and the baths. $\alpha_\eta(t,s)$ is the bath correlation function. The density operator of the system can be recovered from the average of the solutions to the NMQSD equation over all the environmental noises. When the environmental noise strength is weak, the non-Markovian master equation can be written as [36]

$$\frac{\partial}{\partial t}\rho_s = -i[H_s, \rho_s] + \sum_j \{[L_j, \rho_s \overline{O}_z^{j\dagger}(t)] - [L_j^\dagger, \overline{O}_z^j(t)\rho_s] + [L_j^\dagger, \rho_s \overline{O}_w^{j\dagger}(t)] - [L_j, \overline{O}_w^j(t)\rho_s]\}. \tag{5}$$

The first term on the right-hand side of Equation (5) accounts for the coherent unitary evolution, which is ruled by the system Hamiltonian H_s. The other terms on the right-hand side describe the couplings to the environment. For the bath correlation function $\alpha_\eta^j(t,s)$, we choose the ohmic type with a Lorentz-Drude cutoff [37–39], whose spectral density is given by $J_j(\omega_j) = \frac{\Gamma_j}{\pi}\frac{\omega_j}{1+(\frac{\omega_j}{\gamma_j})^2}$. Here Γ_j, γ_j are dimensionless real parameters. Γ_j describes the overall environmental noise strength to the system dynamical evolution process, and $1/\gamma_j$ represents the memory time of the environment. When γ_j approaches to zero, the bosonic bath bandwidth is narrow, which corresponds to colored noise, then the environment manifests a strong non-Markovianity. On the contrary, for a large γ_j, the distribution of the Lorentzian spectrum represents a white noise, which corresponds to Markovian limit. $\overline{O}_\eta^j(t)$ can be numerically calculated by the following equations [40,41]

$$\frac{\partial \overline{O}_z^j}{\partial t} = (\frac{\Gamma_j T_j \gamma_j}{2} - \frac{i\Gamma_j \gamma_j^2}{2})L_j - \gamma_j \overline{O}_z^j + [-iH_s - \sum_j(L_j^\dagger \overline{O}_z^j + L_j \overline{O}_w^j), \overline{O}_z^j], \tag{6}$$

$$\frac{\partial \overline{O}_w^j}{\partial t} = \frac{\Gamma_j T_j \gamma_j}{2} L_j^\dagger - \gamma_j \overline{O}_w^j + [-iH_s - \sum_j(L_j^\dagger \overline{O}_z^j + L_j \overline{O}_w^j), \overline{O}_w^j]. \tag{7}$$

2.2. Spin Chain

The NMQSD approach provides a general theory to deal with the non-Markovian dynamics of an open quantum system. The system Hamiltonian can be taken as different forms for different physical systems. The spin chain model has attracted much attention in experimental and theoretical studies due to its rich and exquisite mathematical structure. It is not just an abstract theoretical model but in fact accurately describe the dominant physical phenomena of metals and crystals like ferromagnetism and antiferromagnetism [42–45]. Here in this paper, we take a one-dimensional *XY* spin chain with *DM* interaction and external magnetic field. For the individual bath model, each spin is immersed in its own baths (see Figure 1). The Hamiltonian reads

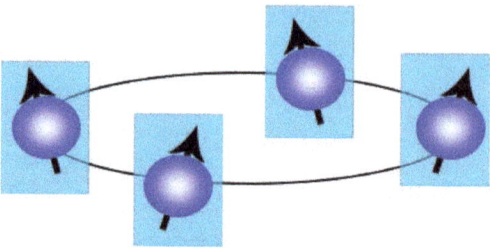

Figure 1. (Color on line) The sketch of the spin chain. Each spin is immersed in its own non-Markovian and finite temperature heat bath.

$$H_s = \sum_{j=1}^{N}\left[J(\sigma_j^x\sigma_{j+1}^x + \sigma_j^y\sigma_{j+1}^y) + D_z(\sigma_j^x\sigma_{j+1}^y - \sigma_j^y\sigma_{j+1}^x) + B_z\sigma_j^z\right], \tag{8}$$

where σ_j^α ($\alpha = x, y, z$) represents the α component of the Pauli matrix for spins and J is the coupling constant between the nearest-neighbour sites. N is the number of site and we assume the periodic boundary conditions $\sigma_{N+1}^\alpha = \sigma_1^\alpha$. The parameters D_z and B_z are DM interaction and uniform magnetic field strength. Note here we consider z-component DM interaction D_z and uniform magnetic field B_z along z direction. Antiferromagnetic spin chain have gained increasing attention in spin technology owing to their advantages over their ferromagnetic counterpart in considerable spin orbit, achieving ultrafast dynamics, and large magnetoresistance transport [46–48]. For this model, we take antiferromagnetic coupling $J = 1$ throughout and $0 \leq D_z \leq 1$.

Now we assume that initially the spin chain is also at thermal equilibrium, with the density matrix $\rho_s(0) = e^{-\beta_s H_s}/tr(e^{-\beta_s H_s})$. $\beta_s = 1/T_s$ is the inverse temperature. The high-temperature approximation can be taken when $\|H_s\| \ll T_s$ ($\|H_s\| = tr\sqrt{H_s^\dagger H_s}$). In this case, $\rho_s(0)$ can be approximately expressed by the first two terms of the Taylor expansion [25]

$$\rho_s(0) = \frac{1}{2^N}\left(I - \frac{H_s}{T_s}\right), \tag{9}$$

where I is the identity matrix of dimension 2^N. Although the thermal equilibrium state is highly mixed, experimental and theoretical studies have shown that this state can be transformed into a pseudo-pure state [49,50]

$$\rho_s(0) = \frac{1}{2^N}(1-\epsilon)I + \epsilon|\varphi_0\rangle\langle\varphi_0|. \tag{10}$$

Pseudo-pure state is still a mixed state ($tr(\rho_s^2) < 1$), but in the whole evolution the state $|\varphi_0\rangle$ appears with probability $(1-\epsilon)/2^N + \epsilon$ and it can carry out some manipulations and quantum algorithms designed for pure states [51]. All of the states orthogonal to state $|\varphi_0\rangle$ appear with equal probabilities of $(1-\epsilon)/2^N$, where the coefficient ϵ is usually small. This pseudo-pure state technique provides a convenient starting point for quantum information processing with less than 10 qubits [52].

For the initial density operator of the system, according Equation (10) throughout the paper we take $N = 4$, and assume

$$|\varphi_0\rangle = (|1000\rangle + |0100\rangle + |0010\rangle + |0001\rangle), \qquad \epsilon = -3\beta_s. \tag{11}$$

Note that the temperature-dependent parameter $\epsilon \to 0$ in the high-temperature limit and the initial density matrix is more inclined to be a mixed state $\rho_s(0) \to \frac{1}{2^N} I$.

2.3. Energy Current

The energy transfer between the system and the environment is important in the study of thermodyanmic properties of an open system. The exchange energy between the open system and environment is accompanied by the exchange of entropy, which is one of the important criteria to evaluate the amount of information stored in a quantum system. Therefore, energy current can indirectly describe the information storage capacity of the environment. Recently, an exactly solvable model was proposed to investigate the quantum energy current between a nonlinearly coupled bosonic bath and a fermionic chain [53]. The adiabatic speedup and the associated heat current with and without pulse control is investigated, where the heat current is defined as the difference of the energy current and the power [10,54]. The energy current can be defined as the derivative of the expectation value of H_s [55,56]

$$E(t) = \frac{\partial}{\partial t} tr[\rho_s H_s]. \tag{12}$$

The above definitions has been proved to be valid for a non-equilibrium spin—boson model and a three-level heat engine model in the case of non-perturbative and non-Markovian conditions [57], where the reduced hierarchal equations of motion approach is used.

2.4. Quantum Coherence

Quantum coherence or quantum superposition lies at the hotspot of quantum theory, and it is a very valuable resource for quantum information processing [58,59]. It is also of equal importance as entanglement in the studies of both bipartite and multipartite quantum systems [60]. Based on the framework of consistent resource theory, the commonly used coherence measure is the l_1 norm coherence, which is a sum of all off-diagonal elements of the density matrix [61]

$$C(\rho) = \sum_{a \neq b} |\rho_{a,b}|. \tag{13}$$

3. Numerical Results and Discussions

Based on the definition of energy current and quantum coherence in Equations (12) and (13), we next numerically calculate the non-Markovian dynamics of the energy current and quantum coherence. Now the model is that each spin is immersed in its individual bath [22]. However, due to the neighbor spins are close to each other, we assume the same environmental parameters $\Gamma = \Gamma_j$, $\gamma = \gamma_j$, $T_b = T_b^j$ for all these jth baths. We also assume there is no initial system-bath correlations, $\rho(0) = \rho_s(0) \otimes \rho_b(0)$. $\rho_s(0)$ is often taken as pure state, and $\rho_b(0)$ is in a vacuum state [22], or thermal equilibrium state [62,63]. As an example, throughout the paper we consider the quantum dissipation model, in this case the Lindblad operator $L_j = \sigma_j^-$. $\sigma_j^- = (\sigma_j^x - i\sigma_j^y)/2$. In this case, the number of excitations is not conserved, and transitions between different subspaces with certain number of excitations occur [64]. We will study the behavior in time of the energy exchange between the system and the baths and the quantum coherence of the system under the influence of the baths.

We first explore the effects of non-Markovianity, environmental temperature and noise strength on the system dynamics when the system couples to warm baths ($T_b > T_s$). In Figure 2, we plot the energy current as a function of time t for different parameter γ (Figure 2a), T_b (Figure 2b) and Γ (Figure 2c), respectively. In the inset of Figure 2 we also plot the corresponding coherence dynamics. In Figure 2, we take $T_s = 10$ and the weak coupling limit $\Gamma = 0.003$, $T_b = 80$ for Figure 2a, $\gamma = 5, \Gamma = 0.003$ for Figure 2b, $T_b = 80, \gamma = 5$ for Figure 2c. From Figure 2, we can see that the energy current between the system and baths increases with increasing parameters γ, Γ and $|T_s - T_b|$. That is to say, more Markovian baths, stronger system-baths interactions and higher temperature difference correspond to bigger energy current, which is in accordance with the case that the initial states of the system is in a pure state [54]. Correspondingly, coherence decreases with increasing parameters γ, Γ and $|T_s - T_b|$. As expected, non-Markovian baths, weak system-bath interactions and low temperature difference will be helpful to maintain the coherence of the system. Note that in most cases the energy current is positive, which indicates the energy transfer from environment to the system. At time $t = 0$, the energy current is 0. In a short time region, the energy starts to increase and reach a peak value. Then it decreases in long time region. For a relatively strong non-Markovian bath (Figure 2a $\gamma = 0.5$), the energy current exhibits a oscillation pattern before it reaches steady state, which has negative values (from system to bath). In this case, the coherence also shows an osillation, i.e., the energy backflow from sytem to baths affects the coherence of the system.

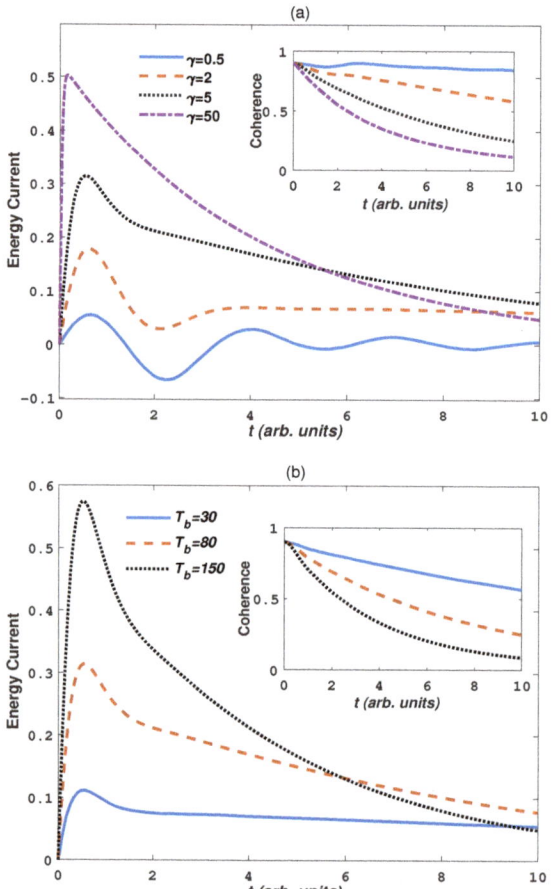

Figure 2. *Cont.*

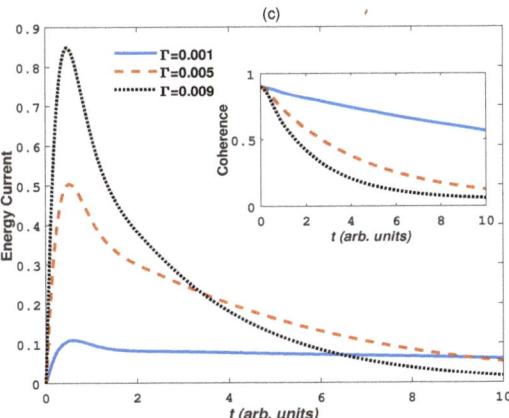

Figure 2. (Color on line) The energy current and quantum coherence as a function of time t in warm baths ($T_s < T_b$) for different values of bath parameters: (**a**) γ, $T_b = 80$, $\Gamma = 0.003$; (**b**) T_b, $\gamma = 5$, $\Gamma = 0.003$; (**c**) Γ, $T_b = 80$, $\gamma = 5$. Other parameters are take as $T_s = 10$, $J = 1$, $D_z = 0$ and $B_z = 0$.

Next we discuss a contrary case that the system is immersed in cold baths ($T_s > T_b$). Figure 3 again plots the effects of the parameters γ, T_b and Γ on the energy current and coherence. Here we take a high system temperature $T_s = 100$, clearly the coefficient ϵ in Equation (11) becomes smaller, pseudo-pure state purity decreases, thus weakening the quantum coherence in the initial state (the initial coherence is now 0.09 from Figure 3). Compared with Figure 2, we find that the same conclusion is obtained that the energy current increases with increasing parameters γ, Γ and temperature difference $|T_s - T_b|$. But a negative energy corresponds to the energy transfer from a warm system to the cold baths. During the calculation, we find that initially positive energy current occurs in a very short time, these initial currents reflect the response of the system to instantaneous coupling to the baths at time $t = 0$. For the coherence, the conclusion in Figure 2 also holds: non-Markovian baths, weak system-bath interactions and low temperature difference will be helpful to maintain the coherence of the system. But surprisingly, the coherence increases with increasing parameter γ and Γ but decreases with increasing T_b. That is to say, for warm system in cold baths, more Markovian, lower temperature, and stronger interaction strengths helps the system to be a more pure state. This phenomenon can be explained as follows: when a small warm system is surrounded by large cold baths, the system energy dissipates into the bath quickly and the system gets cool down, thus the coherence starts to increase due to low system temperature.

The DM interaction is an antisymmetric exchange interaction between nearest site spins, arising from spin-orbit coupling. It emerges in Heisenberg model lacking inversion symmetry and promotes noncollinear alignment of magnetic moments and induces chiral magnetic order [65,66]. Although this interaction is weak, it has many spectacular features, for example, chiral Néel domain walls [67,68], skyrmions [69], etc, implying that a study of spin models with DM interaction could have realistic applications. In antiferromagnetic materials, DM interaction will break the antiparallelism of the spin chain spatial structure. This change enriches the physical properties of antiferromagnetic materials [70,71], such as in coupled quantum dots in GaAs [72]. Next we will discuss the effects of DM interaction on the energy current and coherence. Figure 4 plots the quantum coherence and energy current dynamics for different DM interaction strength D_z in the warm baths ($T_b = 80$, $T_s = 20$) and cold baths ($T_b = 20$, $T_s = 80$), respectively. Other parameters are taken as $\Gamma = 0.005$, $\gamma = 2$, $J = 1$, $B_z = J$. From Figure 4a, for warm baths the negative energy current is obtained by the introduction of DM interaction. Strong DM interaction strength D_z restrains the positive energy current and enlarges the negative energy current. This is due to, as the DM interaction strength increases, strong spin-orbit couplings cause the neighboring spins inverse antiparallel structures to intersect and the system energy is enhanced, as a result it restrains the energy current from the bath to system and enlarges the reversed current. For the cold baths plotted in Figure 4b, the negative energy current always exists and clearly the energy current increases with increasing D_z, which is also caused by the increasement of the system energy. From the inset of Figure 4a,b, the coherence of the system decreases with increasing D_z. Stronger DM interaction will destroy more coherence of the system, i.e., the system energy increase is not conductive to the preservation of quantum coherence, whether in warm or cold baths. In addition, we find that after the evolution time $t > 4$, the quantum coherence in warm bath and cold bath has a significant recovery, which is caused by the non-markovianity of the environment.

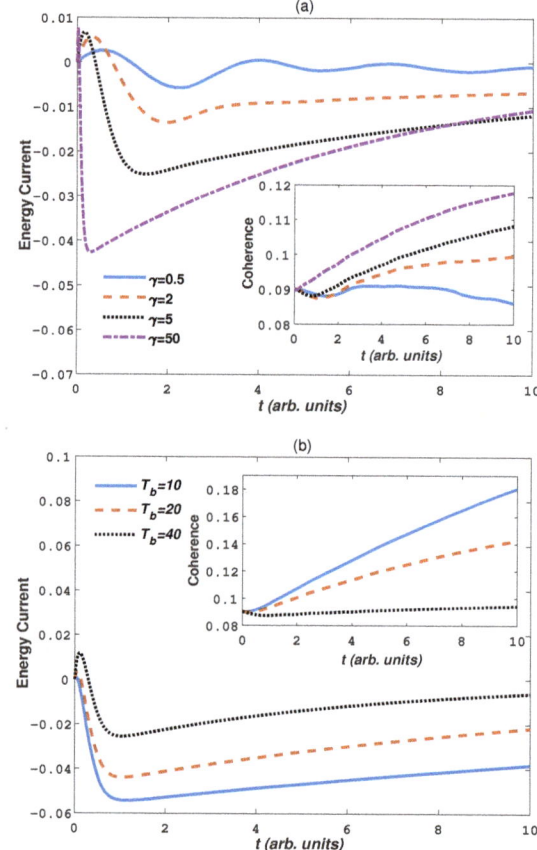

Figure 3. Cont.

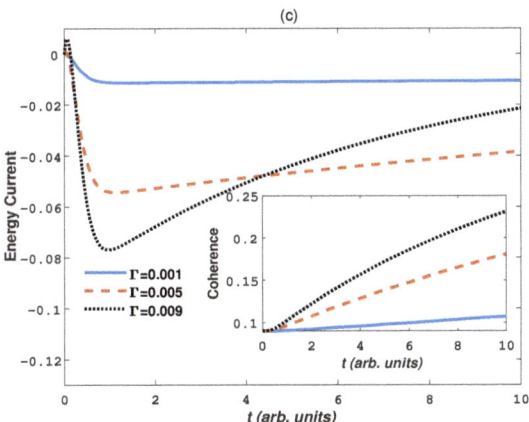

Figure 3. (Color on line) The energy current and quantum coherence as a function of time t in cold baths ($T_s > T_b$): (**a**) γ, $\Gamma = 0.005$, $T_b = 10$; (**b**) T_b, $\gamma = 10$, $\Gamma = 0.005$; (**c**) Γ, $\gamma = 10$, $T_b = 10$. Other parameters are $T_s = 100$, $J = 1$, $D_z = 0$, and $B_z = 0$.

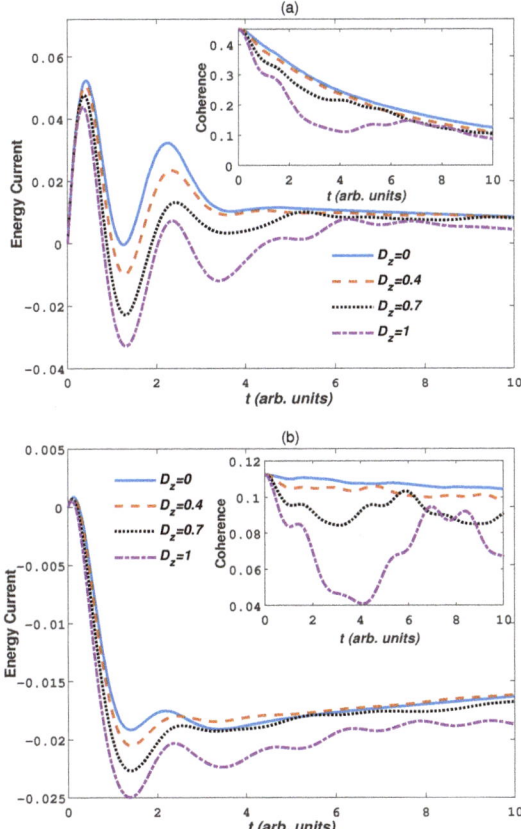

Figure 4. (Color on line) The dynamics of the energy current and quantum coherence with different DM interaction strength D_z in (**a**) warm baths ($T_s = 20$, $T_b = 80$) and (**b**) cold baths ($T_s = 80$, $T_b = 20$). Other parameters are $B_z = J$, $\gamma = 2$, $\Gamma = 0.005$, $J = 1$.

At last, we consider the effects of the external magnetic field, which can also affect the spatial structure of spin chain and show a positive aspect in the study of quantum entanglement and quantum state transport in a spin chain [73–75]. In Figure 5, we plot the energy current and coherence dynamics for different external magnetic field intensity B_z in warm baths and cold baths, respectively. The parameters are the same as in Figure 4 except that $D_z = 0.3$. First from Figure 5a for the warm bath case, the positive energy current decreases with increasing B_z for a weak magnetic field ($B_z = J$). When $B_z = 2J$, the energy current starts to reverse and it increases with increasing B_z. The coherence in the inset of Figure 5a also shows this decrease-increase behavior. $B_z = 2J$ corresponds to the lowest coherence. Why strong field can cause the reverse of the energy current? From Figure 5a the energy transfer from the low temperature system to the high temperature baths always occurs in a strong external field (e.g., $B_z = 5J$). The spin chain is more inclined to be at antiferromagnetic order in thermal equilibrium, but the introduction of magnetic field reduce the antiferromagnetic order. When the external magnetic field increases to the critical field point ($B_z = 2J$), the spin chain polarization flips into the direction perpendicular to the field, and the phase transition characteristics are immediately captured by the evolutionary properties of coherence or the energy current. The spin-flip transition of antiferromagnetic materials under the external magnetic is a first-order quantum phase transition, and can be observed experimentally [76,77]. Strong field causes the spin parallel to the direction of the field and corresponds to a high potential energy, thus the energy current from the low temperature system to high temperature baths occurs. Strong field also corresponds to high coherence and weakens the decoherence of the system. The increase of the energy caused by the field can also fairly explain the results in Figure 5b. The negative energy current always increases with increasing B_z for cold baths. The energy difference between system and baths enlarges the energy current. In this case, the phase transition ($B_z = 2J$) can not be characterized by the energy current reverse, but it can still be characterized by the coherence.

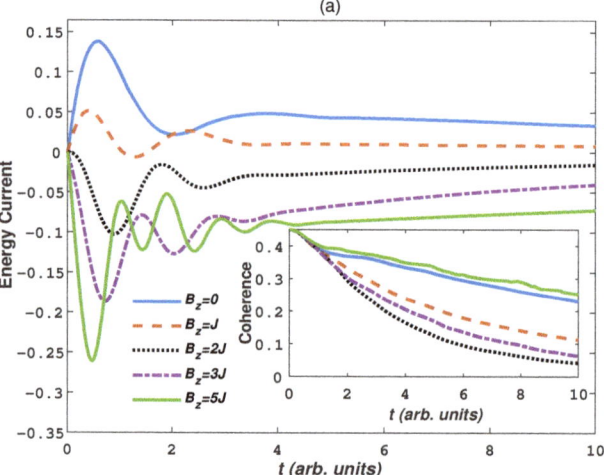

Figure 5. *Cont.*

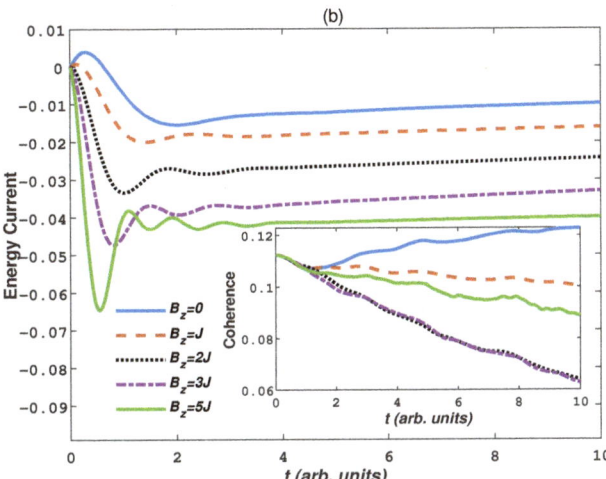

Figure 5. (Color on line) The dynamics of energy current and quantum coherence for different B_z in (**a**) warm baths ($T_s = 20$, $T_b = 80$); (**b**) cold baths ($T_s = 80$, $T_b = 20$). Other parameters are $N = 4$, $\gamma = 2$, $\Gamma = 0.005$, $J = 1$, $D_z = 0.3$.

4. Conclusions

We have investigated the energy current and coherence dynamics in open systems. The system is a one dimensional spin chain with periodic boundary conditions. We have considered the independent bath model, i.e., each spin is immersed in its own non-Markovian bath. Specifically, the spin chain is initially at thermal equilibrium at finite temperature, or equivalently at pseudo-pure state. By using the NMQSD approach, we calculate the energy current between the system and baths and the coherence dynamics in warm baths and in cold baths, respectively. The effects of the bath non-Markovianity, bath temperature and system-bath coupling strength on the energy current and coherence are analyzed. We find that non-Markovianity, low temperature difference and weak coupling correspond to weaker energy current and are in favour of the coherence for both warm and cold baths. However, the coherence will be damaged by the warm baths but in cold baths it can be significantly enlarged. Cold environment will help to boost the coherence. We also consider the influences of the DM interaction on the energy current and coherence. The DM interaction will increase the system energy for antiferromagnetic chain. Then it shows different behaviours for warm and cold baths. For warm baths, strong DM interactions restrain the positive energy current and enlarge negative energy current. For cold baths, it only exists negative energy current, and strong DM interactions also enlarge the negative energy current. The coherence will always decreases with the DM interaction strength D_z. Finally we have also studied the magnetic field effects, where $B_z = 2J$ is a critical value which corresponds to the first a quantum phase transition. The magnetic field can also increase the system energy, then similar as the DM interaction case, for warm baths, strong magnetic fields restrain the positive energy current and enlarge negative energy. For cold baths, strong magnetic fields also enlarge the negative energy currents. It is interesting to note that for both types of baths the coherence demonstrates decrease-increase behaviour with increasing B_z, and the lowest coherence corresponds to the critical value $B_z = 2J$. These investigations, based on microscopic understanding, elucidates the relation of energy current and quantum coherence, which might potentially be a good reference in context of quantum thermodynamics of non-Markovian open quantum systems [78], as well as in study of environment-induced quantum coherence [79–81].

Author Contributions: Conceptualization, Z.-M.W. and L.-A.W.; methodology, A.A. and Z.-M.W.; validation, R.-H.H. and Y.-Y.X.; writing—original draft preparation, A.A.; writing—review and editing, Z.-M.W. and L.-A.W.; supervision, Z.-M.W. All authors have read and agreed to the published version of the manuscript.

Funding: This research was funded by Natural Science Foundation of Shandong Province grant number ZR2021LLZ004, and grant PID2021-126273NB-I00 funded by MCIN/AEI/10.13039/501100011033, and by "ERDF A way of making Europe" and the Basque Government through grant number IT1470-22.

Institutional Review Board Statement: Not applicable.

Informed Consent Statement: Not applicable.

Data Availability Statement: The datasets used and/or analyzed during the current study are available from the corresponding author on reasonable request.

Acknowledgments: We would like to thank Ahmad Abliz, Shen-Shuang Nie and Jing-Wu for their helpful discussions.

Conflicts of Interest: The authors declare no conflict of interest.

Abbreviations

The following abbreviations are used in this manuscript:

NMQSD Non-Markovian Quantum State Diffusion
DM   Dzyaloshinskii–Moriya

References

1. Woggon, U.; Gindele, F.; Langbein, W.; Hvam, J.M. Quantum kinetic exciton–LO-phonon interaction in CdSe. *Phys. Rev. B.* **2000**, *61*, 1935–1940. [CrossRef]
2. Breuer, H.P.; Laine, E.M.; Piilo, J.; Vacchini, B. Colloquium: Non-Markovian dynamics in open quantum systems. *Rev. Mod. Phys.* **2016**, *88*, 021002. [CrossRef]
3. Piilo, J.; Härkönen, K.; Maniscalco, S.; Suominen, K.A. Open system dynamics with non-Markovian quantum jumps. *Phys. Rev. A* **2009**, *79*, 062112. [CrossRef]
4. Tarasov, V.E. General non-Markovian quantum dynamics. *Entropy* **2021**, *23*, 1006. [CrossRef] [PubMed]
5. Czerwinski, A. Dynamics of open quantum systems—Markovian semigroups and beyond. *Symmetry* **2022**, *14*, 1752. [CrossRef]
6. Breuer, H.P.; Laine, E.M.; Piilo, J. Measure for the degree of non-Markovian behavior of quantum processes in open systems. *Phys. Rev. Lett.* **2009**, *103*, 210401. [CrossRef]
7. Helm, J.; Strunz, W.T. Decoherence and entanglement dynamics in fluctuating fields. *Phys. Rev. A* **2010**, *81*, 042314. [CrossRef]
8. Guarnieri, G.; Uchiyama, C.; Vacchini, B. Energy backflow and non-Markovian dynamics. *Phys. Rev. A* **2016**, *93*, 012118. [CrossRef]
9. Guarnieri, G.; Nokkala, J.; Schmidt, R.; Maniscalco, S.; Vacchini, B. Energy backflow in strongly coupled non-Markovian continuous-variable systems. *Phys. Rev. A* **2016**, *94*, 062101. [CrossRef]
10. Wu, J.; Ren, F.H.; He, R.H.; Nie, S.S.; Wang, Z.M. Adiabatic speedup and quantum heat current in an open system. *Eur. Phys. Lett.* **2022**, *139*, 48001. [CrossRef]
11. Schmidt, R.; Maniscalco, S.; Ala-Nissila, T. Heat flux and information backflow in cold environments. *Phys. Rev. A* **2016**, *94*, 010101. [CrossRef]
12. Wittemer, M.; Clos, G.; Breuer, H.P.; Warring, U.; Schaetz, T. Measurement of quantum memory effects and its fundamental limitations. *Phys. Rev. A* **2018**, *97*, 020102. [CrossRef]
13. Passos, M.; Obando, P.C.; Balthazar, W.; Paula, F.; Huguenin, J.; Sarandy, M. Non-Markovianity through quantum coherence in an all-optical setup. *Opt. Lett.* **2019**, *44*, 2478–2481. [CrossRef]
14. Khurana, D.; Agarwalla, B.K.; Mahesh, T.S. Experimental emulation of quantum non-Markovian dynamics and coherence protection in the presence of information backflow. *Phys. Rev. A* **2019**, *99*, 022107. [CrossRef]
15. Yan, Y.A.; Yang, F.; Liu, Y.; Shao, J. Hierarchical approach based on stochastic decoupling to dissipative systems. *Chem. Phys. Lett.* **2004**, *395*, 216–221. [CrossRef]
16. Bundgaard-Nielsen, M.; Mørk, J.; Denning, E.V. Non-Markovian perturbation theories for phonon effects in strong-coupling cavity quantum electrodynamics. *Phys. Rev. B* **2021**, *103*, 235309. [CrossRef]
17. Ricottone, A.; Rudner, M.S.; Coish, W.A. Topological transition of a non-Markovian dissipative quantum walk. *Phys. Rev. A* **2020**, *102*, 012215. [CrossRef]

18. Rivas, A.; Huelga, S.F.; Plenio, M.B. Entanglement and non-Markovianity of quantum evolutions. *Phys. Rev. Lett.* **2010**, *105*, 050403. [CrossRef]
19. Chruściński, D.; Kossakowski, A.; Rivas, A. Measures of non-Markovianity: Divisibility versus backflow of information. *Phys. Rev. A* **2011**, *83*, 052128. [CrossRef]
20. Chen, X.Y.; Zhang, N.N.; He, W.T.; Kong, X.Y.; Tao, M.J.; Deng, F.G.; Ai, Q.; Long, G.L. Global correlation and local information flows in controllable non-Markovian open quantum dynamics. *Npj Quantum Inform.* **2022**, *8*, 22. [CrossRef]
21. Strathearn, A.; Lovett, B.W.; Kirton, P. Efficient real-time path integrals for non-Markovian spin-boson models. *New J. Phys.* **2017**, *19*, 093009. [CrossRef]
22. Wang, Z.M.; Ren, F.H.; Luo, D.W.; Yan, Z.Y.; Wu, L.A. Quantum state transmission through a spin chain in finite-temperature heat baths. *J. Phys. A Math. Theor.* **2021**, *54*, 155303. [CrossRef]
23. Wang, Z.M.; Luo, D.W.; Byrd, M.S.; Wu, L.A.; Yu, T.; Shao, B. Adiabatic speedup in a non-Markovian quantum open system. *Phys. Rev. A* **2018**, *98*, 062118. [CrossRef]
24. Laine, E.M.; Breuer, H.P.; Piilo, J. Nonlocal memory effects allow perfect teleportation with mixed states. *Sci. Rep.* **2014**, *4*, 1–5. [CrossRef]
25. Fahmy, A.F.; Marx, R.; Bermel, W.; Glaser, S.J. Thermal equilibrium as an initial state for quantum computation by NMR. *Phys. Rev. A* **2008**, *78*, 022317. [CrossRef]
26. Genway, S.; Ho, A.F.; Lee, D.K.K. Dynamics of thermalization in small Hubbard-model systems. *Phys. Rev. Lett.* **2010**, *105*, 260402. [CrossRef]
27. Ponomarev, A.V.; Denisov, S.; Hänggi, P. Thermal equilibration between Two quantum systems. *Phys. Rev. Lett.* **2011**, *106*, 010405. [CrossRef]
28. Wu, S.X.; Yu, C.S. Quantum speed limit for a mixed initial state. *Phys. Rev. A* **2018**, *98*, 042132. [CrossRef]
29. Jing, J.; Yu, T.; Lam, C.H.; You, J.Q.; Wu, L.A. Control relaxation via dephasing: A quantum-state-diffusion study. *Phys. Rev. A* **2018**, *97*, 012104. [CrossRef]
30. Jing, J.; Yu, T. Non-Markovian relaxation of a three-level system: Quantum trajectory approach. *Phys. Rev. Lett.* **2010**, *105*, 240403. [CrossRef]
31. Wang, Z.M.; Ren, F.H.; Luo, D.W.; Yan, Z.Y.; Wu, L.A. Almost-exact state transfer by leakage-elimination-operator control in a non-Markovian environment. *Phys. Rev. A* **2020**, *102*, 042406. [CrossRef]
32. Link, V.; Strunz, W.T.; Luoma, K. Non-Markovian quantum dynamics in a squeezed reservoir. *Entropy* **2022**, *24*, 352. [CrossRef] [PubMed]
33. Diósi, L.; Gisin, N.; Strunz, W.T. Non-Markovian quantum state diffusion. *Phys. Rev. A* **1998**, *58*, 1699–1712. [CrossRef]
34. Flannigan, S.; Damanet, F.; Daley, A.J. Many-body quantum state diffusion for non-Markovian dynamics in strongly interacting systems. *Phys. Rev. Lett.* **2022**, *128*, 063601. [CrossRef]
35. Chen, Y.; You, J.Q.; Yu, T. Exact non-Markovian master equations for multiple qubit systems: Quantum-trajectory approach. *Phys. Rev. A* **2014**, *90*, 052104. [CrossRef]
36. Xu, J.; Zhao, X.; Jing, J.; Wu, L.A.; Yu, T. Perturbation methods for the non-Markovian quantum state diffusion equation. *J. Phys. A Math. Theor.* **2014**, *47*, 435301. [CrossRef]
37. Wang, H.; Thoss, M. From coherent motion to localization: II. Dynamics of the spin-boson model with sub-Ohmic spectral density at zero temperature. *Chem. Phys.* **2010**, *370*, 78–86. [CrossRef]
38. Ritschel, G.; Eisfeld, A. Analytic representations of bath correlation functions for ohmic and superohmic spectral densities using simple poles. *J. Chem. Phys.* **2014**, *141*, 3365. [CrossRef]
39. Meier, C.; Tannor, D.J. Non-Markovian evolution of the density operator in the presence of strong laser fields. *J. Chem. Phys.* **1999**, *111*, 3365. [CrossRef]
40. Nie, S.S.; Ren, F.H.; He, R.H.; Wu, J.; Wang, Z.M. Control cost and quantum speed limit time in controlled almost-exact state transmission in open systems. *Phys. Rev. A* **2021**, *104*, 052424. [CrossRef]
41. Ren, F.H.; Wang, Z.M.; Wu, L.A. Accelerated adiabatic quantum search algorithm via pulse control in a non-Markovian environment. *Phys. Rev. A* **2020**, *102*, 062603. [CrossRef]
42. Marchukov, O.V.; Volosniev, A.G.; Valiente, M.; Petrosyan, D.; Zinner, N. Quantum spin transistor with a Heisenberg spin chain. *Nat. Commun.* **2016**, *7*, 13070. [CrossRef]
43. Van-Diepen, C.J.; Hsiao, T.K.; Mukhopadhyay, U.; Reichl, C.; Wegscheider, W.; Vandersypen, L.M.K. Quantum simulation of antiferromagnetic Heisenberg chain with gate-defined quantum dots. *Phys. Rev. X* **2021**, *11*, 041025. [CrossRef]
44. Dyszel, P.; Haraldsen, J.T. Thermodynamics of general Heisenberg spin tetramers composed of coupled quantum dimers. *Magnetochemistry* **2021**, *7*, 29. [CrossRef]
45. Mohammed, W.W.; Al-Askar, F.M.; Cesarano, C.; Botmart, T.; El-Morshedy, M. Wiener process effects on the solutions of the fractional (2 + 1)-dimensional Heisenberg ferromagnetic spin chain equation. *Mathematics* **2022**, *10*, 2043. [CrossRef]
46. Lebrun, R.; Ross, A.; Bender, S.; Qaiumzadeh, A.; Baldrati, L.; Cramer, J.; Brataas, A.; Duine, R.; Kläui, M. Tunable long-distance spin transport in a crystalline antiferromagnetic iron oxide. *Nature* **2018**, *561*, 222–225. [CrossRef]
47. Wadley, P.; Howells, B.; Železný, J.; Andrews, C.; Hills, V.; Campion, R.P.; Novák, V.; Olejník, K.; Maccherozzi, F.; Dhesi, S.; et al. Electrical switching of an antiferromagnet. *Science* **2016**, *351*, 6273. [CrossRef]

48. Olejník, K.; Seifert, T.; Kašpar, Z.; Novák, V.; Wadley, P.; Campion, R.P.; Baumgartner, M.; Gambardella, P.; Nemec, P.; Wunderlich, J.; et al. Terahertz electrical writing speed in an antiferromagnetic memory. *Sci. Adv.* **2018**, *4*, 3. [CrossRef]
49. Wei, D.; Chang, Y.; Glaser, S.J.; Yang, X. Cooperative pulses for pseudo-pure state preparation. *Appl. Phys. Lett.* **2014**, *104*, 242409. [CrossRef]
50. Peng, X.; Zhu, X.; Fang, X.; Feng, M.; Gao, K.; Yang, X.; Liu, M. Preparation of pseudo-pure states by line-selective pulses in nuclear magnetic resonance. *Chem. Phys. Lett.* **2001**, *340*, 5–6. [CrossRef]
51. Cory, D.G.; Fahmy, A.F.; Havel, T.F. Ensemble quantum computing by NMR spectroscopy. *Proc. Natl. Acad. Sci. USA* **1997**, *94*, 1634–1639. [CrossRef]
52. Warren, W.S. The usefulness of NMR quantum computing. *Science* **1997**, *277*, 1688–1690. [CrossRef]
53. Wang, Z.M.; Luo, D.W.; Li, B.; Wu, L.A. Quantum energy transfer between a nonlinearly coupled bosonic bath and a fermionic chain: An exactly solvable model. *Phys. Rev. A* **2020**, *101*, 042130. [CrossRef]
54. Wang, Z.M.; Ren, F.H.; Sarandy, M.S.; Byrd, M.S. Nonequilibrium quantum thermodynamics in non-Markovian adiabatic speedup. *Physica A* **2022**, *603*, 127861. [CrossRef]
55. Whitney, R.S. Non-Markovian quantum thermodynamics: Laws and fluctuation theorems. *Phys. Rev. B* **2018**, *98*, 085415. [CrossRef]
56. Thomas, G.; Siddharth, N.; Banerjee, S.; Ghosh, S. Thermodynamics of non-Markovian reservoirs and heat engines. *Phys. Rev. E* **2018**, *97*, 062108. [CrossRef]
57. Kato, A.; Tanimura, Y. Quantum heat current under non-perturbative and non-Markovian conditions: Applications to heat machines. *J. Chem. Phys.* **2016**, *145*, 224105. [CrossRef]
58. Feng, G.; Xu, G.; Long, G. Experimental realization of non-adiabatic holonomic quantum computation. *Phys. Rev. Lett.* **2013**, *110*, 190501. [CrossRef]
59. Altowyan, A.S.; Berrada, K.; Abdel-Khalek, S.; Eleuch, H. Quantum coherence and total phase in semiconductor microcavities for multi-photon excitation. *Nanomaterials* **2022**, *12*, 2671. [CrossRef]
60. Hu, M.L.; Hu, X.; Wang, J.; Peng, Y.; Zhang, Y.R.; Fan, H. Quantum coherence and geometric quantum discord. *Phys. Rep.* **2018**, *762–764*, 1–100. [CrossRef]
61. Baumgratz, T.; Cramer, M.; Plenio, M.B. Quantifying Coherence. *Phys. Rev. Lett.* **2014**, *113*, 140401. [CrossRef] [PubMed]
62. Yu, T. Non-Markovian quantum trajectories versus master equations: Finite-temperature heat bath. *Phys. Rev. A* **2004**, *69*, 062107. [CrossRef]
63. Sun, Y.J.; Zhang, W.M. Modeling neuronal systems as an open quantum system. *Symmetry* **2021**, *13*, 1603. [CrossRef]
64. Ng, H. Decoherence of interacting Majorana modes. *Sci. Rep.* **2015**, *5*, 12530. [CrossRef] [PubMed]
65. Moriya, T. New mechanism of anisotropic superexchange interaction. *Phys. Rev. Lett.* **1960**, *4*, 228–230. [CrossRef]
66. Dzyaloshinsky, I. A thermodynamic theory of "weak" ferromagnetism of antiferromagnetics. *J. Phys. Chem. Solids* **1958**, *4*, 241–255. [CrossRef]
67. Heide, M.; Bihlmayer, G.; Blügel, S. Dzyaloshinskii-Moriya interaction accounting for the orientation of magnetic domains in ultrathin films: Fe/W(110). *Phys. Rev. B* **2008**, *78*, 140403. [CrossRef]
68. Emori, S.; Bauer, U.; Ahn, S.M.; Martinez, E.; Beach, G.S. Current-driven dynamics of chiral ferromagnetic domain walls. *Nat. Mater.* **2013**, *12*, 611–616. [CrossRef]
69. Yu, X.; Kanazawa, N.; Zhang, W.; Nagai, T.; Hara, T.; Kimoto, K.; Matsui, Y.; Onose, Y.; Tokura, Y. Skyrmion flow near room temperature in an ultralow current density. *Nat. Commun.* **2012**, *3*, 988. [CrossRef]
70. Qaiumzadeh, A.; Ado, I.A.; Duine, R.A.; Titov, M.; Brataas, A. Theory of the interfacial Dzyaloshinskii-Moriya interaction in Rashba antiferromagnets. *Phys. Rev. Lett.* **2018**, *120*, 197202. [CrossRef]
71. Liu, B.Q.; Shao, B.; Li, J.G.; Zou, J.; Wu, L.A. Quantum and classical correlations in the one-dimensional XY model with Dzyaloshinskii-Moriya interaction. *Phys. Rev. A* **2011**, *83*, 052112. [CrossRef]
72. Kavokin, K.V. Anisotropic exchange interaction of localized conduction-band electrons in semiconductors. *Phys. Rev. B* **2001**, *64*, 075305. [CrossRef]
73. Wang, Z.M.; Shao, B.; Zou, J. Anisotropy and magnetic field effects on the entanglement transfer in two parallel Heisenberg spin chains. *Int. J. Mod. Phys. B* **2001**, *27*, 4853–4861. [CrossRef]
74. Abliz, A.; Gao, H.J.; Xie, X.C.; Wu, Y.S.; Liu, W.M. Entanglement control in an anisotropic two-qubit Heisenberg XYZ model with external magnetic fields. *Phys. Rev. A* **2006**, *74*, 052105. [CrossRef]
75. Wang, Z.M.; Shao, B.; Chang, P.; Zou, J. Quantum state transfer in a Heisenberg XY chain with energy current. *Physica A* **2008**, *387*, 2197–2204. [CrossRef]
76. Felcher, G.; Kleb, R.; Jaccarino, V. Observation of the spin-flop transition of MnF_2 by neutron diffraction. *J. Appl. Phys.* **1979**, *50*, 1837. [CrossRef]
77. Welp, U.; Berger, A.; Miller, D.J.; Vlasko-Vlasov, V.K.; Gray, K.E.; Mitchell, J.F. Direct imaging of the first-order spin-flop transition in the layered manganite $La_{1.4}Sr_{1.6}Mn_2O_7$. *Phys. Rev. Lett.* **1999**, *83*, 4180–4183. [CrossRef]
78. Vega, I.D.; Alonso, D. Dynamics of non-Markovian open quantum systems. *Rev. Mod. Phys.* **2017**, *89*, 015001. [CrossRef]
79. Pozzobom, M.B.; Maziero, J. Environment-induced quantum coherence spreading of a qubit. *Ann. Phys.* **2017**, *377*, 243–255. [CrossRef]

80. Latune, C.L.; Sinayskiy, I.; Petruccione, F. Energetic and entropic effects of bath-induced coherences. *Phys. Rev. A* **2019**, *99*, 052105. [CrossRef]
81. Eastham, P.R.; Kirton, P.; Cammack, H.M.; Lovett, B.W.; Keeling, J. Bath-induced coherence and the secular approximation. *Phys. Rev. A* **2016**, *94*, 012110. [CrossRef]

MDPI
St. Alban-Anlage 66
4052 Basel
Switzerland
Tel. +41 61 683 77 34
Fax +41 61 302 89 18
www.mdpi.com

Entropy Editorial Office
E-mail: entropy@mdpi.com
www.mdpi.com/journal/entropy

www.ingramcontent.com/pod-product-compliance
Lightning Source LLC
LaVergne TN
LVHW070639100526
838202LV00013B/837